Colonialism and Cultural Identity

SUNY series

—————————

EXPLORATIONS

in

POSTCOLONIAL STUDIES

—————————

Emmanuel C. Eze, editor

COLONIALISM

and

CULTURAL IDENTITY

Crises of Tradition in the Anglophone Literatures of

India, Africa, and the Caribbean

PATRICK COLM HOGAN

STATE UNIVERSITY OF NEW YORK PRESS

Published by
STATE UNIVERSITY OF NEW YORK PRESS, ALBANY

For information, address State University of New York Press,
State University Plaza, Albany, NY 12246

Production, Laurie Searl
Marketing, Fran Keneston

Library of Congress Cataloging-in-Publication Data

Hogan, Patrick Colm.
    Colonialism and cultural identity : crises of tradition in the anglophone literatures of
India, Africa, and the Caribbean / Patrick Colm Hogan.
        p.   cm. — (SUNY series, exploration in postcolonial studies)
    Includes bibliographical references and index.
    ISBN 0-7914-4459-7 (alk. paper) — ISBN 0-7914-4460-0 (pbk. : alk. paper)
        1. Commonwealth literature (English)—History and criticism. 2. Indic literature
(English)—History and criticism. 3. African literature (English)—History and criticism. 4.
Caribbean literature (English)—History and criticism. 5. Decolonization in literature. 6.
Ethnicity in literature. 7. Culture in literature. 8. Postcolonialism. I. Title. II. Series.

PR9080 .H64 2000
820.9′9171241—dc21
                                                                                                99-056631

10   9   8   7   6   5   4   3   2   1

This book is dedicated to Noam Chomsky

lo mio maestro e lo mio autore

Inferno I.85

CONTENTS

Acknowledgments

I have presented earlier versions of this work in a number of classes. I am grateful to my students—especially Cherif Diop, Kate Smith, and Katie Girard, as well as Bill Dalessio, Tom Drewry, Margaret Groesbeck, Kurt Heidinger, Kathy Koljian, Josh Masters, Ellen O'Brien, and Ken Ross—not only for their comments on my presentations, but for their thorough research and insightful presentations on related topics. I am deeply indebted to Tapan and Dipa Roy for their invaluable help with the Bengali original of *Gora*. Jerry Phillips provided characteristically insightful comments and suggestions on portions of an earlier version. Finally, many thanks to James Peltz of SUNY Press for his quick and careful handling of the manuscript, and to Jane Bunker, Laurie Searl, and Fran Keneston for their work at each stage.

Much of the writing of this work was made possible by release time provided by a Provost's Fellowship awarded by the University of Connecticut Research Foundation for the Spring semester of 1996. I am very grateful for this support.

An earlier version of part of Chapter 1 appeared in *Order and Partialities: Theory, Pedagogy, and the 'Postcolonial,'* edited by Kostas Myrsiades and Jerry McGuire (Albany: State University of New York Press, 1995). Copyright 1995, State University of New York. All Rights Reserved. It appears by permission of State University of New York Press. An earlier version of part of Chapter 3 appeared in *Research in African Literatures*, 25.2 (Summer 1994). Copyright 1994, Indiana University Press. All Rights Reserved. It appears by permission of Indiana University Press.

IDENTITIES AND UNIVERSALISM

Cultural identity is at the center of world politics today, and has been for some time. It underwrites war and revolution. The American bombing of Iraq was in part allowed by an opposition of cultural identities: Christian versus Muslim, European versus Middle Eastern. Vietnam too. Elsewhere, the identitarian elements of violent conflict are more explicit: Igbo against Yoruba in Nigeria, Catholic against Protestant in Ireland. It is the same politics of identity in each case, whether admitted or not. Of course, the effects are not confined to brute force. Often, cultural identity covertly infiltrates national policies, or becomes an overt cause to rally political allegiance, as with the Christian Coalition here, Hindu parties in India, Muslim parties in Algeria. Indeed, cultural identity is broader even than politics—art and education and personal affinities are pervaded by its incarnations: racial identity, ethnic identity, religious identity, national identity. Feelings of a communal self, based in a real or imagined history of shared practices and beliefs, inspire Afrocentric education explicitly, and Eurocentric education implicitly; they guide writers' literary decisions from genre to diction; they constrain friendships and romantic love. In short, cultural identity is at the center not only of politics, but of daily life as well. And it is almost always bound up with colonialism—its historical causes, its ideological justifications, its continuing effects—and with struggles against colonialism.

In the following pages, I have set out to analyze the issue of cultural identity—the structure in which it arises, the manner in which it becomes problematic, the ways in which people respond to this problematization. The first chapter outlines a general analytic or theory of cultural identity in the context of colonialism. It begins with a definition of the colonial condition aimed at clarifying what regions are relevant to the current study and in what way they are relevant. Following this, it distinguishes the primary cultural complexes that are brought to or develop within the colonial situation (metropolitan tradition, indigenous tradition, various syncretistic "contact cultures"), and the different attitudes people in the colonial situation take up toward these cultural complexes (imitation, repudiation, etc.). In undertaking this analysis, I seek to isolate a range of patterns common to all relevant regions, but at the same time I seek to articulate some of the broad differences between Africa, India, the Caribbean, and to a lesser extent Ireland. In relation to this, I pay particular attention to ideas about gender, for these ideas are most often crucial to any group's conception of its own culture, and, indeed, to any group's understanding of other cultures.

In the final section of chapter 1, I discuss some differences between my approach and the currently dominant poststructural strain of "postcolonial theory," focusing in particular on Homi Bhabha's seminal essay, "Of Mimicry and Man: The Ambivalence of Colonial Discourse."

The second chapter considers Derek Walcott's *Dream on Monkey Mountain*, a work that is structured by an analytic of attitudes toward cultural identity. The play is a narrative dialectic in which characters take up and enact one attitude toward identity (e.g., one type of mimeticism), develop it to a practical extreme, then abandon it in the face of new conditions and contradictions. By means of this dialectic, Walcott leads us systematically through a range of responses to colonialism and tradition, responses that have been and continue to be central to considerations of cultural identity, not only in literature, but in practical politics as well. In doing this, he draws heavily on motifs and practices of Afro-Caribbean religion, which concretize his thematic analysis. Walcott's drama thus provides a culturally particularized exploration of the general issues set forth in the theoretical overview of chapter 1.

The next four works, Jean Rhys's *Wide Sargasso Sea*, Chinua Achebe's *Things Fall Apart*, Earl Lovelace's *The Wine of Astonishment*, and Buchi Emecheta's *The Joys of Motherhood*, explore a narrower range of attitudes, but they do so in more detail. They also share a consistent focus on gender.

In the first chapter, I follow the common practice of dividing postcolonization literature into that by metropolitan, settler/Creole, and indigenous writers. Six of the remaining seven chapters concern indigenous writers. However, the third chapter considers Jean Rhys's *Wide Sargasso Sea*. This is the only nonindigenous work treated in detail. It is well suited to the present study, however, because cultural identity is central to the novel. Indeed, *Wide Sargasso Sea* is, in many ways, the story of a woman who is denied positive cultural and gender identity because of her intermediate position in the colonial structure. Her final madness is, in effect, the manifestation of this denial. Moreover, discussing this madness allows us to clarify the constitution of personal identity in relation to cultural identity, colonialism, and gender and it allows us to do this in a way that has direct bearing on the interpretation of indigenous as well as Creole works.

Achebe turns away from the theme of colonialism and madness, shared by Walcott and Rhys, taking up instead the more ordinary practices and beliefs of daily life, the ways people structure their work and play in the context of an expected future. Specifically, *Things Fall Apart* explores the ways in which colonial contact distorts Igbo culture in general, and Igbo gender identity in particular. This distortion, though sometimes subtle, is so severe that it may undermine one's entire sense of purpose, one's entire imagination of a future life, and thus result in complete and psychologically devastating despair—as it does in the case of the main character. Lovelace focuses more narrowly on the degree to which Afro-Caribbean men have lost their sense of masculinity along with their cultural traditions; he considers the causes and the consequences of this loss, and the possibilities for reparation—primarily through specific forms of Afro-Christian spirituality, and through Afro-Caribbean artistic traditions. Emecheta too addresses the loss of indigenous masculinity after colonization, but her greatest concern is with the way colonization has degraded the condition of indigenous women. In each case, the author examines how the development or intensification of colonial contact precipitates a crisis in cultural identity in general, and gender identity in particular, and thereby generates a specifiable range of conflicting attitudes toward and enactments of that tradition.

The works considered in the final chapters are, like Walcott's play, broader in their treatment of cultural identity. However, in these cases, the function of that breadth is to direct our attention away from identity proper and toward universalist considerations of shared or shareable culture, in the case of Tagore, or globally stratified political economy, in the case of Hosain.

Like *Dream on Monkey Mountain*, Rabindranath Tagore's *Gora* provides a dialectically developed anatomy of postcolonization identity. However, in the case of *Gora*, this is a Socratic, rather than a Hegelian dialectic. Through discussions and debates between characters, Tagore articulates the most powerful arguments for a range of opposed positions on cultural identity—including the hyper-traditionalism (or "fundamentalism") that is politically so important in world politics today, but rarely treated with understanding or empathy in political commentary or in literature. Through this dialectic, Tagore advocates a sort of universalism— what Lalita Pandit has called "empathic universalism" (207)—an attitude that is, ultimately, opposed to any narrow advocacy of cultural identity, European, Indian, Hindu, Muslim, Christian, Igbo, or whatever.

In choosing literary works, I have for the most part confined myself to literature written in English. *Gora*, which was written in Bengali, is the only exception. This work treats the issue of cultural identity with an analytic clarity, systematic rigor, and narrative power, that are, in my reading, unmatched. Because of this, I felt it would be too great a loss not to discuss this work. Moreover, Tagore was part of Anglophone, and even English, literary culture. He not only read widely in English literature (*Gora* is in part a response to Kipling's *Kim* [see Pandit]). He translated some of his own work into English, eventually won the Nobel Prize largely for his English-language work, and, in the course of writing, fully expected his novels to appear eventually in English and to be read by English readers. In this sense, his work is part of Anglophone literature even though it was not written in English.

In the final chapter, I turn to Attia Hosain's *Sunlight on a Broken Column*. This novel takes up most of the cultural concerns addressed in the preceding works, but it does so in relation to a systematically materialist, indeed, Marxist analysis. Hosain's treatment of the problem of identity is, in the end, not culturalist, but economic, for she portrays both the use and the effect of culture—European or indigenous—as a function of class. Ultimately, for Hosain, the most important problems are not those of social custom, but of economic empowerment. This is not to say that Hosain's novel turns us away from considerations of cultural identity. These remain crucial. But Hosain urges us to focus our primary attention on the often painful economic conditions that make cultural identity problematic to begin with.

As will become clear in the following pages, my own views are close to those of Tagore and, even more so, Hosain—including their acceptance of universalism. In an afterword, I set out to clarify these views. Specifically, I argue that the problems of colonialism and cultural identity are necessarily complex and in some ways contradictory. Though there are certainly important patterns, the human pain of colonialism is, in the end, always individual, and thus to some degree contextual. Nonetheless, there are some responses that, though partial, are uniformly valuable in opposing colonialism and the human pain it entails. I isolate two such responses. The first might be called "social universalism" and is particularly close to Tagore's views. It includes four components: descriptive universalism, experiential or empathic universalism, ethical universalism, and cultural universalism. The second, democratic socialism, is closer to Hosain's views. Though both are important, the second is the more crucial. Individual empathy or an affirmation of shared world culture become insignificant, almost a mockery, when the practitioners of one culture live in opulence while those of another go hungry.

At the request of several readers, I have included an "Analytic Glossary of Selected Theoretical Concepts" as an appendix. This glossary provides a quick overview of the book's major theoretical concepts, organized in six broad categories. It will, I hope, serve both as a general summary of the theoretical principles that guide the preceding analyses and as a reference tool for readers who need a quick reminder of one or another theoretical term.

Though we will consider universalism more thoroughly in the afterword, it is worth saying a few things about the topic before going on, especially as it is so controversial within postcolonization literary study. Universalism is the view that all people and all human societies share fundamental cognitive, emotive, ethical, and other properties and principles. Clearly, all forms of racism and colonialist ethnocentrism are anti-universalist, for they necessarily assume profound and consequential differences between peoples and/or between cultures. Yet many postcolonial critics and theorists have claimed that colonialism is universalist. For example, in a recent collection, Ashcroft, Griffiths, and Tiffin devote one section to the critique of universalism as an ideological source of the oppression of nonwhite peoples (for a review and criticism of this view, see Jacoby).

Part of the problem is that these critics and theorists seem to have confused universalism with absolutism, on the one hand, and projection, on the other. Absolutism is the view that one culturally particular set of precepts or practices applies to everyone; it is absolute. Projection is the unself-conscious assumption that everyone thinks the same way I do. In contrast, universalism involves a self-conscious effort to understand precisely what is common across different cultures—empirically, normatively, experientially. Of course, one might make mistakes. One might slip into projection or absolutism. Or one might simply lie, referring to projection or absolutism as "universalist." But the problem, then, is not with the pursuit of universalism. Rather, the problem arises precisely with one's *failure* in that pursuit; it arises when *anti-universalist* tendencies arise, consciously or unconsciously. As Kwame Appiah points out, "It is characteristic of those who pose as antiuniversalists to use the term *universalism* as if it meant *pseudouniversalism*, and the fact is that their complaint is not with universalism at all. What they truly object to—and who would not?—is Eurocentric hegemony *posing* as universalism" (58). Indeed, as Appiah stresses, "intellectual responses to oppression in Africa" are almost invariably "grounded in an appeal to an ethical universal" (152).

Appiah—and Pandit—are not alone. A wide range of postcolonization authors and theorists have been adamantly universalist. Rabindranath Tagore is a clear case, as we shall discuss below. Aimé Césaire, a writer very different from Tagore in other ways, shared this attitude, referring to "the 'barbaric repudiation' by Europe of Descartes' charter of universalism: 'Reason . . . is found whole and entire in each man'" (Nandy, *Traditions*, 32)—a repudiation that has continued in current academic fashions. Samir Amin has argued that "Without a truly universalist perspective . . . enriched by the contribution of all peoples, the sterile confrontation between the Eurocentrism of some and the inverted Eurocentrisms of others will continue, in an atmosphere of destructive fanaticism" (146). In keeping with this, Aijaz Ahmad's recent *In Theory* stresses the "universalist character" of socialism and presents a strong, renewed case for active, Marxist universalism.

Moreover, universalism is not merely a conceptual stance. It has been of practical importance among anticolonial activists. For example, Edward Said has repeatedly appealed to universal principles in his work for Palestine (see, for example, "Bookless," 6). Ashis Nandy points out that "Gandhi . . . was no cultural relativist. In the thousands of pages of his collected works, there is hardly a sentence to suggest that he believed in fundamental or irreconcilable differences between cultures. And there is positive evidence that he put all his faith in universal, as distinct from cross-cultural forms of social theory" (*Traditions,* 127). Frantz Fanon, so often seen as the antithesis of Gandhi, expressed much the same view in his well-known call for human universality in *Black Skin, White Masks* (197):

> As I begin to recognize that the Negro is the symbol of sin, I catch myself hating the Negro. But then I recognize that I am a Negro. There are two ways out of this conflict. Either I ask others to pay no attention to my skin, or else I want them to be aware of it. I try then to find value for what is bad—since I have unthinkingly conceded that the black man is the color of evil. In order to terminate this neurotic situation . . . I have only one solution: to rise above this absurd drama that others have staged round me, to reject the two terms that are equally unacceptable, and, through one human being, to reach out for the universal.

Ngũgĩ wa Thiong'o is particularly noteworthy in this context, for he has characterized himself "an unrepentant universalist" (*Moving*, xvii), but at the same time he is insistent in his affirmation of cultural particularity and diversity. "The universal is contained in the particular just as the particular is contained in the universal," he writes; "We are all human beings but the fact of our being human does not manifest itself in its abstraction but in the particularity of real living human beings of different climes and races" (26). This form of universalism—we might call it "particularist universalism"—is equally a form of cultural pluralism. It is not at all a matter of everyone having the same culture. It is, in fact, antithetical to any such absolutism. Rather, it is a matter of all cultures being preserved in their uniqueness. Indeed, universalism provides the most important rationale for such preservation: The many cultures of the world and the people who live them merit the universal, ethical respect that leads to cultural preservation. And they merit this at least in part because all people share universal feelings, propensities, rights, and our various cultures all develop out of these shared feelings, propensities, rights.

It is important to stress Ngũgĩ's idea of the deep compatibility of universalism and particularism. There is a tendency to think of universalism as vacuous—a mere expression of good will—or as a matter of bare subjectivity. In fact, humans share many specific structures and properties, as the array of linguistic universals illustrates. But these may manifest themselves quite differently. To take a romantic example, we might say that it is a universal human tendency to fall in love—as the cross-cultural predominance of romantic tragicomedy testifies. But that does not mean we all fall in love with the same person, or the same sort of person, or that we pursue love in the same ways. Universalism, again, is not absolutism. It does not deny that universal principles will be instantiated differently, in conditions that differ across ethnic groups or regions, or for that matter across families or individuals within a group or region. It does not claim that universals should or even can be instantiated in the same way. Indeed, genuine universalism is the only way in which we can recognize the common humanity and thus the shareable value of distinct instantiations. Respect for different cultures is not the antithesis of universalism, but a *consequence* of universalism.

The point could be put differently—following Pandit's emphasis on empathy—by considering the great Arabic literary theorists who treated the ethics of literature. Al-Fārābī, Ibn Sīnā, Ibn Rushd, and others, argued that, when ethically successful, a literary work fosters a feeling of "*raḥmah*" in the reader. Commonly translated as "compassion," "raḥmah" derives from a root "signifying *tenderness requiring the exercise of beneficence*" (Maulana Mohammad Ali, 3n.3). This feeling, Ali stresses, is universal and unqualified (3n.3). It necessarily places all of us in the same category. Thus, in its nonabsolutist, empathic universalism, it is the absolute contradiction of the colonial belief in profound difference and the colonial attitude of denigration.

Once again, I share with these writers—Tagore, Hosain, Ngũgĩ, and so on—a commitment to universalism. This commitment animates my reading of every writer considered in the following pages, and underwrites the project as a whole. Indeed, my analysis of each individual work is tacitly guided by the empathic universalism of al-Fārābī *et al.* In isolating the experience of *raḥmah*, the Arabic theorists point to one of the most important potential ethical consequences of literature after colonization, and one of the most important tasks of interpretation— enhancing the moral empathy for which literature is almost uniquely well designed. I am not so deluded as to think that a book of literary criticism is likely to have much practical effect on anyone. However, I hope that the following explications will foster the experience of *raḥmah* regarding colonized peoples and their ways of life, especially because this experience is both the deepest source and final aim of so much literature arising from the deprivation and shame of colonialism.

A Note on Terminology

The usual term for the literature and culture discussed in the following pages is *postcolonial*. I would be the last one to object that a term has some sort of intrinsic meaning and that people cannot define a term as they like. Nonetheless, the term does seem misleading (as others have noted; cf. McClintock and Shohat). It appears to imply that the field begins where colonialism ends. But, in fact, the field is largely defined by the continuing effects of colonialism and many central works of "postcolonial" literature appeared before even political independence was achieved—for example, Mulk Raj Anand's *Untouchable* and Raja Rao's *Kanthapura*, both published before Indian independence, or Chinua Achebe's *Things Fall Apart* and Amos Tutuola's *The Palm-Wine Drinkard*, both published before Nigerian independence. The literature that is typically studied in this field was not written after *colonialism*, but after *colonization*. Thus, it seems that the term *postcolonization* is more apt. In any event, it better fits the concerns of the present study. Thus, I shall use it in the following pages, except when referring to a person or group that is self-defined as "postcolonial" (e.g., postcolonial theorists).

CHAPTER ONE

LITERATURES OF COLONIAL CONTACT

Cultural Geography and the Structures of Identity

POSTCOLONIZATION LITERATURE AND CULTURAL GEOGRAPHY

The first problem facing anyone who sets out to write on postcolonization literature is to determine the scope of the field. Unlike most literary
"periods," postcolonization literature is broadly multinational and multicultural. More importantly, not everyone is agreed as to which nations
and cultures fall under the rubric. There are some unequivocal cases:
India, Pakistan, Kenya, Nigeria, Ghana. And there are some almost
unequivocal cases: Jamaica, Trinidad, Barbados, South Africa. But some
writers include New Zealand, Australia, and Canada; some add the
United States; others include Ireland.

These various countries and their literatures can be grouped in different ways, depending upon one's interests and aims. It does not seem to
me productive to try to decide that one or another grouping is definitive,
that it captures some sort of essence—or, conversely, that there is an
essence to the "postcolonial" that can be rightly instantiated in one particular grouping. Rather, the best approach, in my view, is to define the
sort of colonial situation in which one is interested, and then to determine
which regions are relevant to that definition, and in what degree.

By "postcolonization literature," I mean literature emerging from
the historical encounter between culturally distinct and geographically

separated societies, where for some extended period one society con-
trols the other politically and economically; moreover, during this
period, the dominated society remains numerically and culturally
prevalent in its own geographical location, and the dominant society
justifies its control through the denigration of the dominated culture
and through the ideological insistence that the dominated people are an
inferior race. In other words, the body of literature I should like to isolate has the following characteristics: It is the historical result of direct
political and economic domination. This direct domination need not be
in place currently (i.e., the colony may have achieved independence).
However, direct domination must have continued for a long enough
period to establish lasting political and economic structures, as well as
ideological or cultural institutions (schools, etc.) that continue to have
important effects. Moreover, the initial, direct domination was imposed
and maintained through violence or the threat of violence, along with
other forms of coercion. Thus, in its most significant impact, it was relatively sudden; it did not develop slowly out of internal conditions. In
keeping with this, it involves a salient cultural conflict in which the
dominant society claims cultural and racial superiority and justifies its
domination by reference to this putative superiority. Finally, each
group—colonizer and colonized—retains a geographical domain in
which it is clearly numerically superior.

Societies such as India, Pakistan, Ghana, Kenya, Nigeria, and South
Africa fit this definition very well, as does Ireland. Australia, New
Zealand, Canada, and the United States do not fit well, for the indigenous population did not maintain majority status in the colony—a fact
with important political, economic, and cultural consequences. Thus, we
shall not be considering this group at all in the following pages. On the
other hand, there are a number of similarities between these two groups.
Moreover, any literature from the predominantly European colonies
which emerges from an appropriate sort of cultural encounter—not only
early settler literature, but, for example, Maori writing in New Zealand,
African American literature, Australian writing concerned with aborigi-
nal peoples, and so on—could fruitfully be compared with the paradigmatic postcolonization literatures in this respect.

Colonies that retained an indigenous majority and colonies that
were overrun by Europeans do not, however, exhaust all relevant cases.
Somewhere between these lie what we might refer to as "alienated
majority" colonies. These are colonies, primarily in the Caribbean, in

which the colonized people are in a numerical majority, but they have been alienated from their land through forced displacement, and alienated from their ancestral traditions, languages, and so forth through forced dispersal and intermixing. In consequence, there are, as we shall see, some significant differences between alienated majority literatures and the indigenous majority literatures of the paradigm postcolonization countries. On the other hand, since the writers in this region are largely of West African ancestry, they retain many African traditions, and they do so in a way that clearly involves the repeated transformation of these traditions in response to novel circumstances—an important point for any study of cultural identity. Moreover, perhaps even more than African writers, black Caribbean writers—whose ancestors were almost all slaves—have been faced with the justificatory racism and ethnocentrism of Europe in a particularly stark form. Because of this, their treatment of identity is in some ways more paradigmatic of the colonial condition than is that of lighter-skinned south Asians or, even more obviously, the Irish. Indeed, the separate racial status of the Irish was slowly dissolved into a reconstituted "white" race—which, in some versions, includes Semitic and south Asian peoples—all opposed to blacks.

As this definition already makes clear, by its very nature, postcolonization literature is, in a sense, two literatures: one arising from the dominant or colonizer society, the other from the dominated or colonized society. This is, indeed, the most fundamental division, which one must draw in anatomizing postcolonization literature: literature written by members of the oppressor group (i.e., the English) and literature written by members of the oppressed group (Indians, Africans, and so on). As one would expect, these literatures are united by a sort of dialectical tension necessarily produced by the history that defines postcolonization literature. But they also maintain a striking degree of thematic or structural congruence, often centering around the issue of identity. Within the dominated group, we have already distinguished indigenous and alienated peoples. We may isolate two roughly parallel categories within the oppressor group: 1) metropolitan writers—English writers, in the case of Anglophone literature—and 2) settlers and Creoles (i.e., descendants of settlers).

We can render this division more precise, and use it to provide a framework within which to discuss identity, if we consider in more detail the geography of the colonial situation. We may distinguish, first of all, the metropolis, which is to say, the home country of the colonizer, and the region of colonial contact, which is to say, the region of settlement where colonizers live in close interaction with the colonized people. Finally, we may isolate an indigenous region or region of cultural autonomy involving little contact with the colonizer, a region parallel to the metropolis. Regions of contact are most often large urban centers (e.g., Lagos in Nigeria), where the colonized inhabitants (e.g., Igbos) are, like the Europeans, settlers themselves, and not strictly indigenous to the place. Perhaps the most famous example of this general division is Ireland. For centuries, the region of contact—and, for a long period, the region of English control—was confined to the city of Dublin and a small area around the city. This area, referred to as "The Pale," was Anglo-Irish in culture. Outside of this area (beyond the Pale), Ireland remained largely Gaelic in language, customs, dress, and so on. (On the Pale, see, for example, Hayes-McCoy, 176, and Cosgrove, 168.)

Within the region of settlement, we may distinguish regions of high intensity contact and regions of low intensity contact between colonizers and colonized. I shall reserve the term "region of contact" for the former (i.e., areas of high intensity contact). Obviously there is often a continuum in intensity of contact between the contact region and the autonomous region. Indeed, sometimes it will be important to distinguish low intensity contact regions. However, I reserve the term for high intensity contact because the zone I wish to isolate is a zone in which interaction is extensive, structured, even routinized, in such a way that it has structural consequences regarding culture. This sharply differentiates my use of the phrase "region of contact" from Mary Louise Pratt's use of the similar phrase "contact zone." While I am concerned with established, structured contact, which is integral to the daily life of both colonizers and colonized (as in, say, Lagos), Pratt is concerned with the sorts of contact that are not well established, structured, etc. Hence her view that colonial encounters are "improvisational" and her statement that the contact zone is "often synonymous with 'colonial frontier'" (6). At the frontier and in the early stages of contact, encounters may well be improvisational (though they may also be governed by a rigid set of military protocols, known and understood by one side only). My concern, however, is with contact that is not at all improvisational, but highly regulated, and regulated in such a way as to define a system of interaction, for this is the sort of contact that is consequential for one's sense of identity. It is worth noting that the region of contact (in my sense) is typically the region that is under the firmest control of the colonial government, whereas Pratt's contact zone would be the area least firmly controlled.

It is also worth mentioning that, in the region of contact, the relations between the colonizers and the colonized are often partially mediated by some third group, which is also often considered racially intermediate. Mulattos and other mixed-race people often fill this role. Privileged relative to people of fully indigenous ancestry, they can aspire to a higher station than ordinary "natives" and can be used by colonizers as a sort of buffer. Indeed, the mixed-race character who strives to be white and who collaborates with the colonizer is a common figure in much postcolonization literature. On the other hand, this function is not confined to mixed-race people. It can be taken up by any race considered "closer" to being white. In Africa and the Caribbean, this role is frequently taken up by South Asians. Indeed, during apartheid, the South African government strictly distinguished between South Asians and black Africans in precisely this way. But this was not confined to South Africa. As Benedict Anderson has pointed out, "Almost everywhere economic power was either monopolized by the colonialists themselves, or unevenly shared with a politically impotent class of pariah (non-native) businessmen— Lebanese, Indian and Arab in colonial Africa" (116). This colonial division—sometimes exacerbated by extreme collaborationism and anti-"native" racism on the part of some members of the buffer group—often gave rise to considerable (racist) resentment against this group after independence, Uganda providing perhaps the most notorious instance. In the absence of such a racially intermediate group, an indigenous group, often one with a more "European" culture— religion, political structure, dress, etiquette, whatever—could serve the same function, with similar results.

In terms of identity, the most important aspects of this geographical relation are cultural and social. The metropolis and the indigenous region maintain what might be called "basic" culture—English culture in England and Igbo culture in the interior Igbo villages. In contrast, the regions of high intensity contact (e.g., Lagos), develop two sorts of Creolized culture. Most obviously, indigenous culture is affected by metropolitan culture—through English education, forced Christianization, or simply through the partial Europeanization produced by the structure of work and the physical and economic environment. Less obviously, the settler culture is altered by indigenous culture. We may refer to both the modified indigenous culture and the modified metropolitan/settler culture as "contact cultures."

At the same time, despite this cross-cultural interaction and the formation of contact cultures, settlers and contact-region indigenes often form tightly knit, socially rigid, and mutually antagonistic societies which operate to rigidify aspects of basic culture viewed as threatened by contact. Contact leads to widespread modification or even loss of basic culture. But it leads simultaneously to a reification of that culture. Basic culture has always evolved in the metropolis and the autonomous region and continues to do so. In the contact region, the recollection and practice of basic culture often become fixed at a particular moment—the moment when the settler left the metropolis or autonomous region. For example, the English settler/Creole often feels him/herself to be somewhat African (Indian, etc.), and thus to a degree different from the English. But, at the same time, he/she often believes him/herself to be more "truly" English than the English, more genuinely faithful to English custom, etc.

Here as elsewhere, the Caribbean is slightly different from India, Africa, and Ireland. Through slavery, virtually all Africans were, at least initially, thrust into a contact region, and removed entirely from autonomous regions. Of course, slaves—including newly arrived Africans, who carried particularly fresh memories of their culture (see Price, 24)—sometimes escaped from the plantations and formed Maroon communities, and these partially had the function of autonomous regions. Moreover, even plantation work could involve more or less contact. Though extensively routinized, it could be structured in such a way as to make it highly oriented toward European culture (with forced church attendance, etc.), or it could be structured more or less purely as labor, with other aspects of culture not entering systematically into regulated interaction. Nonetheless, there was no strictly indigenous region where an indigenous culture could be revisited, for even the culture of the Maroons was a sort of ad hoc synthesis of different African traditions—Yoruba, Ashanti, and so on (see Price, 29).

We can more fully specify the nature of culture in the region of contact by distinguishing three related parameters. The first is intensity of contact. This is a matter of frequency of contact (i.e., how often Europeans and non-Europeans come into contact), significance of contact types (whether contact involves essential matters of livelihood or more peripheral matters), the diversity of areas affected (e.g., is it merely a matter of commerce, or does it enter into religious observance, education, etc.), systematicity and rationalization (i.e., is it governed by articulated rules that make interactions regular and predictable), and so on. Again, I reserve the term "region of contact" for an area in which contact is relatively intense, in this technical sense.

The second parameter is the degree of severance, the degree to which one is cut off from basic culture. This is a highly complex matter and involves several subvariables. The most obvious subvariable within severance is a matter of the actual lines of connection with the basic culture—the distance, the freedom of travel, the existence of means of transportation, and so on. Clearly, there are differences here between India, with its extensive infrastructure, Africa, with its more limited infrastructure, and the Caribbean, where there was no access to the original autonomous regions at all, for the slaves simply could not return to African villages.

A second subvariable here is the mode of existence of the basic culture, the degree to which it is codified in writing, etc. It is clearly easier to maintain a culture that is preserved in writing than to maintain one that is not—the latter will simply die out if it is not practiced for a single generation. Mode of existence is closely related to a third subvariable, the uniformity of basic culture across communities. It is clearly easier to preserve a culture that is broadly consistent across the indigenous region. Members of many different local communities mix together in the contact region; insofar as they share detailed cultural ideas and practices, they are more likely to repeat and thus preserve them. Though, for ease of explication, I have referred to "basic culture" in the singular, there are significant cultural differences determined by region, profession, economic status, and so on. These differences can impede, and sometimes undermine, the preservation of what is common. For example, if all Yoruba share a particular ritual, then that ritual may be practiced in the contact region, even when the Yoruba there are from different regions. However, suppose that, despite common abstract principles, this ritual is subject to considerable regional variation in its actual performance. Then it is much less likely that the ritual will be repeated and preserved, for its performance will require a high concentration of Yoruba from a particular region.

This is related to a fourth subvariable, the degree to which a tradition may be continued at a distance from the autonomous region. Consider, for example, the difference between Hindu and Igbo practices. Much Hindu ritual is performed within a family, and thus does not require a large community. In contrast, as Isichei points out, in Igboland, "Traditional religion is essentially local—tied to this local shrine, this village festival, this village taboo. A man who left his village for Lagos was almost bound to cease to practice his inherited religion" (169).

Another subvariable affecting the parameter of severance is the degree of linguistic continuity. Irish and Caribbean people, including writers, no longer share the language of everyday culture used by their colonized forebears. Africans and Indians typically do preserve that language in fluent, daily, native use.

Finally, the third important parameter is degree of internalization. Each of us assimilates certain ways of thinking about ourselves and about the world, and certain ways of acting. We come automatically to conceive of people in particular ways, to organize our conception of life in relation to particular structures, and so on. The parameter I wish to isolate here is a matter of the degree to which any given culture has been internalized in this sense. In the region of cultural autonomy, the people have internalized the basic culture—Igbo or Hindu or whatever. The same holds for the metropolis. In the region of contact, however, there will be a variety of internalizations. Some indigenous people will have internalized a culture that is largely indigenous; others will have internalized a culture that is largely metropolitan; and there will be all intermediate cases as well. A simple example should illustrate the point. The story of Romeo and Juliet does not have a place in basic Indian culture. There, the paradigmatic literary instances of romantic love would be Duṣyanta and Śakuntalā or Rāma and Sītā in the Hindu tradition (see Kālidāsa and Vālmīki) or Laila and Majnun in the Muslim or Arabic/Persian tradition (see Nizami). Clearly, there is a difference in acculturation—that is, internalization of culture—between an Indian who spontaneously assimilates lovers to Duṣyanta and Śakuntalā and one who spontaneously assimilates them to Romeo and Juliet. The same holds for settlers/Creoles. It is rare for any colonizer fully to internalize the indigenous culture (though this is an important literary motif—cf. *Gora*, *Kim*, and *Midnight's Children*). Nonetheless, even among colonizers, there will be many degrees of partial internalization of indigenous culture. As we shall see, this has considerable bearing on the attitudes individuals and groups take up toward cultural identity.

Clearly, degree of internalization is in part a function of intensity and severance. However, it is not reducible to these—in derivation, in consequences, or in explanatory value.

IDENTITY AND TRADITION

It hardly needs to be said that colonial contact disrupts indigenous culture, often radically. For many people, it renders traditional ideas uncertain and ends the easy performance of traditional practices. In doing this, it makes cultural identity a problem—an issue on which one almost necessarily takes a stand. While questions about one's relation to tradition may arise at any time, in any context, they arise with unique force and scope as colonial contact intensifies, the degree of severance increases, internalizations of idea and act fade or shift between antagonistic cultures, coming to rest fully in neither one nor the other. In short, under colonialism, in the region of contact, the conflicts are so strong and pervasive that they constitute a challenge to one's cultural identity, and thus one's personal identity.

As we shall discuss in more detail in the following chapters, identity is best thought of as involving a representational or referential component and a procedural or "skills" component. (The distinction is fairly standard in cognitive science, though the terminology varies; see, for example, Johnson-Laird, 166ff.) The procedural component consists in all of one's unreflective knowledge about how to act or interact in typical situations. It includes knowledge about how to greet and address different people, knowledge of how one is to take part in religious activities or work, and so forth. I will refer to this as "practical identity." The representational or referential component consists in a set of properties that define one's self-understanding. This set is hierarchized in that some properties are "more central" to one's self-definition than are others (e.g., one's sex is more central than one's shoe size). I will refer to this as "reflective identity." Clearly, the two are related. For example, much of one's practical identity is based on one's sex, which is correlatively central to one's reflective identity.

Both sorts of identity are the result of common social practices, not individual decisions. Clearly, I do not choose my practical identity. Rather, I am brought up in such a way that I am comfortable in certain situations, know how to behave, know my "role." The same is true of reflective identity. It is standard social practices that define the categories in which I conceive of myself. And it is standard social practices that tell me which of these categories is important. If "male" is centrally important to my reflective identity, this is because sex is generally treated as centrally important in the society around me, because I am regularly identified as male, because my practical identity has been shaped around this categorization.

In terms of both reflective and practical identity, indigenous people in contact culture are caught between two conflicting sets of imperatives. The practices that are normal and natural in indigenous culture are often inappropriate, and are almost always denigrated, in colonial culture. One's reflective identity as defined by the colonizer is often brutally demeaning. And yet the economic and political domination of the colonizers—their widespread control of the structure of work, their system of education, and so on—impels one to accept the colonial categories, their implications and practical consequences. This can give rise to very sharp and painful conflicts in one's self-understanding, aspiration, expectation, action, etc., leaving one almost entirely unable to take coherent action toward humanly fulfilling goals—and thus in effect requiring that one take some sort of stand on the issue of identity. In the very simplest terms, one may respond to this by embracing indigenous tradition, striving for full Europeanization, or combining the two. I should like to discuss each option in turn.

Orthodoxy, Unreflective Conformism, and Reaction

The most obvious way in which one may return to tradition is through a genuine reintegration with the living, changing practices and ideas of the tradition, accepting them in all their precolonial diversity. It is particularly important to stress the open quality of tradition here. As Ashis Nandy has argued, "Those in deeper touch with traditions . . . are, for that very reason, more open to the new and the exogenous" (*Illegitimacy*, 47), for traditions are themselves always to some degree flexible, multiple, various. Bhiku Parekh, following Gandhi, maintains that "A tradition . . . [is] not blind, a mere collection of precedents, but a *form of inquiry* . . . an unplanned but rigorous *communal science* constantly tested and revised against the harsh reality of life" (19). Even if one does not go this far, it seems clear that all traditions necessarily allow some scope for social change, for regional and other diversity, and even for individual choice and idiosyncrasy. Many allow a great deal.

I call this sort of broad and open traditionalism "orthodoxy," and mean the category to encompass a wide range of attitudes toward tradition, including some that are systematically critical. Indeed, orthodoxy, in this sense, can even be "modernizing," for, like Samir Amin and others, I would distinguish modernization from Europeanization or Westernization. As Amin has stressed, the "debate in which 'identity' (and 'heritage') are placed in absolute contrast with 'modernization,' viewed as synonymous with 'Westernization'" is "confused" and is part of "a false construction of the question of 'cultural identity'" (133). Specifically, I see "modernization" as the adoption of practices which, by the broad principles of traditional thought, count as advances on traditional ideas or practices, either for empirical or moral reasons. For example, there is nothing in orthodox Hindu thought that is incoherent with the development of medicine. Indeed, there is a highly developed Hindu science of medicine. To make use of the benefits of Western medicine would thus count as "modernizing," in my sense, and not necessarily as "Westernizing."

In contrast with open-minded orthodoxy—especially modernizing orthodoxy—we might distinguish "unreflective conformism" or "unreflective traditionalism." As I am using the term, "orthodoxy" involves an openness to the reflective consideration of tradition, and genuine attention to the structure and meaning of traditional beliefs and acts. Unreflective conformism, in contrast, is merely the thoughtless repetition of the common ideas and practices of a tradition, not only without criticism, but without an understanding of their relations and purposes. It is roughly what Heidegger called "inauthenticity," doing what "one" does. It is not entirely complementary with orthodoxy, as any given orthodox traditionalist is likely to be reflective about certain aspects of tradition but not about others. Indeed, it is not possible to be reflective about everything. In that sense, everyone is, to some degree, an unreflective conformist. However, there are highly significant differences in degree, with some people—or at least some literary characters—being almost entirely unreflective conformists, and others being highly reflective.

The nature of orthodoxy becomes clearer when we consider the third standard mode of affirming tradition, what I call "reactionary traditionalism"—or, sometimes, "reactionary nativism" or "reactionary racialism." Reactionary traditionalism is, first of all, a rigidification of indigenous tradition. However, it is a rigidification governed by European culture—*not* by indigenous tradition itself—and this in one of two ways: It is either *purgative* or *stereotypical*. If purgative, the reactionary traditionalist tries to eliminate from indigenous culture all elements that it shares with European culture. Simultaneously, he/she stresses all elements of indigenous culture that oppose European culture. If English men and women mix freely, then the traditional practices surrounding the isolation of women and men must be extended and strengthened, with exceptions eliminated. Arguably, this form of reactionary traditionalism is not simply a matter of eliminating Europeanisms, but involves a larger "purifying" practice, in which the reactionary traditionalist purges indigenous culture of anything that seems to make it weak in the face of colonial culture. This would centrally include any element shared with colonial culture, for a point of contact might equally provide a point of entry for cultural "infiltration." But this sort of purgative traditionalism also seeks to eliminate any non-European aspect of indigenous culture that appears to make it vulnerable. Thus, distinctive indigenous traditions of pluralism, nonviolence, and the like, may be purged by reactionary traditionalists, insofar as these are seen as weakening tradition in the face of colonial threat.

Purgative reactionary traditionalism often takes the form of originalism or pseudo-originalism. Originalism is the return to a putatively "pure" form of tradition, an original form that was followed by degeneration. Reactionary traditionalists often see this putative degeneration as the reason for the eventual triumph of colonialism, making the elimination of degeneracy and the return to the origin crucial for the political struggle against colonialism. Originalism is the antithesis of the modernism found among some orthodox traditionalists, for it counsels, not the continuation of development, but its abandonment. "Fundamentalism," in the popular sense of the term, is typically a form of originalist reactionary traditionalism, usually involving some sort of dogmatic textual literalism linked with coercive force.

The stereotypical version of reactionary traditionalism is an adoption of tradition based not on tradition per se, but rather on the colonial, ideological misrepresentation of that tradition. It is typical of the reactionary traditionalist that he/she does not truly know indigenous tradition. He/she has lived away from communal practices for too long, has never studied the sacred texts or learned the holy tongue, has never internalized the ways and stories of his/her ancestors. Indeed, the reactionary traditionalist is typically someone who has tried to become English and be accepted into English society, but has failed. In seeking to become English, he/she has internalized not indigenous culture, but colonialist views of indigenous culture.

Most often, the stereotypes in question involve specific views about the nature of indigenous traditions. But sometimes the stereotype is even cruder than this, for it in effect represents indigenous people before colonialism as living in as state of nature, acting from a sort of brute spontaneity. When an indigenous person takes up this sort of stereotype, it hardly makes sense to refer to this as "traditionalism." In this case, I substitute the term "reactionary nativism." Similarly, when a stereotypical identification by race is the basis for reactionary traditionalism, I refer to this as "reactionary racialism."

Sometimes indigenous "traditions" adopted by the reactionary traditionalist were not precisely what we would call "stereotypes," but were, nonetheless, a byproduct of British administrative practices, which comes to much the same thing, as both involve the substitution of the colonizer's ideas about tradition for tradition itself. Parekh presents a fine illustration from the British treatment of Hindu law. "The complex customary law which the traditional system of administering justice knew how to interpret and enforce" was too flexible and complex for "the British-established courts of law." In consequence, the traditional system was "replaced by the *shastras* and their rigid and sometimes obsolete and impractical norms" (31). In this way, the rigidity of some Hindu reactionary traditionalists was a direct result of this prior, British rigidification of Hindu law, which was entirely out of keeping with living Hindu tradition.

Along the same lines, reactionary traditionalists often unconsciously anglicize indigenous tradition themselves, reformulating it in British terms, shaping it in British categories. As Nandy points out, many traditionalists remade Hinduism in the image of Christianity, "introduc[ing] into Hinduism the principles of organization, proslytization, specialized priestly orders, the concept of religion as a principle of political mobilization, a hard sense of history and even, in some cases, a patriarchal God" (*At the Edge*, 57).

Assimilation and Mimeticism

But, again, one need not accept indigenous tradition; one might turn instead to the metropolis. Directly parallel to orthodoxy is what I shall call "assimilation." Assimilation is the full acceptance and internalization of the other basic culture. For an English person, it is, in effect, becoming African or Indian. For an African or Indian, it is, in effect, becoming English. Some Europeans find themselves drawn to Indian religion, Indian literature, Indian food and customs. Some Indians find themselves drawn to Christianity, English literature, and so on. Though the colonial situation limits the degree to which assimilation is possible in either direction, there are, I think, many cases where it occurs. This is particularly true if one allows the possibility of being truly multicultural—and there is no reason not to allow this. In other words, it seems to happen with some regularity that Indians or Africans or Caribbeans (or even Irish) come to be perfectly at home in English society, think of themselves as English (as well as Indian, or whatever), act with perfect, unreflective ease in English society, and so forth. It also happens that English persons come to be perfectly at home in Indian or African or Caribbean (or even Irish) society, and so on. Though it is more difficult, one can assimilate another culture just as one can become fluent in another language. (Having mentioned that the English may assimilate, I should probably note that all these categories apply to the colonizer as well as the colonized. For example, a settler may adopt a reactionary traditionalist attitude toward English culture. I have not treated the English side here as it has only very limited bearing on the literature we will be examining.)

If we like, it is possible to distinguish a form of assimilation that is critical or deliberative and a form that is unthinking or mechanical. If we wish to make this distinction, we may reserve the term *assimilation* for the former (maintaining its parallelism with "orthodoxy"), and refer to the latter as a type of unreflective conformism—perhaps distinguishing the two types of unreflective conformism as "emulative" and "traditionalist." In real life, both sorts of unreflective conformism are no doubt important. However, the distinction between assimilation proper and emulative conformism (i.e., unreflective, uncritical, but genuine internalization of the ideas and practices of the alien culture) does not have much of any place in literature. This is unsurprising as it is really a distinction important only within the alien culture, and thus has little bearing on the problem of cultural identity as it appears in indigenous literature.

The general nature of assimilation becomes clearer when contrasted with the remaining manner of adopting metropolitan culture—mimeticism. Mimeticism is directly parallel to reactionary traditionalism, but, like assimilation, it moves in the opposite direction. An early account of this response to colonialism was given by Douglas Hyde, in his seminal lecture of 1892, "The Necessity for De-Anglicizing Ireland." As Lyons summarizes, "Hyde protested . . . against the slavish conformism which made the Irish adopt everything English simply because it was English" (*Culture*, 42). More exactly, mimeticism—or, equivalently, "reactionary assimilationism" (I shall use the terms interchangeably)—is closely related to reactionary traditionalism, not least in having two main types, purgative and stereotypical. In the more common, purgative mode, mimeticism is the repudiation of indigenous traditions, and includes the repudiation of those aspects of English culture that overlap with indigenous traditions. It involves the maximization of difference between the two traditions. It is enacted through an emphasis on and exaggeration of the most extreme and non-Indian/non-African/non-Irish aspects of English culture, even to the extent of appearing to be a sort of parody of English custom—as when a Hindu gives up Indian food to sit every evening at a high table with a white cloth and eat vast quantities of boiled beef. This parodic effect is particularly easy to achieve because, much like the reactionary traditionalist, the mimeticist most often has only the most superficial knowledge of the culture to which he/she has devoted him/herself. This is equally evident in the less common stereotypical mode. In this mode, the mimeticist strives to imitate a standard idea of English custom that has little relation to actual British practical identity–as when an Igbo man wears an ill-fitting three-piece suit while at leisure in a remote village on a sweltering afternoon

One particularly important connection between reactionary traditionalism and mimeticism is that reactionary traditionalists are typically reacting against a prior mimeticism. In other words, a colonized person who ends up as a reactionary traditionalist will very often do so after having passed through a period of mimeticism. In general terms, this point was one of the main themes of Fanon's work (see, for example, *Black Skin*, 8–9 and *Wretched*, 217–23). Ashis Nandy's analyses of Sri Aurobindo and Nathuram Godse, the assassinator of Gandhi, provide excellent illustrations of this process (on Aurobindo, see *Intimate*

Enemy, 85–100, on Godse, see *At the Edge*, 70–98). As Nandy put the general point, one group "paid their homage to the alien authorities by identification and imitation," while the other did so "by compulsive and counterphobic rejection" (*At the Edge*, 61, see also 113).

As Nandy's allusion to psychoanalysis suggests, the process here is closely related to—and is often an instance of—what psychoanalysts call "reaction formation," the repression of one impulse or idea and its substitution by the precise opposite. Reaction formation is, in a sense, a sort of hyper-repression. It in effect says, "That is so false that the complete opposite is true!" Suppose, for example, that I have strongly aggressive impulses toward someone, which cause such intense and disturbing conflict that they are repressed. As part of my defense against these impulses, I may come to behave toward this person with excessive affection and care. This is a reaction formation. Though my outward behavior and conscious attitude are solicitous and loving, they are in fact a defense against aggression and hatred. Reactionary traditionalism, racialism, and so on, are directly parallel in that they are outward affirmations of one's cultural or racial superiority, but they are frequently derived from, and in many cases still based on, a prior or underlying belief in one's cultural or racial inferiority.

Syncretism and Alienation

Finally, one might privilege neither indigenous nor metropolitan tradition, but try instead to combine the two, choosing what seems best from each, and bringing them together into a new culture, ideally superior to both precedents—or, if not superior, at least better suited to those people who have internalized aspects of both cultures. This is syncretism. It is the attitude toward identity preferred by the bulk of Anglophone postcolonization writers—predictably, given their background, readership, and so forth. (It should be emphasized that this background is by no means typical of postcolonization people, as Appiah [239], Ahmad [149], and others have stressed; indeed, for this reason, and due to the diversity of opinions and practices in any society, the views of these writers should never be generalized or taken as "representative" of their home cultures.)

For the most part, the nature of syncretism is straightforward and does not require explanation. However, it is worth noting that what counts as orthodoxy and what counts as syncretism is relative to cultural context. In Afro-Caribbean literature, there is no "pure" orthodoxy. Rather, what counts as orthodox (in our sense) is any cultural practice that, however synthetic, preserves elements or structures of African origin. For example, in Africa itself, a religion that combines Yoruba and Christian beliefs would be syncretist and would be opposed to "pure" orthodox Yoruba belief on the one hand and "pure" metropolitan Christianity on the other. In the Caribbean, however, the "pure" Yoruba practices survive, for the most part, only in syncretistic forms. In that context, then, the Yoruba/Christian synthesis would be the only relevant form of "orthodoxy." The overall result is that the alternatives in Afro-Caribbean tradition are more limited than alternatives in India or Africa. Orthodoxy and syncretism are, in effect, collapsed into a single category.

Paired with syncretism is what I will call "alienating hybridity," the estrangement from both traditions, the sense that one can be neither English nor Igbo (Hindu, etc.), the paralyzing conviction that one has no identity, no real cultural home, and that no synthesis is possible. In literature, at least, the condition is linked with madness. This extreme cultural alienation appears to be particularly common in Caribbean literature, unsurprisingly, given the high degree of severance experienced by all colonized people in the region. As Walcott puts it, the "West Indian feels rootless on his own earth" ("What the Twilight Says," 21). Indeed, in some cases from the Caribbean, the alienation is so severe that it might more appropriately be referred to as "alienating denial of identity." In the standard less severe case of alienating hybridity, the character in question internalizes the alien culture after extensive education, typically including a period in the metropolis. His/her racial or ethnic origin prevents true acceptance in the foreign culture, and the internalization of the foreign culture makes him/her (in Achebe's phrase) "no longer at ease" in the home culture as well.

IDENTITY AND GENDER

As Ashis Nandy has pointed out, the colonial denigration of indigenous culture consistently involved an assimilation of cultural hierarchies to sex hierarchies (*Intimate*, 4–11). Specifically, the indigenous cultures were seen as feminine or effeminate and the metropolitan culture as masculine. Colonialists who promulgated this view stressed or fabricated elements of indigenous culture putatively indicative of effeminacy (passivity, weakness, irrationality, wiliness, etc.) and elements of metropolitan culture putatively indicative of masculinity (aggressiveness, strength, rationality, honesty, etc.). Correspondingly, they downplayed or denied the aspects of both cultures that did not fit this schema.

As Nandy emphasizes, colonial ideologists tended to focus particular attention on indigenous men, in effect denying their manhood. On the other hand, the position of women was ideologically important as well. First of all, indigenous women were viewed as the most passive creatures possible. Subservient, even to the point of lacking separate will, they were the shadowy tittering figures on the margins of *A Passage to India*: "All the [Indian] ladies were uncertain, cowering, recovering, giggling, making tiny gestures of atonement or despair" (36). Or "those Indian women . . . silly, pretty, flimsy nincompoops" of Virginia Woolf's *Mrs. Dalloway* (10). At best, they were fitting objects of pity for Western liberals, including Western feminists. In this way, colonial ideology tended to "feminize" indigenous men and "hyper-feminize" indigenous women.

But this feminization did not merely involve seeing indigenous people as passive. As, for example, Homi Bhabha has stressed, the colonizer never views colonized people as simply and unequivocally subservient. He/she always sees colonized people simultaneously as dangerous and uncontrollable. As we shall discuss below, Bhabha identifies these two aspects of the colonizer's attitude with fetishism and paranoia. But, insofar as there is a dualism here, it seems much closer to the dualism of misogynist stereotypes, more like virgin and whore. Indeed, the dissembling or duplicity that allows for this duality is itself a misogynist stereotype. Thus, indigenous peoples came to be viewed in colonial ideology as seemingly passive and subservient, but harboring hidden violence and lust. Out of sight, they were drugged and lecherous, immoral and dissolute. These are the "Eastern excesses," bacchic "opposites" to European "values" (57), the putative "lechery" and "debauchery" (62), explored by Edward Said in *Orientalism*.

This racist and sexist view was applied cross-culturally by colonial ideologues, but there were some important variations in degree. In particular, the more vicious the cultural denigration, the more sexually degraded was the image of colonized people. This denigration reached its nadir with respect to sub-Saharan Africa. Thus, it helped give rise to the racist image of the African rapist or the African man with huge reproductive organs and inexhaustible drives—a psychologically deep, historically persistent, and ideologically functional image, as Frantz Fanon demonstrated in *Black Skin, White Masks*. In this way, the ideological feminization and consequent sexualization of colonized people—which, again, involved a misogynist stereotype of vast and predatory sexual appetites—paradoxically contributed to the apparent hypertrophy of male sexuality in the ideological representation of the African man. This is not to say that women did not suffer from this ideological sexualization. Quite the contrary. Here, too, indigenous women were "hyper-feminized," which in this case means assimilated as a group to prostitutes, or rather to a fantasy of the prostitute, an imago of an insatiable, scheming, threatening temptress.

In part as a result of this colonial imposition of gender models on cultural relations, and in part as a result of a cross-cultural tendency to assimilate important social divisions to the division between men and women, many indigenous Anglophone writers too came to see the opposition between tradition and colonial culture as bound up with gender issues. Indeed, a great deal of characterization in postcolonization Anglophone literature may be viewed as a direct, if partially unconscious, response to this ideological feminization of indigenous people.

Beyond this, gender is in any case a central part of both reflective and practical identity. It is typically the first and most repeated way in which we are defined. In every culture of which I am aware, children are categorized by sex from birth and are consistently referred to in terms of their sex thereafter. Moreover, this categorization is consequential. In a wide range of cultures, sex is one of the most highly stereotyped categories, especially in terms of ideals. In other words, moral and practical ideals appear to be based on gender distinctions far more often than they are based on distinctions of any other sort. Many cultures also have descriptive stereotypes associated with sex. In other words, most cultures assign distinctive normative roles to men and women—obvious instances for women would include serving their husbands and nurturing their children. In addition, a large number of cultures impute distinctive psychological and other traits to men and women—for example, rationality and nonrational intuition respectively in Euro-American culture. Thus, one's reflective identity as male or female is not a matter of simple sexual categorization. Rather, it entails a wide range of beliefs about what one should do and what one is able to do.

In keeping with this, social interactions in work and leisure, in public and in the home, are largely organized according to sex. What jobs one can have, what tasks one is expected to fulfill, what forms of relaxation one can engage in and with whom—these are all at least in part determined by whether one is male or female. Not only one's reflective identity, but one's practical identity is largely a function of one's sex. All this makes gender identity a central concern in deliberations over cultural and personal identity and in responses to crises of cultural and personal identity.

We may conceptually organize the possibilities for gender identity in parallel with the general categories of cultural identity, beginning with orthodox masculinity and orthodox femininity. These are, of course, social categories—not so much because gender identity is "socially constructed," in the sense of resulting from socialization, but rather because gender identity is ideological. In other words, reflective identity is not a matter of what we are made into by culture, but of what we believe we are. In all cultures, conceptions of masculinity and femininity are determined not by what men and women are really like—whether this results from nurture or nature—but by the function of the concepts "male" and "female" in structuring social hierarchies. Thus, "orthodox masculinity" here is masculinity *as understood* in the culture in question; the same holds for "orthodox femininity." Moreover, this category is *normative* within the tradition in question, which is to say, a definition of "orthodox masculinity" or "orthodox femininity" indicates a *standard*, not necessarily a belief about real people—still less any fact about real people.

Orthodox masculinity and orthodox femininity necessarily involve competence, as well as strength and a degree of fortitude, in traditional spheres of activity. This is part of any literary representation of characters of this sort. On the other hand, there are, unsurprisingly, differences in the precise ways this is depicted. This type is usually of two sorts, depending upon the age of the character. A younger woman is chaste and respectful of her husband—though not necessarily, or even typically, subservient. An older woman is most often a repository of spiritual and folk wisdom. Both figures occur in literature by men and by women, but the strength and independence of both is somewhat more likely to be emphasized in literature by women. Moreover, the strength and competence of traditional men is less in evidence, and their abuse of social, economic, and physical power is more likely to be exposed in work by women—though this motif is not absent from writings by men.

Unreflective conformist masculinity and femininity are somewhat rarer than the other categories we are considering. In each case, we are faced with a character's unquestioning conformity to common gender roles, as currently practiced, even when those violate larger social ideals or are directly harmful to the people involved. The most obvious cases of this, perhaps the only cases, occur in feminist writing, where we might find a woman thoughtlessly adhering to patriarchal practices that harm her and other women, including her daughters.

Parallel to reactionary traditionalism, we may distinguish reactionary masculinity and reactionary femininity. Either may involve stereotypical elements. Thus, women may be presented as silent, subservient, chaste, and so on, and men as eloquent, wily, virile, and so on, depending on the specific way the group in question has been stereotyped. However, characters of this sort do not seem to figure prominently in postcolonization Anglophone literature. Whatever the reason, in literature at least, both reactionary masculinity and reactionary femininity are most often "purgative," rather than stereotyped. Thus, reactionary masculinity is typically a refashioned masculinity from which all elements of putative femininity have been purged in order to avoid the threat of feminization. This is closely related to "machismo," with the difference that reactionary masculinity is a part of reactionary traditionalism, involving religious and other attitudes that we do not associate with machismo. Machismo is, in a sense, reactionary masculinity divorced from traditional culture. Reactionary femininity is a scrupulous adherence to a cultural ideal of femininity, purged of any hint of the degeneracy projected by colonial ideologues onto colonized women. It too is clearly a part of reactionary traditionalism. Note that both reactionary masculinity and reactionary femininity are often originalist, calling for a return to "original" culture with its "pure" masculinity and femininity.

In connection with reactionary femininity and reactionary masculinity, it is important to recall that colonial ideologies tend to deny the masculinity of indigenous men and the "purity" of indigenous women. Thus, a purgative reactionary masculinity and a purgative reactionary femininity will operate differently. They are opposed not to one another, but to a set of demeaning colonial stereotypes. These stereotypes have particular force for the reactionary traditionalist, not only because they are demeaning, but because they suggest a form of cultural decline that could account for the triumph of colonialism. In other words, the reactionary traditionalist man defines himself not against the traditional woman, but against the degenerate effeminate (e.g., cowardly) male stereotype promulgated in colonial culture; the reactionary traditionalist woman defines herself not against the traditional man, but against her derogatory characterization in colonial ideology. Indeed, as reactionary femininity is opposed to a colonial "hyper-feminization," it may involve stereotypically masculine traits, such as strength, anger, even physical violence, especially insofar as these are aimed at the colonizer or at other dangers facing tradition. In each case, the opposition to the stereotype is simultaneously a purging of just those elements that may be seen as making indigenous culture weak in the face of metropolitan threat.

To these orthodox, conformist, and reactionary categories, we may add the falling away from orthodox gender ideals that is linked with mimeticism and is typically conceived of as a form of effeminacy—compare Okonkwo's judgment of his Christianized son Nwoye as "degenerate and effeminate" in Achebe's *Things Fall Apart* (159). More exactly, as we have seen, degeneracy and effeminacy have been central attributes in the standard European view of colonized men and women. This view has no doubt been held by reactionary assimilationists as well. However, canonical postcolonization writers rarely treat mimeticism with any sympathy. Thus, they not only repudiate this colonial view, they tend to reverse it. In other words, a number of postcolonization authors see European culture—and *a fortiori* all those who imitate European culture—as lascivious and degraded, and typically effeminate as well. Just as reaction is standardly portrayed as masculinizing—even in reactionary femininity—mimeticism is standardly portrayed as feminizing.

On the other hand, this does not mean that there are not male and female forms. There are. Moreover, just as reactionary masculinity and reactionary femininity tend to be purgative, degenerate masculinity and degenerate femininity tend to be stereotypical, at least in the sense that they tend to be based in part on a stereotype of Europeans as hedonistically self-indulgent, cruelly dominant, and, again, effeminate, which is to say, lacking in putatively masculine virtues and harboring putatively feminine vices.

Degenerate masculinity typically involves excessive intoxication, sexually exploitative behavior, and general dissolution. A good illustration of this is Rushdie's Ahmed Sinai, a mimic even to the degree that his skin turns white (212); in the course of this transformation, he becomes an alcoholic and begins to sexually harass his secretaries (154). This character type is frequently linked with political corruption as well.

However, in that version, the sensuous dissipation is typically much less, and is replaced by the more abstract degeneracy of greed—though the exploitative treatment of women remains relatively constant. Moreover, in the political case, the mimic often conceals his mimeticism behind an insincere traditionalism, reactionary or orthodox.

Degenerate femininity is parallel, but with some predictable differences. Female sensual decadence is more likely to manifest itself in such mild forms of self-indulgence as smoking, rather than habitual intoxication, and sexual dissolution in this case is often a matter of prostitution. Unsurprisingly, when women writers take up the common "Westernized whore" character, they frequently do so in such a way as to criticize the sexist presuppositions that so often underlie the stereotype. For example, Dangarembga's Nyasha is a Westernized young woman who is falsely perceived to be dissolute.

Parallel to syncretism is the synthesis of masculine and feminine properties, sometimes referred to as "androgyny," in other words, a forging of gender identity that combines the putative virtues of both sexes into a new, superior identity. For example, in Tagore's *The Home and the World*, Nikhil is the culturally syncretistic character. He also combines the "feminine" virtues of generosity, kindness, affection, with such "masculine" virtues as physical bravery. In other words, he is not only synthetic in culture, but androgynous in gender. It is worth noting that he is opposed to Sandip, a cowardly mimic who exploits women and indulges mild sensual vices, and who conceals his mimeticism behind a facade of reactionary nationalism and violent masculinity. This sort of opposition—between an androgynous syncretist and a degenerate mimic masquerading as a hyper-masculine traditionalist—is not uncommon in postcolonization fiction.

Finally, corresponding with alienating hybridity, we have the complete loss of gender identity, usually as part of a broader loss of personal identity. Bessie Head's Elizabeth, in *A Question of Power*, is a good example of this—a colored woman with no real home culture, she loses any firm sense of even physical sexual identity. Needless to say, not all cases are this extreme.

Assimilation should find a parallel here as well, presumably in some genuine adherence to metropolitan gender roles and ideals. However, I know of no relevant cases in postcolonization literature, thus I shall leave it aside, as there is no empirical basis on which to develop and specify the notion.

On "Postcolonial Theory":
An Example from Homi K. Bhabha

Some readers of the preceding pages have been troubled, not by what I have discussed, but by something I have not discussed. They refer to it as "theory." One colleague actually went so far as to ask, "Why isn't there any theory in your opening chapter?"

Initially, I found this curious. If one isolates significant general patterns, provides an explanatory framework, and systematically structures a range of seemingly disparate phenomena—well, that *is* theory. What else could theory be? More exactly, I have set out to provide a sort of logico-empirical analysis of colonization, especially its geographical and cultural organization, and of cultural identity after colonization. Too often, I believe, we discuss colonialism with little basic terminological or conceptual clarity. Thus, our arguments and analyses flounder—muddling together orthodoxy and reaction, failing to recognize the symmetry between reactionary traditionalism and mimeticism, and so forth. Most discussions of colonialism do not even keep clear the distinct regions of cultural geography, not to mention the crucial differences of degree in severance, contact, and internalization. Moreover, those writers who do recognize one or another of these distinctions most often do so implicitly, and thus without the full clarity and rigor that are made possible by the sort of explicit analytic undertaken in the preceding pages.

But, of course, this is not what my colleague meant. His objection concerned my references to other theorists, specifically "postcolonial theorists." Admittedly, there are many well-known theorists of colonialism that I do not treat. But this cannot count as an objection in and of itself, for the purpose of this chapter is not to provide an overview of postcolonial theory. Rather, the purpose is to provide a positive account of cultural identity after colonization. Toward this end, I build on the work of Ashis Nandy and, to a lesser extent, Frantz Fanon. In addition, I draw more locally on the work of Samir Amin, Kwame Appiah, Edward Said, and others. Here too, then, it seems odd to complain of an absence of theory.

But even this was not precisely what my colleague had in mind. For "postcolonial theory" is not used to refer to Nandy, Amin, Appiah, nor even to Fanon and Said. Rather, it is used to refer to certain doctrinal principles and certain canonical critics. In recent years, it has come to be used very narrowly to refer to that subset of theorists of colonialism who are also poststructuralist—most obviously Homi Bhabha and Gayatri Spivak. This is what my colleague meant: Why isn't there any Homi Bhabha in your opening chapter? If this were some sort of idiosyncracy on his part, the question would be inconsequential and could be set aside without further thought. But my colleague is not alone in tacitly reducing "postcolonial theory" to a handful of prominent poststructural critics. Indeed, he appears to be in the majority—so much so, that if one sends out an article or book manuscript on postcolonization literature it is very likely that one will be required to treat Bhabha and/or Spivak as a condition of publication, for one is likely to be required to treat "post-colonial theory" and these two figures are increasingly taken as definitive of the entire field.

Though I do acknowledge some of Bhabha's insights here and in subsequent chapters, my colleague was correct when he found that the manuscript did not incorporate any significant amount of "theory" in this extremely narrow sense. This is not a mere oversight. In fact, on the whole, I find the writings of Bhabha and Spivak terminologically opaque, conceptually imprecise, and empirically lax. For these reasons, I did not initially wish to address them at all. In this book, I have sought to draw out what is valuable in the authors I examine. I do not always entirely agree with them, but I have tried to find what is positive and worthwhile in their novels and plays, what contributes to our understanding of cultural identity in various and complex colonial conditions. In keeping with this, I have chosen to discuss literary works that I believe address these issues insightfully. When I began writing this book, I felt that there had been enough negative discussion surrounding the literature and culture of the former British colonies. In connection with this, I wished to write a book that did not focus on tearing down theories and interpretations but on building up theories and interpretations. It is something like Rabindranath Tagore's attitude toward *swadeshi*, the general boycott of foreign goods in Bengal in the first decade of this century. He contended that the crucial thing was to manufacture cloth and other goods in India—"positive *swadeshi*," as it was called—rather than engaging in the "negative *swadeshi*" of burning foreign-made items (see Sarkar, 32–33). I had hoped to confine this book to a theoretical version of the "positive" politics advocated by Tagore.

These were not my only reasons for wishing to avoid such a direct encounter with "theory" in this reduced sense. My criticisms of Bhabha and Spivak are largely my criticisms of Lacan and of deconstruction, which I have already elaborated in chapters 2 and 3 of *The Politics of Interpretation*. Moreover, I share broad political sympathies with Bhabha and Spivak—something particularly significant in this period of increasing political "conservatism," corporatism, and racism. The political issues on which we evidently agree are far more important and consequential than the intellectual issues on which we disagree. Finally, there is something not quite right about criticizing these writers when my primary argument is with those followers who have made their work compulsory in "postcolonial studies"—something I believe neither Bhabha nor Spivak would have done themselves.

Despite this, I have finally been forced to conclude that some statement on the dominant, poststructural strain of postcolonial theory is unavoidable. Clearly, I cannot deal with all the work of Bhabha and Spivak. The book is already lengthy and an extended treatment of these writers would not only increase its size, but distract from its main, positive, purposes. In order to keep my criticism within a reasonable compass, therefore, I shall focus on a single essay by Bhabha, "Of Mimicry and Man: The Ambivalence of Colonial Discourse." This essay, first delivered on a panel organized by Spivak (Bhabha, "Of Mimicry," 126n.), is an important, indeed seminal treatment of identity and colonialism. It serves, therefore, as an appropriate example of the problems with the encompassing set of "theoretical" writings in which it is located.

Bhabha begins his essay with two lengthy epigraphs. The first is from Jacques Lacan and concerns mimicry among animals. Whatever his point in the larger context, here Lacan notes the camouflaging function of such mimicry. This may lead the reader to expect that Bhabha will discuss the way in which some indigenous people might try to mimic the habits of the colonizer as a form of camouflage. But this is not the focus of Bhabha's essay. It is important to note this right at the beginning, for—in this essay at least—Bhabha has very little concern with the thought or action of colonized people. His focus is almost entirely on the colonizer's thought and action. There is, of course, nothing wrong with this—so long as Bhabha is clear, to himself and to his reader, that he is concerned with the perspective of the colonizer. However, the conjunction of this quotation with the next already suggests that Bhabha is not entirely clear about the perspective he is adopting in his analysis. For the second quotation clearly takes up the colonizer's point of view. We will return to this point below.

The second epigraph is from Sir Edward Cust. In 1839, addressing the Colonial Office, Cust stated that the British have "conferr[ed] on every colony of the British Empire a mimic representation of the British Constitution," thereby deceiving the colonized people into thinking that they can "defy the mother country." Cust's point is, in part, that allowing colonized people certain forms associated with independence, giving them a sort of false imitation or mimicry of independence, will almost necessarily lead them to think of themselves as independent, and to act that way.

The two epigraphs seem to have nothing in common but the use of the word "mimicry." They do not speak of the same phenomena, or even of related phenomena. This is worth noting, not only for the reasons already mentioned, but also as it alerts us to the possibility that Bhabha might base some of his arguments on accidental matters of word choice.

In the first paragraph of the essay, Bhabha picks up on the second quotation. It is difficult, however, to isolate any specific argumentative or analytic content in this paragraph. It begins, "The discourse of post-Enlightenment English colonialism often speaks in a tongue that is forked, not false." There are several problems with this sentence. For one thing, it implicitly attributes the ideological import of Cust's statement to the Enlightenment. There are certainly elements of Enlightenment thought in colonial ideology. However, Enlightenment principles also form the basis for a great deal of anticolonial thought and action (for a recent example, one need only think of Noam Chomsky). Thus, Bhabha begins by passing over an extremely complex issue with a sort of careless flippancy.

More importantly, the main claim of the sentence—which turns out to be crucial to his argument—is very confusing. First of all, what does he mean by saying that "The discourse of . . . English colonialism . . . speaks"? Ordinarily, we would say that persons speak, not discourses. Discourses are, after all, things that are *spoken*. Perhaps Bhabha has in mind the idea that colonialists express colonialist ideology when they speak about colonialism. Colonialist ideology, then, is the relevant discourse, and one can say that it speaks, because individuals do not make reasoned choices when repeating ideological commonplaces. Given that there is no real individual agency in repeating colonial propaganda, one might, as a sort of shorthand, say that the discourse speaks. But, of course, if this is what Bhabha meant, he should have said it. In any case, the statement certainly seems rather less profound—less a matter of high "theory"—when clarified in this way.

Assuming that this is indeed what Bhabha had in mind, we are still left with the more important issue of what Bhabha means when he says that this speech is "forked, not false." Let us begin with the simpler part—"not false." One obvious difficulty here is that most of what colonialist ideology "says" is, indeed, false—racist claims about non-European animalism, propagandistic lies about the death tolls during colonial conquests, and, more relevantly, the various deceptions of colonial government regarding the equal administration of justice, the nature of political rights, and so on. Of course, Bhabha only says that this discourse "often" speaks in a forked, not false way. So perhaps these are not the relevant cases.

Perhaps we will be able to determine what speech of colonialist discourse is not false once we have determined what Bhabha means when he says that this "not false" speech is, rather, "forked." Clearly, Bhabha is drawing on the idiom of Native Americans in Hollywood westerns, where some embattled leader is likely to say, "White man speak with forked tongue." But why is Bhabha doing this? In those westerns, the idiom is used to indicate that the white man is deceptive—which is to say, false. Moreover, it is precisely this deceit, this falsity, that seems to be the problem with the "mimic . . . Constitution" mentioned by Cust.

The point is important because it bears directly on the theoretical conclusion of the opening paragraph, in which Bhabha takes up the main topic of his essay—mimicry—implicitly characterizing it as "forked, not false": "In this context," he writes—the context, among other things, of the "forked, not false"—"mimicry emerges as one of the most elusive and effective strategies of colonial power and knowledge." Clearly, mimicry is precisely this forkedness, a sort of intermediate term between truth and falsity. Bhabha presents his conclusion as if it is a radical theoretical revision of standard views. But this is a radical revision only if he has established that the issue with, for example, Cust's "mimic representation of the British Constitution" is not one of its falsity or deceit, but one of something different from falsity or deceit, and something different from truth or sincerity—some third alternative. Moreover, this claim is theoretical only if Bhabha clarifies what this third option is, integrating it into a comprehensible body of hypotheses that is open to communal evaluation and critique. If Bhabha never clarifies the nature of mimicry and forkedness, then he has not formulated a theoretical principle or concept at all; he has not clarified premises, rendered concepts more lucid, extended our conceptual framework, etc. He has, at best, made a remark that is suggestive. On the other hand, if, when made clear, mimicry turns out simply to be a form of deception—as appears to be the case in the quote from Cust—then its potential to become a bold new theoretical alternative is lost. For it is merely a commonplace that has been restated unclearly.

More exactly, the forms of governance, justice, and so on, in the British colonies systematically disprivileged indigenous people in a variety of ways. In some cases, this disprivilege was a straightforward matter of direct discriminatory treatment, the refusal to extend a range of legal rights to the colonized people. Sometimes, this disprivilege was a matter of indirect discrimination—as when Indians were allowed to take civil service examinations, but had to travel to England in order to do so (see Wolpert, 251). Sometimes, it was a matter of discriminatory enforcement of laws, due to the prejudice of administrators. Sometimes, injustice resulted from linguistic or cultural misunderstanding. The list could be extended. But in each case there was some form of falsity, a falsity about what the colonizers were doing in the colony, a falsity about the status and rights and treatment of the indigenous people themselves. In general terms, we have known this for a long time. Our understanding of individual cases can be greatly enriched by historical research. But what theoretical gain can there be in subsuming all of these cases under the rubric of mimicry, somehow understood as distinct from falsity? Such a subsumption seems clearly antitheoretical, for it renders colonial relations, not more lucid, but more obscure.

Indeed, Bhabha's own statement that mimicry is "elusive" suggests just this problem. It is not so much the practice that is difficult to isolate. Rather, it is the concept itself that is difficult to pin down. This difficulty suggests two things. First of all, that the concept is not functioning to aid in the evaluation of hypotheses, to systematize our understanding of colonialism, to clarify our interpretations and render them more rigorous, etc. Rather, it is functioning to obscure precise claims, to baffle rational evaluation, to muddle understanding—like any "elusive" and ill-defined term. Second, it is operating in this way because the phenomena Bhabha is discussing are, in fact, encompassed by ordinary notions of falsity and deceit, leaving no place for a third, theoretically revolutionary concept.

Bhabha's point is not clarified, but rendered more obscure in the next paragraph. There, Bhabha seeks to relate this (ill-defined, non-false, forked) mimicry to a Lacanian notion of castration. I have argued against Lacan's idea of castration elsewhere (see chapter 3 of *Politics*) and will not repeat the criticisms here. But even if one accepts Lacan's idea, the link here is extremely obscure. Indeed, it seems to be purely verbal. In other words, it is akin to the link between Lacan's discussion of mimicry and Cust's—two completely different concepts, yoked together by the chance use of a common term.

Specifically, the colonizer wishes to establish a situation in the colonies that is comparable to that in the metropolis—involving the sorts of administrative and other practices to which he/she is accustomed at home. However, he/she clearly does not wish to establish a system that grants indigenous people the full rights of people at home, or provides indigenous people with the same opportunities for social, economic, or political advancement. As part of this, the colonizer establishes schools and other institutions that are designed to make indigenous people serve well in the colonial structure—but not to make them leaders in that structure. Put simply, these institutions are established to make indigenous people into good clerks and servants for the colonizers, not to make them good administrators who will replace the colonizers. All this is clear. A theoretical discussion of this should make our conceptualization, description, explanation more thorough, more systematic, more encompassing. It should lead us to understand the structures by which such aims are put into practice, the ways in which they succeed or fail, and so on. But Bhabha's "theoretical" discussion seems only to take this relatively clear idea and render it opaque.

Specifically, Bhabha, adopting the viewpoint of the colonizer, writes that "colonial mimicry is the desire for a reformed, recognizable Other, as *a subject of a difference that is almost the same, but not quite*" (126). Once one figures out what Bhabha is referring to—the partial education of indigenous people, an education for service, not independence–this might seem true enough, if somewhat overstated. Bhabha seems to give the colonizer too much credit, reducing colonial bias to some small and limited difference. Indeed, one might argue that the colonial training was designed to produce a group of indigenous people who were "mostly different from Europeans, but not quite," having just enough English language, manners, and the like, to serve their masters well. Still, one is unlikely to complain about Bhabha's phrasing, as the distinction here seems inconsequential. Whether one says "almost the same, but not quite" or "mostly different, but not quite," the main point is shared: Indians were to assume a place in a structure overseen by the British. Thus, there was some degree of integration, but it was incomplete. Of course, we are still left with the issue of how this makes "mimicry" different from deceit, or perhaps discrimination. But, in any case, the precise phrasing seems inconsequential.

However, as it turns out, the precise phrasing is not inconsequential. For it is via this implication of a limited and local difference—implicitly associated with the limited and local difference between male and female—that Bhabha links "mimicry" to "castration," or, more exactly, to "the marginalizing vision of castration" (126). Needless to say, this is no argument. Even if one grants that mimicry is what makes colonizer and colonized "almost the same, but not quite," and even if one grants that castration is what makes boys and girls "almost the same, but not quite," this (forced) verbal parallel provides no reason to see the two as linked. After all, saline solution and water are "almost the same, but not quite." The difference is salt. Are we then to conclude that salt is castration—or, rather, the marginalizing vision of castration? And what could it mean to link mimicry and castration anyway? Does the colonizer have an unconscious fantasy that the colonized person is castrated? That the colonized person will castrate the colonizer? Far from providing rigorous theoretical clarification, this idea is almost impossible to make sense of.

Indeed, it is worth contrasting Bhabha's claim here with the analysis of gender and cultural identity set forth in the preceding section. Both Bhabha and I—following Nandy—posit a connection between colonial hierarchies and gender hierarchies. But Bhabha does so in a way that does not render our conceptualization more precise, or link it with a body of data, or facilitate further research. Rather, he does so in a way that yokes two concepts—mimicry and castration—in a way that is difficult if not impossible to spell out. He bases this, not on empirical evidence, but on accidental features of phrasing. And he does all this in a way that makes it very difficult to say what would count as further research in this field, for he has not made clear any of the consequences of this conjunction. Just how would one seek or recognize instances of this castrational mimicry? One might claim that at least the link with castration does finally provide us with a differentiating criterion for mimicry. Falsity and deceit are not necessarily involved with "the marginalizing vision of castration." But, in fact, even this is not true—for we have no clear idea of just what the link with castration might be and thus how it might function as a defining property.

These problems are not solved when Bhabha does go on to define mimicry further, explaining that mimicry "emerges as the representation of . . . a process of disavowal." One might be able to see how mimicry, as Bhabha is using the term, would involve disavowal in a loose sense. The colonizer has every motive to conceal colonialist mimicry—for example, the falsity of the Constitution—by an ideological pretense that indigenous people are being given full rights, opportunities, and so forth, or that they will be given those rights as soon as they are "ready." However, if Bhabha were saying this, we would again be faced with a situation where his "theory" operates only to obscure commonplace observations, and does not integrate them into a rigorous, clarifying theoretical structure. For, in that case, Bhabha's observation about mimicry and disavowal would be nothing more than an opaque restatement of a standard observation regarding governmental deceit. Perhaps more importantly, this does not seem to be what Bhabha has in mind anyway. Rather, he seems to be extending his obscure linkage of mimicry with castration by alluding to the psychoanalytic concept of disavowal.

More exactly, "disavowal" is a Freudian term, closely linked with the Freudian/Lacanian notion of "foreclosure." It is used to refer to the repudiation of a perception of castration and is linked with the origin of psychosis, as well as fetishism (see, for example, the entry in Laplanche and Pontalis, 118–19). So, evidently, Bhabha is here "theorizing" mimicry as the representation of a psychological defense mechanism that involves the repudiation of a perceived castration. There is a common colonial practice of establishing colonial institutions that are similar to metropolitan institutions, but which do not carry the same rights and possibilities. This practice—or perhaps the denial of this practice, or perhaps the "forked, not false" discourse surrounding this practice—is an image or "representation" of the "process" whereby a child supposedly sees the female genitalia as castrated, but then disavows that sight through a psychological mechanism that leads to fetishism or psychosis. What leads Bhabha to make this connection? What is his argument? What is his evidence? It appears that he has drawn the connection simply on the basis of the term "disavowal," for that term can be used to refer to either the colonial condition or the psychoanalytic condition.

Can this series of identifications, based once again on coincidence of terms, truly be considered theoretical? Is there a real questioning of premises here, a thorough analysis and evaluation of competing hypotheses, an advancement in rigor and explanatory capacity? What reason do we have to believe that British racism, British economic exploitation, British double standards in the administration of justice, etc., are better understood by positing some form of underlying repudiation of castration? Moreover, what would this mean anyway? How could this sort of psychological repudiation explain aspects of colonialism, or anything else?

Of course, Bhabha might respond to all this by saying that he is not literally claiming that there is castration fantasy or repudiation in the psychoanalytic sense. He is merely using these as models for the colonial process. That is fine. But what then do these models show us? How do these models advance a theory of colonialism and identity? Do they lead us beyond the more obvious, literal descriptions—that the British provided colonized people with roughly the degree of justice and self-determination that suited their own interests, that they established colonial institutions that would make indigenous people good functionaries, but not leaders, that they sought to deceive themselves and the colonized people about the nature of colonial rule by claiming that they were far more egalitarian and benevolent than was in fact the case? Does the idea of mimicry, with its associated metaphors of castration and disavowal, advance beyond this obvious (and, in fact, somewhat oversimple) observation?

Later in the essay, Bhabha returns to the issue of castration, but this treatment too is of no help. At one point he refers to "the subject's lack of priority (castration)"(131), casually identifying the two. First of all, what is this "lack of priority"? Is it the colonized person's position in the colonial hierarchy? That would be the obvious interpretation, but it does not fit the rest of the essay. Is it the forkedness of colonial institutions, their mimicry, that makes them diminished, discriminatory versions of comparable, "prior," institutions in the metropolis? That fits the rest of the essay, but not the characterization of this castration as "the subject's." Which subject does Bhabha have in mind? If he is using "the subject" to refer to anyone at all, then how can this be a specific, explanatory part of colonial relations?

Bhabha does say that the questions generated by mimicry go "beyond" this lack of priority/castration "to a historical crisis" (131).

But this too does not clarify anything. It tells us that there is a partial but incomplete connection between castration and these questions, but it does not tell us what the nature of the connection is, where and how it ends, and the like. He does not clarify what the historical crisis is. Or, for that matter, what the questions are—except that they are questions "of authority" (131). Is he saying that indigenous people eventually challenge the rule of colonizers and their vision of marginalizing castrational mimicry? But that does not seem to be the case, for Bhabha's historical crisis is not a material crisis. Rather, it is a "crisis in the conceptuality of colonial man as an *object* of regulatory power" (131). Clearly, then, it is a crisis in the action of the colonizer. But it is not a crisis in the colonizer's control or domination of colonized people. Rather it is a crisis in the colonizer's "conceptualization" of that control. And what does it mean to say that this goes beyond castration?

The situation may be slightly improved if we interpret Bhabha in another way. Perhaps he does not mean that "lack of priority" is to be explained by reference to castration. Perhaps he is saying the reverse. Perhaps in referring to "the subject's lack of priority (castration)," he is defining "castration," saying that, in his usage of the term, "castration" means simply "lack of priority." First of all, if so, then it seems that Bhabha must give up any claim that linking mimicry with castration is theoretical. For if "castration" merely *means* "lack of priority," then, of course, any deceitful repetition of metropolitan structures in the colonies does involve castration, in this sense—for it involves the creation of structures that lack priority. The point is trivial, and obscurely put. Second, if we understand "castration" in this way, then the claim about historical crisis seems almost trivial as well. For, in that case, it seems that Bhabha is simply translating Cust into impenetrable prose. Cust says that mimicry breeds rebellion by leading colonized people to expect justice, equality, and so on. Once colonized people, puffed up with mimic institutions, have "dared to defy the mother country," as Cust puts it (Bhabha, 125), then there is a historical crisis in which the colonizer must conceive of new methods of control. It seems that the best sense one can make of Bhabha's claim here is that it repeats Cust, badly.

In short, whether we interpret castration as lack of priority or colonial lack of priority as castration, we do not seem to be dealing with anything that has conceptual rigor, or explanatory or interpretive value. Rather, we are dealing with an extremely vague phrase, "lack of priority," used with an unclear point of view (probably the colonizer, but perhaps the colonized), and obscurely connected with ill-defined "historical crisis" and an equally ill-defined notion of castration. Perhaps it all works together to repeat a claim made by Cust in the opening epigraph. But, then again, perhaps not. Once more, this simply does not appear to merit the name of "theory."

Of course, these are not the only points at which Bhabha redefines or elaborates his concept of mimicry. But each treatment seems to suffer from the same problems. For example, at one point he explains that colonial educational policies were designed to Anglicize the colonized people, and "to be Anglicized, is *emphatically* not to be English" (128). The point seems reasonable, if somewhat obscure—he does not clearly define what he means by "Anglicized" and thus leaves the reader to fill in. Indeed, the reader is able to understand Bhabha's assertion here only because it is preceded by a famous statement from Macaulay—explaining that education in India will produce "a class of interpreters between us and the millions whom we govern"—and because the idea is itself relatively commonplace.

But thus far, this is not a theoretical statement. Subsequently, Bhabha seeks to develop the point in a "theoretical" fashion. And here as elsewhere, the "theoretical" development does not clarify or systematize the idea, or relate it to broader, explanatory principles. Rather it renders it opaque. Specifically, Bhabha takes up the Lacanian notion of desire as a "metonymy," and asserts that "the difference between being English and being Anglicized" is a "strateg[y] of desire," which is, in turn, a "metonym[y] of presence." Again, the British generally followed educational policies that would not make colonized people English— that is, would not make them full citizens with all the associated rights and opportunities—but merely train them in English social customs and habits of thought in order to make them suitable intermediaries for colonial rule. Clearly, this was not something random and unmotivated. It was animated by goals and interests—minimizing conflict in the colonies, maximizing profit from the colonies, and so on. One can, if one wishes, refer to these goals and interests as "desires." Given this, one could then go on to say that Anglicization, in this sense, was considered a means to achieve those desires or a strategy for achieving those desires—or, more dramatically and less lucidly, a "strategy of desire."

Thus far we are still in the realm of the commonplace. What is not commonplace is the link with Lacanian psychoanalysis, with Lacan's notion of desire. But here we run into the usual problems. To say that the English had "desires" regarding the colony is not to say that they had "desires" *in the psychoanalytic sense*. Perhaps they did. But that requires some sort of argument or analysis, not a coincidence in terminology—and a forced coincidence at that. In this, once more, we see Bhabha's tendency to leap from identity in name to identity in substance. In addition, here as elsewhere, the resulting identification—colonial desire with Lacanian desire—does not seem particularly plausible, nor particularly suited to Lacan.

As if matters were not confused enough, Lacan's notion of desire as metonymy is itself either complicated or, what seems more likely, muddled. It certainly takes different forms. In one form, it is bound up with castration—as when Lacan asserts that a woman becomes the object of desire because of "the absence of the penis" (825, my translation). In another, to my mind more plausible form, it is more general, and is well illustrated by suckling. The infant needs milk and thus comes to desire the breast, which is metonymically associated with that milk (for a fuller account, see chapter 1 of Laplanche). The first, castrational case seems either trivial (heterosexual men desire women in part because of their genitalia) or implausible (sexual desire for a woman develops through a metonymy from a fantasy of castration). Even the more general, noncastrational case (illustrated by suckling), though not implausible, is hardly well established. But let us suppose for a moment that Lacan is correct, that desire really is metonymy—in either or both ways. What reason do we have to assume that this definition of desire has any bearing on the "desire" of the colonizer? What implications does such a connection have for our understanding of the colonial situation? Again, where does castration fit in this? Does the colonizer fantasize that the colonized person is castrated and thus desire him/her? Or, adopting the noncastrational interpretation, what is the colonizer's need, that might be displaced to desire by metonymy? And what precisely is the relevant desire that results from this displacement? What is it directed toward and what does it involve? The connection is rendered even more opaque by Bhabha's assertion that "The desire of colonial mimicry . . . may not have an object" (130)? How can metonymy lead to a non-object? Sometimes Lacanians assert that *demand* does not have an object, as it is always a demand for love (see Laplanche and Pontalis, 483; it is unclear why this does not make love the object of demand). But how does this extend to desire, and how does that extension itself apply to colonial relations?

One might try to seek an answer to these questions by considering Bhabha's characterization of desire as a metonymy of *presence*. But this seems, in fact, to be a further obscuring of the Lacanian idea. Clearly, desire cannot be a metonymy of any presence whatsoever—for then we would desire whatever is next to anything that happens to be around us. Moreover, in the castration-based construal of desire as metonymy, it is clear that desire is not a metonymy of presence. Indeed, it is more apt to characterize desire in this case as a metonymy of absence. Admittedly, in the more general (noncastrational) construal, one could perhaps speak of the breast as a metonymy to the "presence" of the milk. However, even in this case it seems misleading to characterize the satisfaction of hunger as "presence." Thus, the idea of a metonymy of presence does not appear to clarify the issue, nor does it even appear accurate to the Lacanian concept.

Why, then, does Bhabha use this phrase? If there is a non-Lacanian reason, perhaps this will clarify Bhabha's intent—though the fact that the intent requires this degree of hermeneutic scrutiny already suggests that it is not theoretically illuminating. In fact, I suspect that, in referring to metonymy of presence, Bhabha wishes to allude to the notion of presence as it figures in contemporary canonical literary theory, prominently in Derrida's critique of the "metaphysics of presence" through deconstructive *differance*. But there is no conceptual link between a metonymy of presence and a differantial deconstruction of the metaphysics of presence. If this is, indeed, what Bhabha intends, it is yet another instance of identifying concepts based on an identity of terms—and, here again, a forced identity of terms at that.

Once more, it is almost impossible to see how assertions such as these contribute to an illuminating, explanatory theory.

Obviously, we cannot consider Bhabha's entire essay in this textual detail. However, having treated mimicry, we might look briefly at another, related concern of the essay, that named in the subtitle—ambivalence. In order to make the discussion as clear as possible, I shall focus on one of Bhabha's more concrete analyses—that concerning Christian missionary work in India.

Bhabha introduces us to an ambivalent Christian missionary, Charles Grant, who was "Caught between the desire for religious reform and the fear that the Indians might become turbulent for liberty." In consequence, Grant "implies that it is, in fact the 'partial' diffusion of Christianity, and the 'partial' influence of moral improvements which will construct a particularly appropriate form of colonial subjectivity" (127). Specifically, Bhabha tells us, Grant suggested a sort of collusion between Christian teaching and "divisive caste practices" which would "prevent dangerous political alliances" (127). Anticolonial writers have often noted the ways in which missionaries were complicit with colonialism. Bhabha echoes this idea plausibly.

But this, of course, is not the "theorization." Bhabha goes on from here to a "theoretical" restatement of his idea: "Inadvertently, Grant produces a knowledge of Christianity as a form of social control which conflicts with the enunciatory assumptions which authorize his discourse" (127). Here as elsewhere in Bhabha's writing, it is difficult to see how this "theoretical" statement advances the preceding descriptions. Initially, it seems to repeat a fairly obvious—and rather oversimple—point in an obscure way, roughly: Grant taught a version of Christianity that served as a form of social control. In so doing, he violated the very Christian principles—such as those that could be taken to oppose caste—that might have justified his missionary activity to begin with. There is nothing particularly theoretical about this statement. It does not involve conceptual rigor, questioning of presuppositions, or the like. On the other hand, upon closer examination, we see that Bhabha's phrasing of this claim incorporates a number of theoretical terms. These carry with them the theoretical implications of Bhabha's assertion. But it is very difficult to say what we are to make of these theoretical terms, and whether we are to infer that Bhabha is making theoretical statements. Once again, if he is, they do not seem particularly plausible.

First of all, consider the reference to "knowledge." By saying that Grant "produces a knowledge of Christianity as a form of social control," Bhabha implies that Christianity is truly a form of social control. He implies that, when one has "knowledge of Christianity," one knows it, not as a set of mere "enunciatory assumptions," but rather as what it really is. I am not at all certain that Bhabha intended this implication. If he did, it is an obscurely phrased claim about Christianity, for which Bhabha gives no evidence or argument. On the other hand, it may simply be that a more lucid phrase, such as "Grant uses Christianity for purposes of social control," sounded too simple and obvious, whereas "produces a knowledge of Christianity as a form of social control" sounded vaguely Foucaultian, and therefore more sophisticated. In either case, this is not a theoretical statement.

Or perhaps Bhabha actually intended to make a Foucaultian point here. Perhaps Bhabha is analyzing Christian missionary work in India on the basis of Foucault's idea that systems of knowledge are bound up with systems of power—criminology with prisons, for example. One could imagine Bhabha making an argument of this type. For example, he might seek to uncover the specific "sins" interrogated by priests in Indian confessionals and the way these interrogations operated in relation to particular institutions of British social control. But Bhabha does not in fact do any such thing. Moreover, his exact phrasing is not consistent with such an interpretation. Specifically, Bhabha does not speak of Christianity itself as a systematic form of knowledge which contributes to some specific structure of social control, as criminology contributes to prisons. Rather, he says that Grant produced a "knowledge of Christianity"—which presumably means a knowledge *about* Christianity—as a form of social control. If Bhabha intended a Foucaultian implication, he has even obscured that. For, if that is what he meant, he should have said, "Grant used Christianity to produce knowledge about Indians, knowledge that was inseparable from the forms of social control in effect at the time." And, of course, even then he would have had to specify and support this statement.

The other theoretical resonances in this sentence are not Foucaultian, but Lacanian, and they are specifically connected with the Lacanian unconscious via the reference to "a knowledge . . . which conflicts with the enunciatory assumptions." Here, Bhabha is drawing on the structuralist distinction between *énonciation* and *énoncé*. Énonciation is the act of speaking; énoncé is the utterance, what is spoken. Lacan takes up this distinction to treat the subject of the énonciation, which is to say, the speaking subject, and the subject of the énoncé, the subject who is spoken of (see 800). Consider a simple example. Kṛṣṇa has just stolen a large pat of butter. His mother asks him if he has stolen the butter, and Kṛṣṇa says, "No, I did not steal any butter." Here, the subject of the enunciation, Kṛṣṇa, has indeed stolen the butter. But the subject of the énoncé—the verbal construct of the spoken utterance—did not. Lacan uses this distinction as the basis for explaining the unconscious. It is possible for there to be an unconscious precisely because there is a systematic difference between the subject who speaks and the subject as spoken of.

Unlike Lacan's theory of castration, this distinction is, I believe, quite reasonable. Indeed, I draw on this part of Lacanian theory below—in its fuller form, where the subject spoken of is largely the result of social attribution. But how does this relate to Grant? More generally, how is Bhabha using this idea? How does it fit into an encompassing theory of colonialism? Bhabha seems to imply that the "conflict" surrounding the "enunciatory assumptions" is a conflict of the sort that defines repression—with "knowledge" produced "inadvertently," like that in a psychoanalytic session. But that hardly seems to be the case with Grant. And it is certainly not a claim that is theoretically generalizable, in any event. Whatever may have been the case with Grant, it seems clear that the distortion of Christianity in the service of colonial control was not generally involved with repression in the psychoanalytic sense. Or, if it was, we surely need an argument to that effect, not merely a bald assertion.

Of course, here as elsewhere, it is quite possible that Bhabha does not intend the psychoanalytic connection literally. It is simply an analogy. But if it is simply an analogy, then, once again, it cannot have any claims to being theory.

I do not see any reason to continue examining particular claims and chains of reasoning in Bhabha's essay. However, there is one further point that I must address in conclusion, for it contrasts particularly sharply with the anatomy of identity undertaken in the preceding sections of this chapter. Bhabha's discussion centers around the attitude of the colonizer, as noted above. In this way, it is, for the most part, not directly relevant to the concerns of the present volume. However, there are points when Bhabha's assertions seem to touch on the actions and views of the colonized and not merely the attitude of the colonizer. One of these points comes toward the end of the essay. Bhabha has just quoted Fanon on the mummification of indigenous culture. Bhabha goes on to state that "The ambivalence of mimicry—almost but not quite— suggests that the fetishized colonial culture is potentially and strategically an insurgent counter-appeal." At this point, Bhabha appears to have slipped from the perspective of the colonizer to that of the colonized. In doing so, he sees mummified culture as having a potentially "insurgent" effect. Presumably, Bhabha is referring to the valorization of indigenous culture to be found in every anticolonial movement. But, as the preceding analytic makes clear, this valorization can assume a number of different forms. And the differences among these forms are enormously consequential—a point that should become increasingly clear over the course of the following chapters. Indeed, in "Racism and Culture," the very article cited by Bhabha, Fanon discusses what I have called "reactionary traditionalism" with his characteristic clarity, precision, and insight. Far from advancing Fanon's theoretical analysis, Bhabha renders it obscure and blunt.

In contrast with the multiplicity of responses to tradition, as set forth in the preceding sections of this chapter, Bhabha concludes that "What I have called 'identity-effects,' are always crucially *split*" (131). First of all, it is very difficult to determine precisely what "identity-effects" are. Effects produced by identity as cause? Effects produced in identity by other causes? In any case, it seems that these effects have something to do with the response of indigenous people to cultural colonialism, for this statement follows his reference to "fetishized . . . culture" and precedes his utilization of the epigraph from Lacan, which refers to mimicry as "camouflage" (131). Though he returns to the perspective of the colonizer at the end of the paragraph, it at least appears that, here, he is referring to the attitudes taken up by colonized people toward cultural identity. If so, the implication of Bhabha's claim is that these attitudes are always dual only. Far from a clarifying analysis, this is confusion of types, a reduction of the diversity of identity—the many forms discussed above—to a simple duality.

Moreover, this duality is further muddled by its association with fetishism (131–32) on the one hand, and paranoia (132), on the other. This is problematic for several reasons. First of all, it seems to return us to the perspective of the colonizer—for it is precisely the colonizer who fetishizes or fears the colonized person. But at the same time the idea of fetishism was introduced by reference to the fetishization of culture as "potentially and strategically an insurgent counter-appeal" (131), a point that clearly adopts the perspective of the colonized people. All this suggests what we suspected from Bhabha's epigraphs and saw briefly above in connection with mimicry, castration, and historical crisis: he has not kept these two perspectives entirely clear in the course of his essay, but has sometimes shifted from the perspective of the colonizer to that of the colonized without shifting his argument correspondingly. The second problem with these references to fetishism and paranoia is that they return us to the issue of castration—for the fetish is a substitute for the phallus and paranoia, as a psychosis, is, in the Lacanian schema, the result of a disavowal of castration. Once again, it is not clear how castration might relate to these issues, even if we happen to accept a Lacanian view of the topic. Finally, even leaving aside the issue of castration, the precise function of fetishism and paranoia are unclear—for example, it hardly seems that the colonizer treats colonized people as a literal fetish. But what then is the relation? What exactly is Bhabha claiming about colonialism and these two psychological disturbances? How does their relation operate and what does it mean? The idea is only rendered more impenetrable by Bhabha's linking of fetishism with narcissism through the identification of both with mimicry (131, 132). Certainly, the two may be connected. But how is Bhabha linking them? And what bearing does this connection have on colonial relations? Moreover, how does the identification of mimicry with narcissism (132) relate to the idea that mimicry may "destroy narcissistic authority" (131)? Are these statements even reconcilable?

In sum, Bhabha consistently makes theoretical claims that are not clarifying, but obfuscating. They do not increase our conceptual rigor or expand genuinely explanatory principles. More often than not, they involve an implausible identification of some colonial condition or relation with some poststructural and/or psychoanalytic concept. These identifications are neither well supported nor well explicated, and are often based on nothing more than a coincidence of names. It is frequently difficult to see any justification for drawing the connections put forth by Bhabha, and still more difficult to infer precisely what conceptual or explanatory advancement would be achieved by doing so. At best, he presents a dualistic and thus highly impoverished account of identity after colonization and even in this he does not develop the account with a consistent point of view. In short, this seminal essay in "postcolonial theory" does not accomplish any of the things a theory is supposed to accomplish.

Homi Bhabha is devoted to analyzing and criticizing colonialism in the face of increasing economic and cultural inequality throughout the world. His individual observations on literature and on colonialism are often insightful. He is an asset to literary study in general, and to the study of colonialism and literature in particular. However, his "theoretical" work, like that of other canonical poststructural postcolonialists, such as Gayatri Spivak, does not, I believe, merit the name of "theory." It is unfortunate that "postcolonial theory" has come to be identified with this particular strain of thought, and that it is becoming almost impossible to publish in the field of postcolonization literature without adopting its general views and idiom. I hope this book—along with books by Nandy, Said, Appiah, Amin, and others—makes clear that there are other options for the study of literature after colonization, options that are more terminologically clear, more conceptually rigorous, more empirically sound, and greater in explanatory and interpretive capacity.

CHAPTER TWO

DIALECTICS OF
MIMETICISM AND NATIVISM

Derek Walcott's Dream on Monkey Mountain

THE WHITENESS OF BLACKNESS: MADNESS AND DESPAIR

Perhaps above all else, *Dream on Monkey Mountain* is a play that explores—through a narrative dialectic, a "dialectic . . . in the text," as Walcott said in another context ("Figure," 36)—the various ways in which racism defines an unlivable identity for oppressed people, an identity that pushes toward madness. At various points, Walcott makes this theme explicit. For example, he draws the epigraph for part one from Sartre's prologue to *The Wretched of the Earth*: as a result of "always being insulted," the self becomes "dissociated, and the patient heads for madness" (211). Or, as the colored Corporal Lestrade puts it later, in dialogue with Basil, the "figure of death" (208): "My mind, my mind. What's happened to my mind?" he asks; "It was never yours, Lestrade," Basil replies (297). His mind, we may infer, was never his own because it was always defined by the attributed categories of racism, because his identity was always and necessarily a matter of what he was told he was.

On the other hand, there is a degree of ambiguity here. It is not clear to what extent Makak or even Lestrade suffers from mental illness. On the one hand, Makak does seem "out of touch"—but is he out of touch as a social critic and visionary, or as a lunatic, or both? As many writers have stressed, resistance to unjust authority is often characterized by those in authority as madness. The history of Afro-Caribbean religion, and the biographies of its leaders, provide many examples—and Makak clearly fits into this tradition, for he becomes a leader in an Afro-Caribbean religion with affinities to Kele, Sango, Voudou, and Rastafarianism. Campbell gives many instances: "Alexander Bedward . . . had re-interpreted the bible to depict the whites in the society as the devil . . . when his idealism began to become legend, the colonial authorities declared that he was insane and committed him to a mental asylum" (Campbell, 49n.). Leonard Howell, the first Jamaican Rastafari, "was continually harassed by the State, to the point where they committed him to the mental asylum in Kingston" (72). Grover Redding, the leader of a pre-Rastafarian group in the United States, "was declared insane for his unrepentant attitude towards white America" (90n.). Finally, Campbell reports that, in the 1950s, Rastafarians were commonly placed "in the mental hospital at Bellevue in Kingston" (96). Indeed, a standard colonialist view of Afro-Caribbean religions was that they were not religions at all, but some form of group madness. For example, Williams quotes one writer who characterized Voudou as "a racial psycho-nervous disorder" (99).

Nonetheless, there is dissociation in virtually all the characters, dissociation that results from the denigratory identities projected onto Afro-Caribbeans by colonialist racism, identities partially accepted by those men and women themselves. At the very least, many of these characters are trapped within the problematic of mimeticism and reaction, as if those defined the only options for Afro-Caribbean identity.

Walcott devotes much of the play to exploring the absolute valorization of whiteness, and the absolute devaluation of blackness, in colonial racist ideology. Moustique explains: "When I was a little boy, living in darkness, I was so afraid . . . God was like a big white man, a big white man I was afraid of" (290). The consequence, predictably, is a strain and rupture in identity. When all value is associated with whiteness, blacks almost necessarily seek to repudiate their blackness—which is impossible. As Lestrade puts it early in the play: "Is this rage for whiteness that does drive niggers mad" (228).

In connection with this, Walcott explicitly defines the issue of colonial identity in terms of perceptual and cultural self-understanding and self-evaluation, what is called "self-constitution." One's self-constitution is largely derived from other people—their view that one is beautiful or ugly, smart or stupid, human or bestial. Lacan has maintained that this self-constitution centers around the cultural and perceptual poles of one's personal name and one's mirror image. (We shall discuss this point in the following chapter.) In keeping with this, Walcott's play focuses on a character who foregoes his individual and human name for the derogatory and implicitly racial epithet, "Makak" or "Monkey." When arrested for disorderly conduct, he actually forgets his legal name (219). The delirium from which he suffers is clearly at least in part a function of this inability to link himself to family or to culture. He has, in effect, been formed by an ideology that strips him of the individual and human identity implicit in the name and seeks to structure his personal identity around a racial typology according to which black is to white as monkey is to human. Lestrade summarizes Makak's condition: "This is a being without a mind, a will, a name, a tribe of its own" (222). Lestrade is adopting a colonial and racist attitude, but he nonetheless articulates Makak's alienation from any culture that might provide positive identity, an alternative to denigratory ideology.

Moreover, in keeping with Lacan's link between the mirror and the name, Makak also repudiates any visual self-representation, any image that will remind him of his blackness. Shortly after explaining that he lives "Without child, without wife," hence without links to a family and to the culture such a family might imply, Makak explains that he has also lived without an image of himself: "Is thirty years now I have look in no mirror." He foregoes reflection, for that only brings him face to face with his own blackness and thus the impossibility of value in a colonial situation. He even takes care not to glimpse himself in water: "Not a pool of cold water, when I must drink,/I stir my hands first, to break up my image" (226)—the fragmentation of the reflection foreshadowing Makak's subsequent fragmentation in madness.

In part, this studied avoidance of the looking glass is a matter of racist aesthetics, where black was simianly ugly. And there are many references to Makak's ugliness throughout the play. Tigre says to Makak, "You so damn ugly. You should walk on all fours" (226). Moustique tells him, "You is nothing. You black, ugly, poor, so you worse than nothing" (237). Makak calls himself "ugly as sin" (227) and explains, "They calling me Makak, for my face, you see? Is as I so ugly" (322). But the problem is not specific to Makak. As Campbell puts it, "Blacks were forced to deny a decisive part of their social being: to detest their faces, their colour, the peculiarities of their culture, and their specific

reactions in the face of life, love, death and art. All this was done so that
they would idealize the colour, history and culture of Europeans" (39).
More exactly, "The popular version of beauty . . . suggested that a black
person . . . was ugly and offensive. . . . Some black people, both men and
women, went to great lengths to look European" (95; cf. Rodney,
Groundings, 33).

On the other hand, this is not merely a matter of visual aesthetics,
the "right" nose or lips or skin. It is more general, a matter of what
those features imply, what they were taken to tell about mind and virtue
and culture. When Makak looks at himself, he sees what a white racist
sees. He is, in effect, a metaphor for those legions of colonized subjects
who, in Walcott's words, "looked at life with black skins and blue eyes"
("What the Twilight Says," 9), suffering the "contradiction of being
white in mind and black in body" (12)—or, more accurately, in this case,
white in self-perception and black in self-image. As Rodney put it, "It is
as though no black man can see another black man," or, Walcott might
add, himself—"except by looking through a white person. It is time we
started seeing through our own eyes" (*Groundings*, 34). Makak's identity, his understanding of the world, his evaluation of himself and of others, all have been determined by white perceptions, white ideas—which
is to say, by ascriptions that serve to sustain racial hierarchies.

Late in the play, Makak comes to consider the situation of blacks in
a society structured by white racism. In a moment of despair, he laments:
"We are black, ourselves shadows in the firelight of the white man's
mind" (304). One meaning of the line is clear—in a world dominated by
whites, blacks have no more free volition, no more power, than shadows. But there is more to it. The line alludes to Plato's allegory of the
cave, an allegory that, removed from its historical context could almost
seem to have been formed from images of slavery, Africans in the New
World bound to a stake, or shackled in the hold of a ship, unable to
move, literally or figuratively: "Behold! human beings housed in an
underground cave . . . here they have been from their childhood, and
have their legs and necks chained, so that they cannot move and can
only see before them, being prevented by the chains from turning round
their heads" (296; 514a). Glaucon observes, "They are strange prisoners." Socrates replies, "Like ourselves" (296; 515a).

In one way, the image suggests that blacks are reduced to shadows
by the white racist's perception of them. Whites are like the men in
Plato's cave who muddle shadows with reality. The white understand-

ing of blacks is as distant from reality as the understanding of a shadow is from the understanding of a man or woman. But Makak does not say, "We are black, appearing to whites like shadows in the firelight of their minds." Rather, he says that "We are . . . ourselves shadows," implying, again, that blacks have looked at themselves with the same blue eyes that see shadows only and cannot turn their heads to the reality that casts the shadows. Again, the "strange prisoners" are "ourselves." In this sense, blacks are the prisoners in the cave. And the shadows they see on the wall are not images of others, but of themselves, the only images they have of themselves. As Socrates says, "Like ourselves . . . for . . . do you think they have seen anything of themselves, and of one another, except the shadows which the fire throws on the opposite wall of the cave?" (296; 515a). Glaucon replies, "How could they do so . . . if throughout their lives they were never allowed to move their heads?" (296; 515b).

Yet there is more to Makak than a disvalued and disrupted constitution, a disintegrating ego formed from shadows deep in the mines of racist ideology. In complete opposition to all that he is told, Makak experiences himself and other blacks as human, and whites as a force of natural or supernatural evil. Indeed, this is what brings about his delirium, for he can neither resolve this contradiction nor live with it. In his hallucinations, Makak becomes a savior of his people, the man who will revive their culture, return them to the time before colonial degradation, lead them out of the cave where they see only shadows, and bring them into the light where they will see the truth. The dream on Monkey Mountain is both Makak's delusion and this prophetic vision of the light. Early on, in his first flush of hope and fantasy and insight, Makak links himself to his ancestry, proclaiming himself "the direct descendant of African kings." He, at last, can save his race, for he is "a healer of leprosy"; he can cure the disease that turns its victims white with decay and causes them to disintegrate bit by bit. The people he seeks to lead have decayed to whiteness and lost their identity—their names, their link with a tradition. He addresses them: "I see you all as trees,/like a twisted forest,/like trees without names,/a forest with no roots!" (248).

There is, of course, mania in this messianic mission, confusion, lack of lucidity, a sort of vertigo. But how else can one have a vision, as Socrates stressed: "At first, when any of them is liberated and compelled suddenly to stand up . . . and look towards the light . . . the glare will distress him, and he will be unable to see the realities of which in his former state he had seen the shadows. . . . And suppose once more, that he is reluctantly dragged up that steep and rugged ascent. . . . When he approaches the light . . . he will not be able to see anything at all of what are now called realities" (297; 515c, 515e). Moreover, due in part to the madness, but also due in part to the vision, Makak is ridiculed, despised, and subjected to a ludicrous prosecution. This too follows Plato. Socrates demands of Glaucon: "And is there anything surprising in one who passes from divine contemplations to the evil state of man, appearing grotesque and ridiculous; if . . . before he has become accustomed to the surrounding darkness, he is compelled to fight in courts of law, or in other places, about the images or the shadows of images of justice, and must strive against some rival about opinions of these things which are entertained by men who have never yet seen the true justice?" (299–300; 517d–517e). The fate of Socrates himself—Makak too, Bedward, Howell, Redding.

For Makak, the movement from darkness to light has many dangers. Having named them "shadows," he continues, "Soon, soon it will be morning, praise God, and the dream will rise like vapour, the shadows will be real" (304). A hopeful prophesy until, despairing, he catalogues that reality: "You will be thieves, and I an old man, drunk and disorderly, beaten down."

Elsewhere, Walcott speaks about "racial despair," by which he seems to mean the sense of complete loss of hope for one's race, or for oneself as a member of that race; the sense that, being black, all movement from darkness to light is foreclosed, or pointless; the sense that drives Makak mad. Walcott links this to being "rootless," having no connection with a tradition that gives one personal value, of having no home, of being a stranger in a home owned by someone else, by whites (see "What the Twilight Says," 21). After Makak is arrested, Lestrade mockingly asks him, "Where is your home? Africa?" The implication is that he has no home, no homeland. Makak replies, "Sur Morne Macaque" (218), which he translates as "on Monkey Mountain" (219), and that is what it means, certainly. But "morne" also alludes to the French *morne*, "doleful" or "bleak," and thus the phrase could also be translated as "on despondent Makak"—he lives, in a sense, on racial despair. In his delusion or his vision, Makak's first project is to return to Africa, to find his home, his "roots." Later, he tells his followers, "we will see Africa"; he explains that they will be transported, suddenly, when they open their eyes after making a wish, just as if they "have eaten a magic root" (291). Africa is, in effect, that magic root he wishes will fix him deep in the soil of a home and a homeland.

Makak's project is that of many Afro-Caribbean visionaries, including Marcus Garvey and the Rastafarians. Indeed, throughout the play, Makak's religious quest is linked with that of the Rastafarians, one of whose central beliefs is that Africa is the Edenic homeland to which the black diaspora must return. The link is nearly explicit at points. For example, Rastafarians are perhaps most widely known for giving marijuana or "ganga" smoking a central place in their religious-cultural practices. And so Makak advises Souris: "Here, look, you see this plant? Dry it, fire it, and your mind will cloud with a sweet, sweet-smelling smoke. Then the smoke will clear. You will not need to eat" (288). Tigre shouts back at him, "You crazy ganga-eating bastard" (289). Of course, the point of the connection between Makak and Rastafarianism concerns Rastafarian social and religious beliefs, not ganga. Specifically, Rastafarians take up the nearly universal religious image of a primal fall, a time when happiness was lost and human suffering began. They also accept the widespread belief in future redemption, a time when people will return to happiness, through the intervention of a god who directly or indirectly enters into human affairs. The idea clearly has close Christian parallels, and Rastafarians read and cite the Bible extensively. However, they have taken these ideas and related them directly to the real historical condition of black people. In other words, they have fused myth and history. For them, Eden is Africa, specifically Ethiopia. The Fall is the slave trade. The savior is Haile Selassie, the one African ruler who preserved independence during the colonial period. Salvation is repatriation in Africa.

A crucial part of Rastafarianism and a number of other Afro-Caribbean religions, including Afro-Caribbean versions of Christianity, is the re-imagination of God as black. As Marcus Garvey wrote, "If the white man has the idea of a white God, let him worship his God as he desires. . . . We, as Negroes, have found a new ideal. Whilst our God has no colour, yet it is human to see everything through one's own spectacles, and since the white people have seen their God through white spectacles. . . . We Negroes believe in the God of Ethiopia . . . we shall worship him through the spectacles of Ethiopia" (qtd. in Campbell 60–61). One black nationalist in Ghana wrote, "We must worship God according to our conviction, not according to the whiteman's Christianity. We must see Christ as a Blackman and all the Holy Angels as negroes" (75). Rodney and others have made the same point (see *Groundings*, 33).

Along these lines, unlike Souris, when Makak looked at God, he saw not "a big white man," but "blackness" (225). Again, Makak is here taking on the role of Afro-Caribbean religious reformer and visionary. And yet this too is ambivalent. It is difficult to say if this "blackness" is a good thing. As Lestrade asks: "What did the prisoner [i.e., Makak] imply? That God was neither white nor black but nothing? That God was not white but black, that he had lost his faith? Or . . . or . . . what. . . ." (225). The alternatives are significant, but none is satisfactory. As to the last, even those who do not believe in God are likely to admit that a despairing loss of faith is not a good thing. And if Makak has lost his faith, it is almost certainly not a positive development—an achievement of human community, for example, a turning away from the promises of an afterlife to a social affirmation of this life. It is, rather, a sign of racial despair. On the other hand, suppose Makak has decided that God is black. Certainly, this is better for Makak, and for other people of African descent. But one thing that Souris makes clear is that the first problem with thinking of God as white is that it racializes divinity, and thus value. To make God black is to repeat this racialization, if in an inverted form.

The dilemma is repeated later, when Moustique dies. Makak calls on the dying Moustique to tell him what he sees at the moment of death. Moustique tells him, "I see a black wind blowing . . . A black wind" (274). Is this God? Is it the absence of God? Is it a prophecy of the future triumph of black people, or is it future suffering, "a black wind," not in the sense of black men and women, but in the sense of an evil fate? Makak asks, "And nothing else? Nothing?" The question hints at despair. He then decides to seek further, "Let me be brave and look in a dead man eye." The stage directions explain that "*He peers into* Moustique's *gaze and what he sees there darkens his vision. He lets out a terrible cry of emptiness*" (274). Of course, this could simply be death, godlessness, the cliched condition of modern humanity. But, after Makak screams, demons enter, including "a woman with a white face" (275)— the white vision, the white ideal, the image of perfect hope and desire. The horror Makak sees remains the horror of racial despair. This horror is closely linked with spiritual despair, the feeling that one cannot be saved, the conviction that one cannot be loved by God. Indeed, racial despair is in part a version of spiritual despair. Colonialism has racialized all religious feeling and aspiration. For many people, it has given spiritual despair form and force as racial despair.

In short, the insistence on God's racial blackness is typically reactionary, in the sense of "reactionary traditionalism." To insist that God is black, to waiver between an affirmation of divine racial superiority and racial/spiritual despair, is not to rid oneself of the colonialist and racist insistence that God is white. Rather, it is to react against and invert that insistence. Again, reactionary traditionalism is a rejection of colonial racist ideology which presupposes the acceptance of that ideology. It is the obverse of mimeticism. Mimeticism—in its acceptance of the beliefs and norms of the oppressor—is what leads to racial despair, to the sense that one has no value. Mimeticism creates both Makak's madness and Lestrade's pathetic and cruel conformity. It is also what creates reactionary traditionalism—or, in this case, reactionary nativism. As Walcott puts it, "Once we have lost our wish to be white we develop a longing to become black, and those two may be different, but are still careers" ("What the Twilight Says," 20, see also 34–35). To a great extent, the plot of *Dream on Monkey Mountain* is organized by reference to these two careers, mimeticism and reactionary nativism, mapping the development of the latter out of the former. (This general point has been noted by other critics, but developed quite differently. See, for example, Tejumola Olaniyan, who takes the opposition between "hegemonic discourse" and the "inversion" of "hegemonic discourse" as the basis for a poststructural analysis of the play.)

Three Moments of Post-Colonization Identity (I): Racial Despair and Mimetic Collaborationism

In *Dream*, Walcott implicitly isolates three stages of development in the social and personal identity of his characters. In each stage, he distinguishes what we might call "popular" and "anti-popular" versions, which is to say, versions that arise out of or in solidarity with the people or some subgroup of the people and versions that arise out of an individualist or careerist alignment with the foreign oppressors. (As shall become clear, the "popular" versions do not necessarily contribute to the well-being of the people; the fact that they are oriented toward the people does not imply that they operate in the objective interests of the people.) In exemplifying these alternatives, Walcott presents us with a valuable, if tacit, anatomy of postcolonization responses to the problem of cultural identity.

Specifically, Walcott begins with mimeticism divided into the figures of *racial despair* and *mimetic collaborationism.* The former—exemplified in Makak—is what I am calling the "popular" tendency, for those who suffer racial despair identify themselves with the people. Though they see themselves and the people through "blue eyes," they do not set out to distance themselves from the people. In contrast, the collaborationist tendency—exemplified in Lestrade—is marked by an insistence on difference from ordinary folk.

Lestrade is an instance of a common type in Caribbean literature— the mulatto who strives to be white. As already indicated, mulattos are an important transition group in the Caribbean, a nonwhite stratum, largely co-opted by dominant white society to maintain the suppression of the black majority. Campbell repeatedly stresses that the Caribbean is plagued by a "deformed racial hierarchy of whites, mulattos and blacks" (2). He goes on to claim that "Most mulattos clung to forms of behaviour which were even more pro-British than those of the planters in terms of language, dress and religion, in order to identify themselves outwardly as a community with a different heritage from the mass of blacks" (32). Along the same lines, Zora Neale Hurston wrote that "The color line in Jamaica between the white Englishman and the blacks is not as sharply drawn as between the mulattos and the blacks . . . the mulattoes . . . [engage in a] frantic stampede white-ward to escape from Jamaica's black mass" (16). Rodney offers a somewhat more complex portrait, but one still largely in keeping with the views of Campbell, Hurston, and others: "The West Indian brown man is characterised by ambiguity and ambivalence." While "some browns are in the forefront of the movement towards black consciousness . . .the vast majority have fallen to the bribes of white imperialism, often outdoing the whites in their hatred and oppression of blacks" (*Groundings*, 29).

Lestrade exemplifies these tendencies exactly, even stereotypically. (Indeed, the virtual stereotyping of the character might be objectionable, were it not for the fact that Walcott himself is of mixed racial ancestry.) From the beginning of the play, Lestrade shows a deep disdain for blacks, repeatedly characterizing them in brutally racist terms: "Animals, beasts, savages, cannibals, niggers" (216). He refers to their cages as "a stinking zoo" (216) and reiterates racist evolutionary theory: "Some of the apes had straighten their backbone, and start walking upright, but there was one tribe unfortunately that lingered behind, and that was the nigger" (217). His attitude toward English culture, and particularly English law, is almost reverential. Lestrade clearly sees himself as the upholder of civilization and order—which is to say, European civilization and order—in the face of the endless African tendency to slide back into savage chaos (see 219–20, 279–80).

On the other hand, his attitude is not without the ambivalence that Rodney mentions. Lestrade both imitates and mocks the British judiciary when he drapes himself and two prisoners with towels in imitation of judicial robes. His discourse on law is a parodic, pseudo-legalistic deliberation: "when the motive of the hereby accused by whereas and ad hoc shall be established without dychotomy, and long after we have perambulated through the labyrinthine bewilderment," and so on (*Dream*, 221–22). It is not accidental that this obfuscatory nonsense is what Lestrade pronounces when Souris demands, "Let us hear English!" (220). Lestrade's mimetic collaborationism is not unself-conscious. He knows exactly what he is doing. He does not simply and sincerely value European civilization. He has not merely accepted and internalized the racist propaganda. Rather, he has chosen to act in such a way that he will be the one locking up the prisoners, rather than the prisoner being locked up.

Indeed, part of Lestrade's disdain for black people results from his sense that they actually have internalized the racist views, that they are genuine mimics, truly seeing the world and themselves through blue eyes. Thus, he taunts Makak with being a will-less brute who will do anything he is told (223). He mocks the vendors in the market, calling melons "pawpaw," just to watch the cowed merchants agree, and then hate them for doing so. But, of course, this is not the end of the matter either: "I would like to see them challenge the law, to show me they alive. But they paralyse with darkness. . . . They cannot do nothing, because they born slaves" (261). In saying that they are "born slaves," Lestrade reveals that he does accept the racist ideology, at least in part. Moreover, if they did "challenge the law," he would immediately arrest them. Lestrade may indeed hate true mimeticism, from his sense of humanity, and his shared resentment of racism, but he also hates any challenge to the order that puts him above those he calls "Animals, beasts, savages, cannibals, niggers" (216).

As this indicates, Makak's despondent mimeticism is directly linked with Lestrade's mimetic collaborationism. The most obvious manifestation of Makak's mimeticism is probably in his "name," the insult that substitutes for a name and alludes not only to the racist identification of blacks with apes, but also to the adage "Monkey see, monkey do." At one point, Lestrade—representing white power and authority—has Makak imitate him in a series of meaningless actions. He concludes (via the chorus): "Everything I say this monkey does do,/I don't know what to say this monkey won't do./I sit down, monkey sit down too,/I don't know what to say this monkey won't do" (223).

Interestingly, this scene in some ways repeats a scene in Césaire's *Une Saison au Congo*. There Patrice Lumumba, the great hero of Congolese independence, is taunted in jail by two white jailers, called "Poet macaque," and asked "Who taught you to read, macaque?" (19). Then he is mocked again, with "Macaque" this time used as a name, when he is addressed as "excellency, Macaque!" The link is significant, for it associates Makak with Lumumba, as dreamers of revolutionary dreams, as leaders of men. Of course, Makak is not Lumumba, and the link could be interpreted as purely ironic—Makak as a parody of Lumumba, a ridiculous imitation. But I do not take it this way. Makak is too sympathetic for this sort of dismissal. And he contrasts too sharply with the other characters in the play, who, though more realistic, have none of his nobility of spirit and human sympathy. It seems rather that, through this connection, Walcott is indicating affinities that link together a wide range of individuals who suffer colonialist racism and who at some point try to strike out against it, suffering great hardship in consequence. For though early in the play Makak is a despondent mimic, as the play progresses, he becomes more of a visionary, more of a revolutionary, more the brother to that other Macaque, Patrice Lumumba.

Nonetheless, he is, at this point, a mimic. And the most significant image of his mimeticism is no doubt the mask. When arrested, Makak is carrying a white mask, the mask of mimicry, the mask that imitates whiteness. Makak is, of course, not unique in wearing such a mask. It is a mask that almost all blacks learn to wear as children. When Moustique finds the mask in Makak's hovel, he calls it "cheap stupidness black children putting on" (240). Later, Moustique confronts a crowd seeking release from oppression, and makes the connection explicit: "You all want me, as if this hand hold magic, to stretch it and like a flash of lightning to make you all white." Of course, he cannot. All he can do is train them in mimicry. "All I have is this," he says, pulling out the mask: "black faces, white masks!" (271), he explains, implicitly quoting the title of Frantz Fanon's treatise on mimeticism.

Mimeticism manifests itself not only in relation to authority and divinity, as we have already seen in white law and a white God, but also in relation to desire. In other words, within a racist society, the dominant racial group assumes official authority for all evaluation—temporal and eternal—and enforces that authority through police and ministers. For this, the mimic seeks the respect or approval of the oppressor. But there are other cases in which imitation aims rather at love or affection. And just as respect is definitive only if it comes from a white person, so too is love absolute only if it comes from a white person—a white woman, in this case. Thus, for Makak and for other men whose identity has been formed by racism, the white woman becomes a sort of alternative to racial despair. To be loved by a white woman—that would mean one has value. It is like being sanctified by the white God, exonerated or honored by white law. Frantz Fanon quotes Louis-T. Achille to this effect on the specific case of interracial marriage: "Insofar as truly interracial marriage is concerned, one can legitimately wonder to what extent it may not represent for the colored spouse a kind of subjective consecration to wiping out in himself and in his own mind the color prejudice from which he has suffered so long" (71–72).

In *Dream on Monkey Mountain*, one important image for the desired white woman is milk, which also serves in an obvious way to connect her with motherhood. Thus, Souris explains what "they teach me since I small": "To be black like coal, and to dream of milk" (290), milk being the whiteness he can never achieve, but also the white woman and the white mother he can never have.

The most prominent image for the white woman, however, is the moon. At one level, the moon is a broad image of racial whiteness, and all that it entails. When Lestrade is converted from mimeticism to nativism, he explains that, formerly, "I hated half of myself." Taking up the image of the moon as racial whiteness, he characterizes the hated part as "my eclipse" (299), the black part of him that blotted out the white part, and equally the part that "eclipsed" him, the part that made him less successful. Later, in a moment of despair, Makak explains that "I can [never] reach that moon; and that is why I am lost" (304). The connection is even more striking, if one takes into account Robert Graves's etymology of "Europe." As Fox puts it, "Eur-opë = 'she of the broad face'—that is, the full moon" (207).

But, more often, the moon is directly linked with the apparition of the white woman. Thus, Tigre imagines Makak "Masturbating in the moonlight" (225), which is to say, fantasizing the carnal love of a white woman. In keeping with the folk beliefs about the moon, the apparition is ambivalently cause and cure of the madness. When Makak begins to go mad, he hallucinates the apparition. As the moon, she is its cause: "Sirs, I does catch fits. I fall in a frenzy every full-moon night. I does be possessed" (226), Makak explains to Lestrade. And later, Souris says of Lestrade, "He look crazy. . . . Is the moon. Is the moon" (298).

But, as a woman who loves him, the moon is cure as well—if, predictably, a highly ambiguous cure. Her love inspires him, seemingly returns his identity. First, anticipating his messianic image of Afro-Caribbeans as "a forest with no roots" (248), he explains his initial vision of the apparition thus: "I see this woman singing/And my feet grow roots" (227, 235). In keeping with this imagery, he explains, "she call out my name, my real name" (235), thereby restoring to him his culture, the sense of ethnic and racial connection he had lost. In addition, her love gives him pride in this heritage: "She say that I come from the family of lions and kings" (236). This all seems positive and beneficial. But this new ethnic valorization is not unproblematic. First of all, as Brown points out, "It is all aimed at proving some notion of humanity to the White world rather than to himself" (196). The value still comes from a white source, the white woman; it even refers back to that source, as is particularly evident in the touching moment when Makak kneels down and calls, "Lady in heaven, is your old black warrior" (228), elevating himself in the eyes of the beloved white apparition, but simultaneously humbling himself: "Tell me what to do" (228), he pleads. Even the image of his feet growing roots is mixed. It is a rediscovery of heritage, but also a sort of paralysis, an inability to move, to flee, to escape.

Moreover, the apparition takes on an ambiguous religious significance—both European and Afro-Caribbean, both benevolent and harmful, but in each case indicating that the racist valorization of whiteness has defined the entire structure in which the issue of identity is worked out. In part, the apparition is clearly an angel. She is the concrete manifestation of the psychopathology described by Jean-Paul Sartre in the epigraph to Part One of *Dream*, a passage drawn from Sartre's preface to Fanon's *The Wretched of the Earth*: "Thus, in certain psychoses the hallucinated person, tired of always being insulted by his demon, one fine day starts hearing the voice of an angel who pays him compliments" (211). But the conception of angels is not only theological; it is racial, and part of the complex of problems surrounding racism, mimeticism, and nativism. For angels are like God. They should come in all colors. But, as many black writers have noted, they do not. For example, in *La Tragédie du Roi Christophe*, an important precursor for *Dream*, Césaire has one woman sing of "White color, color of the angels" (82, my translation).

Indeed, there are Afro-Caribbean resonances to this as well. It is not uncommon for an Afro-Caribbean person to believe him/herself called in a dream to African practices of traditional healing or to leadership in Afro-Caribbean religion, just as Makak believes himself to be called. In fact, this appears to be one of the standard ways in which one discovers that one has such a vocation. What is most important in this context is that it is not uncommon for this call to result from the oneiric visitation of a *white* angel and, indeed, a white woman. Barrett reports the case of Mother Rita, a seventy-eight–year-old Afro-Caribbean Healer in Jamaica (see *Sun*, 56). Mother Rita first heard the call to do "African work" shortly before her mother died: "I dreamt I saw a white woman come to me; she said, 'Go and tell your mother that I require her to rest'" (61–62). Rita's mother was also a healer and explained the dream to Rita: "Yes Rita, the Master wants me to rest." Rita then goes on to recount that "In the vision . . . the angel said to me, 'Come, Rita'" (62) and so Rita herself became a healer. Her mother's call had been similar, but more dramatic, for in her case the angel of the vision called her to "rise up and heal the people"; she went to a mountain and fasted and received instruction from the angel (54). The story could apply almost directly to Makak.

The stories of Mother Rita and Mother Rozanne (Rita's mother), like the story of Makak, are in some ways typical of such inspiration stories, wherein a divine visitation spurs an ordinary man or woman to spiritual (and, often enough, political) leadership. But what is crucial for Walcott's play is that the divine visitor is white—and this is not merely an incidental fact; it changes everything. It places the entire experience within the context of the colonialist racial hierarchy, which has been projected from society onto the heavens, otherworldly divinities being made white, in imitation of this-worldly rulers. Moreover, this motif is not merely literary, but part of the religious lives of real Afro-Caribbean people—even the most African of those people, practitioners of "African work," such as Mother Rita and Mother Rozanne.

In addition, Makak's apparition is not merely an angel. She is also a demon. We have already noted that, at the end of Part One, Makak

looks into the eye of his dead friend, Moustique, and recoils in horror at
what he sees, at the nature of the "black wind." Again, directly after this
vision, a chorus of demons enters to take Moustique's body. One is "a
cleft-footed woman" (274), a woman with the foot of Satan. Another is
"a man with a goat's head" (274), again Satanic. The third is "a woman
with a white face" (275), an image of what Lestrade calls "the wife of
the devil, the white witch" (319). When Moustique first hears about the
apparition, he wonders aloud, "A white woman? Or a *diablesse*?"
(236). The reference is exact. As Simpson notes, diablesses, female dev-
ils, are among the more prominent evil spirits found in the folklore of
Walcott's native St. Lucia. He goes on to explain that "A *diablesse*
appears to be a beautiful white woman, one who is capable of enticing
a young man to follow her into the woods where he dies or goes mad"
(316–17n.8; the same figure is found in Trinidad and Haiti—see 23–24).

Here as elsewhere, Walcott has taken a common Afro-Caribbean
belief and teased out the racial significance, the way in which the belief
reveals the pervasiveness of colonial racist ideology. In this case, it is the
sexual idealization of the white woman that Walcott sees as giving force
to the figure of the diablesse, defining her as a figure who can lure
(black) men into the wilderness and drive them mad (as Lestrade puts it,
"is this rage for whiteness that does drive niggers mad" [228]).

Indeed, this does not contradict, but reenforce the interpretation of
the apparition as an angel. As noted above, Mother Rozanne interpreted
her daughter's dream as a message from "the Master" (Barrett, *Sun*, 62).
One's spontaneous inclination is to interpret this as God. But, according
to Beck, "the Master" ordinarily refers to "the Devil" (245), at least in
St. Lucia. This indicates that the two figures (the white angel—serving
"the Master"—and the diablesse) may not be as unconnected as might
at first appear. Moreover, in St. Lucia the diablesse appears to be associated with moonlight and Beck stresses the "nice moonlight" when a
diablesse goes out "dancing" (219).

In keeping with her complex function as angel and devil, Makak's
apparition also manifests traits of the Voudou goddess, Erzulie—"the
divinity of the dream, the Goddess of Love," as Maya Deren explains
(134). The most obvious connection here is that Erzulie calls men to be
her devotees by appearing to them in a dream. As Hurston explains, "At
first [the prospective devotee's] dreams are vague. He is visited by a
strange being which he cannot identify. He cannot make out at first
what is wanted of him. He touches rich fabrics momentarily but they flit

away from his grasp" (146). The luxuriant tactility and vagueness of the dream are closely parallel to those of Makak: "I will tell you my dream. Sirs, make a white mist/In the mind; make that mist hang like cloth/From the dress of a woman. . . . Make the web of the spider heavy with diamonds/And . . . my hand brush it. . . . Till I feel I was God self, walking through cloud. . . . I see this woman singing. . . . The loveliest thing I see on this earth,/Like the moon walking along her own road" (226–27). The devotee immediately "falls ill" (Hurston, 227); in keeping with this, the morning of the action of the play, the morning after the dream, Moustique finds Makak collapsed on the ground (231). Moreover, Erzulie comes to her devotees "in radiant ecstasy every Thursday and Saturday night" (Hurston, 145); the events of *Dream* take place in the course of a Saturday night.

Erzulie is associated with the Virgin Mary; in Haiti, diablesses are virgins (see Simpson, 24) and there is certainly a virginal element to Makak's apparition—Lestrade calls her "Nun, virgin" (318). Moreover, devotion to Erzulie is "more or less a vow of chastity." (Hurston, 146–47), for a man devoted to Erzulie is not allowed to have contact with any other woman. In keeping with this, Makak tells Moustique that the apparition "Know how I live alone, with no wife" (236). On the other hand, Erzulie herself is not a virgin. Indeed, she represents luxurious sexuality, an element that is also not lacking in Makak's apparition—after calling her "Nun, virgin," Lestrade adds "Venus" (318), recognizing her dual character. Moreover, there are suggestions in the literature that devotion to Erzulie involves masturbation—in keeping with Tigre's conjecture concerning Makak's "Masturbating in moonlight" (225). It certainly involves some sort of fantastical sexual congress—perhaps in a dream, in keeping with Lestrade's claim that Makak's dream was "obscene" and was explained by Makak "with a variety of sexual obscenities both in language and posture" (224).

But how does Erzulie fit with Walcott's concerns over racism, culture, and identity? It turns out that she too is already racialized in the culture. While not entirely white, this Afro-Caribbean Goddess of Love is, as Hurston explains, "a mulatto." Moreover, this aspect is emphasized in ritual: "When she is impersonated by blacks, they powder their faces with talcum" (145). She is, in short, another variation on the theme of black skin, white masks. Here again Walcott has managed to isolate an important instance of colonialist racism within Afro-Caribbean culture itself, a point in that culture where the colonialist equation of value with whiteness has been accepted and elaborated by blacks, and he has again integrated this into his encompassing critique of mimeticism and reactionary nativism.

Beyond the ambiguous status and cultural origins of the apparition herself, even her positive function of restoring value to Makak takes its place in the context of a debate over the humanity of black people—a debate that has clearly not been initiated or sustained by black people. No group spontaneously doubts or debates its own humanity. Moreover, by the terms of this debate, Makak is still linked with nature in descending "from the family of lions" (236). Indeed, and this is perhaps even more important, in transforming him from a monkey to a lion, this imaginary white woman makes him white. In case the point is not obvious on its own, Walcott subsequently stresses the lion's whiteness. Later in the play, he sets up three parallels: milk and coal, day and night, lion and monkey (283). Clearly, "lion" has value in just the sense the milk and day have value—through whiteness, contrasted with the blackness of coal, night, and monkey. Moreover, the substitution of "lion" for "Makak" is colonial in another way. Etymologically, "lion" derives from Greek and Hebrew roots, making it firmly Judeo-European. "Makak," in contrast, derives from Fiot, a Bantu language; indeed, "Makak" avoids the French/English spellings (used, for example, by Césaire), employing instead the standard transcription of the Fiot (see, for example, the entry for "macaque" in *The American Heritage Dictionary*), thus further drawing our attention to the origins of the word. Moreover, this use of "Makak" is particularly poignant because it operates not only to denigrate people, but to undermine African cultural values as well. The monkey is sacred in parts of Africa—among the Yoruba, for instance (see Ojo, 167 on the monkey in Yoruba belief; see Drewal, 92–94 on the central place of the monkey in Egungun festivals). To use the monkey as a derogatory image is simultaneously to dehumanize the person who is called a monkey and to devalue the culture that considers the monkey sacred.

Of course, as with every other image in the play, the image of the lion is more complex than a mere instance of whiteness. Makak as lion is not only a wild beast, but also the Lion of Judah—as Lestrade makes clear in his mocking reference at the beginning of the play, "Please let me examine the Lion of Judah" (217). And "Lion of Judah" is another name for Ras Tafari, Emperor Haile Selassie, incarnate God of the Rastafarians. As many writers have noted, Ethiopia and Liberia were the two areas of Africa that were not annexed by European colonial powers (see, for example, Oliver and Fage, 171). Liberia, however, was a country carved out of west Africa for repatriated slaves and thus could hardly stand as a positive image for African heritage. Thus, Ethiopia alone provided hope for Africans and the African diaspora; it demonstrated that Africans could remain independent of European domination. The conquest of Ethiopia by fascist Italy in 1936 was a threat to this hope. But when Haile Selassie returned to Ethiopia, and, by 1941, the Italian forces had been driven out (see Oliver and Fage, 207), this only strengthened the image of Ethiopia as indomitable, as the one source and example of African strength.

Selassie had already taken for himself the title "Lion of Judah." As Campbell explained, "the victory over Italy and the return of the Emperor" to Ethiopia gave new significance to that title; these events "showed that [Selassie] was the *Conquering Lion of Judah*" (78). In consequence, the lion became one of the prime symbols of the Rastafarians: "The Rastas declared their identification with the *lion*—in its roar, its hair, its body strength, intelligence" (Campbell 99); "in the rural areas one of the most popular sayings was 'Rastaman a lion,' for the Dreadlocks were supposed to be a 'symbolic reincarnation or imitation of the lion in man form'"(100).

But even here, as Campbell himself points out, "The British, who denigrated everything African, have used this symbol [the lion] to adorn important public buildings and sites of national importance" (100). In this sense, the symbol of African hope and pride is a symbol already valorized by the colonizer. More importantly, Selassie himself is only a symbol of positive Afro-Caribbean aspiration for the pathetic reason that every other African nation was conquered and controlled and demeaned by Europe. It is not any positive virtue on the part of Selassie that gives importance to the "Lion of Judah." It is, rather, the mere fact that his nation did not fall into complete and prolonged subjugation.

Thus, while the value placed on Makak by the white woman does give him a sense of worth, it is worth that for the most part derives from colonial valorization of whiteness and from European culture (cf. Breiner, 79 and Nelson, 55.) This is why Moustique identifies her with the white mask (see 239). The values she allows Makak to celebrate are ultimately mimetic, however antimimetic they may appear. Or, rather, like so much else in this play, they are ambivalent, but deeply bound up with mimeticism—as, Walcott indicates, they are in the broader culture outside the play, the culture in which most Afro-Caribbean people live.

THREE MOMENTS OF POSTCOLONIZATION IDENTITY (II):
ROMANTIC NATIVISM AND OPPORTUNISTIC NATIVISM

Nonetheless, Makak does move out of mimeticism per se into a form of reactionary nativism, in part due to this identification with the Lion of Judah and the implicit link with Rastafarianism or, more generally, Afro-Christian religion. This transition is adumbrated at the beginning of the play in a way that continues the link with the white woman, for in the very opening sequence "the round moon," representative of whiteness and, particularly, the white woman, is identified with "the white disc of an African drum" (212), representative of a rediscovered African tradition. Indeed, the two are linked in Voudou and other Afro-Caribbean religious practices. Hurston notes that some important Voudou rites—which centrally involve African drumming—are "held on a night when the moon is shining full and white," adding that "In Haiti the moonlight is a white that the temperate zones never could believe possible" (240). Williams quotes one visitor to Haiti, who wrote that "Every moonlight night in Haiti you hear in the woods the tom-toming of the Voodoo drums" (84). Moreover, the drums were not merely spiritual. Like Rastafarianism and other Afro-Caribbean religions, Voudou is deeply political. Indeed, the drums themselves have, historically, held a central place in Voudou political struggle against colonial domination. For example, one writer maintained that "During the insurrection in 1916 in Haiti . . . the beating of a drum was the signal to assemble the Voodoo devotees and to incite them to a religious race war" (qtd. in Williams, 87; a more impartial observer might have called it a war of liberation).

In keeping with this imagery, Walcott represents two dialectically opposed "moments" of reactionary nativism as following from the two moments of mimeticism, but preceding national independence. The first, popular form, I will call "*Romantic Nativism*"; the second, antipopular or individualist form, I will call "*Opportunistic Nativism*."

Romantic traditionalism is a celebratory idealization of the culture and history of the subordinated group—or, rather, of what one imagines to be that history, typically as based on colonialist stereotypes. Romantic nativism is an extreme version of this—the celebratory idealization of a stereotypically "natural" state that is virtually cultureless. Walcott is harshly critical of this view. Elsewhere, he calls it "a schizophrenic daydream of an Eden that existed before . . . exile" ("What the Twilight Says," 20), a daydream made possible by the fact that Afro-Caribbeans are not simply and directly African and have little access to their ancestral culture, except through stereotypes: "Even the last one among us who knows the melodies of old songs fakes his African, becoming every season, by Kodak exposure of his cult, a phony shaman, a degraded priest" (27; cf. Ismond, 257).

From racial despair, Makak, spurred by the apparition, takes up romantic nativism. Consistent with his new self-image as the (white) lion, king of the jungle, he accepts the colonial view of black Africans as living in a natural state, at one with the jungle. Specifically, Makak urges Souris to find himself "at home" as "One of the forest creatures" and makes himself, in the words of Souris, "Half-man, half-forest" (290, 289). Along similar lines, when Lestrade is converted to nativism and affirms the racial identity he had previously rejected (see 299), he is suddenly naked in the jungle. Makak then identifies him and all his African forebears with nature, asking: "Don't you hear your own voice in the gibberish of the leaves? Look now how the trees have opened their arms. And in the hoarseness of the rivers, don't you hear the advice of all our ancestors" (300).

In connection with this turn from law to nature, from the court to the jungle, from civil authority to natural authority, the object of love shifts from the nubile white woman and inaccessible moon to Mother Earth or Mother Africa, black with fertile soil. In this context, love becomes a return to the patient, ever-loving mother or motherland, one's origin and destiny. Though only humoring Makak, Tigre presents this theme when he exclaims, "Ah, Africa! Ah, blessed Africa! Whose earth is a starved mother waiting for the kiss of her prodigal" (289–90). And as he approaches his conversion, Lestrade cries out to "Mother Africa, Mother Earth" (298); as he removes his clothes in preparation for his rebirth as African, he announces, "I return to this earth, my mother" (299). Earlier, when Lestrade denigrated Makak, Tigre explained Lestrade's cruelty as a repudiation of parentage: "That is why you punishing this man. You punishing your own grandfather." But now Lestrade calls out to Makak: "Grandfather. Grandfather. Where am I? Where is this? Why am I naked?" Makak explains that it is Africa, the universal mother, and that he is naked in a new birth, naked "Because like all men you were born here" (300).

In contrast with this naive view of the ancestral African "natural man," opportunistic nativism is the cynical manipulation of the people's hopes and desires through an insincere celebration of non-European values and customs—a celebration aimed merely at one's own advancement. The obvious example of this is Moustique's fraudulent preaching and impersonation of Makak, after Makak has achieved success as a political and religious leader. Walcott criticizes such demagoguery. But at the same time he allows Moustique alone to recognize the close connection between romantic nativism and mimeticism. Alluding to the attempt to recover African traditions—including West African mask ceremonies representing the return of the ancestors and continuity with the past—Moustique announces: "All I have is this . . . black faces, white masks!" (271). The mask he reveals is not the Yoruba Egungun mask of the ancestors, but the white mask of mimicry, here transformed to pseudo-Africanism.

Earlier, Moustique had warned Makak, "Some day . . . you will have to sell your dream, your soul, your power, just for bread and shelter . . . love of people not enough, not enough to pay for being born, for being buried" (254). When Makak insists that they will return to Africa, Moustique is exasperated: "Africa! How we going there? You think this . . . [Holds up mask] this damned stupidness go take us there?" (255). The point is well taken, metaphorically and literally. The imitation of pseudo-African customs made out of white ideas—and that is, in effect, what defines romantic nativism—will not return anyone to authentic tradition. And no amount of religious devotion will pay the literal cost of passage back to Africa—as thousands of disappointed Afro-Caribbeans discovered when schemes of repatriation failed (see Barrett, Rastafarians, 95–97).

Moustique's more general cynicism is not entirely misplaced either. Campbell ends his discussion of Rastafarianism with a caution against "the opportunism on the part of certain Caribbean governments on the question of identification with Africa," and quotes Rodney's insistence that "We cannot romanticise the situation in Africa" (230). Walcott himself bitterly denounces opportunistic nativism in "What the Twilight Says": "Now the intellectuals, courting and fearing the mass, found values in [old traditions, such as Carnival] that they had formerly despised. They apotheosised the folk form. . . . Their programme, for all its pretext to change, was a manual for stasis, because they wanted politically to educate the peasant yet leave him intellectually unsoiled; they baffled him with schisms and the complexities of Power while insisting that he needed neither language nor logic, telling him that what he yearned for was materialistic, imitative and corrupt, while all his exhorters made sure that their wives were white, their children brown, their jobs inviolate" (34–35). Though Moustique is one of those opportunists, he is one in lesser degree, and he, not Makak, recognizes the great danger inherent in both colonial forms of nativism—and, as we shall see, in the forms that follow independence.

Indeed, Moustique is a complexly ambivalent character in other ways, not least in his unique connection with whiteness and with Afro-Caribbean religion—including his nemesis, Baron Samedi. Consider, for example, the spider. From early in the play, the apparition of the White Woman is paired with a sort of inverse or complementary image, that of the white, pregnant spider. In effect, the White Woman is to Makak as the white spider is to Moustique. They are, in a sense, opposed aspects of the same imaginary structure. Moustique reaches under the bench in Makak's hovel and this spider sits on his hand: "A spider . . . A big white one with eggs. A mother with eggs." His reaction: "my blood turn into a million needles" (238). In describing his dream of the white woman, Makak had the same experience; he felt "A million silver needles prickle my blood" (235). The connection is clear, and re-enforced when, a moment later, Moustique reaches under the bench a second time and *"withdraws a white mask"* (239).

Makak and Moustique both suffer the psychopathology of racism. But, in the case of Makak, it is a matter of desire (the white woman). While in the case of Moustique, it is a matter of fear (the spider); recall that, when Moustique thought of God, he saw, "a big white man, a big white man I was afraid of" (290). "Is a bad sign?" Moustique asks, apprehensive of the spider. "Yes, is a bad sign," Makak responds (238–39). At the end of the first part, it turns out that Moustique's fears were well founded. He is killed after impersonating Makak, after pretending to be a revolutionary, while being in fact a mere opportunist. The connection between the death and the spider is emphasized by the inarticulate cry that greets both. When Moustique senses the spider, he cries out, *"in horror,"* "Aiiiiiiiiiiiie" (238). Similarly, when he dies, and Makak sees, in Moustique's eye, Moustique's final vision, Makak cries out, in a *"terrible cry of emptiness,"* "Aiieeeeee" (274).

These connections and oppositions are further developed in Moustique's relations with Basil. Basil, the "figure of death" (209), is an instance of Baron Samedi, the Haitian deity (or "loa") of the dead (see Deren, 54). He is first introduced in the Prologue, where "His face [is] halved by white make-up like the figure of Baron Samedi," and he dances "with a spidery motion" (212). Clearly, the spider, though pregnant, is linked with death. In *The White Goddess*, Robert Graves writes that the White Goddess is simultaneously "the mother of All Living" and "the female spider . . . whose embrace is death" (qtd. in Fox, 207–8). This is in keeping with Voudou cosmology, for in Voudou there are two major types of deity or loa, the Rada and the Petro. Hurston characterizes the Rada as, roughly, benevolent and the Petro as, roughly, harmful— though, of course, it is not that simple, as Hurston fully recognizes. Baron Samedi heads the Petro gods. Erzulie—who, as we have already seen, is linked with the white woman—is a Rada deity. Moreover, Erzulie has a Petro counterpart, just as the white woman has the spider as her counterpart in *Dream*. More generally, Samedi and the spider are Petro, death, cynicism, whereas Erzulie and the white woman are Rada, life, hope. The former are brute reality and dire omens; the latter are dream and possibility. The division fits with that between opportunistic nativism and romantic nativism. The spider, in being white, indicates more clearly the destructive aspect of imitating whiteness. Samedi's face—half black, half white (*Dream* 212)—recalls the mixed heritage of the mulatto, and the opportunistic shifting between black and white—though, of course, he is not himself a mimic; rather, he is death, the fate of the mimic, or the outcome of the mimic's acts.

In keeping with this pattern, Basil tells Moustique that they will meet again, "at the sign of a spider" (252). Unsurprisingly, this dialogue takes place when Moustique is counting up the money he has made off of Makak's religious powers. Moreover, the spider returns in the last encounter between Moustique and Basil. Moustique is imitating Makak, working the crowd into a delirium (267). He denounces "a voice, the colour of milk" and insists that he drinks the milk of Mother Africa, which is "brown milk" (267)—clearly, a reactionary inversion of colonialist hierarchies, as is made particularly obvious by the fact that the central image remains "milk," even if we are now told that good milk, African milk, is "brown." But at the culmination of his speech, he is interrupted by the white spider. The scene is a repetition. Earlier, when Makak had spoken of curative faith, the moon appeared, casting its benevolent rays (248). Now, Moustique, imitating Makak, speaks of curative faith—"I cannot cure, except you want to be, except you believe" (268)—and, in place of the moon, the spider appears. Basil "*confronts* Moustique," taunting him with the spider, placing the spider on Moustique's body, moving it around him (269–70). Linking and opposing the spider and the moon, and taking up again the image of the crossroads, Basil says, "Friend, when the spear of moonlight had pinned the white road till its legs were splayed like a spider . . . I tried to direct you" (270). Basil's comment, with its suggestion of death, is prophetic. Shortly after, Moustique delivers his speech, claiming that he has nothing to offer the crowd but mimeticism: "All I have is this [*Shows the mask*], black faces, white masks!" He then "*Spits at*" those around him. The crowd attacks: "Kill him! Break his legs!" (271). When Makak enters, Moustique is "*sprawled on a heap*" (272) like the splayed spider of Basil's metaphor. He dies almost immediately, with his vision of "A black wind" (274).

With the killing of Moustique, the romantic desire and hope associated with the apparition (temporarily) kill the opportunistic cynicism associated with the spider—though, as we shall see, that cynicism will be revived immediately in a more brutal form. Before this happens, however, Moustique insists that "Makak! Makak! or Moustique, is not the same nigger?" (270–71). As usual, the point is well taken. Moustique the cynic, Makak the dreamer—they are, again, two sides of one experience, an experience involving all the insult and degradation implied in the word *nigger*.

The first conflict between Moustique and Basil took place "At a crossroads in the moonlight" (253). Later, the image of the crossroads recurs, now identified with the spider and associated with Moustique's death (270). The recurrence of this image serves to associate both Moustique and the spider with another aspect of Voudou cosmology: Legba/Esu, the Voudou trickster loa, god of the crossroads. Legba is the messenger who links mortals with deities (see Deren, 98) and is frequently identified with Satan (see, for example, Simpson, 38). Moustique himself is more directly linked with Legba—a link that places his opportunism in a different light and makes it still more ambiguous. Most obviously, Moustique is a sort of trickster and an old peasant. (According to Deren, Legba "is an old peasant . . . at the end of his powers" [99].) More significantly, both Moustique and Legba are cripples with a twisted leg (see Deren, 99). Like Satan, both Legba and Moustique limp (see *Dream*, 209, 265). Indeed, when Legba "possesses a person, the limbs are crippled and twisted and terrible to see" (Deren, 99). As Moustique says of himself, he is "a breakfoot nigger" (234), "Small, ugly, with a foot like a 'S'" (237)—"S," perhaps, recalling "Satan."

Indeed, just as Moustique is linked with the trickster, Esu/Legba, there is a suggestion of another great Yoruba deity—Ogun, or Ogoun—

in Makak. In Voudou belief, "Ogoun is the deity of fire" (Deren, 129)—
Makak, of course, works as a charcoal burner. More importantly, "during the struggle for independence" Ogoun came to "appear as the military general" (130), just as Makak has become a militant leader of his
people. Moreover, Ogoun is presented in a "Christ-like image" (131),
much as Makak is repeatedly associated with Jesus. Finally, Ogoun is
opposed directly to any figure of deceit or cunning. He is specifically the
Rada deity of the upright general, and opposed to the Petro deity of
guerrilla revolution (see Deren, 131).

Perhaps more importantly, the connection of Samedi with Moustique's opportunism contrasts directly and revealingly with Makak's
faith and its relation to the hopeful apparition of the white
woman/Erzulie. According to Deren, Erzulie has "exclusive title to that
which distinguishes humans from all other forms: their capacity to conceive beyond reality, to desire beyond adequacy, to create beyond need"
(134). Erzulie is what is distinctively human—the dream, or imagination. Samedi, in contrast, represents what is common to all life—death.
Moreover, the opposition between these two figures is itself of central
importance in Voudou. Though Erzulie is the lover of many loas, she
refuses all relations with Samedi (at least in his form as Ghede; see
Deren, 137).

In *Dream*, the most striking contrast of this sort comes with
Makak's Christ-like cure of the dying man. Makak takes a burning coal
in his hand; "a living coal. A soul in my hand," he calls it (248). At one
level, the coal is there for its literal heat, to be used in sympathetic healing, which is to say, healing in which the suffering of the sick man (in
this case, his fever) is transferred to a medium (the healer) and thereby
purged. But this is not the primary thematic significance of the image.
Walcott hardly wishes to support the idea that sympathetic healing is
medically valid. Rather, the image of the coal, here as elsewhere, is an
image of racial blackness. In this sense the man is sick with racial
despair—the blackness of blackness, one might say. And it is Makak's
job to cure him, through a form of sympathetic healing—through taking
on himself all the pain of being black, he releases the other man from
that pain. Romantic nativism is, in this sense, the cure for the pain of
racial despair.

Indeed, in this context, the image of the serpent is well chosen also.
The man suffers from snakebite—not only the literal bite of a snake,
but the loss of Eden/Africa in a Fall caused by the serpent. Thus,

Makak does not exhort the crowd to pray or to guard against snakes. Rather, he calls to them, "trees without names,/a forest with no roots!" (248) and exhorts them to accept themselves: "Faith, faith!/Believe in yourselves" (249). The cure is entirely a matter of hope and faith in oneself—in short, the overcoming of despair. Note how this takes up and systematically transforms the Christian idea of overcoming spiritual despair through faith in God. Indeed, this is another relevant connection of Makak with Jesus, for the most renowned case of such sympathetic healing of the soul following harm done by a serpent is that of Jesus, who, in Christian teaching, saved the world by suffering for all our sins in crucifixion, thus giving us hope, giving us a way to overcome spiritual despair.

But, as with everything else in *Dream*, this is far from unequivocal. After taking the coal in his hand, Makak announces that the cure must "wait for the moon" and there is a "pause" until *the full moon emerges*" (248). In part, this is merely a reference to the typical timing of Voudou ceremonies. But it also fits in with the broader imagery of romantic nativism deriving from colonialist values. Moreover, recalling the Conradian identification of Africa with darkness, he calls on the people to "sing in your darkness" (248), to celebrate, it seems, the absence of culture that, in the colonialist view, marks African peoples as part of nature.

Finally, Makak's acceptance of his blackness in taking the coal is deceptive, for he can give value to the black coals only if they are seen as turning into "brilliant diamonds" due to their "pressure. . . . In the hand of . . . God" (249). Even God makes something valuable by making it white. (Moustique's vision is in many ways a cynical version of this idea. Instead of moonlight and diamonds, he sees "a road paved with silver" [253]—also valued as whiteness, but in this case the more practical whiteness of cash.) Moreover, the image of coal and diamonds does not occur here for the first time. It refers back to Makak's dream, where the image of the spider is first introduced as well. Makak sees "the web of the spider heavy with diamonds" when he is on his way to the "charcoal pit" (226). The ambivalence, though unrecognized by Makak, is there, not only in the image of the spider, but equally in the immediately following identification of the diamond-studded web with "the chain" (227)—the chain of the web, certainly, but also the chain of slavery, the chain that continues to bind Makak to colonialist structures and ideas, if now in a mental, rather than a physical form.

THREE MOMENTS OF POSTCOLONIZATION IDENTITY (III):
SECTARIAN NATIVISM AND NEOCOLONIAL NATIVISM

And yet, despite this chain, it is Moustique who dies, not Makak. "I take the dream you have and I come and try to sell it," he confesses (273). There is, for whatever reason, a brief triumph of romance over opportunism.

But, again, Moustique's cynicism has much truth in it. And romanticism breeds its own terrors—as suggested already in the horror glimpsed by Makak through Moustique's death (274), in the links between the apparition and the spider, in Tigre's vision of "The moon, that is nothing, but . . . a skull" (283). Indeed, the truth in Moustique's cynicism is made evident when there is a sudden change in the political situation. In Part Two, independence has been achieved. But instead of the expected peace and harmony, Africans are fighting against Africans. There is violence and brutality everywhere. Makak is at the head of an unstable state with many enemies. This is the third moment of postcolonization identity, and it too has a communal and an individual version. I will refer to these as *Sectarian Nativism* and *Neocolonial Nativism*.

Neocolonial nativism is related to both mimetic collaborationism and opportunisitic nativism. Specifically, neocolonial nativists celebrate indigenous traditions in order to advance their own interests as junior partners of the former colonists. They frequently do so by supporting sectarian nativism, the affirmation of small-group identities within the former colony. Sectarian nativism, then, involves the affirmation of narrow linguistic, religious, ethnic, or other identities—for example, Hindu versus Muslim in India or Yoruba versus Igbo in Nigeria. This is clearly the same sort of affirmation as initially created the broader sense of identity in romantic nativism, where an identification with Africa relied on a specific repudiation of Europe. In other words, sectarian nativism continues the identification of all value with one particular culture, but narrows that identification—for example, from "Africa" to "Yoruba." Indeed, it narrows the identification in a way that can be extremely brutal. Finally, it maintains the mimetic basis of romantic nativism. Value is still understood as white value, even though both sectarian and neocolonial nativists may violently reject all whiteness—the former sincerely, the latter cynically.

As with so much else in the play, Walcott manages to integrate different aspects of Afro-Caribbean politics and culture into this scene through a few well-chosen images. The point is largely political, largely a matter of the horrible events that followed independence in many African countries—and, to a lesser extent, the horrible events that followed liberation in other regions, such as Ireland and India. But the episode also functions mythologically. As Deren notes, in Voudou belief, Ogoun as figure of the upright general "has largely given way to the figure of authoritarian force" (131)—exactly what occurs with Makak.

Makak describes the situation after independence, as sectarian nativism spreads: "The tribes! The tribes will wrangle among themselves, spitting, writhing, hissing, like snakes in a pit . . . devouring their own entrails like a hyena" (305). He also explains that this is the direct outcome of the racist ideology of colonialism and the mimeticism of the colonized. They devour "their own entrails" because they are "eaten with self-hatred" (305). "The tribes! The tribes!," he laments, "One by one they will be broken" (306). But Makak too succumbs to sectarianism. The people who "rejected" his "dream" "must be taught, even tortured, killed." The reign of terror begins: "Their skulls will hang from my palaces. I will break up their tribes" (301). In part, the reference here is straightforwardly historical. After independence, a number of African nations descended into cruel dictatorship and civil strife, often ethnically based. By the time *Dream* was first performed, the Central African Republic, Rwanda, Uganda, Chad, Nigeria, the Sudan, the Congo, and several other African nations—including Ethiopia—had experienced dictatorship, significant ethnic conflict, or both (for an overview, see Oliver and Fage, 245–58).

Unsurprisingly, Lestrade, formerly the mimetic collaborationist, is now the neocolonial nativist. He names himself: "Hatchet-man, opportunist, executioner" (307). He initiates the sectarian violence by killing Tigre, and encourages the reign of terror, telling Makak: "Those who do not bend to our will, to your will, must die" (306). His work is to manipulate the nationalist leader (Makak) and the people in his own interests, and implicitly in the interests of the former colonizers. Now when he says, "I have the black man work to do" (307), we can hear, echoing just below the surface, his earlier statement: "I got the white man work to do" (279). The repetition is not accidental. And the two tasks are not as opposed as they may at first appear.

Predictably, Lestrade's "work" is developed in stereotypical terms. Earlier, he had been vehement (if ambivalent) in his celebration and prosecution of English law. In doing "the white man work," he proclaimed himself "an instrument of the law" (279). And he had already identified law per se with "Roman law" and thus with "English law": "the law, the Roman law" (220), "Roman law is English law" (219). The implication is that other systems of justice, especially African systems of justice, are mere natural chaos: "The law is your salvation and mine. . . . This ain't the bush. This ain't Africa. This is not another easygoing nigger you talking to, but an officer! A servant and an officer of the law! Not the law of the jungle, but something the white man teach you to be thankful for" (280). When Lestrade shifts over to the revolutionary government, he adopts the same view, but reverses the value, now championing the brute force which he imagines to be the substitute for law in Africa: "Now we must press on, old man. . . . This is jungle law" (306). And later, when he urges Makak to kill Moustique again, he elaborates the idea: "Justice must be done. Even tribal justice" (315).

Needless to say, this is dishonest and cynical too, just as his devotion to English law had been. At the opening, Lestrade had parodied "English" in a nonsensical speech of mock jurisprudence. In the court of Makak, he presents a similar speech, filled with obfuscation and doubletalk, in this case designed to confuse everyone present, and substitute his will for law: "The law of a country is the law of that country. Roman law, my friends, is not tribal law. Tribal law, in conclusion, is not Roman law. Therefore, wherever we are, let us have justice. We have no time for patient reforms. . . . Elsewhere, the swiftness of justice is barbarously slow, but our progress cannot stop to think" (311). In keeping with this, he establishes his self-serving strategies: "Now, let splendour, barbarism, majesty, noise, slogans, parades, drown out that truth. Plaster the walls with pictures of the leader" (307).

In keeping with the general structure of hypocritical reactionary nativism, Lestrade deploys his rhetoric of nativism in order to support Westernization. He urges, "Onward, onward. Progress" and, in keeping with his idea of progress, faces Makak toward the moon in order to "go forward" (306), clearly connecting "forward" movement and progress with the ideal of whiteness.

Unsurprisingly, in this repetition of European stereotypes about African justice and this pseudo-nativist mimeticism of "progress," the new black rulers remain mere shadows in the fire of the white man's mind. Speaking of Makak, Lestrade says: "He's a shadow now" (306; subsequently, Makak concurs). The pomp and circumstance only thicken the shadows, but do not make them real. Referring to Makak's coronation, he calls out, "Magnify our shadows, moon, if only for a moment" (307). The moon, the dream based on racist ideas and ideals, does not give them real substance, does not return them to themselves, but merely makes them grander shadows, larger insubstantialities in a European imagination. It does not lead them out of the cave, but exaggerates the images they project against the wall, while they themselves remain chained and immobile, mentally if not physically.

Makak has a brief vision of what this means: the breaking of the tribes, the replacing of tradition by commerce, "the gold and silver scales of the sun and the moon . . . that is named progress" (306)—indeed, white commerce, commerce dominated by sun- and moon-colored metals, dominated, not by cowrie shells, but by European currency. But Makak's response to this is equally mistaken, equally part of the colonialist view, for he engages in a deepening of reactionary nativism. He thereby continues to accept colonial racist ideology even as he denounces whiteness more vehemently and completely. As Taylor puts the general point, "The colonizer's myth (black is evil) is the source of the myth of the colonized (black is good)" (204). When praises are sung in the new kingdom, they are pervaded with the images of whiteness. Makak is lauded as he "Whose plate is the moon at its full,/Whose sword is the moon in its crescent" (309). His peace is "gentler than cotton"; his "voice is the dove," his "eye is the cloud," and his "hands are washed continually in milk" (310). And yet, as emperor, Makak proclaims whiteness to be guilt. He presents a list of names, explaining: "Their crime . . . is, that they are . . . white." He continues, explaining the new official history that parallels and inverts the official histories written by whites: "A drop of milk is enough to condemn them, to banish them from the archives of the bo-leaf and the papyrus, from the waxen tablet and the tribal stone" (312). Again, the nature of this rejection is clear. It is a reaction formation; its vehemence is directly proportionate to the force of the mimeticism that it simultaneously represses and manifests. In keeping with this, the dream degenerates further, from a dream of hope to a "dream of revenge" (286) and, finally, to the beheading of the white woman.

Here too Walcott takes up Afro-Caribbean religious practices and their relation to political activity. First of all, a wide range of Afro-Caribbean rituals involve animal sacrifice, often performed through decapitation. In some cases, such as the Kele religion of St. Lucia (Simpson, 315) and indeed in the great Voudou ceremony that preceded Boukman's historic slave uprising in Haiti (Simpson, 236), devotees have been expected to drink the blood of the victim. In keeping with this, after his first revolutionary act, Makak calls on Tigre and Souris to drink the blood of Lestrade, whom he has just stabbed and apparently killed (285–86). Interestingly, however, Makak makes clear that this act of drinking human blood is not the rediscovery of some authentic African practice; rather it is the enactment of a stereotypical, racist view of Africans: "Drink it! Drink! Is not that they say we are? Animals! Apes without law? . . . I who thought I was a man. . . . Christian, cannibal, I will drink blood" (286). He then prophesies, "The blackness will swallow me" (286), the racist myths of blackness will overwhelm and thus define all his ideas and his acts.

More important, however, are the revolutionary and antiwhite aspects of Makak's religio-politics. Taylor rightly emphasizes that Makak's executions recall "the ritual basis of the Haitian Revolution, particularly the Bois Caiman ceremony, which would find its ultimate completion in the slaying of the plantation whites" (213). Simpson notes that, in Haiti, "revolutionary leaders" had found Voudou "rituals useful in promoting their cause" (234). He cites a number of interesting cases, including the relevant case of Riviere. "Claiming to be the godchild of the Virgin Mary, he used to say mass, torture the whites, and maintain all he did was in accordance with the orders of the Virgin" (235; recall that Erzulie was the Voudou correlate of Mary). The parallels with Makak are revealing.

On the other hand, it is important to note that the killing of whites was not as widespread as Makak's proclamations, or the statements by Taylor and Simpson, might seem to imply. Typically, even in uprisings, whites killed incomparably more blacks than blacks killed whites. Consider, for example, the Sam Sharpe uprising. Campbell points out that "During the two weeks that the slaves held control of the plantations, only fourteen whites and three mulattoes were killed. Yet after surrendering thousands of Africans were put to death" (29). Indeed, even in Makak's case, the only white person actually killed is not even a person, strictly speaking, but an apparition. The others are all condemned in absentia, and are dead anyway.

In keeping with the general inversion of mimetic values in these final forms of reactionary nativism, and the new cultural context of national independence, the apparition as object of desire is reconstrued as object of hate and violence. Before his execution, Moustique accuses Makak: "Once you loved the moon, now a night will come when, because it white, from your deep hatred you will want it destroyed." In reply, Makak asserts his blackness, his rejection of whiteness: "My hatred is deep, black, quiet as velvet." But Moustique, as always, recognizes the mimeticism just below the surface: "You are more of an ape now, a puppet," and he sings, "*I don't know what to say this monkey won't do*" (315), recalling the first scene with Lestrade and implicitly indicating Lestrade's manipulative and collaborationist role in the new society.

Subsequently, Lestrade does drive Makak to kill the white woman—indeed, not merely to kill her, but to brutalize her: "Nun, virgin, Venus, you must violate, humiliate, destroy her" (318–19). Like all successful propagandists, Lestrade mixes truth with lies. He is right that this idealization of whiteness "is the mirror of the moon that this ape look into and find himself unbearable" (319); it is "white light that paralyzed [Makak's] mind" (319), and Makak must free himself from whiteness, "as fatal as leprosy" (318), if he is ever to achieve "peace" (319). But this repudiation of an idea is too easily mixed up with the repudiation of people—in this case, a woman, then all women. It turns too easily to misogyny—a frequent component of reactionary nativism, and yet another hierarchization that mirrors or repeats the stratification of colonial racism. Moreover, Lestrade tells Makak that he must strive "to discover the beautiful depth of [his] blackness" (319), but such a project remains squarely within the racist problematic of colonialism: all self-understanding and value are based on race. The supposed purity and "blackness" of this project is denied by the sectarian brutality of the regime and by its imagery of whiteness. When Makak beheads the white woman, he does so with "*the curved sword*" (320), which was described at the beginning of the scene as "the moon in its crescent" (309). It is not the repudiation of mimicry, but the substitution of one mimeticism for another.

THE SENSE OF ENDING

And yet, for Walcott, this reactionary, sectarian, misogynist brutality seems not to be entirely negative. When beheading the white woman, Makak announces, "Now, O God, now I am free" (320). Immediately thereafter, he recalls his name (321). It is now dawn—with all the symbolism this implies. Suddenly, he is part of no organized religion, but, "I believe in my God" (322); he has found an alternative to both religious despair and religious mimeticism. Most importantly, when Lestrade offers him the white mask, Makak refuses it. He leaves, perhaps for the first time since childhood, without the mask. In his final monologue, he claims that he has now found "roots" and a "home" and the chorus sings that he returns to his "father's kingdom" (326), which, one is left to assume, he finds by accepting himself, his image, his name, rejecting the white mask—not imagining an Edenic Africa to which he could return, not envisioning himself as a lion, but simply accepting himself as he is, Felix Hobain, charcoal burner, on this island, at this time.

The general point is made, with variations, by a number of critics. Indeed, most critics appear to view this conclusion as unequivocally liberatory. Taylor, for example, maintains that "When Makak kills the white goddess . . . the myths of blackness and whiteness are both destroyed"; Makak "has made the leap to a liberating consciousness" (204). Brown maintains that "When Makak . . . beheads the Apparition, the self-conflict ends, because in his words, he is now 'free'—free of White value systems and images which have stunted his Black self-awareness" (197; see also Samad, 19, Urbach, 581, Olaniyan, 164).

But, in keeping with the rest of the play, the event seems, ultimately, far more complex and ambivalent. Certainly, part of the point is that Makak/Hobain has accepted his Afro-Caribbean existence, his "normalcy," so to speak. But even this is not as simple as throwing away "white" value systems. Rather, it is, in part, an acceptance of those value systems, for they are part of what he is. Indeed, Walcott seems to be making a very different point from that which critics normally assume: it is not that Makak has found a genuinely nonwhite identity, but that he is no longer conceiving of cultural identity in a narrow, exclusionary, defensive manner. Makak's/Hobain's final "freedom" is primarily an acceptance that, as Walcott once put it, "The question of emphasizing an African or Indian identity is irrelevant, because you are African or you are Indian and no one can take that away in terms of identity" (Milne, 61–62).

In his early, short essay "Necessity of Negritude," Walcott develops the point more fully. He explains that "Many Negro poets are conducting an experiment in racial self-analysis which involves finding those qualities in their personality which they consider distinctive from those of the White writer. This sort of poetry has led to an emphasis on certain modes which the Negro formerly resented when they were applauded by the white spectator or reader; rhythms, simplicity, 'barbarism,' splendour" (20). But, Walcott insists, far from being "natural," this approach is entirely artificial—recall Lestrade's advocacy of "splendour" and "barbarism" (307). Indeed, "It is more artificial when the Negro in the Western World" attempts this, having been "so long cut off from Africa, with his language, religion, customs and politics an entirely different experience" (20). "For us, whose tribal memories have died, and who have begun again in a New World, Negritude offers an assertion of pride, but not of our complete identity, since that is mixed and shared by other races" (23).

But here too there are complications. Perhaps the most obvious problem is that it is difficult to see what Makak has achieved even for himself. We are told that he will live "in the dream of his people"—but, it seems, he will no longer act, no longer encourage his people to struggle for a different and better life. He tells Lestrade that "Other men will come, other prophets." He indicates both their importance and their ineffectuality: "They will be stoned, and mocked, and betrayed." But Makak will no longer take on that role himself. He may no longer feel betrayed. But, it seems, he is also uninspired. He says he is going home, but will he reach "the green beginning of this world" (326)? Is this idea any less deluded than his dream of a return to Africa?

It is, of course, all to the good that Makak is no longer suffering from despair, at least not at this moment. But, in losing his devil, he has also lost his angel, and there seems to be no replacement. Again, the dream was ambiguous, both bad and good, both illusion and vision. Makak suffered "despair in the wake of my dreams" and found himself "Locked in a dream" (305). Yet Souris told him, "But your dream touch everyone" (304). When Makak cures men, "They say it is a dream he have" (259)—a vision. It was his dream that helped Moustique: "You was the only one to make me believe a breakfoot nigger could go somewhere in this life" (234). It was his dream that got him arrested for "urging destruction on Church and State" (225) and "in defiance of Her Majesty's Government, urg[ing] . . . villagers to join him in sedition and the defilement of the flag" (225). Outside of the prison, it is a time of "strikes and . . . cane-burning" (260), a time of revolutionary violence in the factories and the fields. In this context, Makak's message—the message of a dream—spreads "like a cane fire" (262). And the message is resistance: "He give them hope, miracle, vision, paradise on earth, and is then blood start to bleed and stone start to fly" (261).

At the end, Makak/Hobain is going back up the mountain. The action recalls the strategic retreats of many Afro-Caribbean religious leaders. Yet, there does not seem to be any indication in *Dream* that this retreat is strategic. Nor is there any indication that it will be part of some rethinking of his vision. There are parallels with Rasta communities in the hills, including the community of *O Babylon!*, but Makak/Hobain does not seem to have any such community. There is only Moustique. And even Moustique will leave him until the next market day. So, in the end, it is Makak/Hobain alone, Makak/Hobain, without his mask, without his dream. He has regained his name—and perhaps, after many years, the ability to look at his image on the reflective surface of the water before he drinks. That is something. But it is hardly "the green beginning of this world" (326).

Moreover, there is still the matter of the execution, the violence that seems to lead to Makak's recovery, and the apparent misogyny of the execution. Perhaps, Walcott is following Fanon here in linking violence with catharsis. Fanon wrote: "Violence is a cleansing force. It frees the native from his inferiority complex and from his despair," and "is closely involved in the liquidation of regionalism and tribalism." It is what prevents demagoguery, for, "When the people have taken violent part in the national liberation they will allow no one to set themselves up as 'liberators.'" People are "Illuminated by violence" (*Wretched*, 94). Indeed, "Violence alone, violence committed by the people, violence organized and educated by its leaders, makes it possible for the masses to understand social truths and gives the key to them" (147).

Admittedly, revolutionary violence is often unavoidable. And we should not fall into the trap of condemning the small violence of the revolutionaries while ignoring the vastly more extensive and prior violence of the oppressors. Yet, Fanon seems to be just wrong here. The history of revolutions hardly indicates that violence ends mimeticism or demagoguery, that it leads to social harmony or justice. Violent revolution brings the most violent leaders to the fore, habituates everyone to conceiving of problems and solutions in terms of force, power, weapons, terror. At best, violence is an unfortunate necessity. But it will almost invariably function to perpetuate itself. Moreover, it will tend to operate through and thus support the sort of stratified thinking, and identity, promulgated by colonial racism. Indeed, Walcott himself stressed the point in *Henri Christophe*, through Dessalines's despondent words after the massacre of the whites: "Three wars cannot size/Yesterday's horror. . . . Have I gone mad, after long war?/Does murder grow like habit in the hand?" (24).

The ending of *Dream on Monkey Mountain* is written as an affirmation, a claim of secure identity, a recognition of self and culture: "The branches of my fingers, the roots of my feet, could grip nothing, but now, God, they have found ground. . . . I am going home,/To me father's kingdom" (326). But the claim is hollow, the security untenable on its own terms. For here, in the end, there is no culture, no foundation for identity, no rootedness, no common life, no shared ritual or work of complex acts and of ideas. There is only an old man, poor and alone, burning charcoal on the side of Monkey Mountain.

CHAPTER THREE

COLONIALISM, PATRIARCHY, AND CREOLE IDENTITY

Jean Rhys's Wide Sargasso Sea

MADNESS, REFLECTION, AND PRACTICE

In literature, madness is often bound up with loss of the past. Not Freudian repression of memory, or not that only, but a severing of one's connection to practices and habits continuous with childhood and with earlier generations. Those practices and habits constitute identity, or part of it. We have called this part "practical identity," drawing a line between it and "reflective identity." My practical identity is what I usually do, know how to do, am comfortable doing, do automatically—and do in harmony with others in my society. Practical identity is ordinary, habitual, or confident individual action, but individual action interwoven with other individual actions, including those of co-workers, of neighbors, of friends, of different generations in a family. My part in a communal ceremony, my role in daily labor or in the tasks at home, even the common ways of speaking and of listening, which I share, are part of my practical identity.

This is complemented by reflective identity: everything I think of myself, perceptually or conceptually—my visual self-image, my characterization of my feelings, thoughts, and acts. Put differently, it is my "constitution" of myself, a structure of properties and relations which I take to define me physically and mentally. Sartre and Lacan, following Husserl, refer to this as the "ego"—not myself as constituting subjectivity or as speaker, but myself as constituted object, as something spoken of (see, for example, Sartre, 156). This constituted ego is social. It is not the result of a private intuition about one's subjectivity. Rather, it is a recognition of what one is *for others*. It is one's assumption of a place in a culture of social relations.

Lacan famously divides this constitution into two moments. The first is a perceptual constitution, the young child's formation of him/herself as a visual image. This takes place most obviously when the child looks in the mirror and recognizes him/herself—hence Lacan's term, "The Mirror Stage." Here the constitution of the image in the mirror becomes the child's constitution of his/her perceptual self-image. But, as both Lacan and Sartre note, this occurs equally, and still more importantly, through the gaze of "the Other." The child's perceptual self-constitution is a constitution of him/herself *as seen by others*. Indeed, this is true even of the child's self-constitution in the mirror—for, after all, what one sees in the mirror is what other people see.

The second phase of self-constitution, in Lacan's scheme, is verbal. The child comes to constitute him/herself not only as a perceptual object, but as a linguistic object. And just as the child's perceptual self-constitution is a constitution through the eyes of others, his/her verbal self-constitution is a constitution through the words of others. Specifically, the child comes to conceive of him/herself in precisely the terms through which he/she is characterized by others. The child comes to constitute him/herself in terms of sex, race, religion, and similar categories, because of being told that he/she is male or female; black or white or Asian; Hindu or Catholic or Muslim. Clearly, a child does not look into his/her soul and intuit that he/she is Presbyterian. An untutored child does not even look at his/her face in the mirror and recognize that he/she is Asian. These are social categories, cultural identifications, defined by and within society.

According to Lacan, one attribution is particularly important to the constitution of the ego, or what we are calling "reflective identity": the name. In Lacan's view, one's name forms a sort of basis for one's verbal constitution. Unlike the shifting pronoun *I*, one's name is a social marker constant across other speakers. I am "I" for myself only. For others, I am some variant of my name. The name, then, is like the mirror image—not myself as others see me, but, so to speak, myself as others say me. It is a sort of fixed verbal point, to which I am bound as a social person. Moreover, it is not merely a sound, an arbitrary string of phonemes. It locates me in a system. It tells my sex, my parentage, my ethnicity, my religion, even my social standing; it links me from birth with the practical and reflective identities implied by all of these, and with the hierarchies of value and aspiration they manifest and sustain. It is one still point about which my identity can move, retaining fixity and a structure of relations.

It is unsurprising, in this context, that practical and reflective identity are closely interrelated, indeed mutually definitive. More often than not, reflective identity is specified in terms of practical identity—one's profession, one's place in a family, one's physical capacities for work or play. When asked to say who I am, I mention what I do—"I am a Professor at. . . . I have written . . . . I teach. . . ." Or sometimes I name my place in a nexus of practices defined by a country, a region, a family—"I am from. . . . My parents are. . . ." Conversely, one's reflective identity specifies and limits one's practical identity. The definition of one's sex or race or faith implies and permits some sorts of practical identity, while disallowing others. To be defined as a white woman or an Asian woman or a black man is to find some paths open for one's practical identity, and others closed or blocked.

One definition of "madness" is the loss of these identities: a disequilibrating uncertainty invading ordinary practices and properties formerly understood as definitive of the self. Unsurprisingly, then, in literature at least, colonialism breeds insanity. Colonialism is one of the purest forms of cultural destruction and mass human denigration. It forces or seeks to force discontinuity with the practical past by outlawing tradition; it insistently degrades the self-image of those who are colonized; and, in a Lacanian touch, it even changes the names of colonized people, destroys their systems and ceremonies of naming, replacing these with Christian baptism. In consequence, the colonial condition is, frequently, a nervous condition, as Tsitsi Dangarembga has it, following Sartre. Of course, societies always change. Through interaction with other cultures, through internal developments, through response to environmental alteration, they alter. The process may be slow or quick and will lead, at times, to localized discontinuities. But that process is itself continuous, and recognizable as such. Colonial invasion, by contrast, entails an unprepared-for shock of discontinuity, a radical, sudden severance.

Of course, this is not all there is to the matter. It is no coincidence that so many literary protagonists who suffer madness in the colonies are women. For patriarchy too is a structure that effaces the identity of the oppressed. The derogation of reflective and practical identity is the same—misogyny substituting for racism, disdain for women's practices paralleling contempt for indigenous culture. And patriarchy too, at least for certain classes in certain economic structures, severs women from their past and from common practical life, isolating them, to take the most obvious case, in their husbands' homes, away from a structure of women's lives and acts. Patriarchy can be as powerful and pure a force against identity as is colonialism.

Finally, these effects, especially the debilitating effects of colonialism, are not confined to the oppressed. The colonizer also lives in constant interaction with a culture that questions and alters his/her practical identity. However thoroughly they are dominated, colonized people remain a large majority. However much they are denigrated and disrupted, the indigenous, non-European practices of these people remain a pervasive challenge to European habits. Moreover, the obvious and public brutality of the colonial situation continually threatens to undermine European moral self-adulation. The barely concealed hatred seething below the "natives'" polite surface puts the colonizer always at risk, not only of physical harm, but of crippling self-hatred. Both operate to undermine their reflective identity. Indeed, the problem for the colonizer is exacerbated from the other side, for Europeans in the home country most often come to see the European settlers as partially barbarized by "native" culture and partially blackened by a sort of racial contagion. Threatened from above and below, the identities of the colonizer thus grow brittle and risk fracture in much the same ways as those of the colonized, and those of women (cf. Tiffin, 328–29).

Jean Rhys's *Wide Sargasso Sea* takes up and elaborates just this fragility. Antoinette suffers the disruptions of practical and reflective identity that result from colonialism, along with a parallel series of discontinuities derived from patriarchy. Indeed, for her, the two conspire, each worsening the effects of the other (just as, from the opposite side of the colonial dyad, they conspire and exacerbate the condition of Nnu Ego in Buchi Emecheta's *The Joys of Motherhood*). This leads ultimately to her tragic madness, and to the suicide that, in effect, makes physically manifest the already complete disintegration of her identity, both reflective and practical. "There are two deaths," Antoinette tells Rochester, "the real one and the one people know about" (536). We might translate: the extinction of identity and the mere bodily demise.

The Woman in the Mirror, the Gaze of Men, the Place of Names

From childhood on, Antoinette is faced with a distorted image or with no image of herself at all. She is in many ways almost unseen, concealed from others and even from herself. Her dilemma is perhaps most obvious in the convent, for, as she explains, "We have no looking-glass in the dormitory" (489). She is speaking both literally and figuratively. There is no real mirror there (as Lawson stresses [23]). But equally there is no representative of the larger society, the "outside world" to look at her or at her peers, to constitute them as physical persons outside the rituals and routines of the nunnery. In particular, there was no one to look at them as women and thus to give them sexual identity. Indeed, the girls bathe fully clothed so that they cannot even see one another as women. Their unnatural bathing evades sexual identity by concealing the body.

The two meanings of "We have no looking-glass" are linked. For anyone, though especially for a middle-class European woman, to look in a mirror is to engage in a social act. In a society that prizes women for their appearance, scrutiny in the mirror becomes part of a woman's practical identity, preparing a face to meet the faces that she meets. To remove the mirror from the dormitory is to deny that aspect of women's practical identity, the aspect centrally denied in the nuns' virginal devotions.

In part, this denies to the girls a sort of self-constitution, the forming of an image in which they can recognize themselves as physical, as bodily, as sexed, as both objects and agents of desire. In a sense, it reduces each of them to "the skeleton of a girl of fourteen under the altar of the convent chapel"—versions of Innocenzia, virgin child-saint. The other saints they study—"St Rose, St Barbara, St Agnes" (489)—fit here also: Agnes, virgin, martyred at thirteen. Barbara, virgin martyr as well. Rose, who miraculously evaded childhood martyrdom, but died her virgin's death only a year later. One result of such saintly denial is fragmentation—the head severed from the body in martyrdom, then the body shredded into Relics, bits of bone or hair or nail stripped from the corpse, the body breaking into more and smaller pieces. And the pieces, brute material, mere things: "The Relics. But how did the nuns get them out here, I ask myself? In a cabin trunk?" (489).

Of course, the girls do not themselves forget that they will grow into women and return to the swarming life outside, leaving the severed world of Innocenzia, Rose, Barbara, and Agnes. Moreover, though now suspended between one family, where they were children, and another, where they will be parents, they sustain a practical female identity, trading hints on hairstyle, and cultivating functional vanity—not vanity as a moral flaw, or even as a character trait, but as a socially defined and socially required practice.

Indeed, the image of the looking glass extends back further in the novel, with the same thematics and the same problems. The novel begins with Antoinette in isolation from any society. Her father dead, she lived "a solitary life" with no one but her mother and the servants to mirror back to her an image of herself. Her mother was not up to the task (cf. Lawson, 22; on the broader issue of Annette as a "rejecting mother," see Gardiner, 124–33). Annette strained against the solitude "every time she passed a looking glass"—every time she saw herself and saw at once that others were not seeing her. There were no men to recognize that she was "pretty like pretty self" (465). From the very first page of the novel, we are reminded that, far from being solipsistic (as is commonly thought), a mirror is the most thoroughly social of instruments. To Annette, the looking glass shows her not so much herself as the absence of others—and thereby a sort of absence of herself as well.

Yet, there is ambivalence in all of this. For Antoinette, the convent is "a place of . . . death," but also of "sunshine" (490). "Everything was brightness, or dark. The walls, the blazing colours of the flowers in the garden, the nuns' habits were bright, but their veils, the Crucifix hanging from their waists, the shadow of the trees, were black" (491). Her time in the convent recalls a sort of minor literary genre: embittered recollections of an oppressive boarding school. But Rhys's heroine is not embittered. Indeed, this all-woman society is less oppressive, less stifling, and—despite the imagery of martyrdom—even less fragmenting than life with her mother or, worse still, her husband. Certainly, "One of the nuns knew all about Hell," but "another one knew about Heaven and the attributes of the blessed, of which the least is transcendent beauty. The very least" (491). And so, "This convent was my refuge," she says (490). When her step-father speaks to her of leaving the convent and tells her,

"You can't be hidden away all your life," Antoinette thinks, glumly, "Why not?" (492). Rhys referred to her own years in a convent school as "the happiest time in my life" (qtd. in Angier, 21). She admired and loved the nuns, especially Mother Mount Calvary—for whom she named Antoinette's convent—and she learned from them the "love of beautiful words" that led ultimately to her vocation as a novelist. Before deciding on a career in literature, though, she became for a time deeply devout and believed she had a calling to the sisterhood (see Angier, 21).

In the convent, then, Antoinette maintains a sort of tense identity. In a way, this is not surprising. The mirror is part of a woman's practical identity only because patriarchal structures—and men and women acting within those structures—constrain her to a narrow compass of possible achievement, most often involving visual allure. The virgin martyrs struggled bravely for much of their brief lives against just this constraint. And, ultimately, their bodies were neither prettified nor exploited nor erased—the standard modes of patriarchal operation. They were, of course, crushed by repressive forces of authority. However, these forces are precisely those *outside* the nunnery. The mutilated bodies of the martyrs form a sort of objective correlative to the destruction of identity— not in celibacy, but in patriarchy. They are shattered not by cloistral devotion, but by the broader social world that constituted them into the sexual identities they refused. Later, Christophine takes up the imagery of fragmentation directly in this way; Antoinette's life with her husband will "break her up" (553), she says, "tear her to pieces" (555). It is marriage, the outside world, not the convent, which degrades a woman's body to the reliquary.

Thus, the lives of these saints are not a warning only or primarily. More than that, they are an inspiration. And a prophecy as well. For their stories stretch beyond Rhys's novel to Antoinette's fate, death in flames, and to the fate of Rochester, blinded in the holocaust of Thorne Hall—both known to us already from *Jane Eyre*. This is a double fate in which Antoinette, like the virgin martyrs, asserts a sort of will, a sort of strength, though the consequences ultimately overwhelm and annihilate her. "*I'll say one thing for her, she hasn't lost her spirit,*" Grace Poole reports from the attic prison (567); the word "spirit" is well chosen. The most obvious connection is that all these saints were linked with fire. Rose of Viterbo passed successfully through a fire ordeal to defeat an enemy of the Pope; and after death, her body was untouched by the burning of the convent chapel in which it was entombed. When Barbara refused to worship idols, she was imprisoned and executed by her father; in consequence, he was consumed in flames. Agnes too refused to worship the traditional gods, and refused to marry. For punishment, she was given over to a brothel. After her arrival, only one man tried to rape her; he, like Rochester, was struck blind. In the end, according to Pope St. Damasus, Agnes, like Antoinette, died in flames. (For these biographies, see Thurston and Attwater.)

The convent, then, both starved and nourished identity, in different ways—distorting practice and reflection by erasing sexuality, it provided at the same time images of female identity imbued with resolve, independence, and spiritual strength. In many ways, things were worse for Antoinette before the convent. Certainly, they were worse after. As a child, she did indeed have a looking glass. But, one night, she woke and gazed up into the mirror. She saw herself, all in white, and also in the mirror she saw two rats glaring from the window sill. The scene graphically portrays the function of the mirror—an instrument to see ourselves as we are seen. It also shows the ambivalence of being seen, especially of being seen as a woman or as a girl. The image is a variation on a fairy tale motif: the wolf at the door, a thinly veiled image of a predatory suitor. Eyed by the rats, Antoinette flees outside, aptly seeks comfort in the bright light of the full moon: image of Diana, virgin protectress, a pagan, unmartyred version of the saints. Here, as with the nuns, female society, though it denies desire, provides safety; for in occluding sexual identity of any sort, it excludes forced and painful sexuality as well, the brutal and concealed part of practical sexual identity in patriarchal cultures.

But as this already indicates, there is more to perceptual self-constitution than the looking glass. Again, to constitute ourselves is primarily to synthesize self-images from what we see reflected in the eyes of those around us—not a private intuition of what we are alone, but an inference and projection of what we are with others. To see oneself as tall or short, fat or thin, is to see oneself socially, to categorize and judge oneself through the eyes and the ideas of people that one meets or imagines meeting. The mirror image is an element of this self-construal. The gaze of the Other, as Sartre or Lacan would call it, is what gives force and meaning to that image. Antoinette's self-constitution was from the beginning fragmented between an indifferent mother who hardly looked at her—"She kept her eyes shut . . . I touched her forehead. . . . But she pushed me away . . . coldly" (467); the stony hatred of the black laborers who saw her only as the slave owner's daughter—"*Cosways. Wicked and detestable slave-owners since generations—yes everybody hate them in Jamaica and also in this beautiful island*" (515); and beloved Christophine, from whom she was unbridgeably separated by race and by history.

Ultimately, her life in England repeats this childhood scenario. When in the end her husband (absent, like her father) will not see her and her step-brother cannot recognize her (570), when she is isolated from all society and tended alone by a woman—though a woman who is not her mother nor any other kin—she has in effect arrived back where she began. The structure is the same, but with the alienation systematically intensified. In the beginning, she was imprisoned in the colony, in warm nature, and the looks of love and hate that formed her came from dispossessed black women and men. In the end, she is imprisoned in a cold room—not nature, but not culture either ("They tell me I am in England but I don't believe them" [568]), for she is in fact more thoroughly severed from society than ever before. Replacing both her mother and Christophine is Antoinette's new nurse or warden, Grace Poole. Her name, though drawn from Bronte, serves Rhys well, with its perverse suggestions of the catechism and the lives of saints. The suggestions are apt, for, locked in the attic, Antoinette now leads not the cloistral life of the convent, but the carceral life of the martyrs. Locked in a garret by a cruel guardian, she recalls Barbara, imprisoned by her father. Reduced almost to bones and in effect entombed, she mimics the skeletal Innocenzia. And in the attic, just as in the dormitory, she reports, "There is no looking-glass here" (568). Finally, "Grace Poole" is also a name recalling baptism. That too is apt, for Antoinette's final death in flames—recalling Agnes's death and Rose's miraculous life—twists and parodies the sacrament which brings rebirth through water, just as it perverts the almost suicidal devotion of the martyrs.

Between the dormitory and the attic, Antoinette does enter society for a time, her husband's gaze and acts briefly permitting social place and possibility. Indeed, during this time, she makes ample use of mirrors to see herself, and to see herself as her husband sees her: "All day she'd be like any other girl, smile at herself in her looking-glass," he thinks (512). When Rochester begins to reject her, preparing the path for her eventual incarceration, he plots out her isolation from all such self-images, in mirrors or in the eyes of others: "She'll not laugh in the sun again. She'll not dress up and smile at herself in that damnable looking

glass. . . . Vain, silly creature. Made for loving? Yes, but she'll have no
lover, for I don't want her and she'll see no other" (560). To put an end
to vanity is to put an end to seeing and to being seen. And to put an end
to seeing and to being seen is to put an end to all human relations, to
occlude reflective identity, to bind practical identity.

In her living tomb, the attic of her husband's home, Antoinette
struggles to recall her appearance, to constitute herself, to reclaim the
perceptual part of her reflective identity: "I don't know what I am like
now," she laments. "I remember watching myself brush my hair and
how my eyes looked back at me"—again, to look in the mirror is not so
much to see as to be seen. She goes back even further in time, to her first
self-recognitions in the mirror: "The girl I saw was myself yet not quite
myself" (568)—not quite, because this part familiar and part strange girl
in the mirror was herself *for others*. "Long ago when I was a child and
very lonely I tried to kiss" that girl in the mirror, she explains (568);
there was, after all, no one else for her to kiss, or to be kissed by. Despite
her isolation, her childhood in Coulibri left her still with some self-
image, and thus, as she says on the opening page, with "hope" (465)—
hope because, in seeing herself, she could envision the possibility of others seeing her as well. When she kissed herself in the mirror, she could
imagine herself both kissing and being kissed.

But this is not true in the attic. There, all images are gone: "Now
they have taken everything away." She cannot any longer conceive an
answer to the obvious question, "Who am I?" (568). Again, when her
step-brother visits, at first he does not know her; he cannot recognize
her, connect her as identitical with what went before, see her as a single and continuous person. Moreover, even when he does recognize
her, he speaks to her as if she were "a stranger" (570). Here too we see
the alienating transformation from the beginning of the story to the
end. Her childhood isolation left some connection or possible connection, with her natural mother and with Christophine. This final isolation ties her to kin by marriage only—husband and step-brother, both
absent, neither acknowledging her—and to a hired keeper; all human
relationships—all relations that might give substance to her identity in
linking her with others—are attenuated into mere formalities of law
and money.

Finally, the isolation and dissolve of self are only furthered by the
altering of Antoinette's name. As we have seen, according to Lacan, the
name functions as a point of fixity, a basis for verbal self-constitution;

in our terms, a still point of reflective identity in a turning world of practice. But not for Antoinette. The fragmentation of her perceptual and practical identity is paralleled by a continual unnaming and renaming, a continual unfixing of this verbal self-constitution. Here too the unfixing is a direct, if unusually extreme, result of patriarchy. Initially, her name is Cosway, then Mason, when her mother remarries, then Rochester, when she herself marries. In an effort to remove any stability of name and any distinct identity at all, her husband changes not only Antoinette's patronym, but her given name as well: "He says, 'Goodnight, Bertha.' He never calls me Antoinette now" (526). Antoinette recognizes the importance of this, how name is interwoven with identity. She confronts her husband, and explicitly addresses identity, saying, "Bertha is not my name. You are trying to make me into someone else, calling me by another name" (548). He also names her "Marionette" (553), a mere manipulated thing, a puppet, a piece of wood, without reflection or autonomous action, without social connectedness (beyond mere manipulation), without identity.

Antoinette recognizes too how name and identity are linked with self-image, with the social nature of mirrors and of mirroring. In her attic prison, she reflects, "Names matter, like when he wouldn't call me Antoinette, and I saw Antoinette drifting out of the window with her scents, her pretty clothes and her looking-glass" (568). Image and name dissolve concurrently, and their dissolution is central to the severing of social links, a severing enacted through a structure of fathers and husbands.

REFLECTIONS OF RACE AND PRACTICAL IDENTITY

Again, Antoinette's self-constitution is twisted too, and crucially so, by race and by the history of colonial contact. The rats in her childhood dream displace more frightening, because more real, images of hateful blacks, such as those who fire the estate at Coulibri and stone her. In the dream, Antoinette is all in white (506), an image stressing her color, her stark difference from almost all those around her—according to Davy's data, the ratio of blacks to whites on Dominica was roughly thirty to one (499). And, later, the colored man who poisons her husband's mind against her, unknowingly links himself with the dream, calling himself "a little yellow rat" (534). Her practical and reflective identity are

always at risk because of her social position, her race, her parentage—
her role in the nightmare of history from which she and those around
her are trying to awaken.

More important than threat, however, are the intimate pain and personal distortion of her relations with Christophine and with her childhood friend Tia. As we have seen, Antoinette is denied the mirroring of
her parents—her father dead, her mother indifferent. Christophine
would be the obvious substitute, her maternal words and gaze constituting a stable identity for Antoinette. But the mirroring of Christophine
is clouded by the fact that Antoinette can never be Christophine's child.
However loved and loving, Antoinette is always the mistress. Indeed,
Antoinette herself cannot help seeing Christophine as black, and even as
black only. When Antoinette witnesses her distracted mother forcibly
kissed by a black man, she immediately identifies Christophine, not with
her suffering mother, but with the black man, calling her "damned black
devil from Hell" (540). However suppressed, the racial dyad of white
and black is always there in her mind, always structuring and warping
conceptions and relations, even her relation with Christophine.

The same principles remain in force with Tia, her only childhood
peer. Like mirror images, the two are almost interchangeable. Indeed,
Tia provides Antoinette with a mirror image of herself, but black. An
example: after swimming, Tia takes Antoinette's dress, and Antoinette
returns home in Tia's (470), the unplanned exchange of frocks implying
a broader congruence of identities (a point noted by a number of critics;
see, for example, Gregg, 90). More broadly, when Antoinette looks at
Tia, she sees herself. When she looks at herself, she sees Tia.

But there is, again, an inversion in this mirroring, like a photo-
graphic print and negative. When seeing Tia, as when looking in the
mirror, the girl Antoinette saw was herself yet not quite herself—for,
once again, seeing oneself is seeing what others see. And in this case, as
in the case of Christophine, the inversion is consequential. Tia is "black
nigger"; Antoinette, "white nigger" (470): twin figures paired and
opposed across the tain of a broken mirror, a mirror cracked by
Antoinette's easy lapse into racial derogation—"you cheating nigger,"
she calls Tia (470). Cracked too, from the other side, by centuries of
black resentment built into enduring hostility—"Black nigger better
than white nigger," Tia replies.

The tense and impossible identification culminates as Coulibri
burns, and the angry black laborers crowd threateningly around her

family. Antoinette catches sight of her friend, her other self. Then, Antoinette hungers to be black. Despite her invective and her casual white supremacism, when she looks into the mirror, she too often sees only what she is not: not black, not like Tia, not like Christophine. At this moment in particular, her reflective identity chafes against ocular proof of difference and she longs to settle into practical identity with Tia and with Christophine, to be at home: "We had eaten the same food, slept side by side, bathed in the same river. As I ran, I thought, I will live with Tia and I will be like her" (483).

There is, of course, an ambivalence here, forgotten at the moment, during crisis. She both wants and does not want to be black. Later, her response to the black man kissing her mother exemplifies this well. That moment is very much like what psychoanalysts call a "primal scene," the fantasy of one's own conception. It is as if she found the idea of such mixed parentage—a black man begetting Antoinette upon Annette— both thrilling and repulsive.

In part because of this ambivalence, a lingering colonial disdain, and in part because of the more visible hatred of the blacks against the heirs of slavemasters, Antoinette cannot be like Tia. She cannot choose this identity. Not only their personal ambivalence, but what defines and sustains this socially—the systematic supremacism and resentment and violence along the broader lines of contact between black and white—makes such a choice impossible. The options are too polarized; as Brathwaite insists, "Tia was not and never could have been [Antoinette's] friend" (qtd. in Gregg, 36–37). "When I was close I saw the jagged stone in her hand but I did not see her throw it. I did not feel it either, only something wet, running down my face." At that moment, Tia plainly sees Antoinette as white only, white nigger, white cockroach, mere instance of a resented racial category. The stone thrown by Tia shatters finally the mirror in which they try to see themselves as one another, the imaginary instrument of affirmative identity crossing racial bounds.

And yet, fleetingly, the broken glass still reflects back in a distorted form: "I looked at her and I saw her face crumple up as she began to cry. We stared at each other, blood on my face, tears on hers. It was as if I saw myself. Like in a looking-glass" (483). A final moment of constitu- tion. Tia shifts back from the racial dyad to identification: she cries when Antoinette is hurt, the emotions of one imaginary twin paired with the pain of the other. As Antoinette collapses into fever, Tia's gaze wavers between similitude and opposition, offering friendship and forcing exclusion. But, of course, despite this wavering, all events—all history, economy, political relations—lead inexorably to exclusion. In the end, Tia mirrors back only an image of what Antoinette cannot be, a society from which she is excluded, a practical and reflective identity she can neither assimilate nor engage.

Here too, the only, temporary refuge is the convent. It is only there that Antoinette finds some resolution to the racial opposition that rends her identity. She is sent to the convent shortly after the incident at Coulibri. She is walking to the new school for the first time and the incident is repeated, in miniature. Outside the convent gates, she is attacked by a light Afro-Caribbean man and a dark Afro-Caribbean woman. She escapes the situation, and the conflicted society that it exemplifies, through the doors of the convent. The nun who opens the gate and lets her in is "a coloured woman." Subsequently, when she collapses and begins to cry, she is nursed by a "second nun, also a coloured woman" (487). Then there is her convent friend or mentor, Louise, with "her thin brown hands, her black curls which smelled of vetiver" (490), all contrasting with the black girl who attacked her outside the convent: "Her hair had been plaited and I could smell the sickening oil she had daubed on it" (486). However ambiguous, the convent is a sanctuary. "I resented the nuns' cheerful faces./They are safe. How can they know what it can be like *outside*?" Immediately after, she recounts a dream of a man, "his face black with hatred" (493). In the first place, a prophetic dream of her marriage. But the imagery linking hate with racial difference outside the nunnery is not accidental. Here too, she stresses that her dress—implicitly, like its wearer—is "white and beautiful."

Indeed, as the dream suggests, for Antoinette the problem goes deeper than the mutual exclusion of whites and blacks. For the whites too will not accept her, provide a secure space to form and sustain identity. The first sentences of the novel explain: "They say when trouble comes close ranks, and so the white people did. But we were not in their ranks" (465). Excluded from the reflective and practical identity of Tia and other blacks, Antoinette was equally excluded by the white community. Early in their marriage, her husband thinks, "Looking up smiling, she might have been any pretty English girl" (499). The sentence seems to identify Antoinette as English, to provide a racial/national identity and all that this entails. But the idea of Antoinette's likeness to an English girl can arise only because Antoinette is not an English girl. In the English view, she has lived too long in the black culture of the island. She is not European either in category or in habit. Antoinette's husband reflects: "Creole of pure English descent she may be, but they are not English or European either" (496). In the metropolitan view, the Creole is half-sunk into the state of nature, half-regressed to the condition of savages. As Anderson points out, in the home country, it was common "to make the convenient, vulgar deduction that creoles, born in a savage hemisphere, were by nature different from, and inferior to, the metropolitans," that "suckled . . . in their infancy" by dark-skinned nurses, they "had their blood contaminated for life" (60).

Jane Eyre itself instances this metropolitan attitude. There, Rochester claims that Bertha pursued the marriage because he, Rochester, "was of a good race" (202), in contrast, presumably, to the Creole. He insists that she has a "pigmy intellect" (203), meaning, one assumes, an intellect both small and African. He claims that she is a "wild beast" (205), "violent," "unreasonable," and "unchaste" (203). Summing up his attitude to Bertha and all of her kind, he maintains that what is suitable for him and for his race can only be "the antipodes of the Creole" (206).

The exclusion of the Creole from the "good race" of Europe is further thematized in European racist fantasies about black witchcraft and about Creole participation in those demonic practices carried like disease in the ships from Africa. Mr. Mason's credentials as European and as English are unquestionable. In consequence, when he weds Annette, the white people murmur: it is Obeah, witchcraft (473). Later, Esau speaks more loosely of how Antoinette "bewitch" Rochester (516). And when Rochester renounces her, he tacitly imputes to her the practices of witchcraft, implicitly identifying her with the black hermetic practices of Obeah: "No more damned magic" (563), he vows. Desperate, Antoinette does, at last, try Obeah, after the initial accusations. But, far from being the powerful Satanic weapon feared by superstitious whites, the potion is ineffective, or effective only as a poisonous emetic. Bronte had already introduced the general idea, at least in a simile: "The mad lady . . . was as cunning as a witch" (284). And earlier, she had characterized Bertha's laugh as "demoniac" and had wondered if the woman with that laugh was "possessed with a devil" (96, 97).

For the blacks, then, Antoinette is white; for the whites, she is black. As Mary Lou Emery puts it, "White Creoles . . . feel close to a black culture that they cannot be part of and that can only resent them," but when they look to the "mother" country, they find either that it abandons them or "considers them inferior" (13; see also Gregg, 43). Or, more broadly, with respect to race as well as sex, Antoinette is "perceived not for what she is but for what she is not," as Deborah Kloepfer observes (142); standard identities—white and black—define, not a place for her in society, but rather a "lack of place in . . . society" (Emery, 44; cf. Gardiner, 128).

Antoinette herself articulates this complete social exclusion, this denial of identity by both European and African. Her colored servant refers to her as "a white cockroach"(518). "That's what they call all of us," she explains to her husband. "And I've heard English women call us white niggers. So between you I often wonder who I am and where is my country and where do I belong and why was I ever born at all" (519). When her husband has an affair with that same colored servant, the coupling serves as a graphic image of Antoinette's—or, more generally, the Creole's—exclusion from the colonial dyad of white and black or brown, a dyad that notoriously shifts back and forth between oppressive loathing and illicit intimacy (as Fanon and others have stressed).

Here as elsewhere, this exclusion, this complete denial of identity, precipitates madness. Hence Esau's claim that there is "*madness . . . in all these white Creoles*" (515).

ECONOMY, LAW, AND RELIGION

But Rhys does not present the fragmenting of identity in terms of such personal relations alone. The issues range more broadly than her father and mother, Christophine, Tia, Rochester. This fracturing of identity is, again, invariably social. And here the fault lines are defined not only by personal ideologies of race and gender, but necessarily by political economy as well, and cultural practice, without which those personal ideologies would not be sustained or have determinative force.

Indeed, Antoinette lacks racial status—and thus can be repudiated by blacks and metropolitan whites alike—largely because she lacks economic status. Her family has been caught up in an economic transformation that in effect made her class extinct. The Emancipation Act shifted the economic base; by putting an end to slavery, it put an end to the class of slave holders. "Emancipation, at a stroke, undercut the foundation on which the plantocracy was based" (Baker, 105); "Estates began to dwindle in size and cultivation. Some were sold off; some were parceled off into lots; others were held in name but were little more than country residences; still others were abandoned" (103). The change was both radical and sudden. An illustration: exports of coffee, the major crop of Dominica during this period, dropped from 1,612,528 pounds in 1833 to a pathetic 43,079 pounds in 1838 (see Trouillot, 55), the year of full emancipation and the year in which Coulibri burns. (In 1839, Antoinette is already in the convent [489].)

Parallel to economy, law too occludes Antoinette's social identity. Indeed, it further undermines what little economic status she has. Through marriage, she becomes nothing, a statusless nonentity. "I have no money of my own at all, everything I had belongs to him," she explains. "That is English law" (524). That was roughly it. Before the Married Women's Property Act of 1870, by common law, "Marriage was," as Dicey put it, "an assignment of a wife's property rights to her husband" (369–70); "A husband on marriage became for most purposes the almost absolute master of his wife's property. The whole of her income, from whatever source it came . . . belonged to her husband" (371).

There were ways of skirting common law, for property was governed also by law surrounding equity, and, by the time Antoinette wed Rochester, "A woman who married with a marriage settlement . . . retained as her own any property which she possessed at the time of marriage, or which came to her" (381). Antoinette had no such settlement. And here she suffered from a further lack of identity. Judge-made law surrounding equity aimed not so much at increasing women's rights as at securing the rights of a father to pass on property to a daughter, without it falling into the son-in-law's hands (see Dicey, 374). Antoinette had no father to secure these interests, but a step-father only. Thus, while "almost every woman who belonged to the wealthy classes" entered marriage at midcentury with a settlement of property and income (Dicey, 381), Antoinette did not. That is the meaning of Rochester's mental note to his father: "The thirty thousand pounds have been paid to me *without question or condition. No provision made for her*" (498, italics added). The fact that Rochester could work such a deal, that Antoinette could be handed over with no security, is not, of course, due only to her status as a step-daughter; it is also a function of her status as a Creole. A "pure English" woman of comparable wealth could not, in all likelihood, be had so cheaply, even without a living father.

In any case, Rochester successfully evaded equity, to bind Antoinette by common law. Christophine's early reaction to emancipation is fitting here: "No more slavery! She had to laugh! 'These new ones have Letter of the Law. Same thing'" (471). In the end, English law imprisons Christophine and sanctions Antoinette's domestic incarceration, the isolation of both, not only from one another, but from the flow of worldly life. As to the former, religious law, growing from the paranoic fancy of slave owners, dealt brutally with all distinctive spiritual acts traceable to Africa: "Obeah also is a practice, which has, by laws of Jamaica and Dominica, all of a modern date, been constituted a capital offense: and many negroes have of late years been executed for it in the former island," James Stephen noted, shortly before the action of the novel (quoted in Williams, 187).

For Antoinette too, the law is linked to slavery, of a sort. A woman in England at this time, deprived of resources by a tyrannical husband, "had not even the refuge of divorce . . . for every divorce required a special Act of Parliament" (Halevy, 513). Moreover, "For a woman, a parliamentary divorce was virtually unattainable. Only four women ever succeeded in having their Bills passed. Two were based on incestuous adultery, and two on bigamous adultery" (Doggett, 31). Judicial divorce became possible only in 1857, though even then the circumstances were limited (McCord, 338–39). Indeed, in the eyes of the law, Antoinette is a mere function of her husband; he alone has legal identity. "By marriage, the husband and wife are one person in law: that is, the very being or legal existence of the woman is suspended during the marriage, or at least is incorporated and consolidated into that of the husband" (Blackstone, quoted in Dicey, 369). It was called "coverture," the oppressive fiction that a man's status in law "covered" his wife and her legal interests, and it granted him, until 1891, the legal right to imprison his wife.

Thus, Antoinette, imprisoned by Rochester, can take no action on her own behalf. By coverture, it was impossible for a wife to sue her husband (see Doggett, 18)—that would be equivalent to the absurdity of suing oneself. Nor could a wife testify against her husband in a criminal case (see Doggett, 45–49). With no other options, Antoinette appeals to her step-brother to save her "from this place where I am dying because it is so cold and dark" (570). He tells her, "I cannot interfere legally between yourself and your husband" (570). This is technically untrue. He could apply for a writ of *habeas corpus*. And families sometimes did just this (see Doggett, chapter 1). Again, Antoinette lacks a family to act on her behalf, just as she lacks a home, a nation, a race. But, on the other hand, such writs could be denied, and often were. In the important Cochrane case, only a few years earlier (1840), Mr. Cochrane locked up his wife and nailed shut the windows; Coleridge J. refused "to grant a writ of *habeas corpus*," though he fully realized that "he might be sentencing Mrs Cochrane to perpetual imprisonment" (Doggett 16).

Finally, religion. Antoinette lives neither Christianity nor Obeah. Indeed, her life unfolds like a parody of both religions. Neither Jesus nor any soul-possessing spirit provides a valued sense of self or active social engagement. Her Christianity finds its place between the virgin martyrs of the convent and the flaming parrot that descends toward the threatening, black crowd, a perverse image of the paraclete descending on the Apostles at Pentecost. Inspired and frightened, as by an omen, the crowd disperses. Nancy Harrison points out that perhaps the Masons' lives were saved by the spectacular and absurd death of the parrot, struggling to fly with its clipped wings (177).

When Antoinette dreams of her suicidal leap from the burning mansion, just before she jumps, she hears the parrot call "*Qui est la? Qui est la?*" (574, "Who is there? Who is there?"). What she hears, then, is one version of the question of identity, addressed to others and to herself, to the ghost of herself that haunts the passageways of Thornfield Hall. Moreover, this is the question shrieked by her mad mother in the weeks after the destruction of Coulibri, and before her removal to the country and to the embraces of her black guardian (as noted in Harrison, 173, 177). After hearing the parrot's question—her mother's question, her own question—Antoinette's "hair . . . streamed out like wings" in anticipation of the fiery descent from the battlements (574; cf. Kloepfer, 158). The identification with the parrot and paraclete is clear. Yet Antoinette's jump is even more futile than that of the parrot, for she saves nothing through her spectacular and absurd death, except perhaps the marriage of Jane Eyre.

Even before this, she has already shrivelled to a skeleton in her sepulchral attic ("*She sits shivering and she is so thin*")—an unwilling Innocenzia, chaste and nearly martyred ("*If she dies on my hands who will get the blame?*" [566]). But she is different from the saints, just as she is different from the paraclete. Unlike Rose of Viterbo, she will not survive the fire ordeal. Rather, like Agnes, she dies in flames. The only resultant good is purely negative, punitive: the man who brutalized her is trapped in flames and blinded, like the men who brutalized Barbara (patroness of masons) and Agnes. In the end, then, she is a travesty of both the holy ghost and the virgin martyrs—tumbling to a bloody death, violated, insane, uncanonized, successful only in maiming her captor and annihilating herself.

The tragically parodic, alienating pattern recurs with Obeah. As she finds herself more thoroughly removed from society, as her identity fragments through increasing isolation, Antoinette grows more and more ambiguous between life and death, more and more like the living dead who haunt the forests in Voudou belief (see Simpson, 250–51)—"a ghost/undead . . . zombie," as Mona Fayad observes (448) or, in the words read by Rochester from *The Glittering Coronet of Isles*, "*a dead person who seems to be alive or a living person who is dead*" (522). Like Annette after the destruction of Coulibri and the death of her son: "Wherever her soul is wandering . . . it has left her body," Antoinette reflects (491). Just before she passes through the gates of the convent for the first time, the boy that accosts her, makes the link explicit: "Your mother . . . have eyes like zombie and you have eyes like zombie too" (486). After the convent and the marriage, the condition recurs. When she appeals to Christophine's knowledge of Obeah to rekindle Rochester's affection, Christophine observes: "Your face like dead woman" (528). Later, the inhabitants of Rochester's mansion glimpse her wandering the halls at night; they construe this apparition as a ghost (569). Antoinette accepts their interpretation, splits herself in two, both woman and spirit, the former not quite dead, the latter not quite alive, both tottering on the edge, wavering between worlds: "I never looked behind me for I did not want to see that ghost of a woman who they say haunts this place" (572).

Antoinette's final condition is unusually bleak. For her, every aspect of reflective identity has been broken; every relation of practical identity has been cut. While others might find a tentative and partial identity through gender, race, ethnicity, religion, politics, class—*some* well-structured system of social relations—Antoinette is denied all. Yet, this extremity of severance and constraint makes her a perfect case as well, an ideal illustration of conditions under colonial rule and patriarchy. For, denied all respite in untroubled reflection or ease of act, she instances, with rare intensity and fullness, the devastation of identity that threatens everyone who lives within those pervasive and enduring structures.

CHAPTER FOUR

CULTURE AND DESPAIR

Chinua Achebe's Things Fall Apart

CUSTOM AND THE EXTINCTION OF HOPE

Anthropologists tend to see non-Western societies as permeated by religion, governed and regulated by ideas of divinity and worship. Thus, religion becomes a particular focus of conflict, a crucial point of identity. But what colonialism destroys is much larger than what we would ordinarily call religion. It is the broad sway of practical identity that colonialism undoes. It is the entire systematic organization of work, of law, of economy, of personal relations. It is what we call "culture," which is to say, the system of practical identities.

Consider an Igbo village before colonialism. A boy grows up in that village. He learns how to act in typical and recurrent situations; he acquires a practical identity, which intertwines with the practical identities of those around him. He internalizes all the habits of behavior that organize life in the village—how to interact personally, how to cooperate in work, how to compete in games, how to present or respond to official accusation. Thus, he learns how to greet his elders, his agemates, his younger siblings; he internalizes what can be expected of a spouse or a parent or a child; he gains skill in farming; he assimilates his part in rituals and celebrations; he comes to know what of this can change (e.g., his part in rituals) and what cannot, what he can change by his own effort (e.g., membership in a ranked order of exclusive societies) and what the society can decide to change on his behalf, and how all this occurs. He comes to understand what he can hope for in his lifetime (e.g., how high he can possibly rise in village governance) and what joys he can expect recurrently (e.g., a great feast following the difficult work of harvest).

Every part of his life is lived within an ambience of familiarity. His aspirations for the future, the ways he encourages himself in times of sorrow or inspires himself to labor, are all bound up in this. Unexpected events occur, unforeseeable good- or ill-fortune. But they occur within a broader context of what is expected. It is like knowing one's way from house to house in a village, or from the village to the farmland. A snake could appear on the path, a tree may have fallen, impeding access—but the path is the same. It does not suddenly change course or disappear. It is, indeed, the pervasive familiarity that allows him to consider and respond to whatever is unfamiliar or unexpected, allows him to hope and to have confidence that he can respond successfully to difficulty and surprise.

Whether we like it or not, in every society, one's sex is central to the definition of this identity. Reproduction is necessarily crucial to the life of a society. Indeed, if any society arose that paid no attention to reproduction, it would die out in one generation. In and of itself, this does not require that a person's sex assume definitive significance, that work and play and social relations, the broad structures of economy, law, politics, ritual, and miscellaneous customs should be structured by sex. But they are. The village boy we have just imagined does not think of his work in purely generic, human terms, or in entirely individual terms. What he acquires, in acquiring a practical identity, is at least in part the practice of *men's* work. His aspirations and ideals, the social expectations and rewards that challenge and motivate him, are in almost every case based on his sex. He works *as a man*, advances through positions of authority *held by men*, takes up a role in law or ritual *reserved for men*, addresses others *as a man*. Indeed, when Okonkwo and Obierika discuss alien and incomprehensible cultures, they speak of them directly in terms of disrupted gender roles. Obierika explains that, in "Abame and Aninta . . . titled men climb trees and pound foo-foo for their wives." Other men comment, "All their customs are upside-down. . . . That is very bad." Okonkwo extends the conversation to the truly inconceivable: " I have even heard that in some tribes a man's children belong to his wife and her family." Machi, astonished, replies, "That cannot be. . . . You might as well say that the woman lies on top of the man when they are making the children" (76).

Familiarity of place and act and expectation gives us a feeling of security. It provides one condition for what the Greeks called *eudaimonia*—living well, having a benevolent *daimon*, that element of divinity that dwells within, like God or conscience. The concept translates directly into Igbo—having a good *chi*, a beneficent spirit structuring the happenstance of life, a form of individual or "personalized providence" (Isichei, 25). Without ease of practical identity, habit, tradition, we cannot have *eudaimonia*, a benevolent *chi*. Indeed, the rapid loss of habit, the quick undoing of practical identity, produces panic, a sense of disequilibrium and loss, a feeling that too much is new and one cannot react. It is like a nightmare in which, suddenly, the paths have all changed their course or disappeared. The ground itself is unfamiliar. When this feeling is prolonged beyond panic, when the sense of loss persists, it breeds despair.

Thus, one form of despair arises when one no longer knows, with ease of habit, one's place in work and society, when one's former aspirations are no longer attainable and are rendered meaningless in changed circumstances, when one's manners of interaction and expectation no longer hold good. That is why colonialism breeds despair. It suddenly destroys indigenous systems of work, law, politics, ritual, and thus shatters the people's practical identities. Our imaginary villager acts, unthinkingly, in accordance with village customary law—but then the British impose another law, which condemns him; he builds his aspirations around advancement in a secret village society, but the British outlaw the society, or the Christians convert so many members that it is rendered inoperative; he treats his children according to Igbo tradition, but they respond according to English practices; he cannot work, because he knows how to cultivate yams and the British have made him grow coffee or cocoa or sugar cane; he tries to console himself with thoughts of the joyous harvest festivals and other communal celebrations, but now the harvest is at the wrong time, and anyway the British have banned such gatherings, fearing subversion. In a brief time, all his aspirations for achievement are cut short and made impossible, all his competencies are rendered useless, all his basic enjoyments lost.

When sincere, reactionary traditionalism is an effort to stave off the despair that flows from these uncertainties and incapacities. It is an attempt to reassert ideas and practices that return familiarity to life, give us something we can count on, a basis for confidence and expectation that will permit us to work in the present and imagine the future.

CULTURAL PATHOLOGY AND REACTIONARY MASCULINITY

Like all tragic heroes, Okonkwo is a great man, a sympathetic man, but a deeply flawed man. Indeed, he is deeply flawed by Igbo standards—by Igbo standards of gender in fact. He is adamantly masculine, but his masculinity is not orthodox; it is not in keeping with the unchallenged and naturalized practices of Igbo culture. It is, rather, clearly reactionary. One might put the problem this way: in keeping with the reactionary view of things, for Okonkwo, there is no common ground of male and female traits. The two are perfect complements with no intersection. Thus, for Okonkwo, to be a man is to purge himself entirely of all traces of femininity, all considerations, practices, feelings appropriate to women. As we have noted, this is not an uncommon development in postcolonization society. However, what is unusual about Okonkwo is that his reactionary masculinism is not caused by colonial domination; it develops entirely within Igbo society. On the other hand, it is the incursion of colonialism that makes Okonkwo's condition tragic.

Reactionary traditionalism can be understood as a sort of pathology, a pathology, so to speak, of orthodoxy (just as mimeticism could be seen as a pathology of assimilation). There are two ways of conceiving of any pathology in relation to colonialism. The simpler way is to see the pathology as resulting directly from colonialism. Colonial pressures and contradictions build until one's identity is twisted into madness or perverse and self-destructive compulsion. The more complex way is to see colonialism as undermining social methods for defusing personal pathology. Society, any society, structures not only peoples' needs and wants, actions and expectations, but also their neuroses, their compulsions and delusions. Practical identity provides a means for acting out, in more or less benign forms, the unforgotten traumas, emotional distortions, psychic malformations from which each of us suffers. Part of our practical identity is knowing how to respond to melancholy or rage; part of culture is canalizing those emotions, structuring, and rendering innocuous, the actions to which these give rise. All societies partially succeed at this (if they did not, they would quickly disintegrate). No doubt, all societies partially fail as well. But when a culture is disrupted, traditional means of defusing pathology are disrupted as well. In consequence, small problems can grow into great tragedies.

As we shall discuss in more detail below, Okonkwo's reactionary masculinity is, in effect, a classically Oedipal reaction against his father, who had not one prized quality of Igbo manhood. Okonkwo's own son continues this Freudian tradition, engaging in a similar Oedipal rebellion. And his rebellion too is taken up and given shape by colonialism when he turns from his father's reactionary traditionalism to Christianity and assimilation. Indeed, the novel itself could be read as yet a third Oedipal rebellion. Nwoye/Isaac, Okonkwo's son, is not dissimilar to Achebe's father (Isaiah); and Okonkwo represents the generation of Achebe's grandfather (cf. Killam, 13). Achebe himself, in his focus on Okonkwo, in his great sympathy for Igbo tradition, seems to be rejecting his own father. Though, at the same time, he ambivalently accepts many of his father's (and Europe's) criticisms of Igbo tradition and recognizes that a return to a pristine tradition is neither possible nor desirable.

As Achebe's obvious sympathy implies, Okonkwo's position in *Things Fall Apart* is not thematically simple. He is not merely an instance of traditionalist pathology; he is also a sort of corrective to tradition gone awry. A standard view of colonial conquest, promulgated by a wide range of traditionalists and syncretists in a wide range of colonized regions, is that the culture of the colonized people had already declined, had already entered a phase of decadence, had "softened," when the British came, that it was in part their own feminine condition that permitted the British conquest. In fact, accounts of the Igbo wars seem to me to render this view largely implausible in the case of Igboland. The difference in weaponry was vast, and the British did little more than use their automatic weapons to mow down Igbo warriors (see, for example, Isichei, 129). In any case, whether it fits the historical record or not, this is a view suggested at many points in *Things Fall Apart*, even if it is never entirely clear whether Achebe himself agrees with these suggestions.

In part, then, Okonkwo is a reactionary traditionalist, hyper-masculinizing and thus distorting Igbo culture (the general point has been noted by a number of critics; see, for example, Killam; Wren, 59; Muoneke, 102–4; Gikandi, 40). But, at the same time, there are many suggestions in *Things Fall Apart* that the culture of Umuofia has decayed, that it has become weak and emasculated and that Okonkwo's masculinity is not only a violation of gender norms, but also a corrective to the opposite, feminizing tendency of his fellow Igbos.

For many years, the village was a model of Igbo strength: "Umuofia was feared by all its neighbors. It was powerful in war and in magic, and its priests and medicine men were feared in all the surrounding country" (13); "Umuofia . . . the land of his fathers where men were bold and warlike" (168). But, early in the novel, Okonkwo goes to visit Nwaki-bie, "a wealthy man" who "had taken the highest but one title which a man could take in the clan" (20), a true man, by Igbo standards. He praises Okonkwo, saying, "It pleases me to see a young man like you these days when our youth has gone so soft" (23), though it is hard to say how much this is the perennial complaint of an older generation, and how much it is meant to reflect degeneracy. Later, Obierika complains of two other villages, "'In Abame and Aninta the title is worth less than two cowries. Every man wears the thread of title on his ankle, and does not lose it even if he steals.' 'They have indeed soiled the name of *ozo*,' said Okonkwo" (72). As we have already noted, Abame and Aninta are precisely the villages in which Okonkwo and Obierika find sex roles disrupted, with men acting the part of women. The point is clear—the men of these villages, unlike Okonkwo, have gone soft, become "women." It is no accident that Abame is the village destroyed by the British, marking their first incursion into this remote area of Igboland (see 142–45).

After the British come to Umuofia and begin their insidious destruction of the culture, Achebe repeats the theme, first with respect to Okonkwo's mother's village: A Christian had killed the sacred python, who was "addressed as 'Our Father'" (164) and thus was linked with the masculine heritage of the village. Okonkwo insists that the Christians be "chased out of the village with whips" (164). But his peers do not agree. Okonkwo says that they "reason like cowards," that none will do "what a man does." "This is a womanly clan," he concludes (165). It should be noted that Okonkwo's argument is not without a point. Achebe explains that, traditionally, the accidental killing of the python involved a great penalty (164). Intentional killing should have been treated as a serious matter. Moreover, it was a recurrent problem. According to Amadiume, "By far the greatest conflict" between Igbo traditionalists and Christians, at least in some areas, "centered on the Christian practice of killing the python" (121). One of the strongest arguments against taking action is that the gods can fight their own battles (165). But, as Amadiume notes, this is precisely the British view of things. When approached about the murder of a sacred python, the District Officer "would tell the villagers to leave it to the particular deity to deal with the offender" (121). This was not the Igbo way. By Igbo custom, the clan was responsible for acting on the god's behalf, as the Umuofians did in driving Okonkwo from the village and burning his compound when he committed "a crime against the earth goddess" (128). Indeed, if they did not act, they too became guilty of the original violation.

This motif of social disintegration and degeneration recurs too in a passage that is particularly important because it echoes and accounts in part for the title of the novel: "Okonkwo was deeply grieved. And it was not just a personal grief. He mourned for the clan, which he saw breaking up and falling apart, and he mourned for the warlike men of Umuofia, who had so unaccountably become soft like women" (189).

THE STORY OF A STRONG MAN

Whether we accept this judgement of Igbo society or not—indeed, whether Achebe himself accepts it or not—masculinity is clearly a central preoccupation of the novel. And Okonkwo is clearly, in very many ways, an admirable Igbo man, a model of the masculine virtues—for in Igboland, as in most other societies, the virtues are largely distributed according to sex, and Okonkwo's virtues are squarely male. It is no accident that the novel is subtitled, *The Story of a Strong Man*.

In traditional Igbo society, the main areas in which men demonstrated their masculine excellence were productive labor (farming), oratory, sporting competition (wrestling), war, and the taking of titles (on war, sports, and oratory, see Dike, 117). Okonkwo excelled in all except oratory. The novel begins with the legendary story of Okonkwo's victory in the greatest wrestling match "since the founder of their town engaged a spirit of the wild for seven days and seven nights" (3). His victory links him to the greatest ancestor and that ancestor's triumph over the malign spirits of the Evil Forest, who would have prevented the founding of the village. Though the reference is brief, it is crucial.

As to the rest: "He was a wealthy farmer and had two barns full of yams, and had just married his third wife"; the masculine prowess implied by polygamy hardly needs to be stressed. "To crown it all he had taken two titles and had shown incredible prowess in two inter-tribal wars. And so although Okonkwo was still young, he was already one of the greatest men of his time" (8–9).

In farming, Dike explains, "There was a typical Igbo division of labour between the sexes. The men cleared the bush, made farm ridges and cultivated yam, the main economic crop. The women weeded the farm, cultivated and owned cassava . . . vegetables, fruits and cereals" (123). As Achebe explains, stressing the masculine accomplishment of Okonkwo's two full barns: "His mother and sisters worked hard enough, but they grew women's crops, like coco-yams, beans and cassava. Yam, the king of crops, was a man's crop" (24). And, later, "Yam stood for manliness, and he who could feed his family on yams from one harvest to another was a very great man indeed" (34).

In war, Okonkwo had killed five men and taken their skulls as trophies: "In Umuofia's latest war he was the first to bring home a human head. That was his fifth head; and he was not an old man yet" (11). As Isichei explains, "The practice of beheading a fallen foe was very widespread among Igbo communities east and west of the Niger. The skull was valued as a souvenir, and as a concrete and unequivocal proof of personal valour . . . [a] trophy [which] was a proof of a man's courage" (80–81). Indeed, some groups of Igbo divided men into two groups—those who had obtained a head, "heroes," and those who had not, "cowards" (*"dike"* and *"oju,"* 82). Moreover, the prowess indicated by the possession of five skulls is immense. These were not European wars, with corpses counted up by the truckload. As Dike reports, wars often ended with "the killing of the leaders or one to two persons" (22). Okonkwo, lamenting once again the femininity of the current generation, recalls a particularly bloody battle, a "slaughter": "'Worthy men are no more,' Okonkwo sighed as he remembered those days. 'Isike will never forget how we slaughtered them in that war. We killed twelve of their men" (22). Given the limited number of casualties, Okonkwo's five skulls must represent a significant percentage of enemy deaths.

Perhaps more important than wrestling, farming, or war, is Okonkwo's taking of titles. A title was a sign of honor, more specifically, a sign of wealth and character, for each title required the payment of a fee and the successful passage through a ritual ordeal. As Isichei explains, "Usually there was a hierarchy of ascending titles, to be taken in order, with an ascending scale of payments" (22). The higher the title, the greater the honor.

The title system in Okonkwo's clan involved four grades. For all practical purposes, the third, Ozo, was the highest title, for the fourth title was extremely rare: "There were only four titles in the clan, and only one or two men in any generation ever achieved the fourth and highest. When they did, they became the lords of the land" (127). This is not to say that holders of the Ozo title were common. Quite the contrary. For example, in a recent study of the Nri Igbo community Onwuejeogwu found that Ozo men constituted only 2.4 percent of the total Nri population (about 11 percent of adult men).

Titles clearly brought prestige. But they also granted the title bearer specific roles of legal and religious authority. For example, the Ozo title was immediately preceded by the Ndichie initiation (one's initiation into the world of the elders), which "allows the initiate to participate in all secret deliberations, rituals and homages paid to the elders" or ancestors (Dike, 101–2). The Ozo title itself gave the recipient enormous political, legal, and religious authority and power; in many ways, Ozo title bearers constituted a sort of ruling elite (e.g., on their judicial authority, see Dike, 111–14).

Perhaps most interesting for our purposes is the power of Ozo men to decide on matters "without any precedents" and to "amend local customs" (Dike, 110, 111). Through its extensive trading, as well as warfare, Igbo villages came into frequent contact with other cultures in the region. As Dike points out, "A society that has always been in constant contact with a wide variety of other cultures is bound to learn new modes of behaviour. These new modes are by definition undefined and therefore belong to the realm of the *Ozo* men." Indeed, "The *Ozo* men, because of their accumulated honour and esteem, often initiate new rules and standards of conduct" (110). In the opening chapter, we noted that orthodox societies are always changing, altering in response to new circumstances, and that orthodoxy necessarily involves an openness to change, but change regulated by an internal dynamic of the society, not a sudden undermining of that society, as occurs in colonialism. (A number of critics have stressed this openness in traditional Igbo society—for example, Njoku, 29; Muoneke, 107; and Carroll, 40–42.) Igbo society is remarkable for having integrated a formal means of both allowing and regulating change. This was part of the judicial function of the Ozo title society.

Though Achebe never says so directly, it is clear that Okonkwo has taken the Ozo title. He is able to incarnate an ancestor in the Egwugwu dances and in judicial hearings, which implies that he has undergone the Ndichie initiation. He is evidently not allowed to climb palm trees—a restriction placed on holders of the Ozo title (see 71). He imagines "initiating his sons into the *ozo* society" (178), which would, of course, be possible only if he himself is a member. Finally, by the time of his exile, he has only one further title to achieve, for he reflects that "His life had been ruled by a great passion—to become one of the lords of the clan. That had been his life-spring. And he had all but achieved it. Then everything had been broken" (135).

This achievement of the penultimate title, and the approach to the highest title, demonstrate, once again, his masculine vigor and accomplishment. His position as an Ozo man also indicates that, by Igbo tradition, decisions as to the rate and orientation of cultural change, the alteration of custom, work, law, ritual, were partially in his hands. In struggling against the encroachment of Christianity, of European law and government, he was not acting simply on his own initiative. He was fulfilling one of the central duties that adhered to his position as a holder of the penultimate title of Umuofia, a duty which, by all the traditions of the place, he owed to all Umuofians. His obligation extended back, through all the ancestors, to Ofia, who struggled for seven days and seven nights with a spirit of the wild (3) before he could establish this village and its customs for his descendants, his "umu"—hence the name "Umuofia," with a play on the meaning of "Ofia," "bush" (see Wren, 9), the condition of brute nature from which they had been delivered by this struggle and by these customs.

OEDIPAL REACTION

But, once again, much of Okonkwo's strength is a reaction against his father's weakness, an Oedipal repulsion at his unmanly progenitor, Unoka. Unoka had none of the admirable traits of traditional Igbo manhood. In labor, "He was lazy and improvident and . . . a debtor" (4); he was "known in all the clan for the weakness of . . . [his] hoe." In war, he was "a coward and could not bear the sight of blood" (6–7). In the legal and ritual hierarchy, "He had taken no title at all" (8). By Igbo standards, he was hardly a man. Indeed, Okonkwo remembered with bitterness how "a playmate had told him that his father was *agbala*," a woman; "That was how Okonkwo first came to know that *agbala* was not only another name for a woman, it could also mean a man who had taken no title" (14–15). Ultimately, Okonkwo's father is even denied an appropriate burial and a place with the ancestors. He dies of a "swelling in the stomach." "The sickness was an abomination to the earth," an offense to the structure and balance of life—perhaps because it mimics the swelling of a pregnant woman and is thus of a piece with Unoka's incapacity to be a man. He is thrown, unburied, into the Evil Forest (19). "He had a bad *chi*"—he suffered *kakodaimonia*.

Achebe stresses that Okonkwo's hyper-masculinity was a desperate effort to avoid the fate of his father, to keep from falling into unmasculinity, to *make* his *chi* good, his life *eudaimonic*, in his role as a man— "Ibo people have a proverb that when a man says yes his *chi* says yes also" (28). Okonkwo's "life was dominated by fear, the fear of failure and of weakness." This was not a fear of any outward thing, "capricious gods" or "magic" or "the forces of nature." Indeed, "Okonkwo's fear was greater than these. It was not external but . . . was the fear of himself, lest he should be found to resemble his father" (14). (The general point has been noted by most critics, often without much sympathy for Okonkwo. For a more sympathetic portrait, see Njoku, 31–37.)

This fear was twofold. It was, indeed, a fear directly comparable to the fear felt by men and women oppressed by racism—which is one reason why it fits so well with the theme of colonization. When one's race has been impugned as lazy, stupid, effeminate, one knows that any error one commits will immediately be taken up by members of the dominant group and seen as proof that, like others of one's "kind," one is lazy, stupid, effeminate oneself. That is why, at virtually every moment, a black person in a white society must "prove" him/herself, again and again demonstrating that he/she is not incompetent. The same holds for families. One part of Okonkwo's fear is that the slightest error, the faintest hint of sloth or feminine concern, will serve as proof that he is, indeed, the son of Unoka, dogged by the same mischievous *chi*, equally incapable of making his own success, of taking the place of a man.

Indeed, it was a matter of near certainty that the faults of the father would descend to the son. In Igbo society, personal character was widely viewed as hereditary (cf. the repeated references to this in Nwapa). And this had concrete legal and social consequences. For example, as Dike points out, "In most areas of Northern Igboland the norm is that a son may not perform titles superior to those held by his father" (77). Indeed, anyone who was untitled "*in theory possessed the social position of a slave and as such had no social honours or privileges"* (Dike, 92). Of course, Okonkwo was not barred from any title taking, and thus condemned to the status of a slave. In keeping with this, it is possible that, when Achebe says Unoka had no titles, he means no titles beyond the basic Amanwulu title that distinguished free men from slaves. In any case, it is clear the Umuofia allowed a son to "perform titles superior to those held by his father." Nonetheless, the whole orientation of Igbo custom indicates that this superceding of one's father would be rare and difficult, and thus that Okonkwo's title-taking must have been severely constrained, at least informally. For example, it is crucial to achieving the *Ozo* title that the candidate have "good character"; indeed, good character is crucial "above all" (Dike 99). Unoka's well-known profligacy made it far more difficult for Okonkwo to establish a reputation for good character, and potentially much easier for him to lose that reputation.

Beyond concern over communal judgment, Okonkwo suffers a deeper fear that he might truly have inherited his father's unmasculine traits. More profound and more threatening than society's evaluation is Okonkwo's self-evaluation. Here too racism is parallel. Black people living among whites must not only prove their capabilities to whites, they must often prove their capabilities to themselves. When told over and over, directly and indirectly, that one is incompetent, one is likely to develop a nagging doubt about one's competence; one is likely to fear that any new endeavor will demonstrate incapacity. This is the fear that Achebe stresses, the fear that structures Okonkwo's life, the fear that drives him even more than practical concern about the judgment of society. And both lead to the same reactionary results.

Of course, that such a fear lay at the root of Okonkwo's masculine acts and attitudes need not render those acts and attitudes inappropriate or false. But Okonkwo's fear is so great that he cannot allow himself any hint of weakness. No culture, not even a martial culture such as that of the Igbo, can define masculine and feminine traits in perfect complementarity. Some must overlap. An orthodox man must have some "feminine" traits—at least in certain circumstances, he must be merciful or affectionate or conciliatory; he must, at times, take up what is, in his society, most often considered the woman's part. Indeed, if he does not, then he is not a true man; his masculinity is not orthodox, but excessive. Similarly, women must be brave or eloquent or strong at times, or they are not genuine orthodox women. But

Okonkwo's fear is too overpowering. He cannot allow himself to act the woman's part even when it is required by tradition.

Put differently, Igbo cosmology and custom project onto the universe and demand from society a balance of masculine and feminine principles. The two great deities are Chukwu, the sky-father above, and Ani, the earth-mother below (cf. Onunwa, *Studies*, 11, on the preeminence of the Earth Goddess). We need both principles, and in the right balance. As Isichei points out, "In some expositions of Igbo religion, its core is the polarity between *Chukwu* and *Ana* [or Ani]" (27)—a polarity in which both poles are, necessarily, crucial. Indeed, according to some, they are the same deity—female when on earth, male when in the sky (see Onunwa, *African*, 32).

Cosmological disturbance, imbalance of male and female, Chukwu and Ani, causes drought or disease. Both sky and earth must cooperate to bring forth crops: Nwoye "remembered the story . . . of the quarrel between Earth and Sky long ago, and how Sky withheld rain for seven years, until crops withered and the dead could not be buried because the hoes broke on the stony Earth. At last Vulture was sent to plead with Sky, and to soften his heart with a song of the suffering of the sons of men" (55–56). In the fuller versions, which vary in detail, earth and sky have a dispute over ownership. In one version, they dispute inheritance of the entire world (see Onunwa, *African*, 20–21, though in this particular retelling earth is represented as male). In another, Yoruba version, they dispute a mere mouse (see Idowu, 50; the Yoruba version would have been known to Achebe at least from Tutuola's *Palm-Wine Drinkard*, 118–19). In any case, sky retaliated against earth's claim by withholding rain. The rains returned only when people sacrificed to sky, offering him, through the intermediary of the vulture, what earth had previously withheld. The lesson is clear—without balance, equitable portioning to sky and earth, father and mother, there is no life. (For a discussion of the relevance of this story to other parts of the novel, see Weinstock and Ramadan.)

In most versions, it appears to be Earth that has not given up what it should, that has violated equity. In Achebe's novel, however, imbalance is most often a matter of the masculine part taking more than its share. Indeed, as Nwoye remembers the story, there is no clear indication of who is to blame in the quarrel between earth and sky. Perhaps it is merely the (male) sky that is disturbing the balance. Moreover, it is important that the story was told to Nwoye by his mother. Okonkwo told only "masculine stories of violence and bloodshed" (55). Clearly, he does not understand the importance of balance in myth any better than he understands it in life.

Of course, this story does stress the necessity of reverencing sky and thus the masculine principle. But the importance of earth and femininity is equally stressed, through Ani, "the earth goddess and the source of all fertility." Indeed, though one would not expect it from Okonkwo's disdain for all things associated with femininity, "Ani played a greater part in the life of the people than any other deity." And her function was far broader than agricultural fertility. Most importantly, "She was the ultimate judge of morality and conduct," for morality and conduct could not be purely masculine, any more than fertility could be such. Moreover, though female and the embodiment of the feminine principle, she is intimately linked with masculinity as well, indicating the importance of not isolating one gender from the other: "And what was more, she was in close communion with the departed fathers of the clan whose bodies had been committed to earth" (38).

Balance, then, of masculine and feminine is crucial. Death—drought, disease, famine, suffering—is the result of cosmological imbalance. Similar devastations result from parallel social or ethical imbalance. In repudiating his father's unmanliness, Okonkwo seeks to purge himself of all traces of femininity. In doing so, he unbalances the masculine and feminine, both in himself and in those around him.

The first suggestion of this comes in the characterization of Okonkwo's masculinity. Of the orthodox masculine skills mentioned above, he is lacking in one only—oratory. Indeed, he substitutes physical force for rhetorical force: "He had a slight stammer and whenever he was angry and could not get his words out quickly enough, he would use his fists" (4). Oratory, though often used to inspire martial sentiment, was also crucial to avoiding war, defusing tension, limiting conflict. Note that this is exactly the context in which we are told of Okonkwo's oratorical incapacities: he would never substitute words for arms; indeed, he would substitute physical battle for verbal admonition. This is a particularly clear case of excessive masculinity, for it involves the repudiation of an aspect of orthodox masculinity that has a close parallel in orthodox femininity. As Isichei points out, it was, traditionally, Igbo women who lobbied against war (81). And sympathy was linked with femininity—"When a father beats his child, it seeks sympathy in its mother's hut" (Achebe, 138–39). To substitute words for blows, while sometimes eminently masculine in Igbo society, was often feminine. Because of its possible femininity, Okonkwo could never substitute words for blows, even when canons of manliness demanded, for it reactivated his fear of sliding into femininity, of becoming, like his father, *agbala*. In the end, when Okonkwo wishes to do battle with the British, he reflects, "The greatest obstacle in Umuofia . . . is that coward, Egonwanne. His sweet tongue can change fire into cold ash. When he speaks he moves our men to impotence. If they had ignored his womanish wisdom . . . we would not have come to this" (206–7).

Okonkwo's excessive virility, his violation of communal standards, is clearer still in his actions toward others. Okonkwo is guilty of "brusqueness in dealing with less successful men," brusqueness of the sort condemned by the Igbo proverb, "Looking at the king's mouth . . . one would think he never sucked at his mother's breast" (27). It is important to remember here that most of Igbo society, including Umuofia, had no kings. Indeed, throughout Igboland, village societies were hierarchized, largely by the title societies, but there were no supreme hereditary rulers: "The missionaries . . . asked who the king of the village was, but the villagers told them that there was no king. 'We have men of high title and the chief priests and the elders,' they said" (153). In short, by Igbo custom, Okonkwo's demeaning attitude was inappropriate for anyone, no matter what his/her position.

Okonkwo's first disdain is for his own father, an unfilial and irreverent attitude—thus an attitude inappropriate for an Igbo man. In keeping with this, Okonkwo reserves his sharpest words and loathing for those who remind him of his father, and thus of the part in himself that he fears will grow and make him similar to his father: "A man had contradicted [Okonkwo] at a kindred meeting. . . . Without looking at the man Okonkwo had said: 'This meeting is for men.' The man who had contradicted him had no titles. That was why he had called him a woman. Okonkwo knew how to kill a man's spirit" (27–28). The man's name was "Osugo," recalling "osu," the name for a slave. The language is revealing. Okonkwo wished to kill the man's spirit, because he so reminded Okonkwo of his untitled father, Unoka, and of all that followed from Unoka's sloth and cowardice—being *agbala*, slave, without status. Like the ancient ancestor Ofia, Okonkwo too was struggling with a spirit of the forest. When he tried to kill Osugo's spirit metaphorically, he wished to kill the spirit of his father—the wandering spirit, one of those "evil spirits of [the] unburied dead, hungry to do harm to the living" (33), a mystical correlate of what Okonkwo truly fears in communal history and personal memory. Later, when he thinks of his father, he represses the thought immediately: "He had long learned how to lay that ghost" (68)—as if in wrestling. But this struggle is not like that of Ofia. Ofia did not battle his own father, try to kill the spirit of his kin. Okonkwo has gone too far. "Everybody at the kindred meeting took sides with Osugo when Okonkwo called him a woman" (28).

Okonkwo carries this distorted relation with his father over to his relations with his own sons. For he fears them too, that they will be like their grandfather, that they will be lazy and weak, unmanly. He tries to crush any hint of *agbala* in them, just as he has crushed it in himself: "Okonkwo wanted his son to be a great farmer and a great man. He would stamp out the disquieting signs of laziness which he thought he already saw in him" (34). And, just as he wishes to kill the spirit of a man who is *agbala*, just as he wishes to kill his own father's spirit, he will kill his own son, rather than risk another generation of disgrace: "I will not have a son who cannot hold up his head in the gathering of the clan. I would sooner strangle him with my own hands" (35). Later, he worries that "A bowl of pounded yams"—which is to say, the work of a woman—"can throw [Nwoye] in a wrestling match," even though he "is old enough to impregnate a woman." He is too much of *agbala*. To communicate this, he says "There is too much of his mother in him," which is to say, too much woman, and too little man. But, while saying this, he thinks what is even worse, "Too much of his grandfather" (68)—for the grandfather, not the mother, is likely to be judged the source of that unmasculine strain.

After the arrival of British law and Christian missionaries, Okonkwo's masculinity becomes bound up with a fearful defense of tradition as well. In this case, Okonkwo's reaction is rendered more ambiguous, for the threat is real, and malignant. But his brutal actions often aid precisely that cultural destruction he seeks to forestall. He is still cruel; he still confuses a sense of humanity with weakness. Indeed, another way of explaining reactionary masculinity, or reactionary femininity, is as a repudiation of one's humanity, for it is precisely humanity that one shares with members of the other sex; this works for tradition as well, for it is humanity that is shared by all traditions, and it is in the name of human communality that one can justly call for the reformation of tradition.

Once, Okonkwo almost follows through on his threat to kill Nwoye. Nwoye has been to the Christian church. Okonkwo, "overcome with fury . . . gripped him by the neck. 'Where have you been?' he stammered" (157). The stammering is important. It recalls Okonkwo's inability to conciliate. Nwoye says nothing. "'Answer me,' roared Okonkwo, 'before I kill you!'" This second threat is immediately followed up with action: "He seized a heavy stick that lay on the dwarf wall and hit him two or three savage blows" (157). When he let go of Nwoye, at his uncle's command, Nwoye "walked away and never returned" (157).

For Okonkwo, Nwoye's interest in Christianity is the final sign that he is *agbala* like his grandfather: "To abandon the gods of one's father and go about with a lot of effeminate men clucking like old hens was the very depth of abomination" (158). Okonkwo asks himself, "How then could he have begotten a son like Nwoye, degenerate and effeminate? . . . How could he have begotten a woman for a son?" (159). Later, he calls for his five sons, to denounce their oldest sibling and warn them of unmanliness: Nwoye "is no longer my son or your brother. I will only have a son who is a man. . . . If any one of you prefers to be a woman, let him follow Nwoye now." He repeats his threat of filicide, made first against Nwoye, but now generalized and even extended beyond his own death: "If you turn against me when I am dead I will visit you and break your neck" (178–79). He will haunt them, much as he is haunted by Unoka, and they will have to struggle with him as he has to struggle. But while Unoka was weak, he is strong and will crush them. In case there is any doubt that this is excessive, Achebe tells us that the youngest of the sons whom Okonkwo threatened and chastised "was four years old" (178).

One wonders what will be the effect of such threats. Perhaps to drive his other sons along Nwoye's path. Certainly, Nwoye is driven to Christianity largely because of his father's reactionary masculinity. When Okonkwo beats him for attending the Christian services, this incident only serves to intensify Nwoye's resolve, precipitating his final decision to leave home and abandon the customs of his ancestors, Oedipally repudiating Okonkwo, just as Okonkwo repudiated Unoka. The more crucial and deeper causes of Nwoye's conversion bear on Okonkwo's acts also—especially his still more heartless, unorthodox, and hypermasculine treatment of Ikemefuna, perhaps the most egregious case of Okonkwo's repudiation of common humanity, and thus of orthodoxy.

Ikemefuna was a child from an enemy village. Members of that village had killed an Umuofian, and they demanded "a young man and a virgin to atone for the murder" (28). Ikemefuna was given over to

Okonkwo. He was two years older than Nwoye and was raised as part of the family: "Ikemefuna called [Okonkwo] father" (30). But Okonkwo would not reciprocate with paternal feeling: "Okonkwo never showed any emotion openly, unless it be the emotion of anger. To show affection was a sign of weakness; the only thing worth demonstrating was strength" (30). Ultimately, the oracle pronounced that Ikemefuna must be killed. The aged Ezeudu announced the proclamation to Okonkwo, but urged him not to take part: "'That boy calls you father. Do not bear a hand in his death'" (59). Later, Obierika reiterates this view, after Okonkwo has taken part in the murder: "The Earth cannot punish me for obeying her messenger," Okonkwo insists. Obierika agrees, but replies, "If the Oracle said that my son should be killed I would neither dispute it nor be the one to do it" (69). Here, as elsewhere, Obierika presents the orthodox, and human, view. It is fitting that his name means "The heart is great" (Ogbaa, 68)—great enough to encompass tradition and change, law and human feeling, masculine and feminine.

But, as just indicated, fearing that to be human is to be half woman, Okonkwo joined the execution party. When Nwoye heard that his "brother" was to be killed, he "burst into tears"; Okonkwo "beat him heavily" (60) in the hopes of stemming the tide of unmanliness, which he felt also in himself. On the journey, "The men of Umuofia talked and laughed . . . about some effeminate men who had refused to come with them" (61). This is just what Okonkwo feared, why he had to go along. What if they said this about him? What if they connected this with his father?

They told the boy that he was returning to his mother. He sings, thinking about her (63). A man raises his machete and strikes him. The first blow does not kill Ikemefuna. He cries out, "My father, they have killed me!" (63) and runs to Okonkwo for protection. "Dazed with fear, Okonkwo drew his machete and cut him down." The cause of his fear? "He was afraid of being thought weak" (63). When, in the idle season between harvest and planting, he is overcome by remorse, Okonkwo chides himself: "When did you become a shivering old woman . . . you, who are known in all the nine villages for your valor in war? How can a man who has killed five men in battle fall to pieces because he has added a boy to their number? Okonkwo, you have become a woman indeed" (67). Okonkwo is not heartless. Indeed, there are hints, especially surrounding his daughter Ezinma, that he is warm-hearted, tortured by concerns and affections that may indicate there is, in him, something of his gentle, flute-playing father. That is what, in the end, makes him a tragic hero. Nonetheless, the killing of Ikemefuna affects Nwoye more profoundly, and with greater practical consequence. "As soon as his father walked in, that night, Nwoye knew that Ikemefuna had been killed, and something seemed to give way inside him, like the snapping of a tightened bow" (64). What snapped at that moment was the cord that bound Nwoye to the traditions of his people.

When Ezeudu dies, Okonkwo recalls that Ezeudu had told him to refrain from Ikemefuna's murder. With this recollection, "A cold shiver ran down Okonkwo's back" (125). Ezeudu had urged Okonkwo not to join the other men, and in this he was more humane; but he had also announced the necessity of murdering the boy. Okonkwo must have remembered both, blaming himself for one act, and Ezeudu for the other. It is tragically appropriate, then, that Okonkwo should repeat the murder of a boy at Ezeudu's funeral, though now it is Ezeudu's son, not Okonkwo's, who is killed: "It was the dead man's sixteen-year-old son, who with his brothers and half-brothers had been dancing the tradi-tional farewell to their father. Okonkwo's gun had exploded and a piece of iron had pierced the boy's heart" (128).

In the *Poetics*, Aristotle spoke of two types of necessity in literature. One is causal necessity. The other is necessity by design, the structuring of events in such a way as to communicate a sense of necessity resulting from moral principle or thematic structure or some other noncausal con-nection, as when "the statue of Mitys at Argos killed the man who caused Mitys's death by falling on him at a festival" (39). Okonkwo's inadvertent murder of Ezeudu's son is a perfect instance of such neces-sity by design. It is a sort of posthumous rectification, punishing Ezeudu, depriving him of a son who would offer sacrifices to his departed spirit.

Moreover, Okonkwo too is punished at this remove. The killing of Ezeudu's son is a "female" crime and an abomination to Ani, for Okonkwo has "polluted" the earth "with the blood of a clansman" (129). He is therefore exiled for seven years to live with his mother's people; his houses are burned to the ground, his livestock killed, his barn destroyed. He is literally punished for the death of Ezeudu's son. But his guilt is stronger in the killing of Ikemefuna. At the time, Okonkwo protested, "The Earth cannot punish me for obeying her messenger" (69). Perhaps not. But now, the earth, Ani, has punished him, and for a directly parallel crime. When visible signs of his success as a man have been burned to the ground or axed, the friends who perform these acts think of this retribution in terms which seem almost to mock Okonkwo's earlier professions of innocence in the death of Ikemefuna: "It was the justice of the earth goddess, and they were merely her messengers" (129). Moreover, Ani has punished Okonkwo's crime of hypermasculinity aptly by condemning him for a "female" (i.e., unintentional) crime (129), and by exiling him to the village of his mother.

This was not, of course, Okonkwo's first or only offense against Ani. He continually failed to honor the female part of his culture. Once, he beat one of his wives in the "Week of Peace" devoted to the earth goddess. Ani's priest explains, "Our forefathers ordained that before we plant any crops in the earth we should observe a week in which a man does not say a harsh word to his neighbor. We live in peace with our fellows to honor our great goddess of the earth without whose blessing our crops will not grow." He orders Okonkwo to make sacrifices to atone for the "insult" to the earth goddess. "Inwardly, [Okonkwo] was repentant. But he was not the man to go about telling his neighbors that he was in error. And so people said he had no respect for the gods of the clan" (32). But it was not that he had no respect. It was, rather, that he could concede nothing to the goddess or to any principle or instance of femininity for fear that through even the slightest lapse in vigilance, his masculinity would be destroyed.

Later, Okonkwo behaves more recklessly still. At the time of the New Yam Festival, "for giving thanks to Ani, the earth goddess and the source of all fertility" (38), Okonkwo, first beat, then tried to shoot one of his wives. His later punishment for accidentally killing Ezeudu's son recalls, and punishes, through Aristotelian design, this abomination too.

Needless to say, in both these incidents, he not only defies the goddess, he brutalizes real women. This also is part of his always fearful masculinity. "No matter how prosperous a man was," he thought, "if he was unable to rule his women and his children (and especially his women) he was not really a man" (55). He cannot understand the ideal marriage of Ndulue and Ozoemena—a marriage praised, again, by Obierika, the representative of open-minded orthodoxy in the novel: "It was always said that Ndulue and Ozoemena had one mind. . . . He could not do anything without telling her." Okoknwo protests, "I thought he was a strong man in his youth." Ofoedu, seeing no contradiction, replies, "He was indeed." Okonkwo will not believe it. Obierika explains, "He led Umuofia to war in those days" (71).

ACHEBE'S IGBO AND CHRISTIAN UNIVERSALISMS

So Okonkwo, from fear that his son would violate the customs of his people, in the end drove his son to repudiate those customs. He precipitated the very tragedy he set out to prevent. And yet, in all likelihood, he merely hurried a process that was inevitable. It is clear that some principles of Igbo custom should indeed be violated. Okonkwo simply exaggerates and makes more salient the indecencies of his culture. He rubs Nwoye's face in them. But he does not create them; they were there already—the routine abandonment of twins, the sacrifice of Ikemefuna at the mysterious command of the oracle. For Nwoye, Christianity "seemed to answer a vague and persistent question that haunted his young soul—the question of the twins crying in the bush and the question of Ikemefuna who was killed" (151–52). The proselytizers hammer away at these two practices: "All the gods you have named are not gods at all. They are gods of deceit who tell you to kill your fellows and destroy innocent children" (150). And it was not just talk: "They were rescuing twins from the bush" (160).

There are other injustices as well—exile for manslaughter, even without "reckless endangerment": "Why should a man suffer so grievously for an offense he had committed inadvertently?" (129). The practice of defining outcasts or *osu*, each one "a thing set apart—a taboo for ever, and his children after him." His/her marriage restricted to other outcasts, his home located in the quarter of outcasts, "An *osu* could not attend an assembly of the free-born. . . . He could not take any of the four titles of the clan, and when he died he was buried by his kind in the Evil Forest" (163). This, too, the missionaries denounce, addressing the *osu*: "How are you different from other men. . . . The same God created you and them. But they have cast you out like lepers" (163). It is no accident, of course, that "nearly all the *osu* in Mbanta" converted. As Isichei points out, Christianity had the greatest appeal, predictably, for those who were oppressed by Igbo culture: "The bulk of the first Christian converts were drawn from the poor, the needy, and the rejected: the mothers of twins, women accused of witchcraft, those suffering from diseases such as leprosy which were seen as abominable" (162).

Despite his much-quoted denunciations of universalism, Achebe here is clearly universalist. Indeed, he is an extreme universalist. First, he assumes that there is a universal ethical principle that condemns the slaughter of innocents and tells us outcasting is wrong. Second, he assumes that all humans have a sense of this. That is why Nwoye is troubled by the exposure of twins and by the sacrifice of Ikemefuna. Isichei explains the killing of twins in the following terms: "Single births were regarded as typically human, multiple births as typical of the animal world. So twins were regarded as less than human, and put to death (as were animals produced at single births)" (26). But this would not still Nwoye's qualms, which are ethical, not cosmological. His question is the question of Obierika: "He remembered his wife's twin children, whom he had thrown away. What crime had they committed?" (129–30). Others too share these feelings. Nwoye twice felt "a snapping inside him." Once at the death of Ikemefuna, once when he "heard the voice of an infant crying in the thick forest." The women around him at that moment feel the pangs of guilt or sympathy as well: "A sudden hush had fallen on the women, who had been talking, and they had quickened their steps" (64). Uchendu asks Okonkwo, "If you think you are the greatest sufferer in the world ask my daughter, Akueni, how many twins she has borne and thrown away" (139). Even Okonkwo suffers bitter remorse over the death of Ikemefuna; his tragic flaw is precisely that he suppresses such universal ethical feelings. And that, Achebe implies, is part of suppressing his humanity.

Despite the academic unfashionability of the notion that blacks share with whites universal rights, duties, and so on, some critics have noted the importance of ethical universalism in Achebe's work. For example, in his study of Achebe and Igbo folkways, Kalu Ogbaa argues that, as one would expect, Igbo tradition is itself concerned with universality and thus anyone working within that tradition will be concerned with universality also (22–23):

> Being familiar with Igbo village storytelling habits—habits which include giving moral tags to each story—Achebe could not have written about Igbo religious life without raising some universal moral issues. In other words, he appropriated the Igbo world-view as a means of asking, in his own way, some ontological and theological questions which have puzzled man for ages. Initially, there is a tendency for readers and critics to localize the tragedies of the major characters, attributing them to Igbo or African problems. But carefully examined, some of the issues Achebe raises prove to be human problems which are presented as universal parables.

Achebe also seems to adopt a universalist view of the evaluation of empirical hypotheses. For example, he clearly indicates the Evil Forest was not "alive with sinister forces and powers of darkness" and that the Igbo gods are not active beings who strike down their enemies. The missionaries build their church on the grounds of the Evil Forest. The people wait out the month during which they suppose the gods will act. "At last the day came by which all the missionaries should have died. But they were still alive" (156). Note that this empiricism is a universalist view, not a European view, not only because all societies engage in empirical investigation, but also because Achebe's conclusions are not uniformly consistent with European conclusions. Most strikingly, in the case of Ezinma's illness, he presents Igbo medical science as appropriate and efficacious—not mystically, but because of its observable results. It is empirically successful.

It is important to stress that this universalism in no way entails syncretism. Indeed, the themes of the novel seem most consistent with the sort of instantiated or particularized or culturally specific universalism advocated by Ngũgĩ. Perhaps the novel is best understood as presenting a universalist version of orthodoxy, advocating the preservation of Igbo customs and beliefs that have not been purged of common humanity (as in reactionary traditionalism and reactionary masculinity), but that have, rather, been purged of whatever violates that common or universal humanity—the murder of innocents, the outcasting of people by birth, and so forth. Moreover, these universal principles need not be derived from other cultures. Their universality means precisely that they are already present in each culture, that they are already felt by people everywhere—as is perfectly clear from the reactions of Obierika, Nwoye, Ezeudu, the mothers of twins, even Okonkwo himself. Indeed, as we have already seen, Igbo culture had mechanisms for developing and altering Igbo custom. Christianity was not required for this. In fact, Christianity rarely fostered the development of Igbo universalism. Rather, like any oppressive and demeaning structure, it most often operated either to destroy Igbo culture or to inhibit internal development, in part by inspiring reaction, in part by claiming that any progress was not progress toward universal principles, but toward Christianity, conceived of as the one valid religion.

Moreover, Igbo culture did historically change and develop on its own terms, by its own means, until its development was cut short by Christianity. Achebe gives us one important instance of just this sort of internal development. It concerns the treatment of those who break the peace of Ani. Recall that Okonkwo had broken the peace and, in punishment, had been required to offer a sacrifice. Ezeudu, "the oldest man in the village," observes that "the punishment for breaking the Peace of Ani had become very mild in their clan." In part, this may indicate that the punishment is too mild, and thus that the clan has declined in masculine rigor. But, more importantly, it indicates that the tradition has changed because it was judged to be inappropriate. Ezeudu describes a time when the punishment for breaking the peace was death. He explains that this irrational practice was ended "because it spoiled the peace which it was meant to preserve" (33). This anecdote gives a clear instance of the way in which traditional Igbo society could and did change and develop internally, according to universal ethical and rational principles, without the interference of external agents.

Moreover, the thoughts and behavior of Obierika indicate that the exposure of twins, human sacrifice, and other unjust practices might ultimately have been subjected to similar reform. Again, Obierika is Achebe's orthodox ideal—a true Igbo man, but open-minded, reflective, questioning. He refuses to participate in the sacrifice of Ikemefuna (69), despite the mockery this entails (61); in this, he is clearly braver than Okonkwo, who fears these insults more than he dreads killing his own foster child. And later he questions the sense of killing twins ("What crime had they committed?"), or even of punishing a man "for an offense he had committed inadvertently" (129). Though he does not dismiss either practice, it is clear that Obierika's mind is moving toward a universal ethical principle—that the innocent should not be made to suffer or die. Such questioning might have been the beginning of internal change, if the missionaries had not come, putting an end to the process.

Indeed, one story of conversion suggests that the murder of twins was not consistent with Igbo principles, that it was a communal repudiation of cosmic balance, of the feminine principle which should always be honored in Igbo thought, and thus that its abolition would not only be the universally just thing to do, but the deeply Igbo thing to do as well. A pregnant woman "fled to join the Christians" because she "had had four previous pregnancies and child-births. But each time she had borne twins, and they had been immediately thrown away." Her husband and in-laws became "highly critical of such a woman" and were glad to be rid of her (156). The family's attitudes are obviously inhumane, both to the twins and to the woman. That they may be un-Igbo too is indicated by the woman's name, Nneka. The family, which stands for the current practices of Igbo society, or Umuofian society, has rejected both the woman and her offspring, and thus, one might infer, the principle implicit in her name as well, a principle that should be central to Igbo life: Nne-ka, "Mother is Supreme."

When Okonkwo arrives in his mother's village, Uchendu asks, "Can you tell me, Okonkwo, why it is that one of the commonest names we give our children is Nneka, or 'Mother is Supreme?'" (137–38). Of course, Okonkwo, who has repudiated all things feminine, cannot respond. Uchendu answers that "Your mother is there to protect you," and when one's father or one's fatherland is harsh, one goes to the mother and the motherland for comfort. For this particular Nneka, Igbo culture has become the father only, the father who punishes. And the mother to whom Nneka flees is the Christian church. For her, Christianity has taken up the feminine duties of protection and solace, while Igbo society has abandoned these duties. In connection with this, it is perhaps worth recalling that, while Christian missionaries "pushed into the Igbo interior in the wake of the military expeditions" and were thus clearly a part of colonial conquest (Isichei, 172), the very earliest missionaries "on the Niger and in the Delta . . . were Africans from Sierra Leone, often, though not always, of Igbo descent," Africans whose ancestors had been sold as slaves in an earlier perversion of Igbo custom (Isichei, 160).

But, as this incident indicates, Achebe's advocacy of universalist orthodoxy does not lead him to denounce Christianity or European culture. They too have value and they too have faults, both to be judged and evaluated by universal criteria.

As to colonialism, consider the devastation of Abame. The killing of the white bicyclist and the British "retaliation" is based on the murder of Dr. Stewart in Ahiara in 1905. It is unfortunate that Achebe provides no background to the event. He presents it as an unmotivated murder by the people of Abame. This fits the general thematics of the novel, for the murder is ordered by the oracle—or, rather, the oracle speaks vaguely, and the villagers infer that the man is to be killed (see 143)— and Achebe is exploring the theme of the culturally sanctioned murder of innocents. Had he given the background, the innocence of the man killed would have been to some degree obscured. Not because of any guilt on Dr. Stewart's part. But because of broader guilt on the part of the British colonialists, and the villagers' error in taking Dr. Stewart to be the Divisional Officer (see Asiegbu, 335).

Nonetheless, the background is important. The British had been a military presence in Igboland since the middle of the preceding century (see chapter 1 of Asiegbu), shelling Ndoni from a gunboat in 1876, sacking Onitsha in 1879 (Isichei, 119). And by the end of the century, the Royal Niger Company was using violence systematically (Isichei, 119). The Arochukwu expedition of 1901–1902 is particularly noteworthy. Isichei reports that "Ogwe . . . [was] crushed by machine guns," the great oracle in Arochukwu was "blown up with explosives," at Ikwerri, the people "were scattered by machine-gun fire, 'with heavy loss'" (128), "the people of Ngor . . . lost their homes, their food supplies, and their livelihood," "as the [people of] Afikpo tried in vain to come to grips with the enemy, a machine gun mowed them down as they came within range" (129). The examples could be multiplied. When Dr. Stewart's death occurred, the villagers were well aware of the massive and recurrent British war crimes. They killed Stewart, not out of blind devotion to an equivocating oracle, but out of rage against the British, who had slaughtered many people, razed many villages, and imposed over wide areas the corrupt and incomprehensible courts and prisons that appear in Umuofia only at the end of Achebe's novel. Moreover, at the time of Stewart's death, the British were already engaged in another large expedition in the area: "During this expedition, the news of Stewart's death arrived, and the expedition inflicted draconian punishment on Mbaise, *which it had been intended to conquer anyway*" (130, italics added).

It is, again, unfortunate that Achebe excluded this background from his recounting of the incident. Indeed, in rewriting the story in this way, Achebe tends partially to reenforce colonialist stereotypes, by making the Africans' actions superstitious, by making them the initial aggressors, and so on. Wren, who is to be credited with isolating the incident to begin with, also leaves out most of the background (see 26–27). He rightly emphasizes the cruelty of the British policy of collective punishment (see 28); however, it is important to stress that this was not really a matter of punishment, anyway, but part of an ongoing conquest, and that the Igbo, not the British, were the ones responding to prior aggression.

Nonetheless, Achebe's moral point is clear—clearer, in fact, than it would have been had he followed the actual history. For the actual history is a matter of stark brutality on the British side, and a case of mistaken identity on the Igbo side. The revision allows Achebe to show that, just as English/Christian culture follows universal moral principles in its treatment of twins, and is in that respect superior to Igbo culture, Igbo culture follows universal moral principles in certain aspects of warfare, and is in that respect superior to English/Christian culture. Indeed, as it turns out, the universal moral principles followed by the Igbo are more significant, greater in consequence than those followed by the British. To use a distinction drawn by Noam Chomsky and Edward Herman, one might say that the Igbo are guilty of "retail" killing of innocents (a foreigner here, a pair of twins there), while the British are guilty of "wholesale" killing of innocents (a village here, a village there).

Specifically, the villagers have killed one innocent man. The British respond by murdering everyone in the marketplace, virtually all innocent: "They have a big market in Abame on every other Afo day and, as you know, the whole clan gathers there. . . . The three white men and a very large number of other men . . . began to shoot. Everybody was killed" (144). To get a sense of the number killed, recall that the number of men in Umuofia was ten thousand (12). This is not out of keeping with the actual events: "It is alleged that after gathering the local people ostensibly for a public 'palaver' or meeting, the British-led soldiers opened gun fire on the unsuspecting people and mowed them down by the hundreds" (Asiegbu, 335).

Any humane person will find the British action morally obscene. But it is particularly important that the British action contrasts with Igbo practices which, however objectionable in themselves, demonstrate far greater adherence to universal moral principles. As Achebe tells us, "Umuofia . . . never went to war unless its case was clear and just" (13). At the beginning of the novel, we learn that the people of Mbaino have killed a woman of Umuofia. In other words, they have committed a crime identical in kind and in degree with that committed by the people of Abame against the English. The Umuofians do not go to war; they do not attack Mbaino surreptitiously, destroying the town and slaughtering its inhabitants. Rather, they negotiate a settlement, demanding a young man and a virgin in compensation. Mbaino agrees. The young man they send is Ikemefuna. This allows a direct comparison between the moral behavior of the Igbo and the moral behavior of the British. Both suffer the same outrage—one of their own is killed. The British attack; the Igbo negotiate. Indeed, the British dismissal of any possibility of conciliation goes far beyond any such extremism on Okonkwo's part. Moreover, while the Igbo of Umuofia are culpable for killing one innocent person in supposed compensation for their own loss, the British kill hundreds, perhaps thousands. Indeed, the disparity is so great as to render the death of Ikemefuna almost insignificant by contrast.

Moreover, the point can be extended. As we have already noted, even in war, the Igbo kept casualties to a very small number. Again,

Okonkwo was a great hero in several wars, but he had killed only five men. Also in direct contrast with the British, "Among most Igbo communities . . . there was no total conquest" (Isichei, 81). More generally, Igbo warfare was "regulated by many conventions. [Wars] were preceded by negotiations, which endeavored to prevent conflict, and by a formal declaration of war. Women and children were unharmed. Markets and those visiting them were left in peace" (80). All these are conventions that serve to specify the universal moral principle that innocent people should not be killed. And they are all conventions that are blatantly violated by the British. Indeed, the British not only failed to negotiate or declare war, they even attacked on a market day, and thus presumably killed women and children and traders from other villages.

Universal principles apply more narrowly to Christian people and practices as well. Just as there are flexible and rigid forms of Igbo tradition, there are flexible and rigid, humane and reactionary forms of Christian tradition. Just as he draws a contrast between Okonkwo and Obierika, Achebe distinguishes Rev. Smith and Enoch, on the one hand, from Mr. Brown, on the other. Of course, the entire evaluative scale weighs strongly in favor of the Igbo characters. Okonkwo's reactionary traditionalism is far more sympathetic than even Brown's orthodoxy. This is true not only because we know Okonkwo more deeply, but also because Brown, however he might act personally, is objectively part of the colonialist forces that are destroying the Igbo physically and culturally. He and Okonkwo are not parallel. After all, Okonkwo has not done anything to destroy the English and their culture, nor have any other Igbos.

Nonetheless, there is a difference between Brown and Smith/Enoch, and it is not unimportant. Brown "preached against such excess of zeal" as killing the sacred python, and argued respectfully with Akunna about the nature of God. His arguments are, it seems clear, inferior to those of Akunna, precisely because Akunna's arguments are universalist and Brown's are differentialist; Akunna sees the similarities between Chukwu and the Christian God, and explains the other gods as "messengers" (186)—in Greek, the word would be *angeloi*, hence English "angels." But Brown remains fixated on seeing Christianity as superior and True. On the other hand, it is interesting that Akunna passes over a difference in the two religions—the absence of female divinity in Christianity. Implicitly, Igbo tradition shows us that Christianity violates a universal principle of balance between male and female more extremely than even Okonkwo.

Needless to say, both Smith and Enoch share Brown's conviction that Christianity is the one True faith and all others are wrong. But they do not share his opposition to overzealous behavior that leads to the gratuitous desecration of Igbo places and practices. Indeed, Smith saw all Igbo religious beliefs as "stories . . . spread in the world by the Devil to lead men astray" (191). In consequence, "He condemned openly Mr. Brown's policy of compromise and accommodation. He saw things as black and white. And black was evil" (190). This is a reactionary traditionalism harsher than any to be found among the Igbo. It rejects all common ground, all human universality; it asserts one unique and absolute truth, and is vigilant to shelter tradition from all alien elements (see 191).

The psychological background to Smith's exclusionary traditionalism is obscure. Enoch however, clearly suffers from the same Oedipal antagonism that seems to drive so many Igbo men in the novel, and it leads him to the most severely reactionary forms of mimeticism: "His name was Enoch and his father was the priest of the snake cult. The story went around that Enoch had killed and eaten the sacred python, and that his father had cursed him" (185). Indeed, this is not Enoch's only act of sacrilege: "One of the greatest crimes a man could commit was to unmask an *egwugwu* in public. . . . And this was what Enoch did" (192). "Enoch had killed an ancestral spirit" (193). For the Igbo, it was through the Egwugwu that the ancestors came again to contact the living, to guide the course of custom, to decide the law, to celebrate the festivals. The most accomplished men of the village, those who had taken the highest titles, put on the masks of the ancestors and, in putting on the masks, became the ancestors again. As Olajubu says of the parallel Yoruba Egungun masks, "While everybody, male and female, knows that it is a living human being who wears the [mask] . . . he is regarded at the same time by the very same people as . . . a being from heaven, one of the ancestors who has come to visit and bless the people" (155). Unmasking an Egwugwu is like snatching a consecrated host and crushing it into the ground. Even at their most extreme, no traditional Igbo descends to that.

DESPAIR

One final universal principle, if one most famously thematized in Christianity, is that the degeneration of the soul moves between pride and despair. The two are not unrelated to one another, nor to colonialism. Smith and Enoch, the other blasphemers, the performers of sacrilege and desecration, all suffer from the sin of pride. In damning Igbo custom as Satanic, in judging and acting as if they were God themselves, they manifest the sin of Satan, the pride for which he was damned by God. Okonkwo seems initially to suffer from pride too. And his compatriots take his uncompromising harshness as evidence of pride: "'Looking at a king's mouth,' said an old man, 'one would think he never sucked at his mother's breast.' He was talking about Okonkwo" (27). But, as we have seen, his pride conceals fear verging always on despair, the sin of Judas, not of Satan. There is certainly a suggestion of Judas in his suicide, and more importantly in his murder of the innocent Ikemefuna.

Clearly, despair is not only Christian, and is not merely a loss of hope in God. It is, more broadly, a loss of hope in the future. Despair is the feeling that one's aspirations no longer make sense, that one's actions are pointless. One can despair over the state of nature, over children, over one's society. The idea is introduced almost at the beginning of the novel: "That year the harvest was sad, like a funeral, and many farmers wept as they dug up the miserable and rotting yams. One man tied his cloth to a tree branch and hanged himself." It was a "tragic year" and it "surprised [Okonkwo] when he thought of it later that he did not sink under the load of despair." Even Unoka feels that he must encourage his son, saying, "Do not despair. I know you will not despair" (26). Here despair derives from an unpredictable and brutal nature destroying one's work as a man, and the means of sustaining one's own life and that of one's family.

Later, Ekwefi despairs because all her children die in infancy. "As she buried one child after another her sorrow gave way to despair. . . . Her deepening despair found expression in the names she gave her children. One of them was a pathetic cry, Onwumbiko—'Death, I implore you'" (80). Ekwefi, then, despairs when uncontrollable and brutal forces destroy her work as a woman, and the means of reproducing her family.

Thus, despair comes when one can no longer fulfill one's social function, when inscrutable events bring an end to continuity, threatening starvation or barrenness. In *Things Fall Apart*, though, the most crushing form of despair comes from another threat to continuity, the threat that the culture itself will not go on, that all the beliefs and acts that gave form and sense to life will end. What Okonkwo thinks of as "the tragedy of his first son," a tragedy that he fears "might prove too great for his spirit" (178), is searingly painful to him because it breaks two lines of continuity, that of family, and that of culture. The two are clearly related. For the function of one's descendants, their value in the scheme of things, is fixed by the culture: to continue the tradition, maintain the link of belief, ritual, law, custom with the ancestors.

All Okonkwo's life, his every action has been guided by the idea of this continuity. That is the reason to excel in society—to bring oneself closer to the ancestors, first in the communal practices of life, then in death. And that is the reason to leave dutiful children, for they will continue the tradition. Okonkwo's greatest dread is that all this will finish: "He saw himself and his fathers crowding round their ancestral shrine waiting in vain for worship and sacrifice and finding nothing but ashes of bygone days, and his children the while praying to the white man's god." In consequence, "Okonkwo felt a cold shudder run through him at the terrible prospect, like the prospect of annihilation" (158)—for, indeed, it would be annihilation; to end Okonkwo's culture would be to end everything that he was, had been, could be; it would annihilate his spirit, just as famine would annihilate his body, because it would drain the meaning from every property and relation that formed his sense of self; it would leave his ego a forgotten jumble of unmeaning sounds—*ozo, Egwugwu, Ndichie.*

Here we come to the deepest source of Okonkwo's fear that he will become his father, the fear that he too will be dragged by strangers into the Evil Forest, banned eternally from the company of the ancestors, an outcast from both life and death. As Isichei explains (25):

> The ancestors—those who live well-spent lives die in socially approved ways, and are given correct burial rites—live in one of those worlds of the dead which mirror the world of the living. The living honour them with sacrifices. The ancestors watch over the living, and are periodically reincarnated among them. . . . The unhappy spirits who die bad deaths, and lack correct burial rites, cannot return to the world of the living, or enter that of the dead. They wander homeless and dispossessed.

At first, it may seem Okonkwo's tragedy is that, by suicide, he condemns himself to just this fate, that by one rash act he commits himself to the very torment his entire life was lived against: "It is an abomination for a man to take his own life. It is an offense against the Earth, and a man who commits it will not be buried by his clansmen. His body is evil, and only strangers may touch it" (214). His suicide does desecrate the earth and thus continues the pattern of brute masculinity, which marked his life and which was his tragic flaw. And it is triggered by a sense that his people have lost their manhood (211). But the real tragedy is that he knew all this; he knew what it meant to die a suicide; he knew the customs of his people, what it means to be cast into the Evil Forest. Yet he committed suicide anyway. In short, the real tragedy is that he had succumbed to despair, and, indeed, that the despair was rational, for it would be much the same, whether he was buried or not, whether he was given the proper rites or not.

A messenger arrives to halt the meeting of Okonkwo's clan. This is not some innocent errand boy. Court messengers were, as Wren points out, a form of "police" (28), who not only collaborated with the alien government, but used their position for personal advancement, distorting the already alien law to their own purposes (29). The "court messengers were greatly hated in Umuofia"; they "guarded the prison" and beat the prisoners. They used their position as interpreters to decide the outcome of cases in favor of those who offered bribes. In one such case, the British hang a man, then turn over his land to those "who had given much money to the white man's messengers and interpreter" (182).

So Okonkwo kills this collaborator, the officer of the colonial police. But his fellows panic, let the other messengers escape, break "into tumult instead of action." "He discerned fright in that tumult" (211). At that moment, Okonkwo sees not only that once-brave Umuofia will not fight, but that they have lost the will and confidence to resist at all, that his peers will, slowly or quickly, succumb in every way to the foreigners. The ancestors will be reduced to famished shades, unhonored, unremembered, hovering about the overgrown and defiled shrines. With the slow death of their culture, they cannot live their otherworldly lives of ancestors; after death, without reverence, without connection to continuing life, they will be no better than the unburied undead, haunting the abandoned place. Nor can they return to life, be born again into their own lineage—another traditional right of the ancestors—for the home into which they might be born will no longer be home, but an alien place.

Obierika rightly blames the District Commissioner and all he represents; indicating Okonkwo's corpse, he says, "That man was one of the greatest men of Umuofia. You drove him to kill himself; and now he will be buried like a dog. . . ." He cannot complete the sentence, just as Okonkwo often could not; but, unlike Okonkwo, Obierika cannot resort to force. The white man, with his machine gun and his total war, has put an end to that option. Obierika's faltering speech instances the gathering silence of tradition, the erasure of an entire system that gave force and direction to life, that made identity, that drew a line between the reverenced ancestors and the wandering undead, making sense of an aspiration to act rightly for the clan and for one's forebears. The white man, who played by no rules of war, proved a stronger and a crueler foe than the spirit of the wild, for he defeated all the ancestors. As Obierika says, "The white man . . . has put a knife on the things that held us together and we have fallen apart" (183).

In short, Okonkwo's tragedy is not that he lost all status in the Igbo system, was deprived of his rightful place among the ancestors, but that the system itself was lost, that it no longer made any difference if he died a good death or an evil one. Achebe has written that "I would be quite satisfied if my novels (especially the ones I set in the past) did no more than teach my readers that their past—with all its imperfections—was not one long night of savagery from which the first Europeans acting on God's behalf delivered them" ("Novelist," 205). If anything, his novel shows that when the first Europeans came to Umuofia, acting on their God's behalf, they did indeed deliver the "offspring of the wilderness," not from, but into a long night of savagery. A night which, like the superhuman nights of the gods, has already lasted many decades.

CHAPTER FIVE

Worship and "Manness"

Earl Lovelace's The Wine of Astonishment

Lovelace and Achebe

Lovelace not only takes up many of the themes treated in _Things Fall Apart_; in _The Wine of Astonishment_ he, in effect, rewrites Achebe's novel. This is relevant to our understanding of Lovelace's work in several ways. Most importantly for our present purposes, Lovelace's rewriting of Achebe indicates some of the persistent concerns of postcolonization writers, especially black writers, and at the same time highlights some of the differences between Caribbean and African conditions and responses to colonialism.

Briefly, Bolo is Lovelace's version of Okonkwo and Bee is a broader revision of the figures who stand opposed to Okonkwo, most obviously Obierika, but also Ezeudu, Egonwanne, and others. Bolo and Bee are Spiritual Baptists, members of a church that combines Christian and African, especially West African, elements. We will discuss Spiritual Baptism below. At this point, it is enough to emphasize its continuity with Yoruba and other indigenous African practices, and to contrast it with the more purely European Christian denominations of Catholicism, Anglicanism, and so on. The conflict between Spiritual Baptism and the "official" Christianities, such as Catholicism and Anglicanism—Christianities that are linked with English colonists,

English government, and English law—directly parallels the conflict between Igbo custom and Christianity in Achebe. In both cases, European religion, backed by colonial repression and supported by a collaborationist stratum of the indigenous population, threatens to destroy African tradition—Igbo custom, in the case of Achebe, Spiritual Baptism, which is to say, Africanized Christianity, in the case of Lovelace. Bolo, like Okonkwo, urges militant opposition to colonialism and its imposition of European Christianity, and argues that its representative—Prince, in this case—should be killed. Also like Okonkwo, he is voted down by the other men. Led by Bee, they, like Obierika and others, urge various forms of patience and conciliation, and for similar reasons: "Have you not heard how the white man wiped out Abame?" cautions Obierika (Achebe, 182); "You will kill the whole Police Force, Brother Bolo?" asks Brother Sylvester (47).

Just as Okonkwo is a champion wrestler and warrior, Bolo is the great champion of the stick fight. And just as Okonkwo finds the behavior of his fellow Umuofians to be unmanly, Bolo comes to see his compatriots as cowardly and weak in accepting colonial repression. While Bolo does not directly commit suicide, he does in the end so obviously put himself in a position to be killed that he is in effect committing suicide. He too falls victim to despair. There are narrower parallels as well. For example, just as Okonkwo is exiled for a number of years, Bolo is imprisoned for several years, and in each case these are crucial years of change for the home community.

But, again, there are differences. Bee is not orthodox, either in his Spiritual Baptism or in his gender-specific behavior. Indeed, at the beginning of the novel, Bolo is orthodox, and Bee is somewhat cowardly, if human and likable, throughout. Bolo becomes reactionary, extremely so, in fact, especially in his hyper-masculine behavior, but this is clearly the result of colonial brutality and the pusillanimous behavior of his co-congregationists. In other words, in Bolo's case, the pathology of reactionary masculinity is not the consequence of familial psychology, unresolved Oedipal conflicts that are exacerbated by the colonial structure; rather, it is the direct outcome of the colonial structure itself. It is only at the very end of the novel, when the pathology has reached its greatest extreme, that Bolo appears to exhibit the sort of gynophobia and misogyny which are so deeply a part of Okonkwo's masculinity. In fact, early on, his anticolonialism derives a good deal of its emotive force from his affection for his ill-treated mother.

Perhaps the most important difference between these novels is characteristic of the difference between African and Afro-Caribbean views of
tradition. As already noted, because of their high degree of severance
from any sort of basic culture, Afro-Caribbean writers tend not to see
tradition as something tied to a particular time and place, bound to specific, "pure" practices and beliefs. In Africa, the uncolonized village
tends to stand as the paradigm of traditional culture. In consequence,
everything else appears as a falling off, a loss of tradition, an end—the
ancestors crowding around the ruined shrine, seeking the offerings that
will never again be set out in ceremony by the living. Since Afro-
Caribbeans lost this connection with basic culture generations ago—and
since the mixing of different ethnic groups in the slave trade made that
"cultural ancestry" mixed already, not pure Igbo or Yoruba or
Ashanti—Afro-Caribbean writers tend to take a different view of tradition. Specifically, many tend to see African tradition as a complex of
ways of thinking and acting that continually remanifests itself in different concrete practices. Tradition in this context is something more like
what we might call the "spirit" of the African people, a living, collective,
immaterial soul that is continually rematerialized, reborn in different
bodies. Each body may die, but the spirit is reincarnated. When the martial practices of the Igbo or Yoruba or Ashanti are destroyed, their spirit
is reborn in the Trinidadian stick fight. When African religious ceremonies are killed, this is not an absolute ending. The spiritual ecstasy—
and, indeed, even many specific practices, such as ritual ordeals; many
symbols, such as ceremonial chalk drawings (see Houk, 59); many articles of faith, such as belief in the undead—are reborn in Spiritual Baptism, or other Afro-Caribbean religions. And when one of these religions
too is killed, the spirit again revives, in music and in poetry.

More exactly, there is a sense in much Afro-Caribbean literature that
an Afro-Caribbean culture stabilized in the region in the nineteenth century. The slaves brought their various African cultures to the new world
and synthesized them into a new culture that represented a common
African spirit, manifest now in new practical identities—new customs,
rituals, festivals, etc. Initially, these were improvisatory and changeable as
the different groups brought together what they retained of their home
traditions. But ultimately they coalesced into a new, consistent, transmis-
sible culture. The British continually sought to suppress this culture, and
sometimes succeeded in stifling one or another manifestation—killing
one or another incarnation—but the culture continually revived, the

spirit was continually reborn. Laws against Obeah never managed to crush herbalism entirely—there was always a "Ma Kilman" (in Walcott's *Omeros*) or, to take a Francophone example, a Man Yaya (in Maryse Condé's *Moi, Tituba sorcière.* . . .) to carry on the tradition. Laws against Afro-Christianity never succeeded in confining worship to the European churches. This common Caribbean view that African tradition is a spirit that persists and never dies is not mere metaphor or wishful thinking. It derives from a common sense of a history in which African traditions survived despite displacement and continued repression, a sense that, for centuries, there has been a recognizable continuity in Afro-Caribbean practices, leading all the way back to Africa. It derives from a belief that, however hard the British tried, they never did manage to "put a knife on the things that held us together" (Achebe, *Things*, 183); they never did manage to sever the link that tied Afro-Caribbean people to the motherland from which they were, in Othello's words, "taken by the insolent foe/And sold to slavery" (I. iii. 136–37).

This hopeful view is, however, qualified by what might be called "the theme of double imperialism," which is also very common in Caribbean literature and marks another difference from African literature. Specifically, Caribbean writers frequently present the initial phase of colonialism as brutal in its political and economic impact, but as relatively limited in its cultural impact. It did lead to the synthesis of different forms of African religion and their integration with Christianity. But, except for the initial introduction of Christianity, this synthesis was largely the product of Africans themselves, and, again, it continued African traditions, incorporating the same structures and answering the same needs as the native practices, reincarnating the same spirit, or the more inclusive spirit of synthetic Africanism. Unfortunately, however, this more or less culturally stable period of British colonialism was followed by a period of more culturally disruptive American colonialism. American colonialism was not, at least not primarily, political. It was, indeed, perfectly consistent with formal independence of the "colony." But it was more culturally pervasive and destructive.

In this view, under the British, even in cities and on the large plantations, blacks lived their lives largely among themselves. Their speech and stories, their beliefs and memories, their political attitudes and religion, were developed and sustained by internal communication. This relatively autonomous community defined a sort of basic culture even in the midst of contact. The colonial system of education certainly intervened in this basic culture, leading to loss and alienation. But even that was largely isolated in both time and place. It affected a certain percentage of youth for a certain period. But it did not directly enter the home, or the surrounding life.

In the second wave of colonization, this changed. Through the various mass media—radio, film, audio recordings, television—a culture dominated, defined, and for the most part owned by Europeans and, especially, Americans entered every aspect of the lives of even the most isolated Afro-Caribbean people. Politics and poetry, stories and beliefs, were no longer circulated primarily among blacks themselves, but were increasingly determined by the culture industries. Before, white propaganda had been largely confined to the schoolroom, to the highly educated and the collaborators. Now it entered the home, the daily lives, the recreations of ordinary people.

Certainly, Africa and India have been integrated into global capitalism, including global media networks, and are increasingly pervaded by Western technologized culture. But this second wave of colonialism pressed into the Caribbean more visibly and more deeply in part because of the American presence and "interest" in this "backyard" region, and in part due to the small size and limited population of the Caribbean islands. As to the latter, the vast size of both Africa and India, and the relative inaccessibility of many villages, tended to limit this second wave of imperialism to the regions of high intensity contact. America has, of course, been increasingly involved in Africa and India. Moreover, American and other culture industries have increasingly penetrated the (formerly) indigenous regions of every country. Thus, the theme of double imperialism has begun to work its way into these other literatures, and will probably increase in prominence in the coming years. However, it is not nearly as common as it is in Caribbean literature—as one would expect, given the different situations of these regions.

The theme of double imperialism could actually have led Lovelace back to the despairing view of *Things Fall Apart*. Indeed, one common response to this invasion of "modern" culture is to see indigenous or displaced traditions as doomed: having survived political repression and economic hardship for centuries, Afro-Caribbean culture is now falling to the American culture industry; where British guns and schools—and prayers and sermons—failed, American news and docudramas will finally put the knife to the things that held us together. But this is not Lovelace's view. For Lovelace, as we shall see, the new technologies present a means for further manifestations of the African cultural spirit. They will probably bring an end to the current manifestations. But they will foster others.

Of course, not everything is rosy. The new conditions will foster both different modes of African tradition *and* different modes of mimeticism; different modes of resistance *and* different modes of collaboration. It is not only the African spirit that adapts and is reborn, but the spirit of repression too. And, needless to say, the two are closely related. When standard European religion was a, perhaps the, major means of ideological control, then the African spirit manifested its resistance in Spiritual Baptism and other Afro-Christian rites. In this new period, where mass communication, along with schooling, takes up the prime ideological task, it is the artist who, in Lovelace's view, takes up the role of resistance.

POSSESSION

Spiritual Baptism, the main cultural formation with which Lovelace is concerned in this book, involves an extensive syncretism of West African cosmologies and rituals, more or less integrated with Christianity. As Herskovits and Herskovits put it, Spiritual Baptism is "African worship . . . shaped and reinterpreted to fit into the patterns of European worship" (quoted in Thorpe, vii). Or as the narrator, Eva, puts it toward the end of the novel, "The church is Africa in us, black in us" (133).

The Africanness of the religion is clear even from the church building itself: "We have this church in the village. We have this church. The walls make out of mud, the roof covered with carrat leaves: a simple hut with no steeple or cross or acolytes or white priests or latin ceremonies. But is our own. Black people own it" (32). Of course, the most important links do not concern the building, but the practices which take place inside the building. The most obvious and most significant of these are the initiatory practice of "mourning" and the weekly Spiritual Baptist service.

Mourning has nothing to do with sorrow over loss or death. Rather, it is a physical ordeal leading to spiritual realization and renewal. "We never ask nobody to come and join us; but somebody will get a dream, somebody will get a vision, and he come to us and we baptise him in the river and put him out on the Mournin' Ground to pray and fast and wait for the Lord to send him a sign so he will know if his mission is to be a shepherd to the sheep, or a nurse, or a surveyor, or if he call to be a prover to prove out the sheep from the goat and to search out the mock-ers from the true, or if he is to be a warrior like Bolo" (32). Spiritual Baptist mourning derives from various West African ceremonies, which function to induce initiates into the community as a whole or into some special society within the community. Specifically, mourning involves the ritual isolation of the initiate, deprivation of various sorts of food—sometimes, of any food at all—restriction in movement and speech, and the like. The entire mourning time or initiatory period is to be spent in instruction, meditation, and prayer, leading ultimately to a revelation about one's place in society: "During mourning one hopes to receive a 'gift,' that is, to find out what his 'work' is" (Simpson, 149). The ritual ends with a return of the initiate to the congregation and a communal ceremony. Those familiar with African initiation ceremonies will recognize the pattern. But the similarity with Igbo title-societies—which share the ritual deprivation that marks initiation ceremonies, and are in some ways a form of initiation ceremony—is perhaps most important. Mourning, like title-taking, is voluntary, highly costly, and may be repeated for "increased recognition," "enhanced prestige," and to "receive acclaim." Indeed, "One mourns . . . to 'take a higher degree.' For the ambitious, successful experiences in the 'sacred chamber' validate each step up the ladder of the [Spiritual Baptist] hierarchy" (Simpson, 153).

Perhaps even more significant than mourning are the weekly ceremonies, which are centered on possession, the entry of the spirit of God into the worshiper: "We have this church where we gather to sing hymns and ring the bell and shout hallelujah and speak in tongues when the Spirit come" (Lovelace, 32). In principle, "The Holy Spirit is the only spirit that is supposed to appear at a [Spiritual Baptist] service." In practice, however, as Simpson puts it, "the 'mixing' of [more unadulteratedly African] *shango* and [Spiritual Baptist] beliefs and procedures" is common (99). It is probably most accurate to say that there is a range of Spiritual Baptist practices, varying from church to church and from individual to individual. In some churches and for some individuals Spiritual Baptism is more purely Christian. In other churches and for other individuals, it is highly, almost purely African, in effect a form of Shango—Shango being a syncretistic Afro-Caribbean religion combining deities and practices from a number of West African cultures, prominently Yoruba. In any case, "It is not unusual for a *shango* power"—one of the major and minor West African deities, frequently of Yoruba origin—"to manifest on a worshiper at a Spiritual Baptist ceremony" (Simpson, 99n.).

Both mourning and possession serve not only as objects of concern in the novel, but as metaphors for the broader condition of Afro-Caribbean men and woman. In mourning, one is isolated from the group in a sort of exile from the larger community, and tested with continual hardship, much as the Afro-Caribbean community is exiled from the larger community of Africa and tested with continual hardship "in this tribulation country far away from Africa, the home that we don't know" (33). Moreover, mourning is a sort of death that leads to rebirth: "'Mourning' . . . is thought of as a temporary death. The pilgrims are said to be lying 'in the tomb' and there is rejoicing on the third day when they are 'lifted' and 'released'" (Simpson, 147). As Houk puts it, "the most important aspect of the mourning ritual" is "the symbolic or spiritual death and subsequent rebirth of the mourner" (79). Indeed, it is a rebirth that may involve an entire reorientation of one's practical life through the revelation of a new career. As we have already noted, death followed by spiritual revival in an entirely new form—in effect, a new career—is a common image of the existence of the African spirit in Afro-Caribbean society, its repeated destruction in one form and revival in a different form, in different work.

Possession is perhaps an even more fitting image for this condition. The essence or core of Spiritual Baptist ritual—possession by the Spirit, including the spirits of African deities—is, in effect, the condition of all those Afro-Caribbeans who transmit the tradition of Africa. Without self-conscious knowledge of their links with African culture, they are, in this view, possessed by the Spirit of that culture. That Spirit comes upon them, animating their action, revealing itself in their religious preferences, their speech, their beliefs, just as the Spirit comes upon a devotee at a Spiritual Baptist ceremony. Lovelace stresses this link between religious possession and cultural heritage. For example, when the Spirit is on her, Sister Lucas walks "in that sweet, graceful, noble walk that black women alone have from generations of carrying on their head buckets of water and baskets of cocoa" (Lovelace, 62). She repeats a unique pattern of walking which stretches back to African practical identity. When a spirit manifests on her, she manifests the spirit of Africa in one of its aspects. Indeed, the image of walking is particularly relevant here. Simpson notes that "Experienced shangoists say they can identify" people truly possessed and distinguish imposters in part "by the way they walk" (28). Lovelace has chosen to characterize Sister Lucas's possession by reference to her—ancestral, African—walk, not by accident, but because attention to the walk is part of the religion itself, marking the "genuineness" of the possession, and, by implication, of the tradition as well.

Indeed, the imagery of cultural death and revival is present from the very first paragraph of the novel, and, from the outset, it is linked with Spiritual Baptist practices both literally and metaphorically (1):

> God don't give you more than you can bear, I say. 'Cause for hundreds of years we bearing what He send like the earth bear the hot sun and the rains and the dew and the cold, and the earth is still the earth, still here for man to build house on and fall down on, still sending up shoots and flowers and growing things.

Not only is the earth still the earth—a principle of constancy in change, an apt image of the spirit of Africa—but, more importantly, the two things that the earth allows one to do are "to build" and "fall down." Certainly, the building alludes to the building of homes, and of churches, and, more generally, to the progress of ordinary life. And falling down alludes to death, the end of ordinary life. Falling down also concerns sin, especially original sin, referred to in the immediately following questions: "But what sin we commit? What deed our fathers or we do that so vex God that He rain tribulation on us for generations?" (1). But, the most significant meaning in this context is one obvious only within Afro-Caribbean belief and practice: "falling" is one idiom for possession (Simpson, 33). "Building" is the technical name for repeating the mourning rites in order to advance in the Spiritual Baptist church hierarchy (see Simpson, 45). Implicitly, Eva is comparing the life of Afro-Caribbean people to the two main, African experiences carried through or manifest in Spiritual Baptism: possession or falling and mourning or building.

On the next page, Eva continues the metaphor: "The strong suffer most, the weak dies. 'And if He give us this . . . If He give you this, Reggie,' I tell my last boychild, 'is because . . . we could bear it and rise'" (2, ellipsis in original). The tribulations of Afro-Caribbean life—in "this tribulation country far away from Africa" (33)—are a matter of suffering and resurrection, "rising," directly comparable to mourning and building in the Spiritual Baptist church. Indeed, Eva later speaks of the whole Spiritual Baptist congregation *rising* in another sense as well. After many months of abstention, they call again on the Spirit. In doing this, they not only rise from the cultural death into which they had fallen, they simultaneously rise up against the British colonial law that prohibits Africanized worship: "If we clap we hands and catch the Spirit, the police could arrest us" (34). The two senses of "rise," and the two acts, cultural revival and political rebellion, are clearly related, and not incidentally. Thus, Eva celebrates "how we rise, how we rise up, how we dance and sing and how we break the law like the law was nothing" (63).

IVAN MORTON AND THE ALLEGORIES OF MIMETICISM

But, as readers familiar with the novel know well, Bee and the members of his congregation do not break the law, or they do not do so consistently. Indeed, it seems more apt to say that the law breaks them, or nearly does. It is this conflictual relation to the law and to the Spirit that defines the primary alternatives for tradition and masculine identity in the book. The three main possibilities are personified in Bolo, Bee, and Ivan Morton, though there are other relevant, if less important figures as well.

More exactly, there are three obvious mimeticists in the novel: Prince, Mitchell, and Ivan Morton—a police officer, an entrepreneur, and a politician, representatives of the three primary areas of social domination. Of the three, Prince is probably the only sincere mimeticist, the only one driven to become "more British than the British" by his own anguish and self-hatred. Indeed, like the male characters in *Things Fall Apart*, he too becomes reactionary due to a crippling Oedipal hatred. Prince is the newest corporal at the Bonasse police station. The previous corporals were white, and relatively lenient with the Spiritual Baptists: "All of them had their duty to do, but they know we is not criminals and they use a little reason: they leave us alone once we don't broadcast that we have a Baptist church going on in the village. . . . They was police, but they was human too" (35). But Prince, in the typical style of a reactionary—in this case, a reactionary assimilationist—had sought to suppress whatever common strains of humanity he might have shared with other black people and to make himself solely and distinctively white: "This policeman show no sympathy or respect or mercy for people black like he. He was the law. The whiteman send him to do a job" (35–36). The Oedipal origins of this are only suggested, but clear: "Where another policeman mighta hesitate to smash up a church his father and grandfather worship in, Prince had no sense of danger or remembrance or love or fear." It is in this context that Lovelace explains, "It was a sweetness for him to mash up your face or break down your church if you is Baptist." It is no doubt not an accident that his acts of cruelty prominently included striking a boy who tried to protect his father and arresting the oldest members of the congregation (36). Of course, all this has allegorical significance too. Prince's life work is destroying the church of his father and grandfather, which is to say, wiping out the structures, practices, ideas, which are the heritage brought from Africa, remembered by the oldest members of the congregation, and passed on to the children whom filial piety should lead to defend that tradition.

Mitchell, in contrast, is a corrupt mimeticist. He would adopt any idea or practice from the colonizer, fulfill any expectation, as long as it brought him advancement or comfort. Thus, taking up a standard role, he poses as a pure "native" or orthodox traditionalist—when that is what the colonizer wants. When an American officer is writing about Voodoo, Mitchell serves as native informant, despite his complete lack of knowledge on the topic. Because of this, the officer "allow Mitchell to do exactly as he please, and what Mitchell please to do is to not work" (18–19). This could be innocuous enough, in and of itself. But, first of all, Mitchell's misinformation is likely to feed stereotypes about Afro-Caribbean religion, should officer Bob's book ever see the light of day. Second, this behavior is part of Mitchell's willingness to abandon all tradition for monetary gain, which is to say, for the all-defining dollar of the second colonialism. At one point, he shouts angrily at Bolo, criticizing not only Bolo, but the entire tradition for which he stands: "You know what wrong with you? You don't know how to change. You . . . don't realise that things ain't the same and the days you waiting on not coming back again. Why you don't do like everybody and have a good time and try to make some money now that the Yankees giving it away on the Base" (27).

Subsequently, he takes up his role as entrepreneur more explicitly: "Mitchell open a snackette with a juke box in a corner and a girl to serve drinks" (88). Perhaps most importantly, he works with Ivan Morton, in an allegorical representation of the union of upwardly mobile petit bourgeois blacks with petit bourgeois black intellectuals newly elected to political office: "If you want to get anything done you have to be a member of the party group that Ivan Morton form and that Mitchell running" (88).

Ivan Morton, like Mitchell, is a corrupt mimic, but a politician, rather than an entrepreneur. He is one incarnation of a standard figure in much postcolonization literature: a political leader elected to represent his people, but devoted only to his own advancement, in this case a leader who, in the first few pages of the novel, is drained of all his African heritage and sympathies until he becomes indistinguishable from the white rulers he has replaced or joined. Ivan was the "local boy who made good"—"our own boy, son of the soil, our hope, man to save the people" (10). He did well in school, despite some setbacks, perhaps due to his being a Spiritual Baptist, rather than an Anglican or a Catholic (41). After converting to Catholicism, he became a local teacher in a colonialist school (30): "In the school where Ivan Morton teach, they had the little children singing,

> Rule Britannia
> Britannia rules the waves
> Britons never never never
> shall be slaves."

The irony, perhaps too obvious to mention, is that the singing children descended from men and women who were slaves, and who were owned by the very Britons celebrated in the song.

When universal suffrage went into effect after the war, the people of Ivan's village worked tirelessly to have him elected, in part believing that he would put an end to the law banning Spiritual Baptism. In other words, the people of the village of Bonasse saw Ivan Morton as a man who would help them preserve their African heritage, keep their practical identities animated by the African spirit. Not only does Morton do nothing to help the Spiritual Baptists, he in effect repudiates his entire heritage. Bee worked particularly hard on Morton's campaign, "going from daybreak, covering every hill and trace, getting hoarse from talking and red-eye from so much night without a proper rest" (82–83). But when Bee goes to Morton, after the Spiritual Baptists have been raided, Morton tacitly assumes the racist view that Europe equals progress and Africa equals primitive barbarity, and he dismisses the Spiritual Baptist Church: "Ivan Morton look at me and ask what I want to worship as Baptist for. . . . Tell me . . . what worrying him is that I, we should still be in the dark ages in these modern times when we could settle down and be civilize" (12–13). He goes on to articulate the central principle of mimeticism: "We can't change our colour, Dorcas, but we can change our attitude. We can't be white, but we can act white" (13).

Morton's mimeticism, his effort to repudiate all aspects of himself that are specifically African, is both illustrated and allegorized in the story of his acquisition of the old plantation house. There was one big house in the area, the house of the Richardsons—white people, colonialists. But the last Richardson goes back to England, and Morton, due to his new government position, can now move to the big house, "bigger than any house I ever see black people live in" (8). When the white colonialist leaves, the Black opportunist takes his place. Bee insists that Morton will not turn against them, and argues that it is appropriate to Morton's position that he "live like white people" (9). Eva, the more insightful of the two, is unconvinced.

So Ivan moves into the white man's house, leaves "the house that his father build with his own two hands," the paternal heritage, what has been handed down to him and should not be discarded, but refashioned to fit changing circumstances, just as the Spiritual Baptists have refashioned Yoruba and other West African beliefs and customs: "It wasn't bad. It could extend. It could fix." His father "spend his whole life on it"—again, a heritage, a tradition, passed on through the life work of the parent to the child. Unlike the Spiritual Baptists, who were exiled from "Africa, the home that we don't know" (33), but still retained, extended, fixed, that heritage, took it with them—unlike them, "Ivan Morton moved and ain't take one single thing." He "leave the house . . . as if it was a prison or a hotel where you go in and don't own nothing, just a place where you was staying" (9).

The Richardson house has its own things, its own traditions: "old things, dead things, things that generations of Richardson people use"; it is this alien tradition, the tradition of the people who enslaved and brutalized his ancestors that Morton takes up, even though this English house is "falling down," just as the era of British supremacy was coming to an end. "It was as if Ivan Morton was saying to the world that the house his father leave him was nothing, and his father life was nothing and his mother was nothing"—the traditions of his father repudiated, his ancestral mother, Africa, repudiated too. He abandons the entire tradition, forgetting his ancestors, leaving his children without a link to the past. He "just abandon [his father's house and things] like how some women abandon their children, as how some children leave their old parents to beg their bread" (10).

Indeed, the allegory of Ivan Morton goes further. Lovelace takes up what is probably the most common plot of national allegory—two men competing for a woman, which is to say, two political tendencies competing for the heart of the people. Eulalie Clifford is the village beauty (44). Bolo, as we shall see, is the traditional warrior, the champion carrying the tradition of African courage and strength: "Bolo, slim, tall, good-looking, the fastest and the strongest and the bravest young man in Bonasse, a young tiger, the uncrowned king" (44). And everyone expects that "the girl to get Bolo is Eulalie" (44). In contrast, Ivan Morton is the newly educated, the new British-trained young man. He failed his college exhibition examination, twice. But then he converted to Catholicism and went to Teachers Training College in Port of Spain, preparing his career as a mimic. Both court Eulalie.

Allegorically, as the rights of black Trinidadians advance, and as the white colonialists begin to retreat, the people, represented by Eulalie, can choose between the new, educated, mimetic/comprador class and their ideology, represented by Morton, or the African tradition, which sustained them through the long years of tribulation, which links them to their past, and which is represented by Bolo. Unsurprisingly, Eulalie chooses Morton; the people choose the mimeticists: "Nobody know what make Eulalie choose Ivan Morton above Bolo. . . . Some say is the fountain pen she see clip onto his shirt pocket, some say that he talk and impress her with his English" (45). In either case, she chooses him for his Anglicization; the pen and "good" accent are both marks of British education.

Through Eva, Lovelace explains the allegory to us, at least in part: "But when I look at it, I see that what happen with Eulalie was showing something bigger that was happening in the village. . . . [T]he warrior was dying in the village as the chief figure. The scholar, the boy with education, was taking over" (46). This might seem all to the good. After all, education need not mean mimeticism or corruption. But elsewhere, Bee articulates the meaning of this education. His son has been accepted into a high school. Bee is reluctant. In school, he will learn "to turn his back on his family"; in school they teach students "to act civilize like Ivan Morton. . . . So civilize they forget where they come from. So civilize they looking at you as if you is nothing, as if your dreams and hopes and life is nothing" (14; on the theme of ideologization and schooling in the novel, see Thomas, 4). Eva too laments "the bright little ones whose brains they will confuse with their education" (33), and later, "We push these children to this education. . . . And we don't know what this education doing to the heart inside of them" (79).

As in most national allegories, a child—the future of the nation, or part of the nation—is born from the union of the people and their chosen political ideology or leadership: "After Ivan leave and gone back to Port of Spain, Eulalie Clifford . . . in the family way" (46). Literally, Ivan has returned to complete his course in teacher training. Allegorically, the representative of the people has gone off to the capital to guide the political future, leaving the people "pregnant" with hope of the future, with possibilities for a new life, and so on—a scenario played out literally a few years later, when Morton is elected to government. Everyone "was expecting Ivan to put ring on her finger"—to acknowledge and accept the people's hopes, to make them legitimate, to make the union legal, much as the Spiritual Baptists later expect him to make their church legal. Given Morton's character, both literal and allegorical, it is unsurprising that he does not marry Eulalie, does not make the union and its offspring legitimate, just as, later, he will not make the Spiritual Baptists legal. Instead, "Ivan Morton leave her with the baby and take up a light-skin girl from Tunapuna" (46). In other words, he—like many corrupt mimetic politicians in Caribbean fiction, and in Caribbean politics—abandons his own people, and throws in his lot with the mulatto elite, moving as far as he can toward union with the white, colonial structure. After the institution of universal suffrage, this sort of behavior appears to have been the rule. Lewis describes the first decade of full suffrage as "the nadir of Trinidadian life" (207). The new politicians, he explains, "promised the moon to a gullible electorate" but were driven by a "passion for the spoils of office" (208).

The allegory continues a step further. After she is abandoned by Morton, Eulalie is driven to prostitution. The significance of this would be unclear were it not for the fact that the men who buy her services are American soldiers. The implication here is twofold. First of all, once the people have chosen corrupt mimeticists and collaborationists, such as Morton, they will end up exploited by American military and business interests. As collaborationists, politicians such as Morton will not provide the people with economic security (he will not marry Eulalie) or help them to develop economic autonomy; rather, he will abandon them and render them wholly dependent on American imperial power, force them to prostitute themselves. Secondly, as mimeticists, these leaders will not help the people develop their own aspirations, drawn from their own traditions, but rather will foster in them the narrow aspirations of possessive individualism, the central ideology of the second colonialism coming from America: "the Yankees zooming about the place, the village girls parading, stepping out . . . their eyes full with the sickness for money that was the disease taking over everybody. Eulalie was one of them now" (22–23). The statement is, again, both literal and allegorical, for the opening of the American base at Chaguaramas Bay provided "ample opportunities for organized vice" (Black and Blutstein, 71), especially prostitution (see Lewis, 211–12).

THE SECOND WAVE OF COLONIALISM

Again, this prostitution to America—both literal and metaphorical—is part of a broader trend, a second colonialism. In the first, British phase of colonialism, the colonizers had sought to substitute their own traditions (e.g., their own religions) for those of Africa. It had been a conflict of religions, of modes of thought, of systems of traditional belief and practice. In that context, the Afro-Caribbean people could produce a functional synthesis, a syncretism that preserved African tradition in a new form, only partially altered by Christianity. The second wave, however, is different. For in this, American phase of colonialism, the conflict is not between alternative traditions of comparable types (e.g., Christian and Yoruba cosmology and ritual). Rather, it is between, on the one hand, any system of practice and belief continuous with the past, and, on the other hand, the vacuous absolutism and contemporaneity of money. All systems of practical and reflective identity link one to a community, structure one's actions, define goals and opportunities, and thus involve tradition. In this, capitalist "modernity" is no different from "tradition," African or European. But in the sorts of tradition represented by Christianity or the Igbo heritage, the values are broad and multiple. In Igbo society, for example, they derive, for men, from skill in competition and oratory, the taking of titles, valor in battle, and so on. And the practices are equally diverse. Consider the Spiritual Baptists themselves, with their ordeals of mourning to earn prestige, but also to learn one's vocation, and to take one's rightful place in the common worship. Capitalist modernity, in contrast, reduces all values to one: commodities, or their abstract numerical equivalent, money; and it reduces all goals to one: ownership. Obviously, this reduction is present to a degree in British colonialism as well—as we shall see clearly in the case of Emecheta. However, in Caribbean literature generally, and in *Wine* in particular, it is far more closely identified with this second colonialism of the United States.

Lovelace further illustrates and allegorizes this transition in the shift of women's affection from the African hero, Bolo, to the new money-men: "Since the Americans come money start to flow, fellars spring up from nowhere with clean fingernails and pointy tip shoes." They all have the same clothes and wear their hats so low that, "to see their eyes, you have to lift up their hat brims" (22). Women adore them, they are "the new heroes," and everyone ignores Bolo when they are around (22). The account is precise. For example, "clean fingernails" means that they do no manual labor; by implication, they, like the Americans and the British, live off the labor of others. Their deceit is indicated by the fact that they won't look you in the eye. Their faceless impersonality and comic indistinguishability suggest the absolute equivalence, in American capitalism, of all commodities, including cultural commodities, including people—their ideas, acts, "style."

Of course, what is literally important about these men, what gives them literal value in the new scheme of things, and what allows them to displace Bolo, is not their character or their actions or their common style, but their possessions. Possession is, again, the one goal of this second mimeticism. Though the play on words is never explicit in the novel, it is worth recalling that possession is the equal but diametrically opposed goal the Spiritual Baptists as well. The Americans and the new generation of mimics long for nothing but ownership—more and bigger and costlier things. That is Morton's attitude too, discarding the under-valued handiwork of his father for the overpriced and abandoned goods of the English, discarding the undervalued black woman/Afro-Caribbean people for the light-skin girl/mulatto elite. The Spiritual Baptists, in contrast, seek as their highest goal, not possession of, but possession by—possession by the divine world, the tradition of their ancestors, the source of life and human community: the intimate identity with spirit. It is antithetical to the mere thingness of commodities and to the abstract equivalence of all monetary value.

Indeed, the contrast between Spiritual Baptism, on the one hand, and American militarism and capitalist modernity, on the other, is sharper than even this indicates. The *Shouters Prohibition Ordinance* of 1917, which outlawed the practice of Spiritual Baptism, was justified on the grounds that Spiritual Baptism made the neighborhood "impossible for residential occupation," primarily due to the noise, and that worshipers "take their clothing off and commit all sorts of indecent acts" (343, 344).

But, of course, it was not the African traditions that led to chaos and immorality. Herskovits and Herskovits found that the Spiritual Baptists had a "reputation for probity, trustworthiness in personal dealings and high standards of moral conduct" (Thorpe, vii). The disruptions blamed on Africa resulted, rather, from the American presence, the second wave of colonialism. Lovelace's description highlights the degree to which it was the Americans who violated the very principles invoked to suppress Africa-derived practices: "The American soldiers" spent their time in Trinidad disturbing the peace and undermining residential occupation by "driving their jeeps and screeching their brakes like madmen all over the place, waking Christian people up at all hours of the night to hear bottles crash and women scream and guns shoot off." Worse still, they were committing indecent acts with almost religious regularity—"drinking Cockspur rum and fulling up the women," going about "with money in their pocket and guns on their waist to have mother and daughter whoring down the place . . . behind the Yankee dollar" (18).

BEE AND MANNESS

But, again following a standard postcolonization motif, there is a continuing suggestion throughout the novel that this second colonialism can threaten the people's traditions, undermine the moral and cultural structure of the community, only because the people themselves have already degenerated, because the men have lost their courage, their "manness." The epitome of this uncertain, inadequate masculinity is Bee Dorcas, leader of the Spiritual Baptists of Bonasse.

Bee does not initially comply with the law banning Spiritual Baptism. And, as already noted, corporals before Prince tended to turn a blind eye to the Afro-Christian practices. For years, Bee was able to lead his congregation without a test of his resolve and courage. But after Prince arrives, Bee changes the ceremony. "We going to try it their way," he says. "They want us to be Anglican and Catholic, we going to be like Catholic and Anglican. We going to sing how they want us to sing, we going to pray quiet just as they pray. We going to worship like them"

(47). In short, he decides that he and his congregation will conform to colonialist dictates and purge Spiritual Baptism of its African elements. Of course, Bee's position is difficult. As Eva points out, "his is the voice to speak not for himself alone, but for the people. . . . Bee job is to keep the church alive" (46). Bolo proposes killing Prince. To which Brother Sylvester responds, "And when they send another policeman, kill him too? You will kill the whole Police Force, Brother Bolo?" (47). The right solution is not obvious. Still, even Eva grants that Bee is "frighten" and uncertain in "his own manness" (46). And, however unclear the right solution might be, it seems clear at least that capitulating to an unjust law and relying on Ivan Morton is no solution at all. If Bolo's solution shows too much "manness," this easy capitulation shows too little.

Unsurprisingly, as the time of their compliance drags on, Bee and the congregation come to recognize that they are only losing their own practical identity, forgetting the heritage that had remained unforgotten for generations, since Africa: "The more we go on with this type of service . . . the more we realize that we ain't solving the problem. All we was doing was taking away the ceremonies natural to our worship. . . . And what we was becoming?" (48). Giving up possession, they have given up their practical selves.

Bolo attends the ceremonies, but will not participate in their degradation: "every Sunday Bolo is there in church, tall, unbending, his face stiff, his eyes burning. He not singing the hymns; he not praying. He is just there like a hard question staring in everybody face" (49)—a challenge. Indeed, as we shall see, that is Bolo's prime, and tragic, function in the novel: to challenge the men of his community to "be men," not to cower and conform, but to take up the heritage of the African warrior and fight. Bee sees this and is "tired of waiting for this war to end"— both the World War that defers their voting privileges, and this war against Prince and against colonial cultural oppression, this war in which Bolo calls on the men to be warriors. Bee "feel[s] he must give a answer to Bolo, want[s] in a manway to rise to the man-challenge in front of him" (51). So, "battling to be a man," he declares, "I going to break this law" (51). Both he and Eva want their son to "see his father as warrior" (52)—not as a coward, not as Okonkwo sees Unoka. And, though he hesitates, and repeats his resolve without acting for many weeks, until Bolo stops trying to shame him into action and no longer attends the Sunday services, even until his sons have lost the hope that they will ever see their father refuse injustice, despite all this, finally Bee does act; finally he performs the true ceremony, and possession comes: "Like a strong wind, like a mighty water, like a river of fire, like a thousand doves with wings. It come, the Spirit" (61)—Spirit of God, and Spirit of Africa: "to see the people how we rise, how we rise up . . . how we break the law" (63).

The scene, with its images of wind and fire and the dove, calls to mind Pentecost, when the Holy Spirit, traditionally symbolized by a dove, descended among the apostles. According to *Acts*, the apostles "had all met in one room, when suddenly they heard what sounded like a powerful wind from heaven . . . and something appeared to them that seemed like tongues of fire" (2.1–3). The allusion is important, not only to understanding the ecstatic experience of spiritual possession—an experience shared by the early Christians and by African traditional religions—but, perhaps even more importantly, because, in referring to the "acts of the apostles," it refers to the Christian relation to the law, a relation established from the very earliest Christian communities. This relation is simple. Insofar as the law operates to suppress Christian worship, it not only can, but *must* be broken. Much of *Acts* concerns attempts at the legal suppression of Christianity and the early Christians' defiance—their insistence that, in Bee's phrase, they must break the law. For example, in *Acts* 5, the apostles were arrested and "put in a common gaol" (5.18). But they returned to preach in the Temple (5.25). They were arrested again, threatened with death (5.33), "flogged," and "warned . . . not to speak in the name of Jesus" (5.40). But, despite all this, unlike the Bonasse Spiritual Baptists, they were not deterred: "They preached every day both in the Temple and in private houses, and their proclamation of the Good News of Christ Jesus was never interrupted" (5.42). Indeed, when the community first collectively confronts the judgment of the Sanhedrin that they should not preach, they are again "filled with the Holy Spirit" and "proclaim the word of God boldly," even to the extent that their ecstasy surpasses that of Spiritual Baptists: "As they prayed, the house where they were assembled rocked" (4.31). The point is general. In some ways, all of Christianity is founded upon a refusal to follow the law, a refusal that may lead to death, but also leads to resurrection. As Peter points out in the first address delivered after Pentecost, Jesus' persecution was itself a struggle against the legal authorities. And, earlier, Jesus warned his followers, "You will be dragged before governors and kings for my sake" (*Matthew* 10.18). In short, Lovelace's allusion to Pentecost serves to remind us that conformity to the *Shouters*

Prohibition Ordinance violates not only the African sources of Spiritual Baptism, but the Christian sources as well.

For a while after breaking the law, after following the principles of Christianity and the example of the Apostles, "the men holding up their heads in front," not ashamed, not disgraced by acquiescence in oppression and injustice. But Prince soon raids the congregation, rounds them up, drags them to prison. Bolo is the only one to resist, to stand against Prince and fight for his church. But when he is brutally beaten by ten armed officers, none of the other men steps in to help (70). They stand by and watch him savagely kicked and clubbed into unconsciousness. Eva looks at her sixteen-year-old son, "his eyes widening as he watch his father and the other men and realize that they not going to rescue Bolo" (70). Afterward, "feeling his manness and helplessness," he denounces the onlookers: "'All o' you . . .' Taffy say, his voice breaking out of him, 'all o' you stand up there and watch them beat him. And he was fighting for all you'" (71).

But should Bee or anyone else fight against impossible odds? What is the point? "Prince stand up with his revolver pointing at the crowd and the policemen have Bolo on the ground, kicking him, beating him" (70). And even if the congregation had beaten back the officers and avoided Prince's bullets, "The law is not only the police you see in uniform here today. The law is the judges and the magistrates and the British soldiers. The law is the whole empire of Britain" (72). The effect of those words, unintended by Eva, is a stab of despair in her young son: "Walking home, and Taffy ain't saying nothing, his head down . . . he start stammering, 'So . . . so we can't ever fight/ They going to keep on . . . keep on doing us whatever they like, and we going to keep on taking it so? We not going to ever fight" (72, ellipsis in original). This desperation leads first to disdain of family, then criminal violence: "Taffy stab a boy in the week before Easter and run away" (76–77). Taffy has no hope for action within any structure. His rage stretches out to every aspect of his circumstances, to all those around him, to all the acts and ideas and structures that define his daily life in a colonized community. The boy he stabbed, in the week Jesus was crucified, was a scapegoat, the chance victim of a generalized rage that demanded a particular, if random outlet.

So the congregation conforms to the law again, gives up possession. And nothing changes until the ban is lifted, in 1951. The dissatisfaction of the congregation, the challenges of Bolo, the continuing and painful sense that the timid performance of a decorous ceremony is not only inauthentic, but blasphemous—nothing brings Bee to change. He obeys the law. And when the law changes, he proudly takes up his shepherd's crook to lead the congregation to a true service, and he repeats the words and the calls and the congregants to ring the bells and pour the water. But after so long the practical identity, "Africa in us, black in us" (133), is lost, like the knack for playing an instrument or fluency in a language; unused, the capacity, and thus the heritage, fade: "nothing . . . nothing happen . . . it wasn't like old times at all"—old times before the ordinance, or old times in Africa; both are lost. The "Spirit wouldn't come" (144). After the service, Bee laments: "I shoulda never stop worshipping in the true Baptist way. . . . We shoulda fight them" (145).

What troubles Bee at the end is the thought that perhaps the problem all along was that the black men of Bonasse were not men, not African men and not Christian men, not the true heirs of warrior ancestors or of the Apostles, that their *communal* weakness was the cause of the church's oppression, of Bolo's tragedy—even of Ivan Morton's betrayal. These are Eva's thoughts too, reflecting on the change in Ivan Morton: "Maybe is because he couldn't be black like one of us ordinary Bonasse people and be a man too, because the world wouldn't let him" (134–35). Perhaps their own weakness leaves only two possibilities for manhood—Morton and Bolo. In a community without either power or commitment, the possibilities for a life of self-respect dwindle, almost vanish. When Bolo returns from prison, he says that "All he want was to live and be a man, and he want a piece of land to work and a woman to settle down with" (88–89)—one would think that any man or woman deserves this little concession from life: a family, a home, work. And especially Bolo, strong, unafraid, principled, generous. But no. He cannot be granted even this much.

Eva elaborates her thoughts on Morton, blaming the colonialist structure, but blaming even more her own people's inability or unwillingness to fight that structure: "Maybe because his manness was so important to him and because we didn't, don't have no world, no world with power where he could be a man in, where his manness could come out legitimate just from being himself." More generally, "Maybe is our weakness and not the wickedness of our children that turn them away from us and from their self to try to be something else where they could feel that they is human beings" (135). Of course, what Morton fails to recognize is that he is still not a man. He cannot be a man until his people are full people, until they live as people, are fully recognized and understood as people, until they "feel that they is human beings." As Bee puts it, Morton "don't even know that unless black people is people he cannot on his own be a man." One is a man or a woman within a community, a culture, not "on one's own." And, having repudiated black people, Morton cannot make himself into a white man through education and political position: "All the manness that he create with books and position is just a flimsy thing that could break down and crumble any time" (136).

The Story of a Strong Man

From the beginning, Bolo seems to be the one prominent exception to the general emasculation of Spiritual Baptists and the corruption and mimeticism of the rest of the society. Most obviously, he is both a religious man, attending the Spiritual Baptist church with his mother, and an African warrior, a champion at the stickfight. Moreover, his devotion to the stickfight is not egocentric, not a matter of personal triumph merely. Rather, it is devotion to "the beauty of the warrior" (21). Indeed, for Bolo, the stickfight is a celebration of heritage, a rite or "ceremony" (21) directly comparable to the Sunday services of the Spiritual Baptist church: "And he do it with love and respect, more as if he was making a gift of himself . . . as if what he really want was for people to see in him a beauty that wasn't his alone, was theirs, ours, to let us know that we in this wilderness country was people too, with drums and song and warriors" (21–22)—"that we . . . was people too," precisely what Morton fails to recognize: "Maybe Ivan Morton really don't see us as people" (135).

Later, Buntin explains the communal significance of the rite more thoroughly. People engage in the stickfight, Buntin explains, "because they is men. They must test theyself against each other in this dangerous battle, so as to keep alive the warrior in them, in us, to show us again that we have champions, that we have men" (92). It is a sort of communal reaffirmation and reestablishment of strength and bravery—for it is impossible to be brave or strong unless one has seen and engaged in actions of both sorts. "Manliness," like anything else, is part of one's practical identity only when it is practiced. As Eva puts it, "It have spectators plentiful watching as if they come to look for something to remind them of who they is" (93).

Like Spiritual Baptism, stickfighting is appropriate for teaching Afro-Caribbean people "who they is," for it is the product of a long history, extending back through slave revolts to African dance. It combines these different strains, which are important not only to Afro-Caribbean history, but to modern life also. As Hill explains, "The calinda, a stick dance, probably of African origin, was a popular form of entertainment for male slaves." It was "performed to Negro drums, while the dancers engaged in mock combat" (25). As it developed, "The stick fight was both a dance and a combat." Indeed, the fighter "had to demonstrate complete mastery of the art by executing intricate dance steps up to the moment of an attacking or a defensive maneuver." This dance or battle was accompanied by "Calinda chants" as well as drums (27). Moreover, the performance of calinda and of the stickfight that grew out of it was an act of resistance to European cultural hegemony—and not merely in a symbolic way. For a number of years, stick fighters were among the prime antagonists of the colonial police. At the end of the nineteenth century, there were a number of noteworthy clashes between police and groups of stickfighters, or sometimes "individual stick-fighting champions" (Hill, 26). In this sense, even Bolo's individual battle with the police is part of a tradition and a history of Afro-Caribbean resistance. In sum, the stick fight is part dance, part political resistance, part battle; a martial and artistic manifestation of an African and Afro-Caribbean history, used in both the cultural and physical struggles against colonialist repression. Moreover, it too was outlawed by the colonial authorities, if for a shorter period.

The link between stickfighting and Spiritual Baptism is clear not only from their African origins, their function in preserving a heritage of resistance, and their suppression by colonial authorities. In addition, these two represent complementary aspects of a culture's identity and its ability to sustain that identity—war and worship, the communal means of defense and the communal means of self-affirmation, the practical principles defining struggle against destruction of life and culture and the spiritual principles explaining the origin and sustenance of life and culture. They are both means of identity, ways of being oneself, denied "in this Babylon country, where no matter what we do to be ourselves they try to make us illegal, to cut us off from our *God* and self and leave us naked without *defence*" (37, italics added).

Here, Bolo's strength is not reactionary, but fully orthodox and fully human. Unlike Okonkwo, he does not suppress emotion, especially the

deep and pervading sadness at the condition of his people: when he witnesses the false worship of the Spiritual Baptists conforming to the colonial law, his face is filled "with amazement and heartbreak" (17). He is
humanely devoted to the welfare of others, whatever his own condition:
"Bolo was not happy; still, when somebody die he would go to the
wake, and if a man want help on his land or to build a house he would
help him" (30). And he has a deep devotion to and affection for his
mother. When his best friend, Clem, goes to Port of Spain, Bolo is
tempted. But his mother has no one to look after her, so he stays: "In the
end he didn't want to leave his mother in Bonasse alone" (29).

Here too the contrast with Morton is striking and direct. Bolo will
not move away from his mother, hence his heritage; he will not choose
money over home. Morton not only left his parents' house to move into
the house of the white plantation owner, he carried nothing from "the
house that his father build with his own two hands"; again, it was as if
"his father life was nothing and his mother was nothing" (10).

Bolo's devotion to both his community and his mother, and his allegorical position as defender of the African heritage, is presented most
strikingly, and most painfully, in his encounter with Prince. Prince has
rounded up the worshippers and is leading them to prison. Bolo intervenes. He waits for the group to arrive, "like a stickfighter waiting on
the drums to begin the battle" (67).

There is, however, a brief interlude before the battle begins. Ivan
Morton asks Prince what he is doing. Prince responds that he is arresting these people because "It is against the law to worship as a Baptist."
Morton responds, "Well, I suppose you have to carry out your duty"
(68), and leaves. The scene serves not only to further the characterization of Morton as a false representative of his people, but to sharpen the
contrast with Bolo. Bolo continues Morton's questions, but aggressively,
without the polite deference and tacit complicity. When Prince says that
it is none of Bolo's business, Bolo replies, "How you mean none of my
business? I is a Baptist. These is my people. Look, you have my mother
out there too. I want to know where you carrying my mother." When
Prince makes as if to go for his gun, Bolo asks in astonishment, "You
going to shoot me down? . . . You going to shoot me down for asking
you a question? You going to shoot me down because I ask you where
you carrying my mother?" (68). It is not the last time that Bolo will
drink of the wine of astonishment, stunned by the perverse cruelty of
those around him, unable to fathom their extremity. After a while, he

continues, "'What I want from you is what my mother do. She is seventy years. What she do? She thief? Who she poison.' And sudden so his voice burst out of him, 'What my mother do?'" (69).

Prince does not shoot. But in the battle that ensues ten policemen attack Bolo, beating and kicking him brutally. And though he has just identified himself as a Baptist, called them "my people," and sought to protect his aged mother from unjust confinement, no one steps forward to help. The police heave him, like a corpse, onto the floor of the van. Later, Bee is haunted by a memory: Bolo, unconscious, bleeding on the floor of the police van. Bolo is sentenced to "three years with hard labour in jail" (73).

In order to understand the severity of this sentence, it is worth considering a more recent case in Trinidad. A man murders his wife, on the grounds of adultery, and tries to murder his two children (aged one and two). He pleads guilty and is sentenced to three years for attempting to murder the children and five years for murdering the wife. The sentences are to run concurrently, and he is likely to spend less than two years actually in jail (see Khan, 54). Admittedly, this sentence was controversial, and other judges would have been less lenient. Moreover, it is no doubt indicative of the judge's (and the larger society's) sexism. Nonetheless, it gives a sense of the absurd extremity of Bolo's sentence. Or consider an example contemporary with the action of the novel. According to British laws in effect from 1924 until after independence, the abduction of a sixteen-year-old woman for sexual purposes carried a *maximum* sentence of two years in prison (Daly, 9). This is, in effect, what Bolo does at the end of the novel. Whatever one may think of the sentence of two years for such a crime, it is, I would think, uncontroversial that the abduction of a young woman for sexual purposes is far worse than anything Bolo does when his mother is arrested for praying. Again, the obscene severity of the punishment is clear. It is little wonder that, in the end, Bolo is embittered and hateful.

Still, after he returns from jail, Bolo has not yet fallen into the despair that marks his reckless final days of reaction. He is sad, certainly. He has not forgotten that Eulalie betrayed him for a hypocrite with a good accent; that his people voted that same man into office, where he could become a full-blown collaborator; that when Bolo defended his family and his faith and his friends, he was beaten like a dog until he was unconscious, and his fellow Baptists stood by and watched him bleed into the dust of the road and then onto the floor of the van; that, for opposing an unjust law, inconsistent with every principle by which the British sought to justify their rule, he was condemned to three years of hard labor, a far harsher sentence than had he committed kidnapping or even some sorts of murder. This, he cannot easily forget. But he will try to live with it. He will put aside Ivan Morton and all the rest. "He say that now . . . all he want was to live and be a man, and he want a piece of land to work and a woman to settle down with" (88–89).

But, again, even this is denied him. And it is denied because he cannot make himself accept cruelty—not to himself, but to others, especially to others who cannot defend themselves, especially the old. He applies to the government for farming land, but receives no response to the application. He has not joined Ivan Morton's party. After three months of waiting, he goes to San Fernando to check. He stands in line behind a "grey old man . . . in a oversize jacket." The old man is worried and uncertain. He frets over whether he is in the right line, has the correct papers. Finally, "this old man get to the head of the line and as he shove his hand in the pocket of his beat-up jacket, as his fingers bring out the paper, trembling, the clerk start to close the book" (90). The problem was a common one. Eva remembers old people standing all day "in the hot sun, waiting for the officer to come and give them the few dollars they get as old age pension," only to find the office closed, and to hear the clerk address them as if they were "deaf or stupid" (90). Bolo can't bear to see the old man disappointed and disrespected in this way. He grabs the clerk by the collar and drags him back. "That was the end of Bolo and the land" (91).

Because he would not abandon his mother and go to the city to earn money, he could not win the heart of a woman such as Eulalie. Because he defended his family and friends and defended the principle of religious freedom, he was branded for life as a felon. Because he would not join a corrupt political party and could not bear to see a frail old man mistreated, he was denied the rent of land. Bolo's human sympathies and ethical sense—and the orthodox traditionalism that these instanced and allegorized—have slowly narrowed his possibilities. With each event, his future dims. And he knows well that no one he has helped will return the favor. Even his religion, for which he fought unaided against such odds, is lost—tamely complicit with the law. Little wonder that "He was searching for something, like a woman. . . . But it wasn't a woman, it was his life he was looking for" (91–92).

One thing, however, is left. The stickdance. Recall again that, for Bolo, this is not merely a forum for his own glory. Rather, it has all the elements of communal self-affirmation: art and history and ceremony. Bolo's final and utter change comes when this too is lost. When Bolo enters the ring at Carnival, no one will fight him. Here too government suppression has had its effect. The tradition is broken, or at least declined. This, for Bolo, is the final sign that all those around him have lost their "manness," that they will stand up for nothing, fight for nothing. And because they wouldn't fight him in the ring, and because they wouldn't fight for any person or principle, and because he himself was punished no matter what he did, from then on Bolo did everything he could to drive men to battle, to drive them to be men, even if that battle had to be against Bolo himself. "From that day it look to everybody that Bolo had one mission: to force the village stickmen to battle him, to make them face up to that man-challenge that they inherit" (101).

He drinks, gambles, takes goods from shops, and refuses to pay. When, as he expected, no one stands up to him, his disgust and disdain increase—for the aim of his "man-challenge" was not to force acquiescence, but to spark resistance. He befriends one man only—Charleau. Charleau too has suffered for principle and been slandered in the process; he was dismissed from his job with the County Council on a charge of drunkenness, but, "The real reason for losing his job is that he had start to talk out against Ivan Morton" (108). And despite his diminutive size, he stands up to Bolo—not on his own behalf, but on behalf of someone else. When Bolo hits Barber Sonny for no reason, Charleau tells him, "You wrong." When Bolo strikes Charleau, Charleau only repeats the denunciation—and he keeps repeating it as Bolo knocks him to the ground. In the end, without intending to do so, Charleau wins Bolo's respect. "But in Bonasse we didn't have many like Charleau" (109).

Bolo's final tragedy is precipitated by his conflict with the most spineless man in the village: Primus. "Primus don't argue with nobody" (114); "If argument come up while he was drinking, he would agree with both sides," and, in larger groups, "Any side the crowd like—that was his side" (115). Bolo goes to Primus and demands that Primus turn over his daughter as Bolo's wife. Bolo asks for the younger daughter. Primus pressures the older daughter to go, right then, and she packs and leaves with Bolo. Whatever one thinks of Bolo's action, Primus's behavior is worse. He pressures his daughter into a marriage she does not desire. ("But how you could do that to the girl?" Eva asks Primus in astonishment.) He is the epitome of everything Bolo loathes. Given the age of marriage in Trinidad—some marriages are contracted for thirteen-year-olds—the implication seems to be that Primus wants to get the older daughter off his hands. His argument to her is, "She have twenty-three years already" (117). This only makes him more execrable.

Later, when the younger daughter visits her sister in Bolo's home, Bolo detains her as well. Here, of course, if Primus is correct, Bolo is clearly wrong. He cannot expect a seventeen-year-old to stand up to him, to resist. His behavior is grotesque, brutal, morally repulsive.

And yet, when Bee comes to speak with him, Bolo has a point, an argument about hypocrisy and double standards (119):

> The Yankees do as they like with your daughters and you thank them, the police hound you down like beast and brutalise you and arrest you for worshipping your God in your religion and you don't lift a hand against them, the big shots in this island have you catching hell to make a living, you don't open your mouth; but me, I Bolo, I take a girl to live with me and you talking as if I is the devil.

The argument is legally exact. As noted above, according to British laws in effect in Trinidad from 1924, to take an underage unmarried woman "out of the possession and against the will of persons having the lawful care of her with the intention that she should be unlawfully and carnally known by any man" is "punishable by up to two years imprisonment" (Daly, 9). Note that this puts Bolo's crime in exactly the same category as the prostitution of underage women by U.S. servicemen, just as Bolo indicates. And no one calls the police to attack the American GIs. Moreover, while a seventeen-year-old woman was a legal adult for most purposes of Trinidadian law, she was still subject to her guardian for purposes of marriage. Thus, legally, the challenge here is not to the woman herself, but to Primus.

Ignoring Bolo's argument, Bee responds, cruelly, that Bolo is just like Ivan Morton now. "I work to put Ivan Morton in the Council and instead of changing the law . . . he gone up in Richardson mansion to live his own life like a whiteman." Bolo responds simply, "You never put me in no Council. . . . You never did nutten for me" (119). The accusation is painfully true. Even Bee chose the mimic Ivan Morton over Bolo. Indeed, the possibility of putting Bolo in the Council probably never even occurred to him. The only option was Morton. But why? Surely, Bolo would have been a better choice. He had respect for tradition, for the church, for the people; he had compassion; he was not afraid to fight for others and for a principle; he had already suffered in the people's cause. Indeed, his situation is typical, and thus all the more tragic. For all the world is ruled by elites—elites by birth or education or, most often, both. A man such as Bolo has little or no chance of representing his people—for even his people, whom he has affirmed and defended, pass him over, choosing instead a collaborationist with clean fingernails, pointy tip shoes, a good accent, and a light-skin wife.

Bee tries to put off the suggestion with nonsense about Bolo being "a king," due to his stickfighting. "No body didn't have to put you up nowhere, you was there already." But he wasn't there already; he was not in the Council, participating in decisions about the future of the people, "my people," as he (unlike Morton) called them (68). He was in prison, or sitting on the stoop watching Eulalie pass by with American soldiers, or standing in line to ask for his piece of land, and be denied. Bolo merely repeats, in utter despair, "I want to be a man too. . . . I want to be a man" (119)—just what is denied him, by the fact that all those around have denied themselves. Again, to be a man, to have any practical identity, one's actions and beliefs must be woven into the fabric of a culture that structures one's daily life, giving it means and purpose. Bolo calls it "being a people": "We ain't no people, Bee. A people does know what they doing. A people does know why they getting up in the world on a morning. A people does be going somewhere. . . . A people does fight for something. What we fight for?" (120). All along, Bolo—in direct contrast with Morton—believed they were a people, his people, and all his actions were guided by that belief. For him, the loss of that belief is despair.

Of course, Bolo's words and actions here are a provocation too, a challenge—if a mad challenge, a challenge from a man whose mind is dark and chaotic from despair—a challenge to the other men to be men themselves, to fight for something, to make themselves a people: "'You want the girls? . . . Then, you have to take the girls from me. . . . I want you people to be against me" (120). Bee understands the point: "We have to show him we is a people" (122); "He choose out himself. . . . To be the sacrifice. To be the one terrible enough and strong enough and close enough to our heart to drive us to take up our manhood challenge that we turn away from for too long." (122).

But, of course, the challenge fails. It had to fail. Not only is this idea of "manhood" fictional, substituting gender identity for virtue—courage, the defense of principle, respect for people and tradition, these do not have a sex, are no more masculine than feminine. And, anyway, what consequences would it have for a community to attack a man holding a girl hostage, and doing so not out of greed or lust, but to make a moral point through crazed, indecent means? Would it lead them to resist the police? To resist the government? Hardly. Indeed, the situation leads them directly to affirm the very structure of oppression that Bolo wishes them to overthrow. For Primus calls in the police.

This act is the final devastation for Bolo: "'They bring *police* for me,' he say over and over again in that soft voice full of astonishment, looking around him as if suddenly he want to sit down and cry" (126). For now he sees that it is hopeless. This rash act has had the precise opposite of the effect he sought. He comes out of the house behind the two girls, his rifle against the back of the younger one. But he has no intention of killing the girls—"He don't want to shoot the girls, Bee think" (127). Rather, this is a suicide: "On his face is this terrible sadness and rage and water is in his eyes that wasn't from the rain," and he moves out from behind the girls and the police fire. Two shots. One kills Bolo. The other kills the younger girl. So, even here, in his greatest crime, Bolo does less evil than the society around him, than the representatives of justice. Bolo detained the girl against her (or her father's) will. The police murdered her.

"And Mr Buntin was remembering with . . . a kinda sadness and a choking: he was remembering Bolo when he come out of jail and the things he wanted to do and how he wanted a girl to married and some land to build a house on and to be a man. 'He was looking for his life,' Mr Buntin say" (130). Unable to find life, in the midst of a community of cowards and mimics, he chose death instead.

BOLO AND THE GODS

Bolo is, like all tragic figures, a man more sinned against than sinning, a good man driven to despair and cruel acts by the faults of those around him. He is perhaps the one champion of the African and Afro-Caribbean heritage in a place where that heritage is being ground into the dirt. Indeed, Lovelace makes him more than a champion of that heritage, for

Bolo incarnates the Afro-Caribbean cosmology in both its aspects—Christian and African. The community saw Morton as "the saviour" (5). But it was Bolo who took on the role of Jesus—if a Romantic Jesus who was equally a Romantic Satan, rebel against unjust tyranny. Indeed, for the Spiritual Baptists, Jesus was an angel (see 13), and thus more readily assimilable to the Romantics' revolutionary Satan, who warred against the powers of privilege. First, rumors tie Bolo to Satan: "They say he sell his soul to the devil so that nobody could beat him in a battle" (110). And Bolo complains about this unfair identification, when he speaks of how "The Yankees do as they like with your daughters and you thank them . . . but me, I, Bolo, I take a girl to live with me and you talking as if I is the devil" (119). Moreover, the Romantics were not the first to recognize that those who are powerful, act in accord with Satan's wishes, but refer to themselves as angelic, and characterize their opponents as "demons." Jesus himself noted this, asking, "If they have called the master of the house Beelzebul, what will they not say of his household?" (*Matthew* 10.25, in *Jerusalem*).

Of course, there are ways in which the Satanic characterization of Bolo is apt—most obviously in his unequaled temporal power, his absolute spirit of rebellion, and his pride, or what appears to be pride. But, more importantly, there is his challenge, his work of provocation. For there is one tradition that understands Satan not as evil, but as good, not as opposed to God, but as testing humankind for Godly purposes. As Pagels explains, "In biblical sources the Hebrew term the *satan* describes an adversarial role . . . one of the angels sent by God for the specific purpose of blocking or obstructing human activity. The root *stn* means 'one who opposes, obstructs, or acts as adversary'" (39)—as in the case of the testing of Job. In some popular versions, this Satan actually wishes that people would resist his provocations (cf., for example, Marie Corelli's best-selling *The Sorrows of Satan*). Bolo's violent and cruel acts appear in part to be a revision of this adversarial and provocative Satan.

But Bolo is equally Jesus. The night after Bolo tells Bee, "You want the girls? . . . Then, you have to take the girls from me" (120), Bee has a dream: "In my dream I was in a strange place where there was a mountain and Christ was on the cross and I was there with a stone in my hand and he was bleeding and I was alone and I ask him what to do and he say, 'Take these girls from me'" (122). Bolo's death takes up again this imagery of crucifixion: he stands between two girls, like the two thieves, and one is saved, while the other is not; and when he falls, "his two feet close together and his arms stretch out" (128), like Jesus on the cross.

Through Eva, Lovelace explains the function of the image. In this account, Christ's or Bolo's death does not, in and of itself, save the world. Rather, it shows us our own sin, our own refusal to fight. It shows us that we too must take up the cross, that we too must rebel. Indeed, it is part of cowardice and servility to believe that there is a savior, to imagine that another person can take on all our sins and redeem us through his suffering and death, without our taking any action. As Eva puts it (129):

> His death . . . give us the chance, if we so weak to take it . . . to put aside our human challenge and blame it all on Bolo . . . make him Christ who they let the soldiers crucify on the cross because . . . it was easier for Christ to bear the sins of the world than for people to take upon their own self in their own life the burden that is theirs . . . and come against wickedness and come against the Roman soldiers.

Though the links with Satan and Jesus are more obvious, African cosmology is not absent from this portrait. Rather, Christian and African images are linked, both by Spiritual Baptism and by colonialism. Indeed, Bolo may draw his name from the Shango name for Jesus: Abalophon or Obalophon (see Simpson, 18)—the unstressed initial vowel dropped in a typical phonetic development. In any case, early in the novel, "Satanism" is clearly shown to be the colonialists' term of abuse for African practices. Eva remembers: In schools, they teach that "Spiritual Baptist does deal with the devil" (33); in the legislature and the judiciary, they denounce Spiritual Baptists as, in the words of the magistrate, "leading . . . poor people astray, making them jump and prance and shout to the devil as if [they] still in the wilds of Africa" (73).

More importantly, Bolo in his function as challenge to the community "manifests" not only Jesus and Satan, but also, and more clearly, the great Yoruba deity, Ogun. Ogun is one of the central deities for Shangoists. When possessed by Ogun, men act, precisely, like Bolo. As Simpson explains, "Ogun, a warrior, is violent and 'outrageous' when he possesses a follower" (21). His weapon, like Bolo's, is a wooden sword—one of the ritual objects shared by Shango and Spiritual Baptism (see Simpson, 98). And his object, in possessing a worshipper, is most often retributive. He watches for transgressions, then possesses a devotee to challenge the transgressor (see Simpson, 26–27), again Bolo's function.

Thus, Bolo is Jesus (or Obalophon) in dying for (and due to) the community's sins of cowardice; Satan in testing them with evil; and, above all, Ogun, in being a warrior, challenging them with his wooden sword, attacking them for their transgressions. He follows, and instantiates, and symbolizes the African and Afro-Caribbean traditions that have sustained his people, organized and given meaning to their lives.

But Bolo dies. And he dies in despair. However much he may have died for the sins of his people, he too is no savior. His desperate and, ultimately, cruel rebellion and challenge, like Bee's compliance, are in the end no solution either.

Resistance, Culture, and Song

Yet Lovelace is not at all despondent. Filled with despair and remorse at Bolo's death and at the apparent death of Spiritual Baptism, Eva and Bee pass a group of "boys playing on the steelband" and they find "that same Spirit that we miss in our church." It may be gone from the church; it may be gone from the stickfight. But it has revived in the music. Once again, the African heritage seemed to die, seemed finally, after centuries, to have been crushed. But it died in one form only, to be reborn in another: "It is like resurrection morning," Eva thinks, "like if we passing in front of something holy" (146).

This recapitulates other notes of hope throughout the novel. In his youth, Bolo's one close friend was Clem, "a chantwell, a singer leading stickfight chants and bongo songs" (22), songs with their roots in the songs of praise and conflict brought by the slaves from Africa, songs that always accompanied the stickfight—for, again, the stickfight was as much art as battle. Moreover, singing and dancing, including bongo music (see Simpson, 51), were a crucial part of both Shango and Spiritual Baptism, and were central to the experience and enactment of possession. Finally, Clem was not just a musician; he was the village bard, "making up songs about the village girls and the soldiers and the hustlers as it was happening" (23). Clem was the new incarnation of the West African griot, "entertainer, musician, singer, genealogist, spokesman, historian, and teacher" (Hale, 36). The griot was the singer of tales, who played the twenty-one-stringed *kora*, for which Clem substitutes the guitar; sang for the warrior king, as Clem sings for Bolo; preserved the life and history of the people, praised and blamed and exhorted (see Hale, 34–45)—as Clem too preserved the life and history of his people, praised and blamed and exhorted. Eventually, Clem begins to sing calypso, "taking the old music, stickfight tunes, and bongo songs and putting words to them and singing them as calypso" (28). He goes to Port of Spain and, years later, they hear him over the radio singing a song about the way American soldiers have degraded the people's lives, made them prostitute themselves. So, Clem uses new technologies to continue the traditions and purposes of the griot, and to extend them to cultural resistance and ideological critique.

Indeed, Clem is by no means the first to have used the old songs in this way. Calypso operated from the very beginning not only as a manifestation of, but as an exhortation to cultural resistance, especially in the realm of religion. As Hill notes, Calypso descended from the calinda chant that accompanied the stickfight (27) along with "the praise songs and songs of derision of West African natives captured as slaves and brought to the West Indies" (57). More importantly, according the Raymond Quevado, "a leading calypso singer" during the period in which the novel takes place (Hill, 61), the "earliest-surviving calypso" song "expressed the determination of the blacks to take part in their Shango ceremonies against the orders of the planters" (70).

The steel drums fit here as well. Indeed, they are a brilliant instance of cultural death and reincarnation. Steel drum bands, which frequently play calypso music, derive in a very direct way from an African heritage crushed by colonialism, but resurrected in another form. As Hill points out, in 1883, the colonial government outlawed skin drum music. Their objection to African drumming was neatly summarized in a contemporary editorial: "The state of civilization of people whose members can be set in movement by the repetition of such barbarous sounds can easily be gauged" (qtd. in Hill, 44). As a result of this ordinance, Trinidadian musicians began to play on metal containers or "pans." When Carnival was banned during World War II, the "panmen" refused to accept the suppression of their culture and "like the stick-fighting warriors" of the late nineteenth century, they "clashed with police" over the prohibition (Hill, 49). Thus, the image of the steel drum band, especially if it is playing calypso music, brilliantly condenses the African heritage of griot praise songs and calinda chant, battle and dance in the stickfight, the assertion of Afro-Caribbean religious freedom and resistance to colonial repression. It is a nearly perfect symbol for the way Afro-Trinidadians have preserved their heritage, readapting it to changed conditions, fashioning it over and over into new instruments of beauty and identity, and managing to draw, from the details of their historical oppression, new ideas, new practices, new manifestations of their African heritage and their humanity.

Finally, there is another small allegory of the nation in Lovelace's novel. In the standard love triangle of national allegory, Bolo and Morton battled over Eulalie, the heart of the people. In this first battle, Morton moved into the master's house with his mulatto wife; Eulalie became a prostitute; and Bolo ended life mad, ineffectual, and an outlaw. But there is another couple who represent the future, just as Bolo and Morton and Eulalie represent the present and immediate past: Joyce (the daughter of Eva and Bee) and Clyde. Joyce is the child of that tradition represented by Eva and Bee—not the slick, Americanized populace, represented by Eulalie, but what remains of African tradition joined with Christianity and a sense of family or heritage. Clyde was Morton's chauffeur—not the political leader, collaborator, mimic, living in the home of the white people, but an ordinary working man. Clyde, like Clem, plays guitar and sings calypso (82). And Joyce's "belly getting big with her first baby" (139). In Lovelace's Trinidad, that child, not the child of Morton and Eulalie, politics and consumerism, mimeticism and American greed, but rather the child of ordinary people, the child of Afro-Caribbean popular art and Afro-Caribbean popular religion—that child is the possibility and hope for the future, that child is the new incarnation of an undying spirit: Africa that travelled in the slave ships across the seas two centuries ago and, despite many deaths, has survived all the cruel inhumanity devised by Europe.

CHAPTER SIX

LIVES OF WOMEN IN THE REGION OF CONTACT

Buchi Emecheta's The Joys of Motherhood

CULTURE AND THE STATUS OF WOMEN

In many ways, Buchi Emecheta's *The Joys of Motherhood* provides an ideal illustration of the themes we have been exploring. Emecheta portrays the broad colonial structure with particular lucidity in part by clearly demarcating the regions of basic and contact culture. Moreover, she systematically examines the ideology of contact culture, the institutions and other structures through which it is purveyed, and the economic base that sustains those institutions and structures. In doing this, her primary focus is on gender. Here, she shares the view of Achebe (and Lovelace) that men are effectively emasculated by colonialism, that, in contact culture, they lose the character and virtues of men. However, Emecheta is far more concerned with women, with their social position, their conditions of existence, their possibilities for action, achievement, even mere survival.

Emecheta's feminist concerns are twofold. They address both traditional Igbo society and the contact culture of urban Nigeria. Emecheta is critical of each. However, she clearly sees contact culture as far worse for women than traditional society. Specifically, Emecheta recognizes and critiques traditional Igbo patriarchy. However, she simultaneously acknowledges that traditional society had defined an autonomous place for women. Despite the dominance of patriarchal structures, traditional Igbo society provided important structures of economic and political power for women. Moreover, the cosmology and social ideology of traditional Igbo society did not denigrate women.

The standard, liberal Western view on the position of women in colonized societies is that women have much to gain from Westernization and that, however objectionable colonialism may have been in other respects, it did (or could) at least serve the progressive function of bringing some degree of liberation to native women. Ifi Amadiume has recently addressed this issue in an anthropological context, stressing in particular the complicity of white feminists in developing and disseminating this myth. "White feminists were no less racist than the patriarchs of social anthropology," she writes, for "They fantasized a measure of superiority over African and other Third World women" (3). Amadiume therefore calls for a challenge to "what anthropologists and Western feminists were saying about women's lack of power" in Africa (9). Quite the contrary of the standard view, colonialism "undermined [Igbo] women's economic and political power" (Amadiume, 141). First of all, women lost the considerable security and independence they enjoyed in traditional culture. For example, in traditional Igbo society, women owned "livestock, fowls . . . farm and garden crops" (Amadiume, 31). In other words, traditionally, women had often substantial wealth, and at least a measure of economic security, independent of their husbands. As Dike points out, in traditional Igbo society, the women did farming and traded their surplus products and other commodities, all of which "provided the basis for the economic independence of women prior to the British occupation of Igboland" (124). Indeed, Amadiume explains that, in some regions, women marketed not only their own goods (from which they retained all the profit); they also marketed their husband's goods, retaining a part of the profit (39). All this was lost in the contact region.

In short, while colonialism devastates the economy of the subject peoples as a whole, it causes a double hardship for women. At least in this way, colonialism does not improve but worsen the situation of women. One of Emecheta's main aims in *The Joys of Motherhood* is to illustrate this point, to make the reader understand and sympathize with the devastating conditions in which women were often forced to live under the dual oppression of patriarchy and colonialism. (The point has barely been recognized in criticism on the novel, though see Fishburn.)

Of course, the liberal view has typically been that colonialism improves the situation of women in terms of rights and privileges relative to men. In other words, colonialism elevates the status of indigenous women relative to indigenous men, makes, for example, Igbo women less subordinated to Igbo men, Hindu women less subordinated to Hindu men, and so on. But this too is false. And this too is a central theme in Emecheta's novel. Indeed, the relative social status of women is likely to deteriorate significantly under colonial domination. In short, after colonization, women are not only worse off economically in relation to men, they are worse off in their social position relative to men. This is true for three main reasons.

First of all, in contact society, women are removed from the traditional political and economic structures that sustained them in basic culture. In traditional Igbo society, women formed themselves into "village-wide gatherings . . . called 'mikiri' (from 'meeting')" (Van Allen, "'Sitting,'" 169), where they could discuss and work out plans of action concerning "their particular interests," not only as "wives and mothers," but as "traders" and "farmers" ("'Sitting,'" 170), especially as these were "*opposed to* [the interests] of the men" (169). Through their *mikiri*, village women took action against individual men (e.g., men who had mistreated their wives) and against practices of the entire male community (e.g., grazing practices that harmed women's crops). They used "strikes, boycotts and force," as well as humiliation (165), often with considerable success. In keeping with Emecheta's portrayal, Van Allen notes the missionaries opposed *mikiri* ("'Sitting,'" 179) and colonialism "weakened and in some cases destroyed women's bases of strength" (165).

Indeed, one of the most famous acts of Igbo resistance to British colonialism was the "Women's War" of 1929, in which Igbo women attacked the corrupt Native Courts, which were set up by the British in a pretense of regularizing Igbo law; collaborationist Warrant Chiefs, the British substitute for kingship among the relatively egalitarian Igbo; a British factory, and so forth. (On Native Courts and Warrant Chiefs, see Wren, 116–21.) "Basically, it was a protest against taxation and the extortions of the Warrant Chiefs, which escalated into a total rejection of the whole colonial presence" (Isichei, 154). Though it began as a local confrontation, it spread to two dozen villages over some four thousand square miles (see Isichei, 156)—a remarkable uprising, showing great independence, strength, confidence, intelligence, and coordination.

In keeping with this, as Amadiume stresses, women's protests, including the Women's War, were demands for a return to tradition—just as Emecheta's critique of contact culture would suggest. As Amadiume points out, in "the earliest recorded mass protest movement by Igbo women" (in 1925), "The basic demand . . . was the rejection of Christianity and a return to traditional customs" (120). In the Women's War, "Women throughout Igboland were actually demanding the removal of the warrant chiefs and the closure of the native courts and European firms. Women had no place in the colonial government or law courts, and were rapidly losing out in the new economic structure" (140). Indeed, the Igbo women were so much more egalitarian in their thinking than were the British, that their demands were simply not comprehended by the British: "Even when reforms were made in 1933 as a result of the women's struggle, women's demands for a place in the judiciary and government were ignored as they seemed absurd to the British who were ignorant of, or so ethnocentric they could not accept the fact of indigenous women's organizations and their place in the traditional political structure" (140).

Moreover, though indigenous women lose traditional rights and privileges in the region of contact, traditional constraints are unlikely to be removed, and may even be exacerbated. Basic culture is, by definition, orthodox. And, as we have noted, orthodoxy is, most often, flexible. Strange events (e.g., a series of natural disasters) may give rise to short bouts of rigidity and originalism in which people insist that recent sufferings (e.g., drought) are due to social decadence and will come to an end only if society returns to its "original" and "pure" practices. But, despite these occasional periods of reaction, a basic culture is a culture of lived tradition. And lived tradition is always to a degree multiple, loose. In most cases, it is not strictly codified. If it is codified, it is often codified in multiple, vague, partially contradictory ways. Moreover, the codifications are often ignored anyway, for the codes do not have to be consulted as long as the living practices are proceeding in an ordinary, unproblematic way.

Note that, in the broad sense of the term *tradition*, all societies operate by traditions. And typically these traditions are vague and multiple. Think of the United States. We have a wide range of conventions about social interactions and personal behavior. Some of these are codified in law; some are codified nonlegally, for example in books of etiquette; some are a matter of uncodified expectation—that is, some behaviors will seem odd or objectionable to us, even though we could not formulate a principle that they violate. Note that even the codified principles are often very loose. For example, rules of etiquette apply differently depending upon the relations between the people involved and various other elements of context; not all rules are followed or advocated by all people; sometimes we expect a rule to be followed "most of the time," but not all the time. Even rules codified in law are loose to a degree. We feel that a police officer has done something extreme if he/she gives us a ticket for driving fifty-eight m.p.h. where the speed limit is fifty-five, or stops us for jaywalking.

We find exactly the same sort of looseness in any society. Of course, in any society, some things are not loose at all. The point is not that *everything* is up in the air, but that each society implicitly, and in part explicitly, decides what is important to its continuation or functioning and rigidifies its procedures to the degree that seems necessary. The situation is much the same in speech. English has a specifiable grammar and we could all be said to follow that grammar. But, in informal conversation, we follow that grammar only very loosely. A transcript of any discussion would show that we violate grammatical rules constantly, but no one involved has the sense that anything is odd about this. Of course, we cannot violate *any* rule of English. Some rules we observe quite rigidly. Here too there is a, largely functional, distinction between rigid, semirigid, and loose principles and applications of principles. The point seems generalizable to all aspects of social life.

The intrusion of colonial culture, however, alters this situation. Not only does it disrupt ordinary routines and beliefs. The colonizer ridicules and seeks to alter or outlaw aspects of the indigenous culture. One consequence of this is reactionary traditionalism. Practices that had earlier been followed sporadically and loosely may become rigidified and absolute in the face of colonialist objections. This is, indeed, fully consistent with the view of openness and rigidity as largely a matter of function. Practices challenged by the colonizer—including practices harmful to women—can very easily come to be foci of debate over the value of the indigenous culture. In that way, they come to be seen as crucial to the preservation of the culture, even when their position in the culture had previously been of marginal significance. In consequence, colonialist derogation of indigenous practices—including traditional aspects of the treatment of women—can quite easily have the effect of intensifying and multiplying those practices, and forcing the indigenous culture to see them as central to cultural survival. Colonial intrusion can produce such effects indirectly as well, by way of broader social destruction or economic devastation.

Consider the practice of *sati*. Ashis Nandy argues that (*At the Edge,* 1):

> For over 150 years, the legal abolition in 1829 of sati, the Hindu rite of widows committing suicide after the death of their husbands, has been considered the first victory of the modern world over Hindu obscurantism and primitivism. I contend . . . that the epidemic of sati in the late eighteenth- and early nineteenth-centuries was mainly a product of British colonial intrusion into Indian society; that the popularity of the rite and its abolition in response to a reform movement were two phases in Indian society's attempt to cope with large-scale environmental and cultural changes; and that both these changes involved the invalidation and distortion of traditional attitudes to woman and femininity.

Nandy points out that "By the beginning of the eighteenth century [*sati*] had become a rare occurrence" (3). It was only after the development of a massive economic and cultural presence of the British that the rite became widely practiced, breaking out in a sort of "orgy" in the economically devastated, famine ridden, and culturally threatened regions of high intensity contact, most particularly Bengal (4). Nandy argues persuasively that this is not mere coincidence.

Of course, it does sometimes happen that the colonial power has a positive effect on ending a certain form of oppression. But, in such cases, the effect is often little more than one contributory factor in an accumulating development *within* the indigenous society, and it is typically not a matter of direct intervention. Consider purdah, the confinement of women. It seems fairly clear that the absence of purdah among the British, the free interaction between men and women fostered by the British presence in India, Indian travel to England, and, of course, larger changes in economic and social structure—including changes in dress, work patterns, architecture, and other matters not directly relevant to gender relations—encouraged some Indians to question their adherence to this practice (for discussion, see Borthwick). And, indeed, the practice declined considerably over the course of the nineteenth century.

On the other hand, it was not outlawed, and thus never became too obvious a point of contention over cultural identity. Indeed, the issue of cultural conflict was dulled in this case by the view—false, but apparently widespread among Hindus—that purdah was a Muslim imposition and was unknown to Hindus prior to Muslim domination. Thus, Hindus could see the ending of purdah less as a capitulation to English culture than as a return to Hindu culture that had been distorted by the influence of Islam. Moreover, at least to some extent, the decline was related to the shift from a feudal to a capitalist economy, with its different patterns of work and socialization, which almost certainly would have eroded the practice without British cultural presence. Finally, as one would expect, even in this case, British disapproval of purdah led reactionary tradition- alists to insist on its importance to Indian, and more particularly Muslim, culture and may therefore have extended the practice in some areas.

In addition to all this, one should not assume that the British invariably opposed indigenous customs that violated British ethical principles. Some- times, the British opposed indigenous efforts at reform, when they perceived reform as running against British interests. For example, Isichei recounts how "The British trading community opposed . . . vehemently" indigenous efforts to end human sacrifice in nineteenth-century Calabar (97).

Thus, colonized women in regions of high intensity contact are unlikely to be freed from indigenous patriarchal oppression, except in very limited ways and in very limited circumstances. Indeed, European intervention seems, on the whole, more likely to worsen this oppression than to ameliorate it, for it often leads to reactionary rigidification and in some cases blocks indigenous efforts at reform.

In addition to living with the continuing and perhaps even worsened effects of indigenous patriarchy—often without the corresponding rights and institutional support of traditional women's communities—the colo- nized woman in the region of contact is likely to find herself burdened by European constraints as well. For example, in contact culture, an indige- nous woman is likely to be condemned for anything that might be con- sidered a violation of Igbo propriety *and* for anything that might be con- sidered a violation of European propriety. Consider a very narrow issue—modesty. Europeans may find a woman immodest if she does not cover most of her body. Igbo may consider a woman immodest if she exchanges more than two or three brief sentences with a man when they are not part of a group. An Igbo woman in the contact culture is likely to be required to cover most of her body, thus satisfying the European constraint—but disturbing her practical identity as it bears on dress—and to limit her conversations with men, thus satisfying the Igbo constraint.

If she violates either restriction, she is likely to be criticized as immodest or even to some degree ostracized.

In sum, indigenous women are not liberated by colonialism, but triply oppressed. They disproportionately suffer the political economy of colonialism, the exacerbated patriarchy of the home culture, and the patriarchy of the metropolis. More simply, they have the worst of both worlds. In *The Joys of Motherhood*, Nnu Ego has to fulfill all the obligations of Igbo womanhood and simultaneously fulfill all the obligations of European womanhood. Moreover, she has to do so in the midst of extreme economic deprivation and exploitation, for which she and her children suffer far more than her husband.

It is important to stress again that the standard, liberal view—against which Emecheta's novel argues so powerfully—is not only wrong, but is part of a continuing colonialism. It remains part of the liberal ideology of the West that European women are more liberated than non-European women, that white women can provide a model to African, Arab, and Asian women, who otherwise might not think of seeking liberation. This has been a crucial point of contention between white and nonwhite feminists. In literature, it turns up repeatedly in the standard image of the patronizing liberal white woman who tries to befriend and educate a woman of color. Indeed, it works its way into a whole series of evaluations—including such local, but important matters as curricular decisions, hiring, tenure, publication. It colors the way in which Americans, especially white Americans, read literature by or about Third World women, the ways in which they interpret that literature, the Third World women they are likely to hire in literature departments. One important function of Emecheta's novel is to respond to this standard, and highly consequential, view. Indeed, what Emecheta shows us is that, if Igbo women are worse off than Europeans, it is only because of colonialism, and that traditional Igbo society, which was thriving in the mid-nineteenth century, granted far more economic autonomy and political authority to women than did the England of Jean Rhys's madwoman in the attic.

EMECHETA AND NWAPA: WOMEN'S CULTURE OR WOMEN'S ECONOMY

Despite this deep concern with the effect of contact culture on women's lives, Emecheta's approach to women's liberation is not primarily culturalist in orientation. In other words, it does not make culture primary. Rather, Emecheta's is largely a materialist or economic, even Marxist approach. This is particularly clear when one compares *The Joys of Motherhood* with its major precursor, Flora Nwapa's *Efuru*, which is, centrally, a work of culturalist feminism.

Much of the narrative structure of Emecheta's novel, the ironic focus on the "joys" of motherhood, and even the phrase, "the joys of motherhood," itself, are drawn from Nwapa (the last point has been noted by Fishburn [105] and others). For instance, Nnu Ego, like Efuru, is her father's favorite child. In both cases, her special relationship with her father is due to the fact that the girl's mother was the father's one true love. Both go through an initial marriage which fails, and a second marriage that leads to separation after the husband is jailed. Both have a period of infertility, followed by the birth of a child who subsequently dies. The two novels take up many of the same motifs, from slavery to the prohibition on native liquor. Nwapa repeatedly uses the phrase "joy of motherhood," most importantly at the very end of *Efuru*, when she refers to the "woman of the lake": "She had never experienced the joy of motherhood. Why then did the women worship her?" (221). Indeed, this emphasis on the woman of the lake has influenced Emecheta's treatment of the slave woman who becomes Nnu Ego's *chi*.

However, the differences are, in many ways, more important than the similarities. Most obviously, Efuru is a novel of cultural self-affirmation. It is the story of a woman drawing strength from a part of tradition, a part of orthodoxy, that is occluded in anthropological accounts of African culture and in reactionary traditionalism—female cosmology: "The woman of the lake. . . . She was happy, she was wealthy. She was beautiful. She gave women beauty and wealth" (221). Moreover, Efuru is largely a practical and highly independent woman, little given to brooding, emotionalism, or self-pity, and inclined rather to pursue her best interests.

The Joys of Motherhood, in contrast, is primarily a novel of despair. It is the story of a woman whose strength is drained away as tradition of any sort—including female cosmology—becomes inaccessible or irrelevant in economically devastating circumstances. The difference is neatly exemplified in the opposed relations between the two women and their female water spirits. While Efuru envisions an empowering devotion to the woman of the lake, Nnu Ego, trying to drown herself after her first child's death, can imagine a desperate, suicidal reunion only.

One reason for this difference is that Nnu Ego largely accepts the
ideology that oppresses her, and finds that many other women do also—
especially in practice, though also in idea. "But who made the law that
we should not hope in our daughters?" she asks. "We women subscribe
to that law more than anyone. Until we change all this, it is still a man's
world, which women will always help to build" (187). This is one
important reason why Emecheta makes Nnu Ego's female *chi* malevo-
lent, transforms her from the inspiring figure of the woman of the lake
into a figure of cruelty and despair. As we shall see, Emecheta recognizes
and stresses the power and importance of women's solidarity. But she
does not believe that this is in any way easy to achieve. This view is no
less in keeping with Igbo cosmology than that emphasized by Nwapa.
As Amadiume points out, just as Idemili, the river goddess, aids women,
Ogwugwu makes them fail—at work, at child bearing, and so on. Just
as Efuru seeks inspiration and aid from the Idemili-like goddess, Nnu
Ego sees herself as, in part, the victim of an Ogwugwu-like counterpart.

But this is not the only reason for the difference between Efuru and
Nnu Ego. Even more important is the simple fact that Nnu Ego is living
in Lagos, in the contact culture in which women are doubly or triply
constrained. Efuru lives in an area that has certainly been affected,
deeply affected, by colonialism. Nonetheless, it is still predominantly a
culturally autonomous region. Again, the loss of this relative autonomy
in the contact culture, and its destructive effects on the lives of women,
is one of Emecheta's central themes.

Indeed, precisely this theme—and its relation to Emecheta's materialism—is crystallized strikingly in the name of Emecheta's protago-
nist: Nnu Ego. The literal, Igbo meaning of the term is "twenty bags of
cowries" (20). This meaning is important—both for the themes of the
novel and for Emecheta's differences from Nwapa—and we shall return
to it in a moment. However, the novel is written in English and in some
ways its most important meanings are those suggested by its similarities
with English. Virtually every English speaker is likely to pronounce
Nnu Ego's name in such a way as to make it homophonous with "new
ego," perhaps with a hint of "no ego" as well. This is, I think, exactly
Nnu Ego's role in the novel. She is the new ego or new identity—both
practical and reflective—that is imposed on the colonized woman in the
contact culture. And this new identity is, in effect, no identity at all. By
being subjected to the constraints of both indigenous and metropolitan
culture, Nnu Ego/New Ego loses any ability to act for herself. The idea

is expressed clearly at the end of the novel, "The joy of being a mother was the joy of giving all to your children" (224). In the home culture—the phrase happens to be uttered in the indigenous region—a commonplace such as this was severely qualified by the broad areas of autonomy open to women; in contact culture, it became absolute, and absolutely stifling.

Finally, and most significantly, in Emecheta's portrayal of the situation, this complete devastation of female identity is not, again, primarily a matter of culture. Rather, it is a matter of economy. Which returns us to the Igbo meaning of "Nnu Ego," "twenty bags of cowries." This is, first of all, the sum of money paid in a bride price (26, 39). As such, it implies that, even in traditional Igbo culture, Nnu Ego and other women find their cultural identity inhibited because they are reduced to their exchange value, their monetary equivalent. But the resonance of the phrase is much broader than that. For, in reducing them to exchange value, society reduces women not only to bride price, but to labor capacity—what they can produce, both in terms of crops and in terms of children. Clearly, this is inhibiting, restrictive, even in basic Igbo culture. But in the contact culture—where Igbo women assume their "new ego"—women's exchange value, or more exactly their capacity to produce exchange value, their ability to earn and to sustain themselves and their children through productive labor, is devastated. In Emecheta's view, a colonized woman in the contact culture loses her cultural identity, her ego, because she loses her economic identity; her practical and reflective identities are erased—or at least far more thoroughly constrained to routines and ideas that benefit others only—precisely to the degree that her autonomous, productive role in economy is erased. The point is particularly clear when Nnu Ego is contrasted with her mother, Ona, who lived her whole life in the culturally autonomous region. While Nnu Ego has no ego, Ona was "egocentric" (12); while Nnu Ego's name represents her reduction to the bride price of "twenty bags of cowries," Ona's name meant "priceless jewel" (11), a value irreducible to a monetary equivalent.

In keeping with this, the conflicts between women in *Joys*—the conflicts that undermine solidarity—are largely economic. For example, Nnu Ego is unbridgeably separated from Igbonoba's wife by class, by the fact that the latter wears a head tie, the cost of which *"would feed [Nnu Ego] and the children for a whole month"* (163). Her conflicts with Adaku too are, fundamentally, economic—a matter of competition over trade, but also a matter of the benefits of having male children, benefits that, in traditional society, are economic also, for sons stay in the parental home and thus support their parents. The point extends back even to traditional practices, for the conflict between Nnu Ego and her *chi* is the conflict between the daughter of a slave owner and her father's slave—another cultural opposition that is, at base, economic.

At the same time, however, as we shall see in more detail below, economy not only divides women, but provides the possibility for their joining together and altering their condition. Economic cooperation among women can be the basis for women's empowerment, as when the women of Lagos first teach Nnu Ego how to buy and sell goods in the city (see 52). Here too the difference between Emecheta and Nwapa is clear and revealing. Both advocate women's bonding. But Nwapa advocates this in the cultural context of female cosmology, while Emecheta advocates it in the economic context of female cooperative work and business.

In sum, Emecheta's is, in effect, a Marxist view. For Emecheta, Nnu Ego is reduced to the status of a cultureless slave precisely to the degree that her economic security is shattered. She has no secure place in culture, precisely to the extent that she has no secure place in productive economy. In contrast, Nwapa's view in *Efuru* is primarily culturalist. In *Efuru*, women have greater autonomy already, if they are willing to act on it, if they are willing to choose the tradition of women's solidarity and cosmology—as well as women's medicine, and other female cultural practices (for discussion, see my "How Sisters"). The two views are not unrelated. Nwapa clearly recognizes that women need an economic base upon which their traditions can rest. And Emecheta stresses the importance of women's sense of mutual identification. However, even here, the differences are clear. In Nwapa, the economic base is primarily a matter of having enough to eat. It is a brute condition of life. In Emecheta, the economic base is a highly complex determinant of one's options for social action. As to culture, in Nwapa, women's mutual identification is a matter of preserving the vast store of medical and other knowledge held by women, continuing their traditions of tales and wisdom and mutual help in all aspects of life, and subsuming all of this under a female cosmology centered around a female divinity. In Emecheta, in contrast, the sense of identification seems to be primarily the much narrower matter of recognizing common interests and cooperating toward the achievement of concrete economic goals.

Gender in Basic Culture

But, of course, Emecheta does not ignore culture in Nwapa's sense. Quite the contrary. Culture is a central focus of the novel, even if its force and function are always contingent upon economy. As we have already noted, Emecheta clearly delineates the characterizations and roles, the reflective and practical identities, of women and men in indigenous culture. And she systematically differentiates these from the gender identities created in the contact culture. Indeed, the novel begins in the autonomous region, establishing indigenous identities as a standard with which the contact identities can be compared and contrasted. At the outset, indigenous culture remains relatively unaffected by colonialism. The Ibuza villagers are certainly aware of the white man and his culture. Agbadi's friend, Idayi, even declares that "This is the age of the white man. Nowadays every young man wants to cement his mud hut and cover it with corrugated-iron sheets instead of the palm leaves we are used to" (37). But the very fact that this has to be mentioned, that the idea of cement houses must be set out in detail as an aspiration of the younger generation, indicates its distance from the daily lives of the villagers. Much later, we learn that a Catholic school is operating in Ibuza (147), but we hear relatively little about it, and Christian teachings appear to have no impact on the practices and beliefs surrounding Agbadi's death and burial, which occur later still. In Ibuza, it seems, the only significant impact of Europe derives from an earlier period, the period of the slave trade—and in this case the resultant changes are not so much a matter of European cultural influence, as of internal distortion in Igbo tradition.

Nnu Ego's father, Nwokocha Agbadi, is a highly sympathetic representative of orthodox masculinity. He is "a great wrestler," "gifted in oratory" (10), and "one of the bravest hunters the world had ever seen" (154). By Igbo standards, he is great in everything that makes a man. Moreover, he does not surrender any of his authority in personal relations. He is mocking in his speech (17) and refuses to betray his feelings, at least any that would suggest a form of weakness or vulnerability, in some ways like Okonkwo. Indeed, his tendency to excess in this regard is balanced by the more conciliatory attitude of his friend Idayi, who parallels Obierika in this respect. For example, when Ona nurses Agbadi back to health after he has been gored by an elephant, Agbadi will not thank her. She becomes angry, and Idayi intervenes, saying, "We are grateful to you and to your father, I assure you. If Agbadi were to lower himself to thank you, I am sure you would stop caring for him. You need a man, Ona, not a snail" (17).

But, while Agbadi suppresses the verbal expression of feelings, he does not suppress the feelings themselves, or actions based on those feelings. Nor does he fear affectionate intimacy with a woman. He is harsh with Ona, but his devotion to her is obvious. He dotes fondly on Nnu Ego as well. Though fully an Igbo man, he is fully human also, and does not seek to suppress in any way what is common to himself and others, including women. Indeed, he recognizes the importance of affection in marriage. In choosing his own wives, Agbadi sought women who could match his sharp tongue and spirit, but also, "his human tenderness" (10; it is important that Emecheta characterizes this tenderness as "human" and not as masculine or feminine). In seeking a husband for Nnu Ego, Agbadi "wanted a man who would be patient with her, who would value his daughter enough to understand her." Indeed, he recognizes that the ability to love a woman is part of depth in character, and that inability to love is a part of shallowness: "The art of loving, he knew, required deeper men" (36). In keeping with her general themes, Emecheta has Agbadi explain the absence of such of depth not in psychological and individualist terms, but in terms of economics and, implicitly, the economic changes that were being introduced by colonialism. Those who could love were "Men who did not have to spend every moment of their time working and worrying about food and the farm. Men who could spare the time to think. This quality was becoming rarer and rarer" (36).

This humanity of Agbadi is perhaps most obvious at the time of his death. He struggles to keep himself alive until he can see his beloved daughter from whom he has been separated for ten years. He maintains his pride, his orthodox masculine nonexpression of feeling. But the signs of that feeling are, in consequence, all the more powerful. Nnu Ego cries out, "Oh, Father, I did not imagine. . . . Why did I not come earlier?" Agbadi, in contrast, gives his "low, wicked chuckle" (152). But he has held off his death for five days (152) simply to see her, protesting that it is not his own affection, but the need of her long dead mother, whom he will meet when he joins the ancestors: "What will I tell my Ona if she asks me how our only daughter is? How could I tell her that I have not seen our child for the past ten years?" (158). The statement shows not only his feeling for Nnu Ego, but a feeling for Ona so enduring that it structures his very imagination of death. Twice he wakes in the middle of the night "telling Nnu Ego scraps of stories about her childhood and then falling asleep again" (153). He promises her that he will be reborn in her house. And he is reborn, not long thereafter, in the baby boy named "Nnamdio," "meaning: 'This is my father'" (155). And Nnamdio is the only one of Nnu Ego's children who explicitly does not wish for the white man's wealth and education. He longs for tradition; even as a small child, his ambition is "to be a hunter. A hunter with the title 'Killer of elephants'" (201)—that, because, in his life as Agbadi, he had almost been killed by an elephant, but was nursed to health by his beloved Ona. In the end, when Nnu Ego returns to Ibuza, Nnamdio accompanies her.

Agbadi's indirect expressions of love are more sincere, more moving, more human for his suppression of tears and exclamations. It is little wonder that, when he dies, Nnu Ego "let[s] out a loud cry to tell the world that her father . . . the noblest and kindest of all parents, had gone" (154). And also little wonder that Adankwo, the chief wife (now widowed) of Nnu Ego's oldest brother-in-law, though "a woman of few words" who was never "glib of speech" (157), eulogizes him as "a man with such nobility of spirit it defied explanation" (158).

But the point here is not that Agbadi's views and acts were entirely individual, idiosyncratic, removed from the structure of Igbo life. Indeed, the point is just the opposite. His excellence was that he incarnated the tradition in a way few men do. Thus, Emecheta emphasizes that his affection for Ona was not odd, but fully in keeping with Igbo standards. Ona is sharp-tongued, and proud, and independent. But it is not due to some sort of liberalism or strange personal taste, and certainly not due to Europeanization, that Agbadi loves her. It is because he is Igbo: "To regard a woman who is quiet and timid as desirable was something that came after his time, with Christianity and other changes" (10). Even in the next generation, Nnu Ego and other women are "taught to wrestle like men, to learn the art of self-defence" (60). And Nnu Ego herself is able to floor men who try to wrestle with her, as we learn when a man tries to stop her from committing suicide (60).

Of course, this is not to say that traditional Igbo society was not a patriarchy. Igbo women were much better off than English women in the period immediately preceding African colonization, as the case of Antoinette indicates. But they were still oppressed in some degree. First of all, though independence was thought to make women attractive, wives were simultaneously prized for devotion and unobtrusiveness. Thus, despite Ona's obvious attractiveness, "People said . . . what person in his right mind would leave his big spacious household and women who were willing to worship and serve him in all things to go after a rude, egocentric woman who had been spoilt by her father?" (12). Agbadi himself praises his oldest wife as "a good woman. So unobtrusive, so quiet" (22). Moreover, his senior wife, Agunwa, sees Ona as "troublesome and impetuous," "a bad woman" who had "the audacity to fight with her man before letting him have her" (21).

In this way, Ona is an instance of the common literary figure of the uniquely independent traditional woman, the unusual woman who manages to carve out a space of independence for herself within a traditional order, to draw from the loose and partially contradictory tradition precisely those elements that can operate to give women autonomy, much like Aunt Abida in Hosain or Aunt Lucia in Dangarembga or Anjanupu in Nwapa. Moreover, like these other cases of independent traditional women, Ona maintains her independence largely because she remains unmarried—though this too is part of the larger patriarchal structure, in that she remains unmarried for patriarchal reasons: "Because her father had no son, she had been dedicated to the gods to produce children in his name, not that of any husband" (17–18). She was able to remain independent because she was dependent upon her father, rather than her husband.

The situation is similar with respect to Nnu Ego. In Igbo tradition, a woman was a "complete woman" only if she was a mother (see 22). When Nnu Ego fails to conceive with her first husband, she is abused and, in the end, badly beaten (35). Agbadi takes her back home and arranges another marriage, looking for a "deeper" man, a man who can love. Nnu Ego escapes the situation, and retains a degree of autonomy, largely because she remains under the protection of her father.

On the other hand, this protection—like the protection of Ona's father—is not entirely a matter of individual will. It too is a matter of tradition. Agbadi acknowledges common attitudes toward barren women when he says to Nnu Ego's first husband, "Amatokwu, I don't blame you for beating her so badly" (35). But later he denounces the behavior and the people who engage in it: "That marriage should never have taken place. I don't think much of people who illtreat a woman because she has not yet borne a child" (37–38). The implication here is that Amatokwo's attitudes and actions are, in fact, objectionable from the point of view of an orthodox Igbo man, even if they are technically acceptable. In other words, even if they do not, strictly speaking, violate any rules, they contradict the broader values and more encompassing practices of the tradition. Indeed, this conflict might indicate the possibility of a change in the rules. The indecency of Amatokwo's actions occurs to Agbadi much as it occurs to Obierika that the killing of twins is a practice inconsistent with the broader sense of justice in Igbo life. There is even a suggestion, undeveloped, that the ill-treatment of Nnu Ego may have been an indirect result of colonization. "I wish Nnu Ego had been born in our time," Agbadi says to Idayi; "When we were young, men valued the type of beauty she has." Idayi responds, "Nevertheless, the fact is, my friend, she was not born then; she was born in her own time. Things have changed a lot. This is the age of the white man" (37). Moreover, Agbadi's wives immediately welcome Nnu Ego home and make "her feel that though she had not borne a child, her father's house was bursting with babies she could regard as her own" (35). At the very least, this would seem to indicate that social condemnation of a "barren" woman was not so harsh as to impede family affection or bring shame.

Indeed, Nnu Ego's return from her first marriage leads her father to question and reject another "traditional" practice in Igbo society—slavery. First, he offers freedom to his slaves. Then, "All those in his own compound who refused to go were adopted as his children; he had seen to it that proper adoption procedure was carried out, in that they were dipped in the local stream and had the chalk of acceptance sprinkled on them" (35). It is important to stress that Agbadi ends his involvement with slavery in an entirely orthodox way. Indeed, Emecheta stresses the orthodoxy, in pointing out that Agbadi "had seen to it that proper adoption procedure was carried out." Moreover, his act here is the direct inverse of Okonkwo's killing of Ikemefuna. Okonkwo had repudiated his common humanity and treated Ikemefuna as a slave to be sacrificed, even though the boy called him "father." Agbadi, in contrast, accepts his common humanity with the slaves even to the extent of making them his children. In short, Agbadi does not disavow his shared humanity with slaves or with women, and he accommodates this shared humanity within the loose structures of his traditional culture, avoiding both Europeanization and reactionary traditionalism. Agbadi's act here is a fine example of the degree to which orthodoxy is open to change, revision, reform.

Emecheta gives two different, and seemingly contradictory, explanations for this act. One is that Agbadi was acting "for the emotional health of his beloved daughter Nnu Ego" (35). The other is that "the white man says [slavery] is illegal" (51). The two statements can, however, be reconciled. Faced with a law such as that outlawing slavery, a traditional Igbo man may respond in one of several ways. He may simply conform to the law, sacrificing that part of his own tradition, and entering on a process of synthesis or even assimilation. He might rebel against the law and affirm the practice all the more vehemently, taking up a reactionary traditionalist position. Or, he might, so to speak, use the provocation as reason to rethink his own traditions, examining the degree to which he can make the same decision based not on British tradition, but on Igbo tradition. If done sincerely, this is a way in which he can retain orthodoxy, without violating the new law—if he finds it reasonable. Note that Agbadi's actions cannot be explained merely as conformity to law, for the law does not entail his advocacy of slaves returning to their homelands (35) or, even more obviously, his official adoption of some slaves through traditional ceremonies. If he were simply conforming to the British law, there would be no need for these further steps. Indeed, they would hardly make any sense.

But how does his freeing and adopting the slaves bear on his love for Nnu Ego? A *dibia* (a divine and a healer) had explained Nnu Ego's barrenness as the result of her *chi*, a slave woman killed by one of Agbadi's sons: "The slave woman who was her *chi* would not give her a child because she had been dedicated to a river goddess before Agbadi took her away in slavery" (31). Agbadi is "begging the slave woman to forgive him for taking her away from her original home" (35). The remorse is real, though the plea is triggered by his daughter's dilemma. This is not the first time that Agbadi had felt the injustice of practices surrounding slavery, as is clear from the scene in which this slave is killed. When his senior wife died, she was to be supplied with a slave to aid her in the other world. Agbadi made the order himself: "Make sure that her slave and her cooking things go with her" (22). Yet, while "A good slave was supposed to jump into the grave willingly," this woman "kept begging for her life." So, "Agbadi's eldest son . . . in anger . . . gave the woman a sharp blow with the head of the cutlass he was carrying" (23). Though he had not yet fully recovered from being gored by the elephant, "'Stop that at once!' Agbadi roared, limping up to his son." He chastised the son, saying, "What do you call this, bravery? You make my stomach turn" (23). Though he ordained the ceremony, Agbadi even then maintained a sense of common humanity, which could later grow into remorse, and spur social change.

The image of the slave woman, dedicated to a river goddess, stolen into slavery, sacrificed by Agbadi's eldest son, and now determining Nnu Ego's life, is resonant in many ways. Most obviously, Nnu Ego's situation is, in effect, a situation of slavery, her fate that of a slave. It is equally a situation of sacrifice. The slave woman was a human sacrifice, and Nnu Ego's fate is to be a human sacrifice as well, metaphorically at least, for she does give up her own life for her husband and for her children. Indeed, when she initially meets and has painful intercourse with her second husband, it is in a "square room painted completely white like a place of sacrifice" (46).

But there are other implications as well. One leads us back to Nwapa. The slave woman was integrated into the feminine cosmology that Nwapa celebrates, before she was torn away by capture and enslavement. The image is presented too briefly to be entirely clear. But perhaps it suggests a lost tie with a tradition of women, or the way connections between women have been cut, the way men have put a knife on the things that held women together, for, as we shall see, part of Nnu Ego's problem is that she never forges, is never able to forge, links with other women, links of belief and common work and mutual aid.

The image has psychoanalytic resonances as well. In this context, one might say that Nnu Ego is haunted by a too-early separation from her mother, who died when Nnu Ego was still an infant—a too early separation which has taken literary shape, just as it might take shape in a dream, through the figure of the slave who determines her destiny. It is easy to see the connections and the way the image has been transformed by standard dream mechanisms—the slave dies when one of Agbadi's wives dies, shortly after Nnu Ego is conceived. This is a displacement from Nnu Ego's situation, for her mother dies not long after she is born. The slave and this other "mother" are buried together in a sort of inversion of the symbiotic union of mother and child. Moreover, the slave had already been torn away from the river goddess to whom she was dedicated, a metaphoric image of the separation from the fluid, encompassing maternal womb. It is fitting that this too early separation should manifest itself in this literary dream as an inability to become a mother—an inability that first separates Nnu Ego from her husband, and returns her to her home, and subsequently leads her to seek death by drowning in the maternal waters of the river: "She would . . . seek out and meet her *chi* . . . not on this earth but in the land of the dead, there deep beneath the waters of the sea." "She knew her *chi* was a woman" and, as if addressing a cruel mother, "she would ask her why she had punished her so" (9). Indeed, this also fits with Nnu Ego's inability to separate herself at all from her children. And it exacerbates the trauma of their rejection of her—for when her children reject her, the separation in effect repeats her separation from her own mother.

It is no accident that, after her death, the slave woman appears in the novel twice, both times in dreams. By placing her appearance in dreams, Emecheta allows us to interpret her function both cosmologically and psychoanalytically, for dreams may be understood, as they are in most societies, as communications with other worlds—the world of the dead, the future—or they may be understood, as in psychoanalysis, as expressions of the unconscious. In the first dream, Nnu Ego sees the slave woman handing her "a baby boy, by the banks of the Atakpo stream in Ibuza," presumably the stream in which her father performed the ceremony of adoption for his former slaves. But, when Nnu Ego "tried to wade across the stream to take the baby . . . the stream seemed to swell, and the woman's laughter rang out." The slave woman repeatedly "tantalised" her in this way (45). This was before the birth of Nnu Ego's first child. This child, a son, tantalizes Nnu Ego with the prospect of being a mother. But, like Ona's first son, he dies in infancy, evidently an *ogbanje* child, a child from the spirit world who is born only for a short time, usually to be reborn in a continuing cycle of birth and death, which tortures the mother. Tantalos provides an apt image. Suffering from great thirst, he was placed "in a pool of water which always receded when tried to drink from it" (Harvey, 414). It was a punishment for killing his son, Pelops. Tantalos had a daughter, relevant as well—Niobe. When Niobe boasted of her many children, Apollo and Artemis killed them all, leaving her childless. Indeed, the entire complex of myths surrounding Tantalos is relevant to the suggestiveness of the image, for those myths focus repeatedly on the loss or murder of children.

The image of the child emerging from the water also recalls what, in neighboring Dahomey at least, was called the *tohosu* child (see Herskovits and Herskovits, 30ff.). Connected with the spirits of the water, and linked with the *ogbanje*, a *tohosu* in effect sucks his/her parents dry, by consuming everything of theirs and returning nothing. The most famous image of this child is in Tutuola's *The Palm-Wine Drinkard*, the child who eats everything the family owns and is still not satisfied. This image is clearer in the second dream. There, Nnu Ego finds a child abandoned beside a stream—*tohosu* children were abandoned "at water's edge" (see Herskovits and Herskovits, 31). She subsequently gave birth to Oshia, who, like a *tohosu* child, would ultimately suck her dry of everything, take all life out of her, and return nothing—not because of his links with the water spirits, but because of the structure and ideology of motherhood in the region of contact, where "The joy of being a mother was the joy of giving all to your children" (224). In keeping with both the religious imagery and the real conditions of colonialism, in the end, Oshia too retreats across the water, like the child of the first dream, and Nnu Ego loses him to a foreign woman, with skin even lighter than that of the water people.

Perhaps most importantly, however, this psychological trauma of severance from the mother serves as a sort of metaphor for Nnu Ego's severance from Igbo tradition. And here the image of the slave enters again, and more complexly. For the trade in slaves had indeed distorted Igbo society many decades earlier. It had warped the practices and human feelings of those involved, and twisted the traditions that had sustained Igbo life for centuries. It is not at all absurd for Agbadi to free his slaves and simultaneously to seek orthodoxy. Quite the contrary. It was, rather, absurd to pretend that orthodoxy had been maintained despite the slave trade. As Isichei explains, human sacrifice was a relatively limited practice in traditional Igboland, but "In the years of the slave trade, the practice of human sacrifice expanded vastly" (47). Moreover, the practice of servitude to a god—such as occurred with Nnu Ego's *chi*—"underwent . . . distortion and corruption" (47).

In sum, "The nineteenth century was one in which the shadow of the trade in slaves overshadowed every aspect of Igbo life," especially in a general "cheapening of human life" which systematically twisted Igbo culture. In a sense, Nnu Ego is condemned by history, by the cruelties of her forebears who advanced themselves by destroying others, and by perverting their own culture. Her destiny is determined by a dead slave girl in this, allegorical sense too. Her suffering is in many ways a direct result of the sins of her ancestors in the treatment of slaves—not in some mystical sense of spiritual retribution, but in the very material sense that the slave trade distorted the entire society in which she was born and grew to maturity.

GENDER IN CONTACT CULTURE: MASCULINITY

But, again, in contact culture, things are very different from the home culture, and far worse. Colonial ideology is pervasive. Ideology of race, ideology of gender, religious ideology, economic and political ideology saturate the existence of Nnu Ego and her second husband, Nnaife. Sometimes it manifests itself in minor matters, or seemingly minor matters. Nnaife buys native liquor, *ogogoro*, and pours it "into bottles labelled 'Scotch Whisky,'" because *ogogoro* is outlawed. Nnu Ego asks, "Why do they call our *ogogoro* illicit?" Nnu Ego, forced to attend Christian services every Sunday in order to protect her husband's job, and thus subjected to weekly sermons which dealt with a wide range of colonialist issues beyond the text of the Bible, suspects that European gin is purer, and thus that the law is necessary (111). Indeed, not only was native liquor derided as impure, some types of imported alcohol were touted as having an "astonishing array of health-giving properties" and "Nigerians," Isichei tells us, "put pathetic confidence in these promises" (108).

In this case, Nnaife is less fully ideologized, primarily because he has been rendered cynical by years of living in the daily hopelessness and cruelty of the contact culture. In any case, he contradicts Nnu Ego's view, saying that native gin "is even stronger and purer" than the imported variety. He goes on to explain that "If they allowed us to develop the production of our own gin, who would buy theirs?" (111). This, I take it, is Emecheta's account as well, and it is economic. In Nnaife's view, colonial law—in this case, the law governing liquor production and sale—is more or less directly determined by economic interest; the law is superstructure, the economy, base. And Nnaife is right. The profits reaped by British liquor sales in Nigeria were a crucial source of revenue. As Isichei points out, quoting a contemporary English observer, the Royal Niger Company "import what manufactured goods they choose, and practically impose them upon the native, who has a very limited and inferior class of articles from which to select." Significantly, "By the end of the nineteenth century, imports were overwhelmingly dominated by alcohol. In Nembe-Brass, gin accounted for 90 per cent of all imports." This not only profited the manufacturers and importers, but the Niger Coast Protectorate, "in fact, though not in name, a colonial government," (126). In keeping with import percentages, "In 1899, liquor accounted for 90 per cent of its customs revenue" (108).

Sometimes the ideologization is less subtle, and more obviously harmful. Hearing every week the supremacist teachings of the church and hearing every day the "low, patronising" laughter of the white masters and their casual deprecations—"'Good night, sah,' Nnaife said . . . Dr Meers . . . smiled mischievously and answered, 'Good night, baboon'" (Emecheta, 41)—many Africans living in the contact culture come to internalize colonialist views, slowly integrating demeaning characterizations into their own reflective identities. Many "Africans . . . were so used to being told they were stupid in those days that they started to believe in their own imperfections" (83).

Indeed, the contact culture systematically transforms the identity of the colonized people, undermining their practices and self-conceptions, perverting their ideas and habits of gender. The almost immediate effect of contact culture on men, according to Emecheta, is that they are entirely emasculated. First, they lose the loving character that Agbadi showed to be so crucial to orthodox Igbo masculinity; the "human tenderness" (10) that he exhibited and which he sought in Nnu Ego's husband. Agbadi had already noted that "The art of loving," which "required deeper men . . . was becoming rarer and rarer" (36); the implication was that, even in the village, the impact of colonialism was already having a deleterious effect on love. Emecheta expands the point. She directly criticizes the common view that in traditional societies, with arranged marriages, there is no love between spouses, but at best duty, at worst brutality. The hypocrisy of Europeans or Americans criticizing the marriage customs of other cultures is, of course, staggering—as our discussion of Rhys indicates. But Emecheta implies that not only is the stereotype wrong. It is almost exactly backward. It is, precisely, colonialism that undermines the "art of loving," the "human tenderness" prized by such orthodox men as Agbadi.

There are two reasons for this. One, a psychological reason, is the grimness of a constantly demeaned existence. The second, economic, and thus, for Emecheta, more important reason, is the necessity of constant labor in Lagos. The endless round of work for the white man leaves no time for leisure, and thus no time for *ars amatoria*. Moreover, the work itself is alienated into wages. It is not the fulfilling labor of the fields, producing food for oneself and one's family, and for trade which one performs oneself. It is, most often, slave-like labor for others, for the very white men and women whose daily scorn seeps into one's heart and makes one bitter against all life, against one's birth and family and nation and against oneself. And it is labor in the broader context of a commodity culture in which the only distractions and enjoyments come to be based on the purchase of new things, a culture that defines the roles of all men and women not as agents in ritual and law and work, but as consumers, a culture that, as Marx wrote, reduces all relations between people to relations between commodities, relations valued and defined by monetary equivalence. As Emecheta puts it, "That type of family awareness which the illiterate farmer was able to show his wives, his household, his compound, had been lost in Lagos, for the job of the white man, for the joy of buying expensive lappas, and for the feel of shiny trinkets" (52). Just after this, alluding to the commodification of all human relationships, and the reduction of human life to a purely mechanical wage labor judged in purely mechanical terms of monetary equivalents, Cordelia summarizes the situation: "They stopped being men long ago. Now they are machines" (53).

But Emecheta's criticism of colonialism is not primarily a criticism of mechanization. Rather, the cultural effects of colonialism most stressed and damned by Emecheta concern social hierarchies, and the ways in which the new situation transforms, and degrades, the position of Igbos. The two hierarchies on which she focuses are those of owner/slave and male/female. One could understand re-hierarchization in the contact culture in terms of a homology. In the case of gender, this would read: whites are to blacks as men are to women, so that contact culture makes black men into women relative to whites. In the case of slavery, the homology would read: whites are to blacks as owners are to slaves.

We have already suggested that Nnu Ego's *kakodaimonia*, her haunting by a mischievous *chi*, allegorizes her own "destiny" as a sort of slave, due both to her race and to her sex. But the depiction of Africans as slaves in their own country is far more extended. When Nnu Ego finally conceives a child, when she is finally to become a mother and thus make clear to the world that, by Igbo tradition, she is a "complete woman," Nnaife tells her that she must keep the pregnancy a secret, for their marriage is not recognized by the Christian church and thus, by the traditions of the colonizer, her pregnancy is a matter of shame—fornication, illegitimacy. "If I do not marry you in church . . . I may even lose my job," he explains. The whole business gives Nnu Ego "a sick sensation" and she thinks with revulsion "That she had to keep such a joyous thing as this quiet because of a shriveled old woman with ill-looking skin like the flesh of a pig!" She assesses the situation immediately. Nnaife is no longer a man, but an un-man and a slave: "was this a man she was living with? How could a situation rob a man of his manhood without him knowing it?" She denounces him: "You behave like a slave!" and demands, "I want to live with a man, not a woman-made man" (50). Later, she repeats the characterization to Cordelia, "These our husbands are like slaves, don't you think?" And Cordelia extends the analogy noting that, in this context, the women themselves are like the slaves of slaves: "They are all slaves, including us. If their masters treat them badly, they take it out on us" (51).

This is not merely the result of working in a white woman's home. Nnaife labors on a ship for eleven months. It is no better: "Their masters, not able to buy these workers outright, made them work like slaves anyway." Of course, "They were paid," but that only made them "paid slaves" (112)—"wage slaves," in the standard Marxian phrase. Men bound to the owners of capital as if they were themselves owned, for they are dependent for survival on their meager wages. Always teetering on the edge of destitution, their lives are entirely controlled by the demands of the capitalist. As Ubani observes, laughing "bitterly," "I talk like an old slave these days, grateful to be given a living at all" (117). But, of course, he is not "given" a living. He earns his own small wages and, along with his fellow workers, makes a magnificent living for his employers, those who own and control the means of production.

The imperial army is a part of the same structure, a means by which the ruling classes can make use of the underclasses to battle for raw materials, markets, trade routes, territory and further human resources, a means by which capitalists can set workers killing one another for the rival interests of capitalists. And here the slavery is even more obvious. In Lagos, one day, as work ends, Korofos round up the exiting workers, who are "pushed and bundled into the tarpaulin-covered army lorry" (144). The scene is closely reminiscent of a slave raid. The connection does not escape Nnaife: "We don't have slavery any more, so why should grown men be captured in broad daylight?" he wonders (145). Later, Ubani draws the link again: "There is nothing we can do. The British own us" (148). It is, of course, not literally true. But the British own all capital; they control the law; they monopolize the means of legitimate violence. They almost might as well own the people also.

Indeed, while this sort of wage slavery is probably less brutal than, say, American slavery, it may be, at least in some respects, more brutal than the sort of slavery practiced by the Igbo. Nigerians in Lagos lived in hunger and deprivation. Nnu Ego and her children are almost continually undernourished, at points barely evading starvation. In contrast, Igbo slaves "sometimes enjoyed a standard of living little different from their masters, and a reasonable degree of economic mobility" (Isichei, 101). Indeed, Isichei quotes one observer from the 1850s, noting that "Some of the old slaves . . . have themselves become owners of . . . many slaves" (101)—a notion that presents a literal precedent for the metaphorical double enslavement of women.

Of course, Igbo slaves could be, and were, sacrificed, as the case of Nnu Ego's *chi* testifies. But this was not a common practice. Nwakusor, for example, was from Ibuza. But, "He had never seen such a sacrifice." Indeed, he did not even know people who had seen such a sacrifice, he had only "heard of people who had witnessed such an uncommon sight" (59), the implication being that the last human sacrifice in Ibuza was that of Nnu Ego's *chi*. Second, while the British did not sacrifice Igbos to serve as cooks to dead leaders in the afterlife, they killed innumerable Igbos to enrich their leaders in this life—in the conquest of Igboland, in various incidents following conquest, in their own wars. As Isichei points out, "The wars fought to establish colonial rule in Igboland were fought in the name of the abolition of slavery, yet the regime they introduced was marked by the large-scale exaction of unwilling and unpaid labour." Moreover, "They were fought in the name of the abolition of human sacrifice, but no historian will ever be able to count the number of the human sacrifices they exacted" (139).

Again, in Emecheta's view, men are not only turned into slaves, they are unmanned too, "feminized." When Nnu Ego arrives, she sees Nnaife as "a man with a belly like a pregnant cow," whose "hair, unlike that of men . . . was not closely shaved," but long, "like that of a woman." His jaw was weak. She concludes that "marrying such a jelly of a man would be like living with a middle-aged woman!" (42). In Nnu Ego's view the contact culture has entirely feminized Nnaife, made him a pregnant cow, a weak-jawed, aging woman. "She was used to tall, wiry farmers, with rough, blackened hands from farming, long, lean legs and very dark skin" (43). Indeed, she generalizes the point, referring to the city as a "place where men's flesh hung loose on their bones, where men had bellies like pregnant women" (46).

The sources of effeminacy are the same as those that define enslavement. The first is work—initially, Nnaife's domestic service and his absolute subordination to the white woman. When Nnu Ego arrives, Nnaife is ironing (41). Later, her stomach turns to see him washing the undergarments of the white woman, with her skin of a sickly pig, and then to hear him "talking effusively about his treatment of dainty clothes" (47). She chides him, "A man, huh? Some man . . . a man who washes women's underwear. A man indeed!" (48–49). Cordelia expands the point: "Men here are too busy being white men's [and, more importantly, white women's] servants to be men. . . . Their manhood has been taken away from them. The shame of it is that they don't know it." And, of course, they don't know it because, in their new circumstances, the only value is exchange value. There is no longer value in traditional practices, the role and idea of a man. Thus, "All they see is the money, shining white man's money" (51).

The army too is not only enslaving, but emasculating. When they were rounded up, "Men screamed like women as some of them were caught" (144). And when told of their forced conscription to fight a war for their oppressors, "some men wept with tears pouring shamelessly from their eyes" (146).

Nnu Ego imagines her son growing up to be a real man, a traditional Igbo man, entirely unlike his father: "a handsome young man, black and shiny of skin like carved ebony, tall, straight and graceful like the trunk of a palm tree, with no fat anywhere but strong bones set inside his perfect body" (78). She can imagine this masculine physique precisely because she imagines him to be engaged in autonomous and unalienated labor, not the unmanly tasks and wage slavery of Nnaife: "She was not sure whether he was a farmer or a successful businessman in the country's biggest market. . . . All she knew was that this perfect figure of a man . . . was not a washerman, washing women's clothes. And he was not a ship-worker" or grass cutter (78).

But this is no longer possible. Oshia cannot be returned to the past, grow as if he had been born in his grandfather's generation, as his later development and eventual life in America show. The old work is not open to him, the old ways of life. More importantly, Emecheta is not entirely of the same view as Nnu Ego about Nnaife's femininity. Nnu Ego begins to dream again of her first husband, Amatokwu, identifying him as a genuine man and a true "African," unlike the unmanly and unAfrican Nnaife: "Amatokwu . . . That African . . . measured up to the standard her culture had led her to expect of a man." She concludes, "That was the sort of man to respect" (72). But the problems with this

revision of history have already been made clear. Once, when she compared Nnaife unfavorably with Amatokwo, Nnaife replied, rightly, "Pity
your ideal Amatokwo almost beat you to death because you did not bear
him a son" (49). The orthodox masculinity of Agbadi is one thing. The
corrupted masculinity of Amatokwu quite another. There is a degree of
romanticism in Nnu Ego's view of the village—understandable and for-
givable as it is, it is also mistaken, as Emecheta shows.

On the other hand, Nnaife does not always remain a kindly, "feminine" fellow. Emecheta is not presenting us with some sort of new
androgynous ideal. She too loathes his degeneration—though she
loathes the context more than the man, the social and economic conditions more than the personality. Slowly removed from the practical and
reflective identity that had given his life meaning and direction, Nnaife's
ultimate tragedy is not that he is feminized, but that he has no identity
at all, that he went from being the simple "naif" effusing over his skill
at laundering—hence his name, "Nnaife"—to an embittered cynic who
could not sustain faith or hope or affection of any sort, because he had
no structure in which such feelings and aspirations might be sustained.
In the end, "He no longer believed in anything." Nnu Ego thinks,
pathetically, that "She would certainly make sure that a proper shrine
was made for him now that he was the head of the Owulum family"
(151), but to him, it is meaningless.

The man who once was diligent and naively proud of his work
washing women's undergarments degenerates into lethargy and aimless-
ness. The man who was once "an easy-going, generous, simple man,"
according to Cordelia (65), has fallen into bitterness, greed, cynicism,
and cruelty to anyone who is weaker than he is, most obviously his wife.
His life becomes a series of exploitative and insecure jobs, a constant,
boiling resentment, and periodic bouts of impotent rage. Deprivation of
identity leads inexorably to massive and debilitating frustration, and
self-hate—for self-hate is hatred of what others see in us; it is hatred of
the "ego." We do not hate ourselves as subjects, but as objects, as the
objects of other people's disdain and abuse. And because we cannot act
on it, our rage at this abuse pours itself out on irrelevant bystanders,
friends, and family—often those who do not disdain and abuse, but try
to support us. So, through belligerency and outbursts of hyper-masculine aggression, Nnaife takes his irrelevant and unsatisfactory
vengeance. The simplest, most innocuous case of this comes when he is
first unemployed: "Not only did life in Lagos rob him of his manhood

and of doing difficult work, now it had made him redundant and having to rely on his wife. He would find any excuse to pick a quarrel with Nnu Ego" (87). Later, when employed again, the vengeance becomes more physical: "He gained . . . the fear of his wife Nnu Ego. He could even now afford to beat her up" (117). The idiom is precise. He can "afford" to exact physical suffering for his own frustration, because he is employed. Nnu Ego cannot successfully resist or end this brutality, because, though not unemployed, she remains economically dependent, for her children, if not for herself.

The final and most extreme case comes at the end of the novel. Nnaife is declining rapidly into old age and further feminization: "Nnaife was growing old fast." He "acquired stooping shoulders and a protruding belly. He wore no shirt and one could see that his breasts were forming like those of a young girl" (206). His rage and resentment advance at the same pace. He drinks every night, abuses those around him, and cherishes a deep sense of hurt, a deep conviction that even his family has demeaned, abused, and exploited him. Convinced that his daughter has eloped with a young man from a neighboring Yoruba family, he finally engages in an act of manly rebellion. But it is not against the white men and women who cut him off from his family, his beliefs, his way of life. It is against an unarmed Yoruba youth. In a pathetic parody of Okonkwo, Nnaife takes up his cutlass and cuts the boy deep in the shoulder (209). Nnaife shrieks madly that he will not surrender his rights, that he will not allow his tradition to be changed: "I will choose husbands for all my girls" (210). Others try to reason with him, saying, "Look, this is Lagos, not your town or your village." He responds with pathetic irrelevance, "But I come from my village!" (210). It is a final, desperate act to reaffirm the identity he has lost, the sense of place and belonging and unity with others, the sense of community and respect, all that has been stripped from him slowly over the years, before he could realize that it was gone and irretrievable, that his life amounted to wives he didn't know or care for, children he didn't understand. Late in life, he had arrived at a place that he never wanted or imagined, a place he could not even reconcile with the youthful ideas and hopes that had brought him to the city so many years earlier.

The incident has wider significance as well. In part, it transpires as a conflict between Igbo and Yoruba. Nnaife will not permit his daughter to marry a Yoruba. But this is not because he disdains the Yoruba. Rather, it is because he suspects that they disdain him: "No child of mine is marrying a tribe that calls us cannibals. A tribe that looks down on us, a tribe that hates us" (210). Many years earlier, when Nnaife was away, his son Oshia was refused food by a Yoruba family giving a *sarah*. This may imply ethnic hostility or disdain. But Emecheta presents it more as a matter of class than of ethnicity. *Sarahs* "were unofficial parties where food was free for all, especially children. . . . Nnu Ego could see in her mind's eye what must have happened. The other children would have been in smart clothes with neat haircuts, looking very healthy and clean; her Oshia looked like a tramp compared with them," for she could not even wash his tarpaulin (99) and his shirt was badly ripped (98). It does not seem to be a bias against Igbos, then, but rather a refusal to help the poor—even though Oshia himself immediately interprets it in ethnic terms, declaring, "I hate the Yorubas" (100). Indeed, the situation is not dissimilar with Igbonoba, a wealthy relative of Nnu Ego's co-wife Adaku—and, obviously, an Igbo—about whom Nnu Ego thinks, "*God, the cost of that headtie! Whatever she paid for it would feed me and the children for a whole month*" (163). It seems that, in Emecheta's view, ethnic conflict is a displacement from or ideological misconstrual of class conflict.

Thus, more important than any actual ethnic conflict between Igbos and Yorubas is the mode of thinking that drives Nnaife to believe that the Yorubas must despise him. He has lived his entire adult life in circumstances where he has been loathed and brutalized because of his origins. The constant inculcation of European ideology has led him to think of all people in terms of race and of all races in terms of antagonism against and oppression of his own. The daily racism of the Europeans has led Nnaife not to trust the Yorubas, because he can hardly even imagine that anyone would not disdain him, except, perhaps, a member of his own group.

Finally, the conflict acts almost as an allegory for the later civil conflicts in Nigeria. For here, as in so many other newly independent colonies, the different ethnic groups have in part retreated into their own insular ethnicities, into forms of reactionary traditionalism, in response to the devastating impact of European economic and cultural destruction, which they cannot effectively combat. Like Nnaife, they vent their rage and frustration against one another, against fellow Nigerians, because they cannot vent their rage against the metropolis, because in their reactionary traditionalism they have suppressed all sense of shared humanity—and because the former colonists continue to cultivate and benefit from such differences.

In the trial that follows his wounding of the Yoruba boy, Nnaife is ridiculed further. Both he and Nnu Ego appear buffoons. The very group that has deprived him of everything—"the jury, most of whom were Europeans" (218)—now mocks him for his deprivations: "'Your husband is a very strong man,' the prosecuting lawyer said cynically and the court roared in laughter" (217). He is convicted and imprisoned. He does have the good fortune to be released after serving only a fraction of his sentence. "But he was a broken man" (224). He returns to the village, now alien to him, remembering his last, misguided effort at asserting himself and giving meaning to life, an effort reduced to the residue of a criminal record for felonious assault—all that he now has to show for a life that he once thought would lead to a proud old age of comfort and authority.

GENDER IN THE CONTACT CULTURE: FEMININITY

But, however bad Nnaife's situation, Nnu Ego's is far worse. For she suffers with him all the deprivations of colonialism, and in addition suffers all the constraints and cruelties of two codes of female subordination. Again, the traditional hierarchy is carried over. In Lagos, as in Ibuza, a male child continues to be valued over a female child. Adaku laments the loss of her one son, cruelly contrasting his death with the life of her daughters, lamenting that one of them has not died instead (128). Oshia tries to comfort her, saying, "But you still have Dumbi." Adaku snaps back, "You are worth more than ten Dumbis" (128). The children internalize the lesson. Later, Oshia refuses Adaku's order to fetch water, yelling, "Why should I help in the cooking? That's a woman's job" (128). Everyone accepts this. They do not see it as laziness and disrespect, but laugh and murmur "amusedly," "Just like a boy" (128).

Later still, the division of labor is systematized in the family, where the boys are educated, while the girls engage in manual labor. Taiwo complains, "The boys have the evening off for their stupid lessons, and they're let off from going to fetch the wood that we have to sell to feed us." Nnu Ego shouts back, "But you are girls! They are boys. You have to sell to put them in a good position in life, so that they will be able to look after the family" (176).

As these examples indicate, once again, women perpetuate this hierarchy as much, or almost as much, as men—at least the women who are mothers of sons, and not of daughters only, for they too profit from the hierarchy. Nnu Ego and Adaku have a conflict over one of Adaku's relatives. Nwakusor and the other men are called in to judge the case. Afterward, Nnu Ego reflects, "She, Nnu Ego, had been wrong all the way, but of course they had made it seem that she was innocent just because she was the mother of sons" (167).

More generally, women even in the contact culture are "complete" only when they have children. The novel begins with Nnu Ego's despair when she discovers that her one child has died. The first sentence: "Nnu Ego backed out of the room, her eyes unfocused and glazed, looking into vacancy" (7). With her one child dead, she feels that there is no longer any future for her. She backs out of the room not only because her eyes are literally fixed on the dead boy, but also because she cannot "look ahead." All the future had been bound up with the child, with the "joys of motherhood." Now there is nothing there, mere "vacancy," an absence where the future—her son—should have been. This is despair, the sense that nothing any longer is possible which will orient one's life, provide direction and meaning to one's daily acts. When pregnant, at last, Nnu Ego had announced herself "a real woman"—or, rather, had announced, in complete surrender to patriarchal ideas, that Nnaife "has made me into a real woman" (53). When she is finally prevented from drowning herself, she protests, "But I am not a woman any more! I am not a mother any more. The child is there, dead on the mat" (62). She is not a woman, a "real woman," because she has not fulfilled the function of a woman in (patriarchal) Igbo social life. The community concurs: "And they all agreed that a woman without a child for her husband was a failed woman" (62).

But, again, the tradition is not pure. For, in Ibuza, Nnu Ego would not only have suffered, but benefited from the motherhood she eventually achieves. As Dike points out, referring to the "purest" traditions of Igboland, "The child is considered the major social security of the aged parents. He is socialized to eventually assume full economic responsibility of the old parents where necessary" (154). Agbadi had earlier advised his daughter in much the same terms, "When one grows old, one needs children to look after one" (38). Indeed, this too is a reason one needs sons. It is not merely a metaphysical, but a practical preference, given the system of patrilocal habitation. Daughters go to live with the families of their husbands and tend to their aging in-laws. Sons remain in their parents' village. When her first son is born, Nnu Ego feels deep relief and sees a long life of security and respect: "She was now sure, as she bathed her baby son . . . that her old age would be happy, that when she died there would be somebody left behind to refer to her as 'mother'" (54).

But in the new culture of the city, in which tradition is twisted by the cruelty and aspirations of the colonizers, the entire system is undermined. Nnu Ego nearly starves to feed Oshia, works herself to frail sickness and premature old age because of love, and worry, and hope for his future. But in the end he leaves for America, cursing his father. When he is gone, Nnu Ego realizes that all her hopes for the future were false. Oshia would provide her no security, financial or emotional. He would not treat her with the respect due to anyone who has lived to old age through painful times—and, again, the pain had been suffered for him. She recognizes the change in circumstances, then reduces her expectations, alters her hopes, to retain the meaning of her past sacrifices, and to give a different goal to her future, something that is not mere delusion. "Friends and well-wishers . . . predicted that soon her son would be back and driving her about in a big car" (201–2). But "she knew that . . . [s]he was not destined to be such a mother. . . . Her joy was to know that she had brought up her children when they had started out with nothing, and that those same children might rub shoulders one day with the great men of Nigeria" (202).

But even these diminished expectations could not be fulfilled. And Nnu Ego herself can hardly sustain them as a screen against despair. Shortly after leaving Oshia at the airport and reflecting on his future among "the great men of Nigeria," she cries "bitterly from her heart," "He has never given me anything. In fact he was expecting us to give him something before he left. . . . I saw the disappointment on his face. Why do you all make life so impossible for me? Where am I going to run to?" (202). The image of running recalls her attempt at suicide, the long run to the river with which the novel began. The despair is the same. Her life is "impossible" because, without a son, she would have had no future, no social role, no security in age. But also with a son she has no future, no social role, no security in age. For the colonized woman, contact culture is a culture of what is called a "double bind." The possibilities inherent in each culture are foreclosed by the constraints defined by the other.

None of this was foreseeable. Whatever Nnu Ego did was built on what seemed a firm foundation, the ideals and expectations with which she had grown to adulthood, the vision of the future implicit in the developing life stories of all children in her culture. "[H]ow was she to know that by the time her children grew up the values of her country, her people and her tribe would have changed so drastically, to the extent where a woman with many children could face a lonely old age, and maybe a miserable death all alone, just like a barren woman?" (219). A woman's life in the contact culture is indeed an impossible life, or, if not impossible, it is the worst of all possible lives. "It seemed that all she had inherited from her agrarian background was the responsibility and none of the booty" (137).

The tragic impossibility or contradiction of Nnu Ego's life culminates in descent into senility, and in a miserable death where she is not only "all alone, just like a barren woman," but even without a bed or home. She dies beside a road, without any shelter, removed from all society—an appropriate place for a woman whose life has been stripped of every meaning, whose every social function and value has been denied or undermined. To the end, she struggles pathetically to maintain the fiction that her children provide meaning for her past, promise for the future. Indeed, it was this hope that drove her deepening despair: "What actually broke her was, month after month, expecting to hear from her son in America, and from Adim too who later went to Canada, and failing to do so. It was from rumours that she heard Oshia had married and that his bride was a white woman" (224). Oshia's final repudiation of his family and the traditions of his people. Nonetheless, she tries to persist. "She used to go to the sandy square called Otinkpu . . . and tell people there that her son was in 'Emelika', and that she had another one also in the land of the white men." One night, "After such wandering," Nnu Ego "lay down by the roadside, thinking that she had arrived home. She died quietly there, with no child to hold her hand" (224).

Oshia, who has abandoned Igbo traditions entirely, who has sought to assimilate himself completely to European ways, returns upon his mother's death. As is so often the way with mimics, he flaunts an exaggerated traditionalism. He, Adim, and the others "were all sorry she had died before they were in a position to give their mother a good life." And so, to convince others and themselves that they were dutiful children, respectful of all their mother had done for them, they give her "the noisiest and most costly second burial Ibuza had ever seen" and they establish "a shrine . . . in her name" (224).

The Economy of an Impossible Life

In contact society, the colonized woman gradually loses all possibilities for action and identity; her position degenerates to that of the slave, or prisoner. When her first child is born, Nnu Ego accepts "old babies' clothes" from Mrs. Meers, the white mistress. "She forgot that in her culture only slaves accepted worn outfits for a newly-born baby" (54). The act itself is hardly significant. But it implies something larger, an allegory of Nnu Ego's new life—she has already begun to dress her Igbo children in the cast-off garments of the colonizer. To paraphrase Frantz Fanon, one might say, "Black skin, white clothes," or to allude to Ivan Morton, one might say, "We can't be white, but we can dress white." As an emblem of her life, it is an act of slavery.

She is also reduced to slavery by tradition—first through marriage, through her "sale" to Nnaife. Early on, Nnaife demands of her, "Did I not pay your bride price? Am I not your owner?" (48). That, again, is one way the different suggestions of her name fit together. She has no ego in part because she has no identity other than her bride price—"nnu ego," "twenty bags of cowries." Then there are the joys of motherhood, the tradition of duty, along with the genuine human feeling that makes it unbearable for her to watch Oshia suffer; these too "were like her chain of slavery" (186). Elsewhere, Emecheta varies the metaphor to the same end: "it occurred to Nnu Ego that she was a prisoner, imprisoned by her love for her children, imprisoned in her role as the senior wife" (137); "I have many children, but what do I have to feed them on? On my life . . . . I have to give them my all. . . . When will I be free? . . . Never, not even in death. I am a prisoner of my own flesh and blood" (186–87). Finally, she accepts these servitudes and incarcerations. But it is not only because of Igbo tradition. In this resignation too she suffers the effects of both cultures, for "Her new Christian religion taught her to bear her cross with fortitude" (89).

Once again, underlying this multiplied constraint, for women as for men, is economy, an economy dominated by European capitalism and, thereby, European culture. Initially, Nnu Ego brought with her from Ibuza the traditional Igbo idea that women, like men, work in the public sphere, that they work together and trade and sustain economic autonomy. At first, she joins in "monthly meetings . . . with her fellow Ibuza wives" (52), recreating in Lagos the traditional women's *mikiri* of the villages. As a result, she is able to take up trade: "The other women taught her how to start her own business so that she would not have only one outfit to wear. They let her borrow five shillings from the women's fund and advised her" (52). She is successful and happy in her trading, and in her engagement with the other women. As one woman says to Nnu Ego, "We are like sisters on a pilgrimage. Why should we not help one another?" (53).

But after Oshia is born, Nnu Ego succumbs to European and Christian ideology, and, even more importantly, the social and economic structures which define and constrain life in the contact region. First, she takes up the view of her oppressors that economic dependency is to be preferred to economic autonomy: "Were they not in a white man's world where it was the duty of the father to provide for his family? In Ibuza, women made a contribution, but in urban Lagos, men had to be the sole providers." And yet, she is ambivalent; she cannot entirely accept this view. She reflects, "This new setting robbed the woman of her useful role"—and, one might add, her independent role. But the ideology is insistent, and compounded by the deeper ideology of maternal duty, which is harder to dismiss, emotionally, if not logically: "The life she had indulged in with the baby Ngozi had been very risky: she had been trying to be traditional in a modern urban setting." Most often, oppressive ideology comes to be accepted by colonized people precisely insofar as it becomes linked with ideas and feelings they already held. Like anyone in any culture, Nnu Ego worried over her responsibility in Ngozi's death. Any trauma makes us ask how we are responsible, how we might have acted differently. Nnu Ego asks those questions too. And the Christian, European ideology of maternal duty seems to give her an explanation. "It was because she wanted to be a woman of Ibuza in a town like Lagos that she lost her child." In consequence, "This time she was going to play it according to the new rules" (81).

Unsurprisingly, given this cultural conflict, and given her own natural aspiration toward autonomy, doubts assailed her mind still: "She would sometimes ask herself how long she must" refrain from trading. But the social and economic structure is final arbiter: "In Ibuza after the child was weaned, one could leave him with an elderly member of the family and go in search of trade. But in Lagos there were no elderly grandparents" (81). There is no structure to sustain both motherhood and economic autonomy. So, at least for a time, autonomy is sacrificed.

But, of course, the economy is too devastating for Nnu Ego to remain unemployed for long. Eventually, she must return to her trade.

But now it is not only a forced choice, it is an impossible profession. First, it is a contradiction of her European and Christian duty. Second, it is itself enslaving. Merely to keep her family undernourished, but alive, she works without respite. At one point, Oshia begins to starve. Nnaife is gone; the only work available to him required a year-long absence on a ship. Nnu Ego, despite her own weakness and exhaustion, redoubles her efforts, even selling "all her clothes at a fraction of their cost to the Fulani street-walkers, telling herself that if her sons should live and grow, they would be all the clothes she would ever need" (104). Clearly, this is not fulfilling work, but misery and desperation almost worse than slavery.

Nnu Ego herself contrasts this desperate condition with life in the indigenous culture. "She would never lack in her father's house," she thinks (106). The point could be generalized. Though any community can be devastated by mass starvation in times of natural disaster, not all societies are inclined to create want out of plenty, to make some starve while others prosper. Colonial society is highly prone to the uneven distribution of comfort and misery. Nnu Ego's home culture, in its traditional forms, was not. As Isichei notes, "Igboland was a society which lacked extremes of wealth and poverty" (34). Clearly, the same could not be said for colonial Lagos.

But there is one clear exception to this grim picture of women's lives in the contact culture—Adaku. She is another instance of that recurrent literary figure, the lone independent woman. Though traditional Igbo society offered women far more autonomy than contact society, Ona had still been an exception in her extremes of freedom and pride. Adaku is a parallel exception in the contact society. Right from the beginning, Nnu Ego recognizes that Adaku is singularly self-assertive: "'This woman knows a thing or two,' she thought. So independent in her way of thinking" (127). But, of course, in Emecheta's novel, it is not mere psychological predisposition that causes Adaku to rebel. It is circumstance. She is driven to revolt by a system that accords her no status as the mother of daughters only. "I will spend the money I have in giving my girls a good start in life," she explains, announcing her departure from the family (168). "I am not prepared to stay here and be turned into a mad woman, just because I have no sons" (169).

In this particular scene, it is unclear what we are to think of Adaku. She blasphemes against her *chi*, and declares—evidently in anger, and without meaning it—that she is "going to be a prostitute" (168), despite her obvious skills at trade, and the unsavory consequences of this choice for her daughters. But just two pages later, she explains that her trade is thriving, so she "won't have to depend on men friends to do anything" (170). And it is clear afterward that she is a successful businesswoman, not a prostitute. Indeed, far from keeping them in a brothel, Adaku sends her daughters to a "convent school" (189).

It is important to note that Adaku's action here is not so much a violation of Igbo tradition as of British and contact culture. Nnu Ego sends her sons to school, but not her daughters (see 189). This was fairly typical of the period (see Amadiume, 134). But why? Judith Van Allen has argued that "At least part of the answer must lie in the values of the colonialists, values that led the British to assume that girls and boys, women and men, should be treated and should behave as people supposedly did in 'civilized' Victorian England. Strong male domination was imposed on Igbo society both indirectly, by new economic structures, and directly, by the recruitment of only men into Native Administration. In addition, the new economic and political structures were supported by the inculcation of sexist ideology in the mission schools" ("'Aba Riots,'" 80). Thus, Adaku is not necessarily breaking with tradition. She is, rather, refusing to accept the double oppression of contact culture.

This is not to say that Adaku is ideal. She is not. For example, seventeen-year-old Okpo, Nnaife's youngest wife, shows, by contrast, the lack of human warmth and respect that goes with Adaku's pride and independent spirit. Okpo is kind and respectful to all the children, though they are not her own. "Nnu Ego loved the way she never called the male children of the household by their names without the prefix 'My little husband.' Even little Nnamdio was well respected by her. So unlike Adaku, this one" (197). As Nnu Ego knows well, it is difficult to combine independence with a kind heart.

Nonetheless, Adaku's life points toward some solutions to the woman's dilemma in contact culture, and elsewhere. First of all, having left Nnaife, she, like Ona, is unmarried. Second, she is economically self-sufficient. Third, she has joined in solidarity with other women, especially with those of the next generation. This, I think, is Emecheta's position too on women and identity. (Clearly, I do not agree with those critics, such as Allan, who see Emecheta as "fail[ing] to provide any possibility of rescue from" patriarchal oppression [104].) Again, it is not a culturalist position, but an economic strategy. Emecheta wishes to elevate the position of traditional Igbo culture, to foster admiration rather than denigration, to make us see it as less oppressive, more open for women's autonomy and self-realization, than European culture. But she does not wish to advocate any particular practice regarding women and tradition. She is not orthodox or assimilationist or syncretist. Rather, her practical advocacy is a sort of Marxist/feminist universalism. The principles she identifies, at least those relating to economic autonomy and solidarity, apply to women in all societies at all times. This could be called assimilationist or syncretistic, insofar as it draws on Marx. But it could equally be called orthodox Igbo, for it takes up and extends principles already implicit in the practical identity of Igbo women in traditional Igbo society. As Amadiume stresses, there is "a strong cultural bond of female solidarity in traditional Igbo systems" (179)—a bond founded upon economic structures. In any case, whether one conceives of such economically based solidarity as orthodox Igbo or orthodox Marx, its application is global. All women should be part of mikiri; all women should engage in their trade.

Even Nnu Ego recognizes this, though she does not act on that recognition. Looking back over the fragments of a life that no longer had meaning, "Nnu Ego told herself that she would have been better off had she had time to cultivate those women who had offered her hands of friendship" (219). She reflects on her daughters' lives as well, affirming solidarity across generations: "But who made the law that we should not hope in our daughters? We women subscribe to that law more than anyone. Until we change all this, it is still a man's world, which women will always help to build" (187). And she tells Adaku, "I am beginning to think that there may be a future for educated women. I saw many young women teaching in schools. It would really be something for a woman to be able to earn some money monthly like a man" (189).

But, again, all this remains unacted. In despair, she only cries out to God, to Chukwu or, more likely, to the Jehovah of the Christians—certainly not to the divine woman of the lake, recalled by Efuru; she pleads, "God, when will you create a woman who will be fulfilled in herself, a full human being, not anybody's appendage?" (186). But she does not pursue the idea, take steps to create such a woman on her own, in herself or in her daughters. When Adaku asks her if she has sent the girls to school, she replies, "Oh, no. . . . The most important thing is for them to get good husbands" (189). In the end, she does allow her son-in-law, Magnus to raise her youngest daughter to become "a well-educated Miss" (223). But this is a late and minimal change, and an ambiguous one—why does one have to be a Europeanized "Miss" to be "well-educated"?

Nnu Ego's inaction—despite her recognition that solidarity and women's education are important—illustrates how our acts are not based so much on the beliefs we self-consciously affirm as on the beliefs we have internalized, beliefs deeply integrated into our sense of the world and of ourselves, beliefs based on, but false to the real conditions in which we live. It is not hypocrisy that Nnu Ego does not act on her occasional insights. It is human. And it is precisely because of this human failing, because she does not or cannot act on these insights, that she dies a miserable death, homeless, "with no friend to talk to her": "She had never really had many friends, so busy had she been building up her joys as a mother" (224). For Emecheta, the tragedy of Nnu Ego is not unique, not even peculiar to colonized countries. It is, rather, repeated daily in every culture in every part of the world. And while cultural identity plays a role in these tragedies, their ultimate source is in the material conditions that shape our lives, and our societies everywhere, to painful inequality.

CHAPTER SEVEN

ORTHODOXY AND UNIVERSALISM

Rabindranath Tagore's Gora

DHARMA IN THE AGE OF CRUELTY

Rabindranath Tagore's *Gora* is the story of an Irish boy raised in India by a Hindu couple after his natural parents have died in the 1857 uprising or "Sepoy Mutiny." His name is "Gora," meaning "white." His parents never tell him that he is European. As he grows up, his love for those around him, his compassion for their suffering under British rule, lead him further and further into Hindu tradition. He becomes an active and influential advocate for strict Hindu doctrine. In a series of dialogues with comrades and antagonists, he argues brilliantly that unbending traditionalism is necessary under colonial rule. What is unusual about Gora's cultural rigidity is that it is not based on hate or on resentment or hypocritical self-interest, but on love. It is Gora's overwhelming love of the ordinary people around him that makes him burn with fury at their denigration and rebel against their oppression. But there is, of course, a conflict here, because part of Hindu doctrine enforces denigration and oppression within the Hindu community itself. Thus, part of Hindu doctrine runs directly contrary to the humane impulses that animate Gora's Hinduism. This conflict is played out not only abstractly, in Gora's ideas, but concretely, in his love for a young woman of the Brahmo Samaj, a religious group perhaps most easily characterized as mixing elements of

Hinduism and Christianity. The dilemma is resolved when Gora's increasingly traditionalist foster father decides that Gora must be told of his origins, must be told that he has no place in Hinduism.

In my view, *Gora* is one of the greatest novels of ideas ever written. Tagore develops the arguments for and against strict traditionalism with an insight and power unmatched even in treatises on the topic. He carefully teases out the varieties of tradition, the contexts and implications of reaction, the motives and consequences of reform, orthodoxy, and mimeticism. Moreover, *Gora* does one thing that few works of literature and few discursive works have managed to do. It articulates the strongest arguments of all sides. It is true dialectic, not the fake dialectic of Plato, where the result is known beforehand and the author steers all arguments around to Socrates' point, making his antagonists buffoons. That is what makes this such an indispensable book for the study of colonialism and identity—it articulates all positions so that one can understand why people would adopt them, so that one can see their genuine force, their attraction, their value, as well as their errors, their false turns, and the misfortunes to which they might lead.

Or, rather, it portrays the value of all positions within a particular frame. For every position valued by Tagore is valued for its universalism. Not only syncretism, not only liberal orthodoxy, but the extremest reactionary traditionalism he defends by an appeal to what humans share. As with Ngũgĩ, it is a particularized universalism, a universalism necessarily instantiated in different daily practices of speech and habit, just as the universalism of language and of linguistic structure is particularized in different lexical items and details of syntax. But it is, nonetheless, universal.

More exactly, *Gora* is a book about colonial identity. And colonial identity specifically conceived of as *dharma*. "Dharma" means, most concretely, nature—the principles a thing follows because of what it is (cf. Monier-Williams, 510). It is the dharma of water to flow, of heavy objects to fall to the earth, of fire and smoke to rise into the air. It is the nature of humankind to act according to principle. Hence, for men and women, dharma means duty, what I should do—not only, as we would say, "morally," but in respect of every social link. My dharma guides or should guide my action as spouse, son, teacher, author—positively, not simply in negative terms of avoiding ethical errors or "sins." It provides the pattern of life. It is all that is in accord with my "nature"—as spouse, son, teacher, and so on.

Both in popular Hinduism and in European understanding, dharma is most often reduced to *varṇadharma*, the dharma of caste. And this is certainly important. The dharma of the Brahmin or priest is different from that of the *Kṣatriya* or warrior, the *Vaiśya* or cultivator/craftsperson/trader, the *Śūdra* or servant. The other form of dharma that is widely recognized both within popular Hinduism and in the West is the dharma of the wife—devotion to the husband's dharma. This is often misunderstood in the West (and probably in India as well) as devotion, even subservience to the husband. And in practice it was no doubt often true that this and other religious principles were interpreted in such a way as to justify such subservience—just as happened in the West. But in principle this is not the case. Rather, the wife is the *sadharmiṇī* of the husband. The term is common in contemporary Hindi but the idea, at least, is more widely familiar, and it perfectly captures a central aspect of spousal dharma. It means, in general, a "virtuous wife" (see McGregor). More importantly, however, it means a wife who fully shares the dharma of the husband and serves as an aid to his achievement of that dharma. In a more egalitarian construal, we would say that both husband and wife may be characterized as *sadharmi*, that is, as "having similar natures or religious duties" (see McGregor) or, more exactly, sharing dharma. The point is made in Sanskrit through the term *sahadharma*, meaning "community of duty" (Monier-Williams, 1194), especially that between husband and wife (see also the entry for *sahadharmiṇī*, 1194), or *sadharma*, which has roughly the same meaning (1140). In keeping with this the *Dharma Shastra* states that "The wedded couple should be one in spirit in respect of all matters of piety, gain, and desire" (510). Unsurprisingly, the *Dharma Shastra* goes on to specify this dharmic unity in straightforwardly patriarchal terms, and in relation to *varṇadharma*. This means that the kṣatriya wife behaves in such a way as to further her husband's strength and bravery in war, his ability to protect the people, and so on. A Brahmin wife, in contrast, must aid her husband in his spiritual development, his piety, his learning.

We might refer to both *varṇadharma* and the *sahadharma* of wives as "birth dharmas," for they are determined by one's condition at birth—one's birth caste and one's biological sex. There are other forms of birth-specific dharma as well—most obviously, those relating to the family, for example, the dharma of a son or a brother. These too are stressed in popular Hinduism and in Western summaries of Hindu belief. Another widely known form of dharma relates to stage of life.

The dharma of a student differs from that of a householder, which in turn differs from that of an older person who has retired to a contemplative life.

In common understanding, birth and stage of life dharmas exhaust both the idea and the practice of dharma. But the notion of dharma is, in fact, much broader than these two types. And this is crucial, both to the concept itself and to our understanding of Tagore's novel. We have repeatedly stressed that indigenous traditions are always much more diverse than either the colonizer or the reactionary traditionalist will allow. Moreover, traditions typically have ways of conceiving of and evaluating this diversity. The Hindu tradition has an elaborate conceptual system for understanding and debating this diversity. It also has something like a judicial mechanism for very local disputes; this is spelled out at the beginning of the *Dharma Shastra* (3). However, for our purposes—and for the nationalist writers and activists with whom *Gora* is concerned—it is the conceptual system that is most relevant.

Beyond those mentioned thus far, there are four other important categories of dharma: *mānavdharma* (or *sādhāraṇadharma*), *sanātanadharma*, *yugadharma*, and *āpaddharma*. *Mānavdharma*, human dharma—or, equivalently, *sādhāraṇadharma*, universal dharma—is opposed directly to any form of dharma determined by caste, stage of life, and the like. *Mānavdharma* is precisely the form of dharma that applies to all individuals, not to those of a particular stage or birth category. Bhiku Parekh states that, in conflicts between *mānavdharma* and *varṇadharma*, "The *shastras* . . . assign the former higher authority" (16). The matter was not as unequivocal as Parekh indicates; in practice, *varṇadharma* more often superceded *mānavdharma* (see O'Flaherty, "Clash," 97). Nonetheless, the notion and the principles of *mānavdharma* could always be invoked to dispute *varṇadharma* or any birth-specific dharma. For instance, the principle of mercy or compassion, or the principle of *ahiṃsā*, refusal to cooperate with the commission of violence—both being principles of *mānavdharma*—may be invoked against merciless or violent actions which appear to be sanctioned by *varṇadharma*. Thus, within Hindu tradition itself, there is a way of doing precisely what Achebe advocated in Igbo tradition—revising aspects of tradition not by reference to other traditions (e.g., those of the colonizer), but by reference to universal human ethical principles.

Parekh notes that "The *shastras* . . . also distinguish between *sanatanadharma* (eternal principles) and *yugadharma* (historically specific principles)" (16). This too is an important distinction. It is the difference between duties that apply at all times, and those that apply in this particular age, or more generally in the unique conditions of the present. There are four major *yugas* or ages lasting hundreds of millennia, according to Hindu cosmology. We live in the last of these ages, the Kaliyuga, the losing age, the age of ill fortune, strife, discord (see Monier-Williams, 261), an age in which goodness is almost gone from the world, and what little is left declines daily, an age of cruelty and injustice and untruth, an age of adharma. Given the change in objective conditions, *The Laws of Manu* stress, dharma cannot be the same in the four ages (12). This is perhaps most obvious in the current age, the Kaliyuga. An act that, in another age, would bring forth justice, may be perverted into injustice in this evil age. Thus, contradictions arise in dharma. One's duty becomes unclear.

But one can generalize the idea, as Parekh and others have done. Then "*yugadharma*" refers not merely to our place in Kaliyuga, but to the more specific historical conditions in which we find ourselves, at least insofar as these are a part of the condition of the Kaliyuga. Indeed, *yuga* need not refer to one of the four great ages, but may refer to a much shorter period (see Monier-Williams, 854). Moreover, the Sanskrit theorists explicitly allow for the alteration of dharma in specific *personal* situations—"in extremity," as when near to starvation (see Doniger with Smith, liii). This is *āpaddharma*, "a practice only allowable in time of distress" (Monier-Williams, 143). Thus, it is perfectly in keeping with the principles of the classical theorists to see dharma as partially relative to historical conditions. An obvious case of this is colonial occupation. Indeed, colonialism is arguably the most intense manifestation of the Kaliyuga—and that from every point of view. It violates *mānavdharma* in destroying compassion; it violates *varṇadharma* in undermining social structure; it wears away at customs and beliefs that sustain *sahadharma*. Indeed, colonial occupation was widely seen in this light by Indians: as a further triumph of darkness over light, of falsity over truth, of injustice over justice, a further instance of the horrifying but inescapable pattern of Kaliyuga. And, as such, it continually recreates the conditions of extremity or moral conflict that permit—indeed necessitate—*āpaddharma*.

Beyond these various types of dharma, tradition itself is of many sorts, and not all of these are of equal value or authority. Specifically, we may distinguish *paramparā* which "refers to a practice which is handed down in unbroken succession from unknown times" (Parekh, 15) along with *ācārā* or custom, on the one hand, and the various written texts concerning dharma, on the other. *Paramparā* and *ācārā* (henceforth, I shall use *ācārā* for the general concept) refer to living practices. They largely coincide with what we have been calling practical identity. Specifically, they constitute that part of practical identity that is generally seen to have ethical force as "tradition," along with the beliefs, and so on, by which people understand and justify that tradition.

The *śāstras* and related writings (to which I shall refer by the synecdoche of *śāstras*), in contrast, are written codifications of tradition, prescriptive records of practices and principles. Just as, in principle, *mānavdharma* supersedes *varṇadharma* in cases of conflict (at least according to some authors), the *śāstras* supersede *ācārā* in cases of conflict. However, as with the varieties of dharma, this is not as straightforward a matter as may initially seem. First of all, while the *śāstras* are a higher court of appeal for the learned Brahmin, they are, for most Hindus (even highly educated Hindus) an obscure set of esoteric texts, controlled by an elite group. While ordinary Hindus may respect the learning of these elite scholars, their teachings can hardly be expected genuinely to change widespread traditional practices which are firmly a part of practical identity. The point is not that you cannot teach an old dog new tricks. Rather, the point is simply that teachings alone, even teachings which are widely accepted, are unlikely to change long-standing habitual practices. In theory, *śāstras* supersede *ācārā*; in practice, however, *ācārā* is far more likely to supersede the *śāstras*.

In addition, the *śāstras* themselves are multiple and often conflict. Sometimes they advocate different practices; sometimes they articulate different principles; sometimes they explain principles and practices differently. Some *śāstras* are understood to supersede others, and thus in some of these cases the contradiction is resolvable. But there is no hierarchization of sacred texts that is universally accepted. Moreover, there is the further dilemma, familiar to literary critics, that interpreters are likely to give even the same text rather different meanings. Consider, for example, a well-known passage from the *Mahābhārata*. Yudhiṣṭhira is being interrogated by his father, Dharma, who has concealed himself in the form of a Yaksha (a minor forest deity): "The Yaksha asked,—'By what, O king, birth, behaviour, study, or learning doth a person become a Brahmana?'" "Yudhishthira answered,—'It is neither birth, nor study, nor learning, that is the cause of *Brahmanahood*, without doubt, it is behaviour that constitutes it'" ("Vana Parva, 610). Such a passage could be used to oppose the entire system of defining caste by birth. But it would be contradicted by other, equally canonical passages. Moreover, even on its own, it could be interpreted to mean merely that a Brahmin is not a true Brahmin if his behavior does not follow his *varṇadharma*.

Indeed, there are even alternative canons, different and contested bodies of written teaching, some of which radically oppose central tenets of *ācāra* and of the standard *śāstras*. For example, one set of sacred texts important to *Gora*, at least in their general attitudes, are the tantras of Śaivism. These texts, which are accepted as authoritative by some devotees of Śiva, are explicitly and vehemently opposed to the determination of dharma by birth. Indeed, they revile and in effect outcaste anyone who denies women or the "low born" the opportunities to pursue spiritual enlightenment. As the *Mahānirvāṇa Tantra* puts it, "Any member of the Kula [i.e., any Tantric practitioner] who will not allow into the Kula an untouchable or a Greek [i.e., a foreigner], thinking them low, or a woman, despising her—he, being truly low, goes to the lowest place." They also typically displace caste with a hierarchy of spiritual achievements—and, unlike the passage from the *Mahābhārata* cited above, they do so unambiguously: "By becoming Kaulas, all the classes of men on the earth, whatever the different dharmas that they follow, are released from their bonds and go to the highest state" (in O'Flaherty, *Textual*, 137; cf. Avalon, 8.191–95).

The general situation regarding the determination of dharma is summarized well by Yudhiṣṭhira: "Argument leads to no certain conclusion, the *Śrutis* [written texts akin to *śāstras*] are different from one another; there is not even one *Rishi* [religious sage] whose opinion can be accepted by all; the truth about religion and duty is hid in caves" ("Vana Parva," 610).

As Parekh points out, Hindu authors in the colonial period invoked all of the varieties of dharma and all of the ambiguities and inconsistencies of tradition in order to argue that some aspects of *ācāra* or custom should be changed—not because the British insisted that they should be changed, not because they conflicted with Christianity, for that would be to grant Indian traditions too little moral authority and European traditions too much. Rather, they should be changed because they conflicted with unbreachable principles of *mānavdharma*, the unfortunate necessities of *yugadharma*, or the teachings of the *śāstras*, or of some particular *śāstra* that could be argued to supersede its rivals.

For example, "Ishwar Chandra Vidyasagar took full advantage of this when he based his campaign for widow remarriage on the argument that not *Manusmriti* but *Parasharasmriti* was relevant in the present *kaliyuga*" (Parekh, 16). It is interesting that, when Gora travels into the countryside, one of the practices to which he objects most strongly is the ban on widow remarriage. Indeed, it is possible that Tagore intends to allude to Vidyasagar, when he speaks of a learned Brahmin named "Vidyavagish," who leads Gora away from the Brahmo Samaj and toward Hindu traditionalism. Gora had taken to attacking various Brahmins who pretended to great learning, profundity of thought, and propriety of action. He had nothing but disdain for the whole lot of them. Until he met Vidyavagish whose "great learning" and "liberality of mind" were "wonderful." "Gora had never imagined that any one, read only in Sanskrit lore, could have such a keen and open intelligence," marked by "power and peace . . . patience and depth" (23). For present purposes, the most important points in the description are Vidyavagish's "liberality of mind" and "open intelligence," his liberal orthodoxy—a liberal orthodoxy that, we may assume, is based firmly on the Hindu universalism according to which *mānavdharma* is the highest of all dharmas.

But Gora does not, for most of the novel, adopt Vidyavagish's liberal orthodoxy. And he does not do so for reasons having to do with his awareness of the complexities of *yugadharma* under British rule. Specifically, Gora's view throughout most of the novel, the view most powerfully articulated in the novel, is roughly that the *yugadharma* or *āpaddharma* of Hindus is to defend and preserve *ācārā* so that the ordinary men and women of India can feel confidence in themselves and in their culture, so that a sense of human dignity, shattered by colonialism and European supremacism, can be restored, so that Hindus will not be driven to mimeticism or hypocrisy or purgative traditionalism. But this defense of *ācārā* is never final, for Gora. It is a historically specific dharma, which should lead ultimately to a reformulation of custom, bringing custom into accord with *mānavdharma*, reconciling it with the universal. Gora's is, one might say, a form of *strategic* reactionary traditionalism; reactionary traditionalism in the ultimate service of liberal orthodoxy. (A number of critics have, in effect, noted the relation of Gora's views to what we have termed "reactionary traditionalism" [see, for example, Raizada, 67], but not the strategic nature of this reaction and its ultimate justification in relation to liberal orthodoxy.)

As we have already suggested, there is a problem with this. For the insistence on preserving *ācāra* is an insistence on extending the violation of *mānavdharma* (cf. Nandy, *Illegitimacy*, on the suppression of women in Gora's version of tradition). Yet, at the same time, under conditions of British and Christian domination, any criticism of *ācāra* may be used by the colonizers to support their own authority, to advance their destruction of indigenous culture; any such criticism may drive Indian people further into racial and cultural despair. Colonialism creates an irreconcilable conflict between *yugadharma* and *mānavdharma*. Indeed, it exacerbates the conflict between *mānavdharma* and *ācāra*, by rigidifying *varṇadharma* (caste dharma) and the dharma of wives. For example, as noted in the preceding chapter, the practice of *sati*, previously in decline, spread and intensified under British rule. The conflicts are not easy to resolve. In short, colonialism—that great intensification of adharma in Kaliyuga—has made all real options adharmic. That deep and pervasive contradiction is what initiates and guides the dialectic of this novel.

The Brahmo Samaj: Synthesis and Mimeticism

On the other hand, this is not to say that there are no easy cases. Some choices are worse than others, and these may be eliminated at the outset. Thus, Tagore represents and critiques mimeticism, purgative traditionalism, and even unreflective conformism—for, though unreflective conformism is sympathetic in being central to *ācāra*, its errors are precisely what create the conflict between *ācāra* and *mānavdharma* to begin with. His treatment of the Brahmo Samaj is central to understanding these criticisms.

The Brahmo Samaj was a religious movement co-founded, initially under a slightly different name, by Ram Mohan Roy and Tagore's grandfather (see Kopf, 287). It had a number of distinct strains, and is therefore difficult to characterize in a few words (for a detailed overview, see Kopf). One thing all strains had in common was a determination to turn Indians away from practices Brahmos considered objectionable. Frequently, they sought to isolate these practices by looking at other religions, primarily Christianity. On the other hand, many Brahmo writers drew deeply on Hinduism, paying particular attention to universal dharma, as may be seen from the "unqualified universalism" of Akkhoy Kumar Dutt's *Dharma Niti* (Kopf, 52) or of Debendranath Tagore's *Brahmo Dharma* (Kopf, 106; Debendranath was Rabindranath's father). In any case, as regards Hinduism, the movement repudiated caste, child marriage, taboos on widows, polytheism, and "idol worship." All were aspects of Hinduism that had been condemned in British and Christian propaganda. Some may be seen as violations of sādhāraṇadharma; others appear only to conflict with British, Christian, and/or Muslim beliefs.

On the other hand, the differences among Brahmos were as significant as their common beliefs. Some Brahmo Samajis characterized the movement as a reform of Hinduism. Others were more Christian than Hindu in their orientation. Some Brahmo Samajis, especially of the latter sort, appear to have had a rather crude understanding of Hinduism, colored more by European views than by Hindu scriptures or even Hindu practice. At the same time, a number of erudite Sanskrit scholars were members of the Samaj as well.

The "Hindu" wing of the Brahmo Samaj tended to conceive of the movement's function in two radically different ways—as returning Hinduism to its purer origins ("originalism") or as bringing Hinduism into the twentieth century ("modernization"). Both factions of this wing opposed Westernization and saw needed reform as Hindu. On the other hand, they too drew on European and Christian ideas in obvious ways, at least in terms of what they chose to criticize and reform in Hinduism. In other words, even for the Hindu wing, the terms of debate were largely set by the colonizer. Nonetheless, the "Hindu" Brahmos were right to stress that there is a difference between originalism or even modernism and Westernization. Even if one's attention is drawn to certain issues by colonialist propaganda, one might still legitimately study one's *mānavdharma* with respect to those issues. The fact that the colonizer has raised the issue of caste or widow remarriage does not mean that Hindus must ignore that issue.

The ideas of the Originalists, as we might call them, were more or less continuous with those of liberal orthodox Hindus, though syncretistic elements did enter into the Samaj almost of necessity. A good example of this sort approach was Rajnarian Bose, who repeatedly argued for "the superiority of Hinduism to all other religions" and maintained "that Brahmoism was the true reformed Hinduism" (Kopf, 181); he also advocated a "program of general Sanskritic revival" and "urged giving up English food, dress," and the like (Kopf, 180).

The Modernizers were more clearly syncretistic. Again, "Modernization" is primarily a matter of altering tradition in such a way as to reconcile it with the current state of society, most importantly including the current state of scientific knowledge. In this sense, it is related to *yugadharma*, even if, in actual practice, it invariably involves some incorporation of European practices and ideas. Tagore himself articulated the difference between modernization and Westernization particularly well: "Modernism is not in the dress of the European; or in the hideous structures where their children are interned when they take their lessons; or in the square houses with flat, straight-walled surfaces, pierced with parallel lines of windows where these people are caged in their lifetime; certainly modernism is not in their ladies bonnets carrying on them loads of incongruities. These are not modern but merely European. True modernism is freedom of mind, not slavery of taste. It is independence of thought and action, not tutelage under European schoolmasters" (qtd. in Kopf, 305–6).

Opposed to the Hindu strain of the Brahmo Samaj, in both its forms, was a more or less straightforwardly Christian strain. Brahmo Samajis of this orientation based their ideas and practices on the Bible and on the teachings of European and American ministers, eschewing Hindu ideas and practices, in a manner fully in keeping with European colonialist views. Even among Brahmos who did not necessarily see themselves as taking a stand on this issue, there appears to have been a strong Christian bias. Indeed, many Hindus considered Brahmos to be indistinguishable from Indian Christians. The characterization certainly fits the characters in Tagore's novel. Consider Paresh, one of the characters that Tagore most admires and one who is, in principle, syncretistic in orientation, not Hindu or Christian. He has hung on the wall of his sitting room "a coloured picture of Christ," but no Hindu religious figures, and his bookshelf prominently displays "a complete set of Theodore Parker's works" (33); we are not told of any comparable collection of work by a Hindu author. Paresh is not by any means unusual in this. Kopf points out that "It was the discovery of Parker by Brahmos—his collected works in Bengali translation in the 1860s—which provided them with a vital and powerful bond of common values and ideals." This is not to say that Parker was in any way objectionable. Indeed, Kopf stresses that "There was no other minister of any church in the world at that time as actively committed to the equality of all men, to women's rights, and to the idea of man's perfectibility" (27–28). The

problem is simply that all or almost all intellectual and religious authority here is European or filtered through Europe. Paresh's reading of the
Mahābhārata to Sucharita (75), provides only the slightest qualification
to this general point.

In between the Hindu and Christian groups was the fully synthetic
tendency, which self-consciously sought to bring together Christianity
and Hinduism, along with other religions. A good example of the syncretistic group is Keshub Sen, most obviously during the period when he
advocated the formulation of a "universal" religion, a synthesis of all
major religions which could be adopted by everyone. This group was
particularly vehement in its antisectarianism. Seeing the devastation
caused by Hindu/Muslim conflict, members of this group often viewed
religious sectarianism as the prime enemy of any sort of religious feeling,
belief, or practice—hence their hope for a single religion that would
encompass and supercede all others. The problem with this is the problem with all syncretistic absolutism—it tends toward vacuity. As soon as
this synthesis says anything beyond "We must strive toward a spiritually
transcendental order" or the like, it tends to become a form of one or
another particular religion. For example, if it accepts one God, it can be
reconciled with Hinduism, but not with certain sorts of (agnostic) Bud-
dhism. If it accepts that God had a single incarnation in Jesus, then it
becomes a form of Christianity, eliminating Hinduism and Islam. If it
accepts that, say, Kṛṣṇa and Jesus were both incarnations, then it
becomes a form of Hinduism, eliminating Christianity and Islam—for
Hinduism can always add *avatāras* or divine incarnations, while Christianity cannot.

In sum, the Brahmo Samaj included an originalist group that was
very close to liberal orthodox Hinduism. And it included a modernizing
group that was also primarily Hindu and anti-Westernizing, even if it did
involve some syncretistic elements. At the opposite end of the spectrum,
we find groups in the Samaj that were strongly Westernizing and Chris-
tianizing—indeed, mimeticist. Between these extremes were the syncretists, who tended toward a somewhat vacuous synthetic absolutism.

Tagore's attitude toward the Brahmo Samaj was ambivalent, and it
varied greatly in the course of his life. At times, Tagore was adamantly
Hindu. At other times, he was a leader of the Brahmo Samaj, edited its
newspaper, gave sermons in its services, and so forth (see chapter 10 of
Kopf). Tagore is reported to have said that his greatest intellectual weakness was inconsistency, whereas his greatest intellectual strength was

inconsistency. This is more than a *bon mot*. His weakness was his inability to commit himself consistently to one position. His strength was his openness to a unusual variety of ideas and his ability to see the strength in a broad range of views. Hence his vacillation on the Brahmo Samaj. Hence also his ability to portray with sympathy and insight many different and opposed positions on culture and identity.

This is not to say, of course, that Tagores' opinions varied randomly. For the most part, they varied from liberal orthodox Hinduism, to Brahmo Hinduism and Hindu modernization, to syncretism—and all, again, within the context of universalism.

Perhaps in keeping with his inclination toward inconsistency, Tagore's portrait of Paresh Babu is a strange mix of criticism and not only praise, but reverence. Indeed, at the end of the novel, he has Gora virtually worship Paresh. Nonetheless, Tagore did not fail to recognize that there was a strong colonialist/mimeticist strain in the Brahmo Samaj and he criticized it harshly in *Gora*.

Indeed, it is Paresh who describes the purgative mimeticism that characterizes many Brahmo Samajis: "There are plenty of . . . people amongst Brahmos . . . [who] want to sever all connection with Hinduism without discrimination, lest outsiders should mistakenly think they condone also its evil customs. Such people find it difficult to lead a natural life, for they either pretend or exaggerate" (88–89). So anxious to impress their colonial masters, so disgusted by their own origin, they seek to purge themselves of everything Indian, and thus to purge their new religion of any element it might share with Hinduism. The more striking cases of mimeticism may be found in Haran-chandra Nag and Bordashundari, Paresh's wife.

We are first introduced to Haran at the home of Paresh. Those present have just been discussing the first Bengali to pass the British civil service exam (an inside joke—in reality, that person was Rabindranath Tagore's older brother, Satyendranath [see Dutta and Robinson, 38]). It is worth noting that the entire exam process was highly prejudicial. Until 1921, no exams were given in India, so candidates had to travel to England in order to sit for the examination, a requirement that effectively eliminated almost all Indians. Moreover, when Indians did succeed in passing the exam, they were sometimes subjected to extreme prejudice, including disqualification for minor infractions of rules. (See Wolpert, 251–52, on the notorious case of Surendranath Banerjea, which would have been known to Tagore's readers.) Haran insists that the entire discussion is pointless, not because of the prejudicial nature of British governmental policies and practices, but rather because "Bengalis. . . . will never be any good as administrators"—not merely a British position, but a right-wing British position. While snacking on the un-Bengali dish of "bread and butter," Haran goes on to a racist discourse on "the various defects and weaknesses of the Bengali character" (44). Gora responds that if he truly believed this, he would succumb to despair and hang himself. Rather, he insists, Haran is merely aping the English: "What you say about evil customs . . . you have merely learnt off by heart from English books." Indeed, Haran, with his fistful of bread and butter, is hardly Indian at all, hardly familiar with Indian culture: "You know nothing at all about the matter at first hand" (44). Finally, Gora points out the double standard that vitiates all such criticism: "When you are able to contemn all the evil customs of the English with as much honest indignation, you will have a right to talk" (44).

Indeed, Haran has sought to purge himself of all Indian tastes and culture—and not only by preferring bread and butter to Bengali snacks. Elsewhere, he is referred to as a "storehouse of English learning" (74), but certainly not of Indian or Hindu learning: "Amongst the scriptures of the world-religions his only support was the Bible." Indeed, "He wanted to banish" the *Bhagavadgītā*, *Mahābhārata* and "all such books from Brahmo households" (75). Moreover, he considers acceptance by the British to be the highest demonstration of an individual's value. He maintains to Gora that the British disdain Indians because "We have so many bad customs and superstitions that we are not worthy." However, "Those who are really worthy are received with the highest regard by the English." Gora replies, "This kind of regard for some persons which only accentuates the humiliation of the rest of their countrymen, is nothing but an insult in my eyes" (99). In keeping with the standard character type of the corrupt mimic, Haran is a hypocrite also. He has written against the Hindu custom of child marriage, and insisted that no one be married before the age of eighteen. But when Sucharita seems to be showing interest in Gora, he wants to seal the pact and marry Sucharita while she is still underage.

The conflict between Haran and Gora over acceptance by the British is not a purely theoretical matter. Haran and Paresh's family have been invited to a little celebration at the English magistrate's home—"The Magistrate, Mr. Brownlow . . . was in the habit of inviting to an occasional garden-party at his house a few of his respectable Bengali acquaintances" (139). In keeping with their colonial role as performing monkeys, the Bengalis on this occasion have been asked to provide entertainment for the white guests. Bordashundari takes an active part, organizing her daughters and Binoy: "It had been decided that Binoy should recite in a dramatic style Dryden's poem on 'The Power of Music,' and that the girls in suitable costumes should present tableaux illustrative of the subject of the poem. In addition to this, songs and English recitations were to be given by the girls as well" (122). "Haran . . . offered to recite a passage from *Paradise Lost*" (126). It is important to note that the Dryden poem in question is "Alexander's Feast or The Power of Music." It deals with Alexander's festivities following his conquest of Persia and, worse still, leads up to a vengeful torching of Persian homes and "glitt'ring temples of their hostile gods" (l.145). In other words, it is a poem celebrating a European colonial conquest of a great Eastern nation and the victor's brutal treatment of the subject population—centrally including a violent, physical attack on their religion and a destruction of their places of worship.

Needless to say, the evening does not include English people performing work by Kālidāsa or reciting from the *Gītagovinda*—still less, the acting out of scenes representing rebellion against colonial rule and the burning of Christian missions. Indeed, the situation is all the more repugnant when one recalls that indigenous theater had been one of the explicit objects of British colonial suppression. As Kopf points out, "one of a series of acts that infringed upon" Indians' civil rights was the "Dramatic Performances Act of 1876, which gave police commissioners the power to stop any performance they considered objectionable" (197). In short, had Paresh's family wished to take part in an evening of nationalist theater, they would have risked its disruption by that very Magistrate for whom whey were now going to perform.

As preparations for this entertainment proceed, Gora has been visiting Bengali villages. He has come upon a dire situation in Ghosepara: the villagers have had their harvests stolen, and have themselves been beaten or arrested, by the British or their agents. The problem is that they have refused to turn over their lands to Indigo Planters (133–34)—a typical conflict in colonized countries. Gora stops the Magistrate when the latter is out for a walk and asks him to intercede for the Ghosepara villagers. When the Magistrate refuses, and threatens Gora, Gora responds that he has no choice but to return to the villagers and urge them to stand up for themselves. As it happens, Haran had accompanied Mr. Brownlow on this walk. Ignoring the possibility that human feeling and a sense of justice are involved in Gora's actions, Haran explains to the Magistrate that the problem with men such as Gora is that "their education is not going deep enough." They remain Indian barbarians, and have not been fully transformed into Englishmen: "These fellows have not been able to assimilate the best in English culture. It is because they have only learnt their lessons by rote." In consequence, they fail to "acknowledge British rule in India to be a dispensation of Providence" (141). It is difficult even to imagine a more thoroughly reactionary and collaborationist attitude. And this from one of the acknowledged leaders of the Brahmo Samaj.

Subsequently, Gora is arrested and imprisoned by the Magistrate. Lolita, who plays the role of nonconformist in Paresh's family, is the only member of the family to see the disgrace in attending the Magistrate's garden party after this action. "How can you ever go to that Magistrate's house?," she asks in disbelief, "And then to stand on the stage, all dressed up, and recite poetry!" (150). She refuses to cooperate, and follows Binoy onto a steamer returning from the Magistrate's home to Calcutta. In this act of defiance, Lolita takes up feminist ideas, along with the idea, learned from Gora, that if one does not act against injustice, one will only lose self-respect, and sink into despair: "I don't see why, because I happen to have been born a girl, I should have to put up with everything without protest. For us, also, there are such words as possible and impossible, right and wrong. It would have been easier for me to commit suicide than to have taken any part in that play of theirs" (151). Later, she says to her father that "The relationship between the Magistrate and the people of our country is such that his patronising hospitality does us no honour. Ought I to have stayed on there, and put up with such patronage, after I had realised this?" Unfortunately, Paresh's political understanding is not as advanced as that of his daughter, for to him "The question was not an easy one to answer" (167). Haran, of course, remains adamant in his commitment to the Magistrate.

So too does the other chief mimeticist in the novel, Bordashundari, who considers Lolita's departure an unspeakable disgrace. We are first introduced to Bordashundari when Sucharita's background is mentioned. Sucharita is an orphan from a Hindu family. Her name was originally "Radharani," after Rādhā, an incarnation of Goddess Lakṣmī and the beloved of Kṛṣṇa, himself an incarnation of Viṣṇu. Rādhā's longing for her beloved and her sexual union with him are among the most common images of the devotee's relation to God in Hinduism. ("Rānī" merely means "queen.") Bordashundari was so uncomfortable with even the suggestion of the Hindu story of Rādhā and Kṛṣṇa, that she changed the "Radharani" "to the less aggressively orthodox name of Sucharita" (5), meaning "one who leads a virtuous life" (see Monier-Williams, 1223). For Bordashundari, this is probably a virtual antonym of "Radharani," for she would no doubt define "a virtuous life" directly against the sensual example of Rādhā.

This renaming is part of a broader reactionary pattern: "She was always careful about keeping clear the distinction between things that were Brahmo and things that were not" (35) and purging herself and her environment of the latter. Indeed, she identifies all forms of error with Hinduism: "From her childhood [Lolita] had heard Mistress Baroda [Bordashundari], whenever she wanted to be particularly scathing about any fault of Lolita's, denounce it as fit only for girls of Hindu homes." This tactic had the expected effect on Lolita, for, as a child, whenever she was compared to a Hindu, she "thereupon had always felt duly humiliated" (178). When Harimohini, an orthodox Hindu woman and aunt of Sucharita, comes to live in her home, Bordashundari and "her Brahmo lady friends" show nothing but "contempt" when Harimohini "would try to help in making [the guests] welcome" (195). Not only in worship, but in her treatment of the natives, Bordashundari is a virtual memsahib.

Moreover, like Haran and most other mimics, her mimeticism is hypocritical and self-serving, in this case a fairly crude matter of class aspiration: "She had lived quite a simple life in her early days, and then had all of a sudden developed an anxiety to keep pace with advanced society," wearing "high-heeled shoes," "putting powder and rouge" on her face and on the faces of her daughters, and in general aping the manners of the British (35). In keeping with her class aspirations, "The sons-in-law of her dreams were enterprising knights-errant whose one object of pursuit should be a deputy-magistrateship" (43).

Orthodox and Reactionary Hinduisms

Tagore's criticism of Brahmo mimeticism does not, of course, prevent him from criticizing orthodox and reactionary Hinduism. Indeed, the criticisms are established with remarkable parallelism. The major reactionary assimilationist man, Haran, is paired with an equally important reactionary traditionalist man, Gora's adoptive father, Krishnadayal. The major mimetic woman, Bordashundari, is paired with Harimohini, who begins as an unreflective conformist, but soon reveals herself to be a corrupt traditionalist, adhering to tradition with unthinking conformity, insofar as that suits her self-interest, but quite willing to violate tradition for personal gain (see 352–53). More positively, the flawed, but admirable syncretist Paresh is paired with the flawed, but admirable traditionalist, Gora. And the more unequivocally admirable nonmimeticist Brahmo, Lolita, is paired with the almost idealized liberal Hindu, Anandamoyi, Gora's adoptive mother.

The most obvious parallel is between Bordashundari and Harimohini. Both are deeply concerned with the opinions of their respective communities; both seem to have no concern for justice or injustice, humanity or humane feeling, but reduce all decisions to matters of social prestige, and wealth—in short, class standing. The only difference is that Bordashundari is focused on class standing in the Brahmo community and with the British, whereas Harimohini is concerned about class standing in the Hindu community. The most striking example of this is in the way both try to advance their social standing through Sucharita's marriage. Bordashundari is insistent that Sucharita marry Haran, thereby capturing for her family the most prestigious young Brahmo leader, and an acquaintance of the English Magistrate. Harimohini is equally insistent that Sucharita marry Harimohini's brother-in-law, Kailash. Harimohini hopes by this marriage to reenter the mainstream of Hindu society—to reenter the house of her father-in-law, both literally and metaphorically. It is worth noting in this connection that she had earlier gotten her own daughter killed by effectively forcing her to return to the home of an abusive husband (187). The proposed marriage of Sucharita to Kailash is not much more promising, for he is the same sort of corrupt traditionalist as Harimohini. For example, when he comes to Calcutta to see Sucharita, he is far more interested in ascertaining the degree of Sucharita's wealth than in learning anything about her as a person.

Moreover, just as Bordashundari has nothing but disdain for orthodox Hindus, Harimohini has nothing but disdain for those who are not orthodox Hindus. Indeed, she is in an almost continual panic about losing caste. She is endlessly fearful that she will be polluted by contact with someone who is of the wrong caste, someone who does not follow proper customs, and so on.

In the character of Krishnadayal, Tagore criticizes reactionary traditionalism as well. As with many reactionary traditionalists, Krishnadayal began as a mimeticist. He had worked for the British government for many years and "won the approbation of his English masters because of his unorthodox" behavior. As a consequence, "He gained promotion." But when he "retired in his old age with a heap of savings," he "suddenly turned orthodox and intolerant" (12). Indeed, "There had been a time, while his work [for the British] kept him upcountry, when in the company of the soldiers of the regiment he had indulged in forbidden meat and wine to his heart's content. In those days he used to consider it a sign of moral courage to go out of his way to revile and insult priests and *sannyasis.* . . . But nowadays anything savouring of orthodoxy had his allegiance" (21). As Paresh explains, in college, he and Krishnadayal "were the worst pair of iconoclasts you could imagine—we had no vestige of respect for traditions—we regarded the taking of unorthodox food as our actual duty" (40). Now, he is so thoroughly reactionary that he bases his religion on mantras, sacred ceremonies, and punctilious avoidance of pollution—even the pollution brought on by the touch of his adoptive son (109).

Unsurprisingly, his Hinduism is not particularly learned, nor even coherent. At one point, he says to Gora, "Whatever religion is really yours according to your own *karma* [thus as a result of the accumulated effects of your own actions in past lives], to it you will have to return sooner or later,—no one can stand in your way. God's will be done! What are we but His instruments?" (25; "religion" here rather misleadingly translates Bengali "dharma"). As Tagore, or the narrator, comments, "Krishnadayal had a way of accepting, with equally open arms, the doctrine of Karma and trust in God's will, identity with the Divine and worship of the Divinity,—he never even felt the need for reconciling these opposites" (25). The doctrine of karma, as articulated by Krishnadayal, says that one's present life is entirely determined by the accumulated effect of one's actions in past lives. The doctrine of divine will says that one's life, past or present, is merely the working-out of a divine plan. Superficially, at least, the two ideas—that we are determined by our past lives and that we are determined by divine will—are inconsistent. Moreover, even Krishnadayal's interpretation of karma as determinative is not uncontroversial within Hinduism. For example, in the

Mahābhārata, Brahmā, creator of the world, speaks against any absolute determinism, stating that "Everything can be secured by Exertion: but nothing can be gained through Destiny alone" ("Anusasana Parva," pt. 1, 16–17); "So there is no authority inherent in Destiny. . . . Destiny follows Exertion" (18).

In this case, as elsewhere, the hypocrisy of reactionary devotion is clear. Formerly, Krishnadayal was a mimeticist for personal gain; now he is a reactionary traditionalist for gain, filled with "greed for finding some short cut to salvation" (21). Despite all the problems which it causes for his observance of strict caste taboos, Krishnadayal will not tell Gora that his parents were European for fear that it will affect his own material comfort and security (342). It is only at the horrible prospect of eternal pollution, should Gora take part in his funeral obsequies, that Krishnadayal relents and reveals the secret.

As already noted, Gora's orthodoxy is more loosely paired with Paresh's syncretism. And, much as Paresh has a strain of mimeticism and collaborationism (cf. his reaction to the Magistrate's garden party), Gora has a strain of purgative traditionalism. Gora's earliest interests had been in the Brahmo Samaj (22). This may indicate a degree of initial mimeticism. Though Brahmos were not necessarily mimeticist, there was a strong component of mimeticism in the Samaj, as we have seen. Indeed, Krishnadayal had been a Brahmo during his mimeticist period (41). Moreover, Gora's entire attitude toward tradition, when he took it up, was marked by reactionary rigidity of just the sort one would expect from a converted mimeticist. As Sucharita observes, "In this protesting orthodoxy there was a spirit of defiance . . . it had not the naturalness of real conviction . . . it did not find its full satisfaction in its own faith . . . it was assumed in anger" (47–48). Harimohini too notices that "When Gora discoursed on matters of faith his words did not sound so sincere as to be palatable to her. It always seemed as if there were some adversary in front of him, and as if he were merely fighting against this opponent" (327).

But this is not all there is to Gora's Hinduism. Indeed, for the most part, his reactionary traditionalism is, as we have already noted, strategic, a reaction, not against his earlier self, but against the colonialist politics of ethnocide, which threaten to destroy all forms of Hinduism. Moreover—and this point is crucial—Gora commits himself to tradition with absolutely no thought of personal gain. Quite the contrary, in fact. Right from the beginning, we are told that "Gora snatched at every opportunity for casting away all his diffidence, all his former prejudices, and, standing on a level with the common people of his country, to say with all his heart: 'I am yours and you are mine'" (29). Gora considered it "a regular social duty . . . to visit the poor people of his neighbour-hood" every morning (77). He did this out of "desire for their companionship"—in contrast with the patronizing attitude of the Magistrate toward even upper-class Indians. "In fact, he was hardly so intimate with his circle of educated friends as he was with these people." In his sports club, "He had introduced these sons of carpenters and black-smiths on a footing of equality with the well-to-do members" (78). Most strikingly, when he is imprisoned, he refuses to accept a lawyer to plead his case: "I don't want to get free merely because I happen to have friends or money . . . I want my fate to be the same as the fate of those who are without means in this empire" (144–45). When he is released from prison, he refuses to take part in Abinash's celebration of his great sacrifices for mother India and quickly puts an end to the proceedings (261–62). His sacrifices, he insists, are of no greater value simply because he is not poor.

In short, Gora's reactionary position is disinterested, and thus crucially different from the reactionary views of Harimohini, Krishna-dayal, Haran, and Bordasundhari. Indeed, as we have already noted, he is not even a genuine reactionary traditionalist. His is actually a particularist universalism whose final orientation is toward the liberal orthodoxy of *mānavdharma*.

THE NECESSITY OF REACTION

The most important aspect of Gora's work and ideas is his insistence on strategic rigidity with respect to *ācarā*. Again, for Gora, English colonialism puts all Hindus in *āpad*, distress or extremity, and thus triggers *āpaddharma*—not, however, the typical version in which some rules are suspended or loosened, but the reverse, where all rules are observed with every possible strictness. When Harimohini senses that Gora is always arguing against an adversary, she is right. But the adversary is not a figment of Gora's imagination. The adversary is real. It is the pervasive, racist criticism of Indian culture by the colonialists and the mimetic stratum of upper-class Indian society. It is the Magistrate and Haran and the groups they represent. Indeed, this is why Gora's populism is so important. It is a defense and affirmation of the dignity and worth of the people who are most despised in the Hindu population. It is also why he has to defend not merely Hindu metaphysics and *mānavdharma*, but popular *ācarā* also. Binoy characterizes his strategic reactionary traditionalism well, when he says that Gora "insists on rigid indiscriminate observance, lest, by his yielding on minor points, foolish people may be led to feel a disrespect for more vital matters, or lest the opposite party [the colonialists and the mimeticists] should claim a victory" (88). It is not that Gora feels Hindu *ācarā* can never be questioned. Rather, he insists that "So long as we are subject to some foreign nation we must observe strictly our own laws, and leave the question of their goodness or badness till later" (338).

In present circumstances, Hinduism cannot develop along the lines of liberal orthodoxy and *mānavdharma*; if not maintained with rigid discipline, it will only degenerate into mimeticism. Thus, Gora asks all Hindus to "come inside India, accept all her good and her evil: if there be deformity then try and cure it from within." Mimics who approach India "with Christian ideas" will "stand opposed and . . . view it from the outside." They will "never understand," but "will only try to wound and never be of any service" (102–3). Change, "reform," is always important. But it is crucial that such reform be *Hindu* reform, not English and Christian reform, that it be a rethinking of *ācarā* in terms of *mānavdharma*, not in terms of English political economy and Anglican casuistry. "I want the changes in India to be along the path of India's development, for if you suddenly begin to follow the path of England's history then everything from first to last will be a useless failure" (330). Put differently, negatively, "Let me tell you that we are not going to submit to outside attempts to reform us, whether it be from [the Brahmo Samaj] or from foreign missionaries. . . . We can take correction from our parents, but when the police come to do it there is more of insult than of improvement in the process. . . . First acknowledge kinship with us, then come to reform us, else even good advice from you will but harm us" (51).

The central problem for Gora is that the criticism of Indian culture is external, demeaning, and part of colonialist domination. Early in the book, he argues vehemently (23):

> We must refuse to allow our country to stand at the bar of a foreign court and be judged according to a foreign law. Our ideas of shame or glory must not depend on minute comparisons at every step with

a foreign standard. We must not feel apologetic about the country of our birth—whether it be about its traditions, faith, or its scriptures—neither to others nor even to ourselves.

Tagore carefully illustrates the pervasiveness of English culture and the explicit or implicit denigration of Indian culture that goes along with this. We have already seen the gross colonialism implicit in the entertainments at the Magistrate's garden party, with the "natives" called upon to perform Dryden and Milton. The same bias is clear in education, at least in the education undertaken by the Brahmo Samaj. Bordashundari shows Binoy her daughter's school notebook—"English poems of Moore and Longfellow" (45) and boasts of her youngest child's most recent accomplishment, the ability to recite "Twinkle, twinkle, little star" (46). This from a child in Bengal, which has one of the most beautiful traditions of poetic song in the world.

This denigration is explicit elsewhere in the disdain shown by the English and by mimetic Indians to ordinary Indians, a disdain deeply repugnant to Tagore (cf. S. Ray, 21), and illustrated early on in the incident concerning the steamer. Pilgrims are travelling in overcrowded conditions to celebrate a Hindu festival. Some slip off the plank into the river, "while others were actually pushed over into the water by the sailors." The pilgrims' "faces betokened hopeless harassment, their eyes a pitiful anxiety. . . . Gora was the only one who was doing his best to help these pilgrims in their distressful plight." "Leaning over the railings of the upper first-class deck stood an Englishman and a modernised Bengali babu. . . . Every now and then, when one of the unfortunate pilgrims got into a specially awkward predicament, the Englishman laughed, and the Bengali joined in." Gora, unable to bear this insult to his fellow Indians, ascends to the upper deck and says "in a voice of thunder: 'Enough of this! Aren't you ashamed of yourselves?'" (38). Neither man will admit any error. When Gora leaves, the "modernised Bengali" makes pathetic attempts to gain the attention and respect of the Englishman, by seeking ways "to prove that he was not on the side of the common herd of his countrymen" (39). But his efforts are rebuffed by the Englishman, who later stops Gora and apologizes: "I beg your pardon for my conduct. I *am* ashamed of myself" (39).

The Bengali *babu* is like the deputy magistrates who, Gora later says, "are gradually coming to look upon their fellow-countrymen as little better than dogs" (102). But, again, the efforts of the Bengali *babu* are pathetic—he tries to order roast chicken, runs to retrieve the Englishman's newspaper when it blows away. His disdain for his fellow countrymen betrays a fear that he may be like them, that he may be the same sort of inferior creature disdained by the Englishman. He will treat his fellows like dogs because of a nagging fear that he himself has the worth of a dog in the eyes of the Englishman.

As this indicates, the constant devaluation of Indian culture and Indian people leads inevitably to despair. "I once believed there was no hope either for our country or for our society," Binoy confesses, "that we should always be regarded as minors, and the English would ever remain our guardians. And this is still the opinion of the majority of our countrymen" (101). Indeed, Binoy continues to suffer from such cultural self-doubt. Ultimately, this leads him to bend down "in obeisance at [Bordashundari's] feet" and request that he "be initiated into the Brahmo Samaj." He goes on to tell this unscrupulous mimic that "I know I am not worthy but my hope is that you will make me so" (284), almost deifying her in what is likely to strike Christians as a ludicrous allusion to the centurion's profession of faith to Jesus: "Sir, I am not worthy to have you under my roof" (*Matthew* 8.8) or a perverse misuse of the communion rite based on this profession. The result of Binoy's self-abasement is palpable: "Along with the waning of his own self-respect it was as though his respect for every one else had abated" (290). Despair brings with it a generalized cheapening of life, a broad denigration of humanity. In failing to recognize the kinship of myself and other humans, I demean both myself and them.

Gora's entire struggle is against this communal despair. Once, Binoy confesses to Gora his tendency to lose hope: "I have not the courage . . . to keep my faith erect in face of such widespread and terrible misery" (79). Gora responds, "I shall never bring myself to believe that misery is eternal. . . . Binoy, I urge you again and again, never even in your dreams think it is impossible for our country to become free" (79). Indeed, though Gora's traditionalism might, upon superficial acquaintance, appear to be a rigid legalism, based on the authority of law and a desire to keep people in line, nothing could be further from the truth. His motive, from beginning to end, is love. When Binoy criticizes Hindu customs, Gora refuses to take up the position of judge (267):

> What I want is India, no matter how you may find fault with her or how much you may abuse her. I don't want any one greater than her, whether myself or another! I do not wish to do the least thing which might separate me from her even by a hair's breadth! . . .

When the whole world has forsaken India and heaps insults upon
her, I for my part wish to share her seat of dishonour—this caste-
ridden, this superstitious, this idolatrous India of mine!

It is a complete compassionate love for India—and since she has been
brutalized and scorned, he will not criticize her, but must instead comfort her, protect her, heal her. Indeed, for Gora, love is the only means of
reforming Hinduism toward *mānavdharma* (50–51):

> Those whom you call illiterate are those to whose party I belong.
> What you call superstition, that is my faith! So long as you do not
> love your country and take your stand beside your own people, I
> will not allow one word of abuse of the motherland from you. . . .
> Reform? That can wait a while yet. More important than reforms
> are love and respect. Reform will come of itself from within, after
> we are a united people.

Gora's compassion for India is like that of the parrot for the withered
tree in the story from the *Mahābhārata*. Yudhiṣṭhira addressed Bhīṣma: "O
thou that knowest the truths of religion, I wish to hear of the merits of compassion." Bhīṣma responded with the following tale: A hunter shot a poi-
soned arrow at an antelope. The arrow missed its target and lodged in a
tree, which slowly "withered away, shedding its leaves and fruits."
Nonetheless, "a parrot that had lived in a hollow of its trunk all his life, did
not leave." Indra goes and asks the parrot why he remains in this withered
tree. The parrot responds, "Here, within this tree, was I born, and here in
this tree have I acquired all the good traits of my character, and here in this
tree was I protected in my infancy from the assaults of my enemies. . . .
When it was capable . . . it supported my life. How can I forsake it now?"
("Anusasana Parva," pt. 1, 15–16). Gora's relation to India and its culture
is directly parallel to the relation between the parrot and the tree. It bore
and nurtured him and provided him with what is best in his character; how
can he abandon it now when it is wounded and suffering and in need?

ŚIVA AND THE GODDESS

Gora's intellectual defense of reactionary traditionalism is perhaps the
most forceful articulation of such an argument in a literary work; it is

certainly the most forceful in the works with which I am familiar. Moreover, its rhetorical effect is furthered by Tagore's consistent development of Gora as a Śiva figure. Just as European works often involve heroes who are Christ figures—characters who in some ways recapitulate the ideas and sufferings of Jesus—Indian works often include Rāma or Kṛṣṇa figures. Gora is a clear case of a character who is defined in such a way as to recall the great god of discipline, Śiva.

Śiva is often characterized as the god of destruction, in contrast with Brahmā, the creator, and Viṣṇu, the preserver. But this is inaccurate. In the view of Śaivites (worshipers of Śiva), Śiva is creator. Moreover, Śiva holds a central role as preserver in all Hindu traditions. Specifically, in the very earliest time, the world was threatened with destruction by a great poison. Śiva, alone among the gods, agreed to take the poison into his throat and hold it there until the end of time, thereby preventing the destruction of the universe. Śiva is associated with destruction in part because of his anger, which on occasion leads him to reduce opponents to dust by a glimpse from his third eye. Moreover, in one aspect, he is Rudra, the storm god, and his personality is stormy too, prone to indignant fury. According to the Śaivites, he is the most powerful of the gods. But his time is spent in ascetic discipline or yoga in the Himalaya mountains. His sacred books are the Tantras, which, as already noted, advocate the equal treatment of all castes and of both sexes in religious matters (on the latter, see O'Flaherty, *Textual*, 130, 131, 137). Moreover, the Tantras are all dialogues between Śiva and his consort Pārvatī—the one woman, the one being, who can draw his mind away from ascetic practices. These dialogues provide the great classical Indian examples of intellectual dialectic between a man and a woman. Finally, Pārvatī herself has different forms, including the destructive Kālī, who subordinates Śiva himself. The Goddess is widely worshiped in Bengal in her cruel forms as Kālī and Durgā. Ultimately, Śiva and the Goddess are one deity only, not two, a single divinity, god/goddess, represented as the divine androgyne.

Gora's connection with Śiva as Rudra is perhaps most obvious. He becomes indignant regularly in the course of the novel and he is repeatedly associated with storms or represented through images of storms. As Sucharita stands and looks out on the rain, "Gora's face . . . flashed out" just as "the lightening flashed" (50). When he visited Binoy's lodgings, he "burst like a storm into his room" (63), then "went off like the wind" (64). At one point, when Anandamoyi looks at "Gora's face . . . she knew that a storm had raged" (96). This is important because it gives

his indignant anger a resonance that elevates it. It is not merely a cho-
leric disposition, but an aspect of the uncompromising, furious,
supremely disciplined god, Śiva.

Another obvious link is Gora's color. Śiva is a white-skinned god,
and Gora "was outrageously white, his complexion unmellowed by even
the slightest tinge of pigment" (6). Because of his white color, "One of
his college Professors used to call him the Snow Mountain" (6), alluding to Śiva's Himalayas. Moreover, Gora's intellectual eye has a destructive effect similar to that of Śiva's third eye. As Sucharita thinks at one
point, regarding an article by Haran, "Gourmohan Babu could have
powdered this article into dust!" (128).

Sometimes, the connections are more explicit. At one point Anandamoyi says that she has "shaped" both Gora and Binoy "like the
images of Shiva which girls make for their own worship" (177). More
strikingly, when Harimohini sees Gora for the first time, "She was
astonished." For Gora, "was bright like the flame of some sacrificial
fire! He resembled Mahadev [i.e., Śiva] in his lustrous radiance!" (292).
And Abinash thinks of Gora, "Our guru's face is like that of Shiva"
(388). Indeed, there are suggestions that Gora was, in effect, a gift to
Anandamoyi from Śiva. Here, Tagore takes up and varies a theme from
the *Mahābhārata*. In that work, the main characters are born to mortal
women, but their fathers are gods, called down from the heavens by
their mothers. Thus, through union with Dharma, Kuntī gives birth to
Yudhiṣṭhira. When Anandamoyi wanted a child, she explains, "Daily I
used to worship the emblem of Shiva, made with my own hands." But
Krishnadayal, then in his mimeticist phase, "used to come and throw it
away" (12). She never conceives a child of her own. But "One day in a
dream I saw myself offering to God a basket of white flowers"—white
flowers are typically offered to Śiva (I am grateful to Lalita Pandit for
this point). "After a time the flowers disappeared, and in their place I
saw a little child, as white as they were" (26). Within a fortnight of the
dream, Gora was born, and became her son.

Finally, this link with Śiva colors Gora's relation to Sucharita and to
the nation, for they are both versions of Śiva's relation with the goddess.
As to Sucharita, the connections are simple. Gora's icy aloofness to all
women and all sexual matters parallels that of Śiva, and his enchantment
by Sucharita parallels Śiva's sole weakness, for Pārvatī. More significantly,
the dialectic between Gora and Sucharita takes as its classical model the
Śaivite Tantras; we shall return to this dialectic in the next section.

The connections with the nation are more extended and more complex. Gora himself represents his relation to India in terms of the Goddess as Durgā or Kālī: "The goddess of my worship does not come to me enshrined in beauty. I see her where there is poverty and famine, pain and insult. Not where worship is offered with song and flower, but where life's blood is sacrificed" and when he thinks of this, his "heart leaps . . . it is Śiva's dance of life" (71). This is a brilliant use and revision of the mythology and ritual surrounding Kālī worship. Kālī is the goddess in the form of death and destruction, the loss of all things and conditions to which one is attached (see Danielou, 273). In her different forms, she manifests hunger, disease, poverty (see Danielou, 274–83). Gora here uses the image of Kālī-worship—and, implicitly, the worship of other forms of the goddess (e.g., Tārā, who represents hunger)—*not* as the worship of her cruel power, not as some form of self-serving appeasement, but as an image of love for those who suffer. This worship is, for Gora, an acceptance of the "cruel and terrible" in life, a refusal to be seduced by the pleasant and beautiful—for to love and worship what is decayed and diseased and poor, to throw in one's lot with the miserable, is difficult; it is not the easy worship of health and prosperity, the worship of the self-serving mimics and corrupt traditionalists.

Moreover, just as Kālī worship at times involved animal or even human sacrifice, Gora refers to a place "where life's blood is sacrificed," "Not where worship is offered with song and flower," as in the standard ceremonies (71). Of course, Gora is not advocating animal (or, still less, human) sacrifice. Rather, he is using the imagery of Kālī worship to urge real engagement in struggle for the Indian people, active political and cultural work among those whose blood has already been sacrificed. He contrasts this "true" worship, active and devoted to the people, with the rarefied worship that is confined to a temple.

In keeping with this, Gora compares his feeling of bliss in unity with his country to "Śiva's dance of life." As Ananda Coomaraswamy and Sister Nivedita (one model for Gora [see Pandit, 207]) note—in a volume illustrated by Abanindro Nath Tagore—there are "many legends of Shiva's dance." Some legends stress its creative function, as does Gora; others emphasize its preservative or destructive function. But in each case, "Its purpose is to release the souls of men from illusion." In Hinduism, the feeling of bliss—such as that felt by Gora in connection with Śiva's dance—is the feeling of unity with god; it is the dissolution of the individual soul or *ātman* in Godhead. In standard Hindu belief, the individual soul and Godhead are, ultimately, one. It is only in ignorance that we think ourselves separate from Godhead. And this ignorance causes suffering. Gora uses this idea as an image of the relation of the individual to the nation. As individuals, we are one with the nation, though we fail to see this, due to ignorance. Thus, we must continually strive to experience our oneness with the group. Not for altruistic reasons, but for ourselves. For not to experience that oneness is to suffer. To experience that oneness is to experience *ānanda*, "bliss" or "joy," as it is translated in the preceding passage. Indeed, ānanda is used as a technical term to refer to a stage of our experience of oneness with godhead (see Eliade, 80–81). It is on this analogy with blissful *samādhi*, the ultimate spiritual realization of the unity of *ātman* (individual soul) with Brahman (all-encompassing divinity), that Gora tells Binoy, "It is the one desire of my life that my truth may come before me . . . vividly." Thus far, he has "only a book knowledge of the love of country," just as an aspirant, practicing yoga and seeking realization of his/her identity with Godhead, will have a book knowledge of *samādhi*. Once "you have experienced the real thing, you realise how much more true it is than the thing you read about," for truth is, in Hindu metaphysical usage, not merely a matter of facts, but a matter of direct experience. This true experience "claims nothing less than the whole of your universe; there is no place where you can get away from it." As he imagines this absolute union with the community, this transposition of *samādhi* from transcendence to immanence, theology to culture, Gora's "whole life, its consciousness, its power, seemed to lose itself in the bliss of . . . supreme beauty" (70). In sum, Gora sees spiritual realization in social engagement, unity with Godhead in unity with ordinary Indian humanity, the cosmic "dance of life" in the real material conditions and active living of those around him.

This is not the only point at which Gora implicitly compares the work of cultural preservation with Śiva's work of preserving life. In an earlier discussion with Binoy, Gora insisted that "At present our only task is to infuse in the unbelievers our own unhesitating and unflinching confidence in all that belongs to our country. Through our constant habit of being ashamed of our country, the poison of servility has overpowered our minds. If each one of us will, by his own example, counteract that poison, then we shall soon find our field of service" (19). Here, Gora implicitly (via the word *bis*, Sanskrit *viṣa*, poison) links the work of cultural preservation with the earliest mythic salvation of existence—Śiva's counteracting of the primal poison.

The culmination of this revision of Hindu metaphysics into cultural nationalism is spoken by Gora to Binoy. But it refers beyond these two friends to all the vastly diverse nation of India. All the former British colonies have some problems with the cultural coherence of their populations. In some cases, the population is relatively homogeneous, except for a Creole minority. In other cases, there are two or three major ethnic groups. But in India, this cultural diversity is staggering. There is not only the matter of religion—Hindus, Muslims, Sikhs, Parsis, Christians; there are differences among Hindus, by caste, by major deity, by ritual or other orientation; there are regional and linguistic differences, and so on. In consequence, Indian writers tend to focus much more insistently on the possibility of reconciling those differences into a coherent national identity. In this dialogue with Binoy, Gora implicitly takes up this theme—or, rather, Tagore uses Gora's speech about his friendship with Binoy to make a point about national identity (71):

> Our natures are different, it is true . . . but a supreme joy will make our different natures one. A greater love than that which binds us to each other will unite us. . . . Then will come a day when, forgetting all our differences . . . we shall be able to stand together, immovable in an immense passion of self-abandonment. In that austere joy we shall find the ultimate fulfillment.

Allegorically, the unity that binds Hindu, Muslim, Sikh, Christian, Brahmo, will not merely be the unity of individual ties, friendships between individual Hindus, Muslims, and so on. It will be the unity of the nation. Moreover, that will be a unity of "self-abandonment" (*ātma-parihār*, the abandonment of one's *ātman*) because it is akin to the blissful loss of self in Godhead ("the ultimate fulfillment"), but also because it will lead individuals to devote themselves first of all to the nation of India, in its unity and diversity, and not to their narrowly communal or individual self-interests.

It is no accident that Anandamoyi enters at the culmination of this dialogue. "Ananda-moyi" means "full of bliss," the very bliss of divine union to which Gora alludes in this passage. Moreover, it is clear from early in the novel that Anandamoyi, the adoptive mother of both Gora and Binoy, is at least in part an allegorical representation of "Mother India." Towards the beginning of the novel, Binoy makes this connection explicit. He thinks to himself, "May the love-light of [Anandamoyi's] face guard my mind from all distractions. May it be as the reflection of my motherland and keep me firm on the path of duty."

Binoy had earlier argued with Gora over whether or not he should take food with Anandamoyi. Gora had said that Binoy must strictly observe the injunctions of his caste. Binoy had protested, "But she is your mother!" To which Gora responded, "You needn't remind me of that! How many possess a mother like mine! But if I once begin to show disrespect for tradition, then one day perhaps I shall cease to respect my mother also" (14). Rejecting the idea that he should refuse Anandamoyi's food, Binoy thinks, "No scripture shall prove to me that food from your hand is not nectar for me" (16). Here, Binoy alludes to the myth of the primal churning of the ocean. First, a poison had appeared, and it threatened to destroy all life—that was taken by Śiva. Then *amrita* appeared—the nectar of immortality; it was taken by Viṣṇu, or Bisnu, in Bengali pronunciation. Literally, Binoy—"Binu," as he is sometimes called (9)—is making the hyperbolic claim that food from Anandamoyi is like *amrita*, the nectar of the gods; allegorically, Tagore is indicating that immortality comes from Mother India, from one's accepting her "food"—her traditions, practices, beliefs, all the things that nourish one's humanity. Or, rather, some of her traditions—her traditions as modified and fully humanized by the universal principles of *mānav-dharma*. Indeed, the difference between Gora and Binoy can be understood in terms of this myth. Gora is like Śiva and stresses the need to neutralize the poison. Binoy is like Viṣṇu and emphasizes the delight of the nectar. (Later, there is a further suggestion of this link when Binoy is associated with the sound of the *śankha* or conch shell, the instrument of Viṣṇu [154, where it is unfortunately translated as "trumpet"].) Both are right, but partial. Indeed, they are both right even literally. Binoy is right that it is shocking, and unHindu, for Gora to reject his mother's food. But Gora is right that, once one succumbs to the criticisms of the racist colonizers, one risks falling into such decadence and self-loathing that one will soon not only reject a mother's food, but despise the mother herself.

Later, Gora articulates the link explicitly, identifying Anandamoyi with Mother India and with the Goddess, the maternal divinity to whom the soul is joined in *samādhi*. Indeed, just as the unity with godhead releases the soul from suffering, in Gora's meditation, the unity of the individual with Mother India releases that individual from cultural and racial despair (269–70): "The servant came saying that his mother called him, and on receiving this message Gora started suddenly, and repeated to himself, 'Mother has called me!' and it seemed to him that the words had a new significance." Hearing of this call, "Gora's heart was so full that tears came to his eyes and all despondency vanished from his mind." He thinks, "'Mother is calling me! Let me go to where the Bestower of all food, the One who maintains the Universe, is seated . . . the One who sheds the glorious light of the Future on the imperfect and miserable Present'" (269–70). And in this mother—Mother India, Anandamoyi, Goddess Śakti—Gora finds all the sectarian conflicts of personal life, of Indian culture, of religion, resolved; not suppressed under a single dogma, but united and harmonized: "In the midst of this joy Gora felt . . . all the trifling differences of that day being merged in a complete harmony" (270).

In connection with this harmonization of difference, it is crucial that Anandamoyi is the mother of adopted children only. Tagore's point here, I take it, is that no one is the natural child of "Mother India." All the people who claim to be her children are at least in part the descendants of invaders. As Tagore put it in his lectures on nationalism: "The history of India does not belong to one particular race but is of a process of creation to which various races of the world contributed—the Dravidians and the Aryans, the ancient Greeks and Persians, the Mohamedans of the West and those of central Asia" (27). That is why we can all put aside our differences when joined together in Mother India; she is the adoptive mother of all of us in being the natural mother of none. This is also linked, directly and obviously, with Anandamoyi's liberal orthodoxy, most obviously with her rejection of birth-caste. Indeed, it is the moment when she accepts Gora as her child that she rejects caste. "But do you know that it was when I first took you in my arms that I said good-bye to convention?" she asks him, continuing, "When you hold a little child to your breast then you feel certain that no one is born into this world with caste" (13).

PARTICULARIST UNIVERSALISM AND LIBERAL ORTHODOXY

This allegorization, almost necessarily, leads to a particularist universalism, a universalism that finally allows the deepest respect for diversity, because it sees in diversity multiple expressions of shared humanity.

And, indeed, this is Gora's view. Gora's universalism comes out most clearly in his dialogues with Sucharita, which, again, echo the dialogues of Śiva and Pārvatī. Articulating the particularist universalist position, he explains, "That which transcends country, which is greater than country, can only reveal itself through one's country. God has manifested His one, eternal nature in just such a variety of forms." He is insistent that imposing any single, absolute form is wrong: "Those who say that Truth is one, and therefore that only one form of religion is true, accept only this truth, namely that Truth is one, but omit to acknowledge the truth that Truth is limitless. The limitless One manifests itself in the limitless Many." Indeed, in Gora's view, this recognition is itself particularly Hindu; it is Hinduism that most clearly articulates universalist particularism. As Gora puts it, "In other countries they have tried to confine God within some one definition. In India no doubt there have also been attempts to realize God in one or other of His special aspects, but these have never been looked upon as final, nor any of them conceived to be the only one. No Indian devotee has ever failed to acknowledge that God in His infinity transcends the particular aspect which may be true for the worshiper personally" (103).

In a later dialogue with Sucharita, Gora takes up the theme again. Haran wishes to shape Sucharita to a particular Brahmo view of everything; he "could forgive almost anything, except the following of an independent path, according to their own judgement, by those whom he had tried to guide aright" (198). In direct contrast with this, Gora says, "I want you to understand yourself in your own way, and not to belittle yourself, misled by other people's opinions. You must realise in your own mind that you are not merely a member of any special party!" Here, as in Lovelace, we have, in a sort of miniature form, the standard plot structure in national allegory—a love triangle serving as metaphor for the struggle over the hearts of the nation's people. Haran and Gora are two different ideologies that the people of India could follow. Sucharita stands for those people. Haran wants them all to conform to his will and become Bible-reading Brahmos, rejecting Indian culture. Gora wants them to take up their own *ācāra* and dharma and faith and philosophy, their own practical and reflective identity, without apology to anyone else, to consider their own views, what they want and what they do not want, and to do so in the context of a broad national union that is not exclusive in the way that Christianity is exclusive.

Gora goes on to explain that "A Hindu belongs to no party. The Hindus are a nation, and such a vast nation that their nationality cannot be limited within the scope of any single definition. Just as the ocean is not the same as its waves, so Hindus are not the same as sects" (294). Taking up the allegory of Mother India, Gora continues (296, altered):

> You must understand that the Hindu dharma takes in its lap, like a mother, people of different ideas and opinions; in other words, the Hindu dharma looks upon man only as man, and does not count him as belonging to a particular party. . . . Christians do not want to acknowledge diversity; they say that on one side is the Christian religion and on the other eternal destruction, and between these two there is no middle path. And because we have studied under these Christians we have become ashamed of the variety there is in Hinduism. We fail to see that through this diversity Hinduism is coming to realise the oneness of all. Until we can free ourselves from this whirlpool of Christian teaching we shall not become fit for the glorious truths of our own Hindu dharma!

When the god Dharma interrogates Yudhiṣṭhira, he asks, "what is hypocrisy?" Yudhiṣṭhira answers, "The setting up of a religious standard is hypocrisy" ("Vana Parva," 609–10). Christianity is defined by such a single, all-encompassing standard, the imposition of one view on all humanity. Gora's argument is that Hinduism should be defined against such absolute standardization. For Gora, Hinduism, as a particularist universalism, must be defended, not as a sect, but as a human possibility, a possibility for the multiple interests and needs of humankind (294–95):

> Do you want to impose the authority of your own sect upon everybody else? Do you want to shut your eyes and imagine that all men are alike and have been born into the world in order to become members of the sect known as the Brahmo Samaj? If that is your idea, then in what way do you differ from those robber nations who refuse to admit, because of their pride in physical force, that the differences between nations are of inestimable value to the whole of mankind, and who imagine that the greatest blessing for humanity is that they should conquer all other nations of the world and bring them under their undisputed sway, thus reducing the whole earth to slavery.

Gora's project of preserving Hinduism does not serve Hinduism alone, but humanity in general, for the loss of Hinduism would be a loss to all men and women. The needs of humanity are vast and the ideas and practices satisfying those needs must be equally vast: "So you too ought to consider whether you are acting in the interests merely of your own sect or of the whole of mankind. Do you realise what the whole of mankind means? What a variety of needs it has, what different kinds of natures, what innumerable tendencies?" (294). Some are drawn to asceticism, some to mental disciplines, some to ritual, some to dialectic. The more paths that are available, the better it is for all—though all such activities share common principles. One might draw an analogy with music. It would be a terrible deprivation to reduce all music to one period (e.g., Baroque) or one tradition (e.g., Japanese). And yet all periods and traditions share common principles, principles that allow us to benefit from the differences. "God has created men differing from each other in ideas and in actions with a variety of beliefs and of customs, but fundamentally one in their humanity. There is something in all of them which is mine, which belongs to India as a whole, which, if only we can see it in its truth, will pierce through all littleness and incompleteness" (296).

Tagore too advocated just this sort of particularist universalism. As Mukherji explains, Tagore maintained "that the distinct character of a religion need not work against its universality. There could be no real difference between the highest ideals of Hinduism and other religions. Every religion is the product of a land and its people, a country and a culture, and expresses itself through a particular idiom and language; yet it may indeed be universal as well" (105–6).

But this leaves the reader in a quandary—can universalism, even particularist universalism, be reconciled with reactionary traditionalism, even as a strategy? For while one is protecting Hindu ācāra against external attack and trying to maintain Indian self-esteem in the face of colonialist disdain, any injustices of that ācāra itself are continuing, with their own corrosive effects on self-esteem, with their own imposition of religious standards on others—most obviously women and members of the lower castes. However correct Gora's arguments may be, Paresh is right too when he says that "The Hindu Society insults and abandons men, and for that reason nowadays it is becoming increasingly difficult to preserve our self-respect" (356).

Consider the condition of women. In the Brahmo Samaj, women were educated and allowed far broader freedoms to develop their capacities in social interaction and in work. Though there were differences of opinion on the rate at which women's liberation should proceed, for virtually all the major Brahmo leaders the emancipation of women was a central task in the Brahmo program. For example, speaking of the founder of Brahmoism, Kopf notes that "One has only to read Rammohun's works on social reform to realize that most of it deals with one aspect or another of man's inhumanity to women in Bengal" (15). Strains of this egalitarian attitude may be found in Hinduism as well—for example, in the tantras, as already mentioned. But in popular Hindu ācāra, the woman's dharma is to be "light to the home" (9) only. When Lolita and Sucharita, raised as Brahmos, wish to start a school for girls, Harimohini protests, "I have never heard of Hindu gentlewomen wanting to teach in a school—never in my life!" (227). Indeed, in Harimohini's view "education was not only not necessary for girls but was positively injurious" (278). Harimohini recognizes that in Hindu society there is a vast difference in the standards used to judge men and women, but she seems to find this entirely unobjectionable: "Were not the stronger sex privileged to break all rules and evade all discipline, imposed even by orthodoxy?" (223). Indeed, before he finally accepts Sucharita and the implications of his own universalism, even Gora writes that "For women the path of life's true realisation is the welfare of all. The world may be full of joy or full of sorrow—the virtuous and chaste woman will accept it all and make it her chief religious duty to give form to her religion in her home" (397). As Binoy points out, dominant strains of Hindu ācāra, including that which was taken up by cultural nationalists, "look on India as a country of men . . . entirely ignor[ing] the women . . . we do not give the women of our country their rightful place in our consideration" (83). And any system that so thoroughly subjugates and ignores half of its members is necessarily at best "a half-truth" (83).

Indeed, the faults in Hindu ācāra themselves contribute to the continuation of British rule and to the undermining of Hinduism. For example, the dowry system bankrupts fathers of daughters and makes daughters despised. As Mohim says, "This is what is called manliness! To ruin completely a girl's father! Is that a small matter? Whatever you may say, brother, I can't go about with you singing victory to the Hindu society day and night; my voice all of a sudden becomes weak at the suggestion" (339). In one of the villages Gora visits, a Brahmin man works as rent collector, oppressing his fellow Indians. He explains, "After a few years I shall have earned enough to pay the expenses of my daughter's marriage and then I and my wife can retire to a religious life in Benares." His monetary need, a need created by Hindu society, has driven him to this, and not without a price in self-esteem: "Sometimes I feel inclined to hang myself and end it all!" (138).

More generally, Gora decides that, in the villages, "Night and day without ceasing every act of eating, drinking, social ceremony, and touching, in every home, was under the vigilant eyes of society" (367). Gora may be mistaken about the situation being so dire in the villages. In fact, Tagore's attitude toward the villagers, as expressed through Gora, is rather biased and hardly presents a complete picture of villagers or village life. Yet, there was certainly a degree of this Foucaultian panopticism in the villages, and any deviation from *ācarā* was often punished cruelly. Kopf cites many examples of brutal treatment of Brahmos in villages—cut off from their inheritance, their trades boycotted, their property burned, they themselves physically attacked (97–101). Clearly there are problems with the rigidity of Hindu *ācarā* ("*ācarā*" is the term used by Tagore in this passage, in this case translated as "traditional customs" [367]). And Gora sees this when he encounters that *ācarā* removed from direct British threat—in other words, when he moves from the region of contact to the region of cultural autonomy.

Due to the various divisions within Hindu society, and due to the common idea that one's sufferings in this life are fair retribution for sins committed in previous lives, "No one had the least pity for any one else" (367). "Gora saw that society offers no help to a man at the time of his need, gives him no encouragement at the time of his misfortune, it merely afflicts him with penalties and humbles him to the dust." Indeed, popular Hindu *ācarā* is in direct violation of true Hindu dharma: "He could see nowhere any trace of that dharma which through service, love, compassion, self-respect and respect for humanity as a whole, gives power and life and happiness to all" (368, altered). Thus, to defend *ācarā* is, at times, to defend the direct violation of Hindu dharma, and practices that prevented Hindus from uniting against the British. Thus, "Gora who in the educated community [i.e., in the region of contact] had not wanted traditional custom to be relaxed in any respect was the very man who gave to custom a direct blow here in the villages" (369). He could not act differently. "The very intensity of his love for his country" (370) forced him to see the faults and to oppose them. Even earlier, Gora had realized that following dharma in the villages demands liberal orthodoxy: "'What terrible wrong have we been doing,' he said to himself, 'by making purity

an external thing! Shall my caste remain pure by eating from the hands
of this oppressor of the poor Mahomedans, and be lost in the home of
the man who has not only shared their miseries but given shelter to one
of them at the risk of being outcasted himself?" (136). Compare Śiva in
the *Mahānirvāṇa Tantra*: "O Devi! purity is of two kinds, external and
internal . . . what need is there to say more about the rules of purity and
impurity? Whatever purifies the mind, that the householder should do"
(8.70, 8.74).

Thus, despite his arguments for rigidity, even Gora's own ideas point
to liberal orthodoxy, at least as the final goal. Certainly, that is the form
of Hinduism that Gora wishes to preserve, a form in accord with
mānavdharma. Moreover, it is a genuine possibility for Hinduism. As
Binoy says, "Hindu society has always given shelter to new sects, and it
can be the society of all . . . communities" (308). And, elsewhere, "The
very day I come to regard Hinduism as consisting of prohibitions with
regard to touching, and prohibitions with regard to eating, and a lot of
other meaningless rules and regulations, I shall become, if not a Brahmo,
then a Christian, a Mussalman, or something of that sort. But I have not
yet such a lack of faith in Hinduism" (280). His marriage to Lolita is in
part a demonstration of just this ideal—a union of liberal orthodox Hinduism and an antimimetic Brahmo Samaj, a metaphor for the larger
unity that Tagore envisions for India. This is paralleled in the coming
marriage of Sucharita and Gora. It is articulated in Gora's final acceptance of Paresh's tolerance: "Make me your disciple! To-day give me the
mantram of that Deity who belongs to all, Hindu, Mussulman, Christian, and Brahmo alike—the doors to whose temple are never closed to
any person of any caste whatever—He who is not merely the God of the
Hindus, but who is the God of India herself!" (407). And even more so
in Gora's return to Anandamoyi, the culmination of the allegory of
Mother India. "Mother, you are my mother!," he exclaims. "The
mother whom I have been wandering about in search of was all the time
sitting in my room at home. You have no caste, you make no distinctions, and have no hatred—you are only the image of our welfare!"
Making the connection explicit, he concludes, "It is you who are India!"
(407). And, at last, Gora breaks his rigid adherence to cast taboos; he
will drink water drawn by the casteless, Christian woman, Lachmiya,
named, like Sucharita/Radharani, for the Goddess Lakṣmī: "'Mother!'
went on Gora, after a moment's pause, 'will you call Lachmiya and ask
her to bring me a glass of water?'" (408).

Of course, a problem remains. As Paresh points out, while Hinduism may accommodate all varieties of sects for those who are born Hindus, "there is no way of obtaining entrance into the Hindu Society." And in that way it is not at all universal; "That society is not one for all mankind—it is only for those whose destiny it is to be born Hindus" (355). Krishnadayal makes the same point, "But, my boy, simply to call oneself a Hindu is not to become one. It is easy to become a Mohammedan, easier still to become a Christian—but a Hindu! Good Lord, that's a different matter!" (25). On the other hand, there are even options here for liberal orthodoxy, for "In olden times the back entrances to the Hindu Society were left open, and it used to be considered one of the glories of this country that one of non-Aryan nationality could become a Hindu" (356). This is precisely the sort of open Hinduism advocated by Anandamoyi when she supports the *Hindu* marriage of Binoy and Lolita, explaining that Binoy "can marry a Brahmo girl while remaining a Hindu . . . If he is willing to do so" (255). In other words, for Anandamoyi, in direct contrast with Krishnadayal, Hindus are precisely those who call themselves Hindus, whatever their birth or practice. It is a matter of action, not of birth. It is up to these Hindus to accept Hinduism and then to change it themselves, to decide on what they want it to be, following *mānavdharma*—which is, again, following "nature."

Indeed, it is precisely Gora's sense of the unnaturalness of reactionary traditionalism that leads to his most profound doubts about cultural rigidity. After cutting himself off from Sucharita and, at Harimohini's insistence, urging her to marry (397), Gora felt that had done something wrong. But clearly "This wrong was not a violation of rules and laws, it was not a blunder against the Shastras, or something opposed to religious practice"; rather, "It was a wrong which had been committed within his own nature" (400), which is to say, it went against something deeply and universally human. (The Bengali word for "nature" here is *prakriti*, not dharma, but this term is equally suggestive and relevant, for, in addition to signifying "nature," *prakriti* refers to the "feminine principle"—what is, typically, repressed in reactionary traditionalism, but is strongly affirmed in Tantricism.)

Of course, the final resolution has been brought about only because Gora discovers that he is not born a Hindu, because his entire sense of identity has been shattered (402):

> In a single moment Gora's whole life seemed to him like some extraordinary dream. The foundations upon which, from childhood, all

his life had been raised had suddenly crumbled into dust, and he was unable to understand who he was or where he stood. What he had called the past seemed to have no substance, and that bright future which he had looked forward to with such eagerness for so long had vanished completely. . . .

As Gora puts it, in one of the most moving passages in the book, a moment of near total despair, "From one end of India to the other the doors of every temple are to-day closed against me—to-day in the whole country there is no seat for me at any Hindu feast" (405). And yet this is what allows him to say that "To-day I am really an Indian! In me there is no longer any opposition between Hindu, Mussulman, and Christian. To-day every caste in India is my caste, the food of all is my food!" (406).

Allegorically, Gora's condition is generalizable. No one is fully Hindu; no one is unpolluted; all have foreign ancestors; there is no truly "authentic" Hindu. (Some critics—for example, Chakravorty, 198–99—have faulted the novel for having Gora's change of heart rest on an accident. I take the whole point to be that the nature of the realization is necessary and universal.) The revelation of his origins, in leading him to see his previous life as a dream, operates as a sort of enlightenment, directly parallel to the realization that the separate existence of the individual soul in the material world is an illusion, a sort of dream. Indeed, the conclusion develops through images of *samādhi*, as Pandit has shown (231). Gora thus achieves his unity with Godhead through achieving at last a genuine realization of his unity with India. Moreover, this fits well with the implicit references to tantricism, for, in the *Mahānirvāṇa Tantra*, Śiva says to Pārvatī that the enlightened person "is free of all injunctions and prohibitions" (Avalon, 8.273) and that the ascetic "should eat without making any distinction as to the fitness of place, time or person" (8.282)—a dictum that Gora follows immediately with respect to Lachmiya.

Indeed, this allegory of spiritual union with India is doubled in Gora's relation to Sucharita. In hearing of his birth, he realizes that he can truly join with Sucharita in *sahadharma*, in mutual fostering of dharma. Simultaneously, he realizes that it is only in a casteless union with India that he can join India and her people in *sahadharma* as well.

Just after this, Gora turns to Paresh and asks to be Paresh's "disciple" (407). This near devotional attitude to Paresh, an admirable, though flawed character, may seem excessive. Nonetheless, it makes sense in context. Paresh is highly tolerant and nonsectarian. Moreover, he accepts universalism (see 309). Indeed, it is his broad, if somewhat vacuous, sense of universality that allows Paresh to reject sectarianism. "Because of the union with the Supreme which Paresh Babu's life consistently sought. . . . The freedom which he had himself gained . . . made it impossible for him to seek to coerce others in regard to belief or conduct." For this reason, "He often drew on himself the censure of sectarian enthusiasts" (208). Or, as Paresh puts it later, "Sectarianism . . . is a thing which makes people entirely forget the simple and obvious truth that man is man—it creates a kind of whirlpool in which the society-made distinction between Hindu and Brahmo assumes greater importance than universal truth" (242).

Indeed, it is this view that allows Binoy and Lolita to marry: "they forgot they were Hindu or Brahmo, and only remembered that they were two human souls" (306). Gora's rigidity, would not have allowed this marriage and thus would have violated nature—dharma, or *prakriti*. As Binoy argues, "If it is not wrong for me to marry Lolita, if indeed I ought to do so, then it would be actually adharmic for me to be deterred from doing so merely because it happened to be unfavourable to society" (266, altered). Or as Paresh explains, "I know . . . that it will land us all in a great difficulty, but when there is nothing wrong in Lolita marrying Binoy, when in fact she ought to do so, then I cannot think that it is my duty to respect an obstacle which society puts in the way. It can never be right that man should remain narrow and confined out of regard for society—rather society ought to become more liberal out of regard for the individual" (316).

Moreover, it is important to recall that, in the end, Paresh is not the only one to receive Gora's veneration. The figure of Anandamoyi indicates that Tagore hoped that Hinduism as well as Brahmoism would allow for nonsectarian, particularist universalism. Indeed, as Nandy argues, Gora comes to revere both Paresh and Anandamoyi because they affirm a "moral universe" that is "universal" and, at the same time, "in continuity with Indian traditions" (*Illegitimacy*, 41). Early in *Illegitimacy*, Nandy draws a distinction between "homogenized universalism" and "distinctive civilizational . . . universalism" (x xi). The former is roughly what we have referred to as "absolutism"; the latter is particularist universalism. Nandy's point in the passage just quoted is, in our terms, that Gora reveres Paresh and Anandamoyi precisely because they represent for him a "distinctive civilizational" or particularist universalism in the realm of dharma. In keeping with this, Nandy maintains that "A central theme in Tagore's reaffirmation of a moral universe was a universalism that denied moral and cultural relativism and endorsed a large, plural concept of India" (81).

Pandit draws an in some ways more suggestive distinction between "empathic universalism" and "imperialistic universalism" (207). In these terms, we might say that Anandamoyi and Paresh manifest the natural empathy of all humans that is a necessary condition for dharma and that is directly opposed to the imperialistic imposition of dharma—whether by the British Christians or by Hindus or by Brahmos—the hypocritical establishment of a religious standard, as Yudhiṣṭhira put it. Indeed, one could go so far as to say that the universal condition of dharma is empathy and thus that its fulfillment is universal *sahadharma*. In this context, the reverence for Paresh does not have any special significance, beyond the reverence one owes to all people and practices that instantiate dharma and foster human empathy, whether Hindu (Anandamoyi) or Brahmo (Paresh), female (Anandamoyi) or male (Paresh), joyful in union ("Anandamoyi") or respectful from a distance ("Paresh," meaning "the Almighty" [see Shanta]).

And yet, Gora's arguments echo in the reader's mind. The problem of colonialism remains. If one criticizes Hinduism, imperialists will say, "Even the Hindus see the barbarity in their cult." If one does not criticize Hinduism, they will say, "Those Hindus are so barbaric that they do not even recognize what is barbarous in their own practices." Moreover, ordinary Hindus are likely to find the pronouncements of Western-educated gentlemen—whether Indian or not—to be haughty, patronizing efforts to interfere in something that is none of their business. And, what is worse, they would not be entirely incorrect.

In a perverse way, I suppose this releases one from any obligation to base one's decisions on strategy. If all outcomes are the same anyway, one should, rather, base one's action on universal ethical principle, *mānavdharma*. But to say this is not to solve the problem of colonialism and culture. It merely indicates that the efficacy of our efforts at transforming society will be very limited if we focus entirely on affirming liberalism or reaction or any other particular relation to tradition. Indeed, it may indicate that the most strategically important response to colonialism is not culturalist at all, that the problem will remain intractable as long as we consider it in culturalist terms. It seems that if one society dominates another economically and politically, prestige will attach to the dominant culture, and all dominated cultures will be devalued no matter what cultural response they might offer. Certainly today, however much we might assert cultural diversity, European culture—in a somewhat debased, commercial form—spreads like poison through the indigenous cultures of the rest of the world by means of television and textbooks, movies and politics.

Culture is important, certainly, but it is not, I think, primary. For the value we attach to a belief or practice does not determine relations of political authority or economic domination; rather, those relations of authority and domination determine the values we attach to ideas and traditions—when and how we observe them, the degree to which we are punished if we do not observe them, and so on. Emecheta indicated just this, as we have already seen. And there are suggestions of this in Tagore's treatment of Harimohini's hypocritical traditionalism, the issue of dowry, and the events in Ghosepur. Hosain, however, places this idea at the center of her novel, forming plot and character simultaneously around the themes of cultural identity and economic determination.

CHAPTER EIGHT

THE ECONOMICS OF
CULTURAL IDENTITY

Attia Hosain's Sunlight on a Broken Column

INTRINSIC AND CONTEXTUAL CONCEPTIONS OF IDENTITY

Attia Hosain's only novel, *Sunlight on a Broken Column*, is different
from the works we have considered thus far. It is, in effect, transitional
between two major genres of postcolonization literature—works focusing on cultural identity, such as those we have been discussing, and
works focusing on political/economic transformation. Cultural identity
is a deep and persistent concern in the novel. But Hosain's view of cultural identity is almost entirely contextual. She portrays identity largely
as a function of economic conditions and economic interests. Identity in
Sunlight is not, for the most part, a deeply internalized sense of self, but
a provisional manner of dealing with circumstances in relation to relatively constant goals.

More exactly, we may distinguish two broad tendencies in the conception of identity. In the more common view, one's identity is, in its
essentials, determined early on. Both reflective and practical identity,
formed with family in early childhood and extended or re-formed in
more public institutions (e.g., school) during later childhood and adolescence, are relatively constant throughout the course of one's later life.
Changes in circumstances can be radically disorienting and may lead to

great suffering to the extent that the new circumstances degrade or exclude the identity on which one has based one's life. Similarly, there may be a contradiction between the identity acquired in the family and that acquired in school, with similar effect. But in each case the identity in question is, in a sense, a permanent formation of the person. We might call this the "intrinsic" view of identity.

The "contextual" view, in contrast, sees identity as open to considerable alteration throughout one's life. It is not something fixed in childhood and adolescence, but something that can alter almost freely as one's circumstances alter. In this view, one's self-concept or ego can change fairly radically as society changes around one. While this view is in many ways counterintuitive, it is, in fact, reasonably well supported by research in cognitive and social psychology. While this research has focused on "personality traits" (e.g., compassion), not cultural identity in the sense relevant to the study of postcolonization literature, it seems generalizable. According to this research, one's modes of behavior are not determined by one's self-conception or longstanding ideas about the world, but by very narrow circumstances. For example, suppose twenty people are stopped by someone who needs some sort of help. Which of the twenty will offer aid? It turns out that it is not a matter of which person feels most committed to compassionate action. Rather, the best predictor of who will help a person in need is—who is not in a rush. In other words, people who are hurrying to an appointment are unlikely to help, no matter what their commitment to compassion, while those who are not pressed for time are the ones who are likely to help, again independent of their self-conscious commitment to helping others (see Holland, Holyoak, Nisbett, and Thagard, 226–27, discussing research by Darley and Batson).

This research could be interpreted in different ways. For example, it certainly indicates that our behavior has relatively little to do with our reflective identity. Whether we think of ourselves as compassionate has little if anything to do with whether or not we try to help others. On the other hand, this sort of research does not necessarily indicate that reflective identity is not relatively fixed and psychologically crucial nonetheless. After all, it could be that reflective identity has little to do with our specific behavior but is crucial to our sense of well-being and broader abilities to act in the world. Now, it would seem that having a fixed reflective identity would, at least in part, involve having a sense of fixed personality traits. But, as it turns out, even this is not true. We do not typically think of ourselves as having fixed personality traits. Rather, we tend to think of *other* people as having fixed personality traits and tend to think of ourselves as responding flexibly to circumstances (see Holland, Holyoak, Nisbett, and Thagard, 222–24). This would seem to indicate that reflective identity is itself flexible and varies with circumstances.

On the other hand, there is another set of data that points in the opposite direction, indicating that we do attribute fixed traits to ourselves. However, they are not personality traits, but various sorts of group properties (e.g., gender traits related to being male or female). Consider, for example, research on people's judgment of their own speech behavior. In keeping with other studies, it turns out that people's judgments here have very little to do with their actual behavior. For example, when people are asked how often they use certain words or phrases, their answers do not reflect their actual use of those words or phrases. However, their answers do indicate a sense of fixed reflective identity, one based on gender stereotypes. Thus, men standardly report that they speak in ways commonly conceived of as manly; women standardly report that they speak in ways commonly conceived of as womanly (see Cameron, 34; see also Epstein, 88).

The apparent contradiction here suggests that there is merit in both the intrinsic and contextual views. The contextual view appears to be correct in emphasizing the degree to which behavior is determined by context, not by reflective identity. Moreover, the contextual view appears to be correct in indicating that a great deal of reflective identity is fluid, open to reconstrual or redefinition with relative ease. On the other hand, the intrinsic view appears correct in indicating that there are a few categories—such as sex—which serve crucially in our understanding and evaluation of ourselves. It seems likely that these categories guide our aspirations and sense of possibilities as well. It is more difficult to say whether these categories are rigidly fixed and, if so, when that fixation occurs.

One possibility, an extension of the contextualist view, would be that reflective identity—and thus self-description and self-evaluation—is a function of practical identity. In other words, it seems plausible to hypothesize (pending further study) that the categories through which one understands oneself are the categories that define one's practical identity—what one does, what one is able to do. We tend to think that reflective identity precedes and guides practical identity. Indeed, the most common view is probably that "real" identity determines both reflective and practical identity: being a boy determines that one conceives of oneself as a boy and that one acts like a boy, pursuing masculine goals in a masculine way, which in turn leads to taking up and being integrated into masculine forms of play, work, and so on. As we stressed at the outset, reflective identity cannot be straightforwardly determined by real identity, for the simple reason that any individual falls into infinitely many categories. "Male" is selected out of these categories by society, and it is for this reason that it is a crucial part of my reflective identity in a way that the other categories are not. So, that part of the common view seems to be mistaken. Of course, it could still happen that practical identity is determined by intrinsic properties of men and women. This is an empirical question. It could turn out that men and women think differently, for example—that men are more or less likely to follow principles of inferential reasoning—and that these differences partially or wholly determine practical identity. And, indeed, there are instances of this. For example, women have the social role of feeding infants for historically intrinsic reasons—before baby bottles, there were no other options. However, despite the persistence of gender stereotypes, these intrinsic differences do not appear to extend beyond the reproductive facts on which the male/female division is initially based. For example, despite the persistence of stereotypes, they do not appear to extend to cognition (as discussed by Epstein, Faludi, Fausto-Sterling, and others). The same is true for racial differences.

Thus, the standard view of the relation between "real" identity, reflective identity, and practical identity, does not seem to be plausible in most cases. Rather, something along the following lines seems to occur. Society is structured by reference to specific sorts of categorization—most obviously and universally, sex, but also race, and so on. One's reflective identity comes to be defined by precisely those categories that govern the practical activities in which one is trained and the possibilities one is offered in society. In other words, the causal sequence is almost the reverse of the standard view. We first acquire a certain practical identity (through activities in the home, at school, and so on). This practical identity is defined by reference to certain categories—sex, race, and so forth. Insofar as these categories segregate practical identities (e.g., boys' games and girls' games, men's work and women's work), they involve beliefs and evaluations that serve to systematize and justify that segregation. In other words, they are part of systems of ideology.

These categories—with ideological beliefs and evaluations—come to define our reflective identity as a consequence of their having already defined our practical identity.

This is clearly inconsistent with the most extreme versions of intrinsic identity—those based on some sort of biological necessity. However, it is still possible that, once formed, one's practical and reflective identities become intrinsic. In other words, however contingent their genesis, they may acquire permanence and crucial psychological importance. Indeed, it is at least clear that they are not merely ephemeral. Certainly, Hosain recognizes that they have a significant degree of fixity and psychological weight. Yet, she is able to accommodate both the fixity and the psychological importance within a contextual view.

To understand how this can be done, we need to analyze practical identity somewhat further. Specifically, we may divide practical identity into two components, one social, one cognitive. Practical identity, once again, is one's ease of action in certain sorts of common social behavior. Take, for example, the simple case of table manners. Eating practices vary from culture to culture. Part of my practical cultural identity involves eating habits. What I am calling the "cognitive component" of these eating habits consists in my own "competence" in table customs. What I am calling the "social component" consists in the patterned behavior of other people, behavior from which my own actions are inseparable.

More exactly, the cognitive component could be understood as defined by internalized procedural schemas and prototypes, combined with cognitive and noncognitive abilities to execute these schemas or follow these prototypes. Schemas are general structures; for example, the broad definition of "bird" would be a schema. Prototypes are typical instances of schemas; for example, robins are prototypical birds. Conceptual schemas are schemas defining objects of thought, such as "bird." Procedural schemas are schemas guiding action—or example, "putting on pants" or "going to a restaurant." Procedural schemas incorporate conceptual schemas. Thus, the procedural schema for "putting on pants" incorporates the conceptual schema for "pants." We have internalized a procedural schema when we can follow it unreflectively. For example, most men in the United States have probably internalized the schema for tying a necktie. However, all of us who have learned to tie a necktie recall a time when we had not yet internalized the schema and had to think through each step of the process. Finally, we are able to execute a schema, follow a procedure, because of other cognitive and noncognitive abilities. For example, if I break my hand, I will not be able to tie a necktie, no matter how thoroughly I have internalized the schema.

The social component of practical identity consists in the patterned roles of everyone else in culturally defined practices. While tying a necktie or putting on pants are individual activities, most culturally defined practices are not. In most cases, my practical identity relies on other people acting in certain predictable ways, and accepting my actions as part of their practices. It involves their cooperation and, less crucially, their acceptance or approval as well.

The point is clearer if we consider eating practices. Note that eating practices do not merely involve etiquette. Indeed, the very fact that etiquette is largely artificial and self-conscious means that it is marginally relevant to practical identity. If I have to keep reminding myself to follow a certain rule of etiquette, then it is not part of my practical identity. Rather, the eating customs relevant to practical identity involve such issues as when one eats, where one eats, which people eat together, who eats first, who serves, how much one takes, how one takes it, and so on. Again, they involve procedural schemas that incorporate conceptual schemas. The conceptual schemas allow us to identify different foods, utensils, and so on. The procedural schemas allow us to act appropriately with respect to those foods, utensils, and so on. And the actions resulting from these schemas are not merely solipsistic. For example, we expect the hosts to serve different courses without being prompted to do so. It would be considered rude for a guest to ask that the entree be brought out, now that the salad is finished—though it is easy to imagine a society in which the reverse would be the norm, where it would be considered rude for the hosts not to wait for a request from the guests. On the other hand, it is not considered rude for a guest to ask that something on the table be passed. Our ease in these situations is largely dependent upon our expectations meshing with those of other people, our practical identities cohering on these and other matters.

Now we are in a position to say something more precise about the relation between practical and reflective identity. My hypothesis would be that reflective identity does largely, though not entirely, follow changes in practical identity. And the maintenance or alteration of practical identity is largely driven by economic interests and class aspirations. But there are obstacles in the way of changing practical identity.

First of all, it can be difficult, even in some cases impossible, to internalize new procedural schemas. Second, in some cases, even when one has internalized such schemas, communal cooperation may be lacking. Reflective identity, then, becomes a problematic issue in fairly specific circumstances—when there is a disruptive conflict between one's internalized schemas and communal cooperation.

Here we can return to the colonial situation. The colonized person who sets out to internalize English customs is likely to do so for economic benefit. Indeed, as Hosain shows, there are complex class dynamics governing the partial internalization of English behaviors, the partial acquisition of English practical identity. The Taluqdari families, who are at the center of Hosain's novel, were feudal landlords. Each Taluqdar owned several villages. The ownership was guaranteed by the British and, in exchange, the Taluqdar served as the official in charge of collecting revenues from those villages and depositing it in the government treasury (see Kurian). The Taluqdars had an interest in acquiring a certain sort of practical ease with the British. However, it was necessary for them to maintain a certain sort of practical identity with lower class Indians as well. In addition, the men in these families had reason to wish for the maintenance of male and female practical identity within the home. As these different group interests shifted, from person to person or across time, practical and reflective identities shifted as well.

Beyond articulating a contextual and economic view of cultural identity, Hosain is entirely in keeping with classical Marxist thought in emphasizing universal principles of human need and desire—for food, freedom, love, and so on—underlying and motivating the relevant procedural schemas, and in invoking universal ethical principles to evaluate them, or rather the practices they entail. For example, early in the novel, Laila's cousin Zahra insults a sweeper woman. Sweepers are very poor and at the bottom of the caste hierarchy—a status that often affects Muslim treatment of sweepers, even though Islam does not, in principle, accept caste. The woman's poverty is stressed in the passage: "Behind her trailed two of her children, naked, thin-limbed, big-bellied" (45). Laila objects to Zahra's treatment of this woman. Zahra cannot understand: "She's used to it." Laila reflects that, "If I gave her a chance now, Zahra would mockingly reduce to mere printed hieroglyphics those books which had taught me to think of human dignity" (45)—not the dignity of a class or caste or religious group, but *human* dignity, understood as a universal property with universal ethical consequences.

Neither the contextualism nor the universalism should be taken to imply that Hosain discounts cultural issues. However, she clearly sees them as secondary. She is, ultimately, a cultural syncretist. But she sees cultural identity as superficial, as a sort of surface manifestation of underlying conflicts between human universality and economic hierarchy. In Hosain's novel, crises of cultural identity appear to arise at just those points at which there is a conflict between internalized schemas and communal acceptance, in precisely the manner we have suggested. But even here, the conflict is ultimately economic, ultimately a matter of class interest stifling human aspiration. For example, as we shall discuss below, Sita, through living in England, has internalized the courting practices and marital expectations of the English. But her own community in India will not cooperate with her marriage to the man she loves. At one level, this is a crisis in cultural identity—English versus Indian. But Hosain makes it clear that, in her view, love is a human aspiration, not an English idea, and the stifling of that love in Indian society serves to maintain class hierarchies. Thus, what appears to be a conflict of cultural identity—and is such a conflict, precisely in the sense we have discussed—is at the same time and more significantly, a surface manifestation of an underlying conflict between individual interests and class interests.

In sum, Hosain's novel leads us to reconceive the issue of cultural identity. Hosain certainly seeks to preserve elements of the Arabic, Persian, and Indian cultures of which she is the inheritor—especially the literary traditions of these cultures, synthesized with the literary traditions of Europe. But, at the same time, she sees economic issues as primary, and cultural issues as largely derivative. This is true for three main reasons. First of all, in her view, cultural identity is a sort of epiphenomenon of class aspiration. Second, crises in cultural identity are for the most part a matter of conflict between one's cognitive/practical abilities and social cooperation; they are not the result of some deeply intrinsic sense of self. Finally, the most crucial problems in any society are the problems of economic exploitation and brute oppression. It is those people who are starving or impoverished or beaten or raped who should be the author's primary concern. Crises of cultural identity, however real and painful, are, in a sense, the privilege of those who do not have to worry about food or clothing or brutality.

Hosain and the All India Progressive Writers' Association

The basic principles of Hosain's view of society, culture, and art are closely related to, and in part derive from, the Marxist principles of the All India Progressive Writers' Association (AIPWA). As Hosain notes, "I was greatly influenced in the 30s by the young friends and relations who came back from English schools and universities as left wing activists, Communists and Congress socialists. I was at the first Progressive Writers Conference and could be called a 'fellow traveler' at the time" (qtd. in Desai, "Introduction," viii). The AIPWA was a "front organization" for the Communist Party of India (see Coppola, 1) and, as such, promoted literature that undertook to articulate class analyses and to advocate for the oppressed classes. Perhaps the most important theoretical document produced by the AIPWA was its early manifesto, which appeared in several different versions, in several different outlets and languages, in 1935 and 1936. One version was adopted as the official document of the first AIPWA convention at Lucknow on April 10, 1936. This was the convention attended by Hosain.

The *Lucknow Manifesto*, as it is called, set forth the basic goals of the association, and thus the basic goals to which its members had committed themselves as writers. We may divide these, for ease of exposition, into social/cultural and economic/political goals. (I shall set out only those goals which bear on Hosain's novel.)

In the social/cultural realm, the manifesto states that "It is the duty of Indian writers to give expression to the changes taking place in Indian life and to assist the spirit of progress" by supporting "scientific rationalism" and opposing "reactionary and revivalist tendencies on questions like family, religion, sex," as well as "communalism, racial antagonism," and related tendencies (40). Hosain intermittently supports rationalism in the course of the novel, most obviously through her advocacy of medical science. There are three important incidents in the novel where people die or nearly die because tradition prevents scientific medical treatment. In the first case, Nandi's mother dies of tetanus because Nandi's father calls an exorcist rather than a physician (135–36). In the second, Aunt Abida falls seriously ill after a miscarriage "because the only woman doctor in the near-by township was away and [Abida's] mother-in-law refused to allow a man to attend to her" (204). Finally, Saliman dies, due to the same "hypocrisy and bigotry that . . . nearly killed Aunt Abida" (204–5).

The importance of changing tradition to accommodate modern/Western medicine is a common motif in postcolonization literature. In this case, however, there is something more going on. First of all, it is no accident that the three cases all involve women and childbirth. Saliman herself put the "traditional" view well: "Go to hospital to have a baby with men standing round looking on? Be shameless and be seen by all those doctors and half-doctors? Better to die at home." But, in keeping with her Marxist outlook, Hosain does not leave it at that. She has Saliman add, "And who cares for the poor in hospitals anyway?" (136). Thus, it is also no accident that Abida is the only one of the three to survive. For she is the only one of the three who is a member of the exploiting class rather than the exploited class. In short, the conflict is not only, not even primarily, between tradition and modernity, but between universal rights to medical care and the anti-universalist structures of patriarchy and capitalism, the division of society into unequal classes.

As to the treatment of women, it is important to point out that feminist concerns were a significant part of the early AIPWA. The first collection of AIPWA writings, *Angare* (*Embers*), published in 1932, included two pieces by Rashid Jahan, a physician as well as an author; both pieces treated feminist themes, as did Ahmed Ali's two stories (see Coppola, 3). The appearance of Jahan's works was of considerable importance. As Ralph Russell explains, "There had been women writers before her but none who portrayed so bluntly the callousness and injustice women suffer at the hands of their menfolk" (207). This is not to say that Hosain's feminist impulses are derived from the AIPWA. They would no doubt have been there in any case. However, the AIPWA encouraged her to express these impulses in her writing and, more significantly, encouraged her to understand her feminist concerns in Marxist terms. Hosain does not simply reduce the oppression of women to economic circumstances. However, she always places her feminist critique in an economic context, and sees economy as the dominant factor in any sort of oppression, including the oppression of women.

Returning to the list of social/cultural principles set out in the *Lucknow Manifesto*, we find that conflicts over "progressive" and "reactionary" views of "family and sex"—most often related to issues of individual autonomy (e.g., in arranged marriages)—define the central plot elements of Hosain's novel. This is most obvious in the forbidden romance of Laila and Ameer, but it appears also in the various unhappy marriages and liaisons discussed in the course of the novel. Moreover, the relatively pure relationship of Laila and Ameer, contrasted with the unhappy licentiousness of Sita and Mrs. Lal, serve to some extent to oppose "sexual libertinism" as well—another "duty of Indian writers," according to the *Lucknow Manifesto*. (There was a strong puritanical element in the orthodox communism of the period.)

Finally, Hosain consistently criticizes communalism and racism. Indeed, she is particularly concerned with the conflict between universalist socialism and communalist socialism, which is to say, socialism based in some noneconomic—usually religious—community. She goes so far as to manifest this conflict, almost allegorically, in the opposition of two cousins, Asad and Saleem. Communalist socialism has not typically been much of a force in European politics. In South Asia, however, it surfaced in Islam. As Russell points out, "Hasrat Mohani, perhaps *the* greatest *ghazal*-writer of the first two decades of this century . . . had by the middle twenties deduced from Islamic premises that communism was the answer to the world's needs" (209). More importantly, one of the most influential literary advocates for the formation of Pakistan was the great Urdu poet, Iqbal, who was simultaneously a devout Muslim and an admirer of Marx and Lenin (see Russell, 209). In 1922, he read his long poem, *The Guide of the Way* to a crowd of twenty thousand people. Following a section on "Imperial Rule," there is a section on "Capital and Labour," which is a fairly straightforward Marxist critique of capitalism and imperialism (see Russell, 184, for a summary).

This "Islamic socialism" was directly opposed to the universalist and secular socialism advocated by the AIPWA. This is clear not only from the positive religious references of the work and the political and social affiliations of the authors—for example, *The Guide of the Way* makes repeated reference to Islamic beliefs and legends and was read before the Society for the Support of Islam. It is clear also from the casual anti-Hinduism of some of this work. For example, in the section on "Imperial Rule," Iqbal says that those who do not rise up against false masters are disobeying the law of Allāh and are "more of an infidel than the Brahmin himself" (qtd. in Russell, 183).

Though this anti-Hinduism may in part respond to a pro-Hindu bias on the part of the Congress-led nationalist movement, it has no similar bearing on the AIPWA, which did not have any Hindu orientation. Indeed, the earliest AIPWA writers were themselves Muslim or at least from Muslim families. On the other hand, this first-hand familiarity with Islamic practices, combined no doubt with a personal need to break definitively with their origins, led these early AIPWA writers to oppose Islamic tendencies, it seems, more vehemently than would secular writers of Hindu origin. For example, in *Angare*, some writers set out to criticize and even satirize Islam, most notably Syed Zaheer, "the major figure in the development" of the AIPWA (Coppola, 1). Zaheer's treatment of Islam was considered so extreme that it resulted in "public burnings of the book by those whose religious sensibilities were offended and . . . threats to the lives of the contributors" (Coppola, 3).

Interestingly, however, the primary contrast in Hosain's novel is not between Islamic (thus Pakistani) socialists, such as Saleem, and secular (thus, largely, Indian) communists. Rather, Saleem is opposed to Asad, a Gandhian. Indeed, the opposition is particularly sharp at the end of the novel. Having done "educational work among the poor" and other "work in the Eastern riot-stricken areas," Asad worked with the new government, and "was sent as a delegate to the United Nations" (318). He is continuing his work of devotion to the people and the nation. In contrast, Saleem is "one of the senior executives" in a law firm. This does not necessarily mean that Saleem's earlier Islamic socialism was hypocritical or insincere. But it casts it in a different light, making it more similar to the forms of self-serving traditionalism so common in postcolonization literature, and in real political life.

Hosain no doubt chose a Gandhian for several reasons. The most obvious is simply that Gandhism was probably the most powerful and popular force in the independence movement. Moreover, Gandhi was intensely anticommunalist. Indeed, as Hosain is Muslim, and her main characters are all Muslim, it was important for her to choose a Hindu, such as Gandhi, as a symbol of anticommunalism; otherwise her own portrayal would risk a sort of communalism itself. After all, indicating that anticommunalism is Muslim could be tantamount to a communalist claim that Muslim culture is superior to Hindu culture.

More importantly, Hosain seems to have been genuinely drawn to Gandhi's idea and practice of *ahiṃsā*, "nonviolence," or, as it might be translated, "refusal to cooperate with the commission of violence or cruelty." Indeed, one of the most moving passages in the book concerns the death of her friend Nita after she is beaten by the police while taking part in a Gandhian campaign (166). The choice, it seems, was not only a matter of communal "balance," but of sincere sympathy. Moreover, by the time Hosain was writing the novel, the brutally coercive nature of official (Stalinist) communism was entirely clear. She no doubt wished to present an alternative to this that was still genuinely socialist. Socialist Gandhism was particularly appropriate due to its very non-Stalinist emphasis on *ahiṃsā*. And Hosain particularly stresses Asad's nonviolent and noncoercive thought and action. For example, after Asad has been beaten and bloodied during an independence march, Laila asks him, "Why do you not taunt me about inaction as Nita does?"; he responds, "Because the urge for action must come from within you. It cannot be created by taunts" (165).

Finally, Gandhi was an important influence on AIPWA writers from the outset, primarily via the most important and influential of the writers associated with the movement, Munshi Premchand, widely considered to be the greatest Indian novelist of social realism. Premchand had been influenced by Gandhi from as early as 1921 (Swan, 83). For the next decade, his fiction was imbued with Gandhism (Swan, 106–7). The connection is even stronger in the case of some associated writers. For example, the poet, Prabhakar Machwe, wrote, "I was attracted to the writings of Marx and Engels, but the pacifism of Gandhi and his philosophical resemblance to Buddha and Christ appealed to me most" (46). Machwe even wrote a 400–line poem, "Marx and Gandhi." In the Indian context, at least during this period, sympathy with Gandhism was not opposed to, but a central tendency within, Marxist literary activity.

Indeed, Gandhian socialism was at the time probably the most direct and appropriate counter to Islamic socialism. This is particularly true for a writer raised in the Urdu tradition, for these two tendencies—Islamic and Gandhian socialism—found representatives in the greatest modern Urdu poet, Iqbal, and the greatest modern Urdu novelist, Premchand. Asad himself is a writer and his few statements on money economy seem to echo the views of Premchand. Asad's initial devotion to the independence movement and Gandhism is precipitated by the realization, announced to Laila, that "Everything else we are taught is lies. . . . Money is the only truth" (54)—not only a central motif of this novel, but also the theme of Premchand's late essay "Moneylender's Civilization." As Russell summarizes, in this essay, "The features of capitalist society—detestable to [Premchand]—which exalt the greed for money above everything else, are contrasted . . . with the more humane relationship between man and man which . . . [characterizes] the new socialist society" (209).

Turning to the political/economic goals of the AIPWA, we find these stated succinctly in the *Lucknow Manifesto*: "The new literature of

India must deal with the basic problems of our existence today—the problems of hunger and poverty, social backwardness and political subjection" (41). By referring to these as "basic problems," the manifesto indicates that they are problems of the economic "base," not of the social/cultural superstructure; they are the fundamental problems that underlie all of the association's other concerns. Hosain does not treat hunger in this novel. There are two likely reasons for this. First of all, famine probably appeared to be a greater threat before independence than after, especially given the moderately socialist orientation of the Nehru government. Perhaps more importantly, Hosain was writing for an English-speaking readership whose image of India was already too filled with images of starvation. There are similar problems with the representation of poverty and social backwardness. Too great an emphasis on destitution contributes to a sort of dehumanization of the Indian peasantry, almost blotting out the human subjectivity and cultural lives of the people, almost reducing them to their animal needs. Too great an emphasis on "social backwardness," such as caste rules, is likely to reenforce the stereotype of a superstitious and retrograde Indian society. Each of these issues is crucial, but its treatment can be politically problematic, depending on one's readership. Indeed, the same holds for such social issues as communalism and the treatment of women. In an English-language novel, too harsh a critique in any of these areas could all too easily contribute to a European supremacist ideology.

Nonetheless, excepting hunger, these are the central issues of Hosain's novel, just as the *Lucknow Manifesto* urged. She overcomes the practical problem of how to deal with them in several ways. First of all, she is careful to humanize those who suffer oppression. Moreover, her writing is understated, presenting incidents of oppression in brief, moving vignettes, but not dwelling on them. She makes clear their importance, but does not expand upon them in such a way as to eclipse the rest of Indian life. Finally, she not only works to portray oppressed and suffering people as fully subjectively human, she is also careful not to present them simply as victims. In keeping with Marxist and feminist principles, she emphasizes the will and strength of oppressed people, especially oppressed women. This is a politically necessary emphasis, because it is crucial that oppressed people not think of themselves solely as victims, but recognize that, in solidarity, they have the strength to force social change. For example, though ultimately suppressed by patriarchy, both the servant girl Nandi and the narrator's aunt Abida clearly have dignity and power. Though Hosain never explicitly advocates a solidaristic joining of forces against patriarchy or other forms of oppression, the potential is clearly present in such brave, intelligent, and strong-willed women.

In keeping with this awareness of audience, and of the AIPWA goals, Hosain is also careful to balance criticisms of traditional culture with criticisms of European culture and acknowledgment of the strengths of indigenous ideas and practices—"the best traditions of Indian civilization," as the *Lucknow Manifesto* puts it. For example, as we shall discuss below, the strength of Aunt Abida is the strength of a woman within Indo-Persian culture; it is a strength based upon that culture. Indeed, one recurrent theme in the novel, reminiscent of Emecheta's views, is that the most difficult period for oppressed people is likely to be the period of transition from one set of cultural practices to another, a period in which oppressed people—especially women—may be deprived of the benefits of both societies.

Finally, Hosain links oppression and suffering—"poverty, social backwardness and political subjection"—not to uniquely Indian conditions, nor to some particular rapaciousness on the part of the English, but rather to universal categories of Marxist economic analysis, primarily the broad, structural categories of feudalism and capitalism. Indeed, for Hosain, the primary conflict between English and Indian practices is not so much a cultural conflict, as a conflict of economic structure, a conflict between capitalist modes and feudal modes. There is, of course, a cultural conflict there, but, in Hosain's view, this is largely the result of a deeper conflict between different economic systems. Moreover, the "English" customs advocated by Hosain, in her version of cultural syncretism, are largely those that Marxists see as a necessary and beneficial part of the transition from feudalism to capitalism. In this sense, they are not a matter of Westernization, even partial and syncretistic Westernization, but, rather, modernization. Indeed, the primary instance of this in the novel, the advocacy of love marriage over arranged marriage, concerns a fairly straightforward instance of a custom that is economic, not national, in origin. Love marriage was not an ancient English custom, but had arisen relatively recently, along with the shift from a feudal to a capitalist economy. Indeed, the conflict between love marriage and arranged marriage is a recurrent motif in early modern English literature (e.g., *A Midsummer Night's Dream*).

Thus, even in her emphasis on the problems of the period of transition, and in her advocacy of altering certain indigenous practices, Hosain is following Marxist economic principles—and, once again, universal ethical principles—not culturalist principles.

Culture and Identity (1): Europeans

But, again, Hosain's focus on universal categories of economic structure does not lead her to ignore or dismiss issues of culture. To accept that the economy is the base is not to deny that there is a superstructure or that the superstructure is important. Cultural identity is a central theme in of the novel. Indeed, it is an important consideration for writers of the AIPWA, for in the *Lucknow Manifesto*, the Progressive Writers pledge themselves "to be the inheritors of the best traditions of Indian civilization" (40). Here, the progressive writers envision a selective approach to indigenous culture—the preservation of "the best," but the rejection of all that is bound up with "hunger and poverty, social backwardness and political subjection" (41). It is a modernizing view of culture and tradition, and a view that places modernization in the service of the economic and political goals of communism, judging tradition by reference to universal ethical standards. But it is not, except in limited ways, a Westernizing view. In keeping with this, Premchand published a version of the AIPWA manifesto that explicitly denounced mimeticism, "blind imitation" (11), as a reactionary tendency.

This is, of course, in keeping with Marxist economic analysis. Communist society does not merely discard all that went before. In its "dialectical progress," it both "negates and incorporates" previous stages. It would hardly do for a communist to fully accept capitalism and all aspects of bourgeois culture. Nor can a Marxist, intent upon dialectical analysis, simply dismiss all aspects of prior economic and cultural formations. Indeed, a Marxist must recognize not only the universal elements of economic structure, but also the historically specific conditions that are to be found in any given region, so that what is done in one region (e.g., the Soviet Union) cannot simply be repeated in another region (e.g., India). Marxist universalism does not, or should not, deny or ignore particular historical conditions; it is, after all, *historical* materialism. Rather, it seeks to understand these historical conditions in relation to universal structures, and act on them in accordance with universal principles.

Indeed, Hosain's implicit typology of character and culture is not significantly different from that of more purely culturalist writers, and her characters fall into a set of fairly standard types. However, the typology is more complete than usual, especially with respect to Europeans, for *Sunlight* includes more white characters, and more fully differentiated white characters, than most postcolonization works.

First of all, *Sunlight* includes the standard "one good European" character in the person of Mr. Freemantle. This character type is used by a number of syncretistic and critical or liberal orthodox writers to express a sort of dual critique of imperialism and indigenous culture. While portraying white society as oppressive on the whole, many authors include one or, less commonly, two beneficent white characters representing what there is to learn from Western society—often medical science, though sometimes other practical scientific disciplines, such as agriculture (cf. Kenny in Markandaya's *Nectar in a Sieve* or Eugene in Head's *A Question of Power*).

Mr. Freemantle differs from other characters of this type in that he is not a physician or otherwise a representative of what is different and valuable in English society. Rather, he is one of two English characters who partially adopt Indian customs. Indeed, Hosain presents him as, in our terminology, "genuinely assimilated." Moreover, he managed to be assimilated into Indian culture without forsaking his prior assimilation into English culture. He was bicultural, just as one might be bi-lingual. He was a "lawyer, a scholar of Sanskrit, Persian and Arabic, who wore Indian clothes when he visited the houses of dancing girls, and prim Victorian clothes at other times. He held frequent *Mushairas*, soirees where poets recited their verse in Urdu and Persian" (34). He was a good friend of Laila's grandfather. The character is in part modelled on Sir William Jones, also a lawyer and a great scholar of Sanskrit, Persian, and Arabic, who was largely responsible for introducing Indian and Persian literature to Europe, and was a founder of Indo-European comparative linguistics and mythology. Hosain also associates the character with Tagore's Gora by explaining that Laila called him "*Gorey Dada*, white grandfather" (34). This furthers the sense that he is genuinely assimilated—for, after all, who could be more Indian than Gora, despite his whiteness? And who could be more representative of one's cultural traditions than one's grandfather?

But Freemantle's "authenticity" is not a simple or direct result of his benevolent devotion to Indian culture. Hosain explains that this alone "would have reduced him to being a tiresome eccentric." Rather, "Mr. Freemantle's scholarship and his brilliance as a lawyer were the measures of his worth" (34). Indeed, this is what differentiates him from "the bearded English poet searching for the 'Soul of the East'—who antagonised the English community by wearing Indian clothes and eating with his fingers" (203). The bearded poet is a reactionary assimilationist or mimeticist—though a mimeticist of Indian, not English culture—directly parallel to colonized mimeticists. Indeed, Hosain tacitly draws this connection by pairing this poet with a more standard, Indian mimeticist. She is discussing the men in Sita's social circle, and explains that they "varied in type from the bearded English poet . . . to the young subaltern with . . . cultivated English drawl . . .who was as near a copy of his senior Sandhurst-trained officers as they were of their English prototypes" (203).

The characterization of Mr. Freemantle as genuinely assimilated is important for two complementary reasons. First of all, it indicates that no culture is bound to a particular group of people. Second, it indicates that no group of people is bound to a particular culture. Indian culture is no more bound to Indians than English culture is bound to the English; and, conversely, English people are no more constrained within English culture than Indians are constrained within Indian culture. Assimilation can go in any direction. Biology is not cultural destiny. Nor, even, is upbringing. Indeed, Hosain's brief example of Mr. Freemantle makes the universalist point even more forcefully than *Gora*, for Mr. Freemantle was able to enter into Indian culture, not through childhood training in an Indian family, but through his own adult scholarship. Thus, in keeping with the general contextualism of the novel, Hosain goes beyond the view that parentage does not determine culture to the view that early cultural training does not foreclose the possibility of later cultural assimilation.

Moreover, fluency in one culture does not preclude simultaneous fluency in other cultures. Freemantle is able to function with ease in both English and Indian culture. This also reenforces the view that all particular cultures are manifestations of universal principles, and thus that all cultures are available to every human being—not only sequentially, but simultaneously. Different cultures are neither mutually contradictory nor mutually exclusive, but surface variations on underlying needs, aspirations, relations that are common to everyone. Of course, to achieve Freemantle's status, one must recognize the common humanity of all people.

And one must be willing and able to gain the necessary level of scholarship—one must be able to isolate and internalize the relevant schemas. Assimilation is not a simple matter. But it is possible, and it is possible because of the broadly universal patterns that underlie all cultures.

Complementary to this, the bearded poet may be unable to function fully in either culture. His emphasis on cultural difference—indicated by his positing a "Soul of the East"—undermines the universal humanity of East and West, and his airy mysticism gives one little sense that he is likely to pursue scholarship with much devotion.

Needless to say, not all English people are like Mr. Freemantle or the English poet. Hosain uses two English women to portray other common attitudes toward Indian culture. The first is a common type in postcolonization fiction, especially fiction by indigenous women—the patronizing white woman, a sort of inversion of the "one good European" character. Many authors, especially women of color, include a (usually liberal) white woman who sees herself as the friend of the natives, but who is insufferably patronizing and arrogant. We find characters of this sort in Head's *A Question of Power* (Camila; see, for example, 77–79), Emecheta's *The Slave Girl* (Mrs. Simpson; see, for example, 104), Amma Darko's *Beyond the Horizon* (Gitte; see 99, 102), and so on. Mrs. Martin is different from many instances of the type in that she is not a paternalistic liberal. She is, rather, a straightforward colonialist, completely devoted to the British Raj. However, like other instances of this type, she is thoroughly unconscious of her own ethnocentrism.

Mrs. Martin is first introduced, not without mockery, in a "flowered dress and feathered hat" (46; European women's hats are not infrequently the object of aesthetic scorn from non-European writers). Almost the first words out of her mouth involve the mispronunciation of Laila's name: "Are you coming, Lily dear?" (46)—"I felt my cheeks burn, hearing the alien name she had given me," Laila recalls. Despite living her whole life in India, she still considers herself wholly English (48) and has not managed even the minimal accommodation to indigenous culture of learning her former student's proper name. Speaking with Abida, she reminisces further on "Dear Lily," exclaiming "Who would think this is my little girl whom I taught her first words of English" (47). Entirely unaware of the tradition of Urdu poetry and of its importance in Laila's family, she recalls with pride her indoctrination of Laila into English custom—"Do you remember, Abida, when she recited her first poem to her dear parents?" She remembers what Laila wore on that occasion, not Indian clothes, but "a white frock" (47). The scene recalls the recitations of "Twinkle, Twinkle, Little Star" in *Gora*. Later, Laila recollects how Martin "had so carefully taught me 'God Save the King' when I was four." She recalls this on Indian Independence Day, 1947, when her own young daughter "join[s] the other children in singing their country's anthem" (308). The point of the contrast is clear.

Just in case the issue of clothing seems innocuous—after all, one might ask, what difference does it make, really, if Laila puts on a skirt or a *salwar*—Hosain reminds us a few pages later of the coercion that underlay such simple matters as wearing a frock. Mrs. Martin is speaking of watching the Muḥarram procession. The procession in question is the deeply serious religious commemoration of the martyrdom of Ḥusayn, a grandson of the prophet Muḥammad (for a brief summary, see Ronart and Ronart; on the lighting of the Imāmbārās, see Gibb and Kramers). Mrs. Martin views it largely as entertainment—"lovely lights, like fairyland!" (50)—or as a cultural curiosity: "My friend . . . is very interested in the customs of this country" (50). She complains that "In the old days one could avoid the terrible crowds and go on a special day." Laila, implicitly recurring to the earlier mention of her white frock and other English manners, responds "aggressively," "We needed passes that day if we didn't wear European clothes" (50). Indians were kept from witnessing their own religious procession if they did not show themselves willing to imitate English customs. English colonialists were obviously aware of the degree to which thoughts are determined by practice, reflective identity is shaped by practical identity.

At other points, Mrs. Martin's patronizing attitude toward Indians, and her boorishness toward her hosts, are shocking. She complains to Abida, Majida, Zahra, Laila, that her current place of residence is unbearably "primitive," with "no Europeans to talk to." Though she herself was born and raised in India and had spent no more than a few months out of India in her entire life, she could not live in a place where there were no Europeans, for any place without Europeans is "primitive." Moreover, she says this directly to Indians. She makes matters worse by explaining that, when she worked for Laila's father, that was different because "Lily's father, well, he was just like one of us" (48). It is not a stray comment. On Indian Independence day, 1947, Laila happens to meet her again. Concerning the end of the Raj, Mrs. Martin remarks that, at least, it is "comforting . . . that the man at the helm of affairs is so much like a British gentleman" (308). The highest compliment she can pay to an Indian is to say that he is almost a European. Those who are not like Europeans are mere primitives.

The contrast between Mrs. Martin and Mr. Freemantle is obvious without being mentioned. But Hosain stresses the point, noting that Martin "disapproved" of Freemantle "because of his 'non-European' ways," while Freemantle dismissed her, with the contention that "no human being could have married that woman" (48). It is apt that Freemantle's evaluation, though not untinged by sexism, concerns general humanity ("no human being"), while Martin's concerns racial and ethnic difference ("'non-European' ways").

On the other hand, Mrs. Martin is not entirely unsympathetic. Hosain, despite her clear dislike of the character, or the character type, is careful to show that Mrs. Martin is as much a victim of the imperial economy as anyone else. When she speaks about Laila's first English recitation, she recalls how Laila's mother gave her a "gold brooch." "I always wear it," she explains. It is "a tiny golden bird, holding a pearl in its beak" (47). A trifle for the Taluqdar. The degree to which she prizes the token indicates both her relative poverty, and the degree to which she had no community to which she genuinely belonged. Though a thoughtful gift, it should not have been so valuable to her, either materially or emotionally. Indeed, in context, her insistence on European company, and her statement that Laila's father was almost like a European, are perhaps less objectionable than pitiable. Who else would have treated her as an equal? To her employers—except, perhaps, Laila's parents—she is merely a hired tutor in elementary English language and manners. Freemantle, in contrast, was a brilliant lawyer and scholar. To other Indians, she is a casteless foreigner. The ethnocentrism is mutual. And, unlike Mr. Freemantle, she is not protected from Indian ethnocentrism by economic class or administrative power. Moreover, her criticism of some leaders of the nationalist movement—that they are motivated by business interests, not selfless devotion to the country (51)—is entirely correct, and fully in keeping with Hosain's views.

Of course, Martin is on the side of the colonizer, which makes all the difference socially and politically. But, at a personal level, she too is a victim of colonialism—and, more importantly, of class. In the end, she takes up what is, in effect, a form of stereotyped and unself-conscious mimeticism, a parodic twist of Freemantle's assimilation. In the retirement home, "her sole interest" is pseudo-Eastern mystic Spiritualism, in which she attends seances and calls on the spirits of Indian rajas (309).

If Mrs. Martin is a sort of inverse parallel to Mr. Freemantle, the second important white women, Joan Davis, is, in a sense, an inverse parallel to the bearded poet, at least in being partially alienated from both cultures. However, while the bearded poet is alienated because he falsely thinks of himself as Indian, seeking the Soul of the East, Joan is alienated because she falsely thinks of herself as English—a point she partially recognizes at the end of the novel. Joan "passionately believed in the rightness and the greatness of the British Empire," and she praised the English in India "because they have brought peace and justice and unity" (126). Her views are repugnant to anyone who is opposed to imperialism. And yet Nita's response, in context, seems overly harsh and personal: "In any case, how can one be loyal to aliens?" She may not intend to include Joan among the aliens—but even if she went on to say that Joan is "almost like an Indian," the affront to Joan would be painfully close to Mrs. Martin's statement about Laila's father. Of course, Nita has a point—the British rule India from a distance and consider themselves to be different. But then the question should have been, "How can Indians be loyal to people who *consider themselves* to be aliens?"—or, better still, leaving aside the issue of ethnic origin and affiliation and replacing with universal ethical principles, "How can one be loyal to an undemocratic and racist government?"

Of course, Joan is only receiving back her own prejudice. She too considers Indians "a race apart" from the English (127). And, yet, Laila explains that "Joan's weakness in arguments came from the very quality that gave her personal strength. She did not hate as we did. She did not hate Indians as we hated the British" (127). Moreover, there is no possibility of simply identifying Joan with the colonial oppressor and Laila or her friends with the subjugated masses. Laila, again, was from a Taluqdar family. "Joan's mother was a widow, a matron at the Medical College. Joan had been awarded a scholarship and was very conscientious, simple and generous." In contrast with the great estates of Laila's family, "Her home was small and unpretentious" (126). Indeed, Laila goes so far as to say that Joan's "friendship blunted the sharp points of prejudice. I could not make Sylvia the excuse for hatred [of the British] when Joan provided a reason for respect" (127; "Sylvia" here is Sylvia Tucker, a mixed-race character whom we shall discuss below).

Moreover, Joan was by no means culturally at ease in an English identity. She suffered from the sort of "alienating hybridity" which is often characteristic of colonized people who have been educated abroad, but then return to a nation in which they find themselves "no longer at ease" (in Achebe's phrase). She was raised in India. Even her parents were raised in India. Her family "still talk[s] of England as home" and, she insists, "We have more in common with the English than with Indians." And yet they are not English: "It makes one feel like those riders who canter round the ring of a circus, balanced on two horses, except that those horses are trained to keep in step, and their riders are respected" (127). Joan's sense of disrespect from both groups is clear, as is her practical discomfort with both.

Moreover, ultimately, despite her claims, she is more Indian than English. There is a deep difference, which she does not recognize, between her reflective identity, on the one hand, and her practical identity and feelings of affinity, on the other. When Nita is expelled from school for participating in a protest against the British Raj, Joan, despite all her loyalty to England, helps Nita pack before leaving the hostel. Nita writes a brief note to Laila before departing. She chides Laila for holding the right views but engaging in no action. She sees the opposite fault in Joan. "Your actions will, I hope, one day coincide with your beliefs," she tells Laila, "and Joan's beliefs will change to fit her actions" (166). Hosain, of course, is not a Christian, but Joan was, and in the context of Christianity, it is difficult not to think of Jesus' parable of the two sons: "What is your opinion? A man had two sons. He went and said to the first, 'My boy, you go and work in the vineyard today.' He answered, 'I will not go,' but afterwards thought better of it and went. The man then went and said the same thing to the second who answered, 'Certainly, sir,' but did not go. Which of the two did the father's will?" (*Matthew* 21: 28–31).

In the end, Joan and her parents return to England. (The fact that both parents are alive at this point is one of the annoying inconsistencies in the novel.) "She had not wanted to leave, but . . . she had too strong a sense of duty to leave [her parents] alone in their old age" (307–8). She writes, sadly, but without self-pity, of her alienation in England, and indicates that she finally has a sense of her Indian identity: "It is not possible—at any time, at any age, to forget the place and the atmosphere where one was born and brought up. I find myself comparing, and contrasting everything with India; and—would you believe it?—when my parents now talk of 'home' they do not mean England!"

As we have already seen, Laila directly contrasts Joan with Sylvia Tucker. Indeed, she comments that "Joan neutralised in me the remembered venom of Sylvia Tucker" (127). Sylvia too is a standard type from

postcolonization literature—the mulatto striving to be white. Sylvia has
nothing but disdain for nonwhites, because she has nothing but disdain
for the nonwhite part of herself. Even in later life, one of Laila's most
galling memories is of "Sylvia Tucker who had called me 'nigger'" (308).
It is only one of a long series of insults. Sylvia laughs at Laila's Indian
clothes, suggests that she wear a *burqa*, mocks her for not being allowed
to date, hums "'Rule Britannia' each time she saw us after Sita's uncle
had been arrested" in a Satyāgraha campaign, and scolds her sister,
Myra, saying "Can't you keep away from wogs?" (52). Indeed, Sylvia
goes further than Lestrade, because she pretends that she is pure European. Myra is the one who whispers the secret: "Sylvia's a liar. Our
mother isn't Italian. Sylvia won't let her come to school, or meet our
friends. She's—you know what—she's a dark woman" (52).

But here too the act is more to be pitied than despised. No wonder
Sylvia hates the part of her that is Indian. Even Myra has been brought
up to think of her own mother as "a dark woman." Her subsequent life,
though largely comfortable, is also sad. Zahid sees her out with British
soldiers, "each time with a new one" (55). The implication is clear, if
perhaps unwarranted. Later, she turns up as the second wife of Raja of
Bhimnagar. The raja's "good looks had crumbled with dissipation"
(181–82), but he "could buy anything; even [Sylvia's] colour prejudice."
She walks with the senior Rani, "a painted pathetic doll," "both . . .
were like chandeliers of precious stones" (182). Later still, she "left the
bankrupt Raja of Bhimnagar for an American Air Force Sergeant"
(308). Her life is almost an allegory of postcolonization mimeticism in a
wide range of countries, with its shift of dependence from the British to
the indigenous aristocracy to the American military.

CULTURE AND IDENTITY (2): THE ISLAMIC-PERSIAN TRADITION

Hosain's treatment of indigenous tradition is in keeping with our typology of postcolonization literature as well, with some variations. In treat-
ing "traditional" men, Hosain's main critical emphasis is on their dissipation. This emphasis, while probably based in part on her own actual
experiences, is in part a result of her Marxist orientation as well. The
classical Marxist view of the aristocracy, especially at the period immediately preceding the transition to a capitalist economy and the domination of the bourgeoisie, is that they are largely decadent. Indeed, part of

their defeat at the hands of the bourgeoisie is a result of their consumption of all surplus wealth, primarily in sensuous enjoyment; the bourgeoisie, in contrast, reinvest surplus wealth, expanding their enterprises, thus ultimately achieving broad economic and, subsequently, political domination. Note that this too is not so much a matter of individual character or culture as a matter of economic structure. Feudalism fosters personal expenditure of excess wealth; capitalism fosters the reinvestment of excess wealth.

We have already noted in passing one instance of this sort—the dissipation of the Raja of Bhimnagar and his eventual economic ruin, leading to Sylvia's elopement with an American sergeant. The Raja of Amirpur, a relative of Laila's beloved Ameer, provides a less tragic case. He was "a poet and a builder of palaces who had his zenana guarded by negro eunuchs." Hosain explains that "When he had succeeded his parsimonious father he had lived riotously. . . . It was said he had made naked women roll the length of the throne-room in a race" and "had played chess . . . with nude girls and youths as pieces" (33). Later, he "curbed his sensual extravagances" and instead endowed "schools, hospitals and orphanages" (33), thereby shifting to morally admirable, but still economically unproductive investments. Thakur Balbir Singh fits the pattern as well. He spent his time and money hunting, flying pigeons, cultivating fighting cocks, and ordering "embroidered cotton *Angarkhas* and delicate caps" that "cost the sight of many workmen and more than the dowry of their wives and daughters" (33). In the case of men such as these, it is entirely clear that "tradition" is nothing more than class privilege; specifically, the self-indulgent privilege of a decadent feudal aristocracy.

Laila's uncle Mohsin too is a decadent aristocrat. In keeping with the pattern we have been discussing, he "never did any work," but instead visited "the dancing girls of the city" (21). Indeed, Mohsin seems to go beyond the other aristocrats. For he is a lascivious patriarch who bolsters his power with religious orthodoxy, but who, hypocritically, takes sexual advantage of women subordinates. He is, in this way, a version of the hypocritical traditionalist character. The most despicable case of Mohsin's decadent and hypocritical sexual behavior concerns the servant girl Nandi. Hosain emphasizes the degree to which all attractive female servants are subjected to casual sexual harassment. Nandi in particular is subjected to a series of humiliations. However, in keeping with Hosain's Marxist/feminist aims, Nandi is never presented as entirely helpless in the face of these cruelties. "Not long ago . . . the groom of the English family . . . had peeped over the wall while she bathed"; a few days later "the postman . . . had attempted to molest her." In response, Nandi throws "an accurate and sharp stone" at the former and bites the latter (27). While Nandi's father does not appear to be of much help at these times, he takes decisive action when Nandi responds positively to a man's interest. He abuses her loudly and angrily and, by his own admission, "would willingly have killed her" (27), because she has been found alone with a man (28). Abida turns the matter over to Mohsin. Abida envisions Mohsin investigating the accusations. He does no such thing. Rather, he "contemptuously" prods Nandi "with his silver-topped stick"—the reference to the silver emphasizing their stark class difference—and calls her a "slut of a girl . . . a wanton." Knowing well the power of Mohsin and her own weakness, Nandi replies, "A slut? A wanton? And who are you to say it who would have made me one had I let you?" Mohsin does not reply, but beats her cruelly with his silver-topped stick.

The religious hypocrisy of this act is emphasized by Baba Mian's repetition, in the course of the preceding scene, of the two primary epithets of Allāh, as given in the opening invocation, the "Bismillāh," of the *Qur'ān*. Baba Mian, another uncle to Laila, is a gentle representative of orthodox tradition—"His tight flannel pyjamas were crumpled at the knees, through sitting with bent knees in long hours of prayer" (19)—and he is contrasted directly with Mohsin: when Laila entered the room, she "moved out of reach of Uncle Mohsin's outstretched arm, and went over to Baba Mian" (18). He repeatedly punctuates the familial discussion with the exclamation, "Ya, Rahman, Ya, Rahim!" (20, 22, 25). As Maulana Mohammad Ali explains, referring to the Bismillāh, *Raḥmān* and *Raḥīm*, meaning, roughly, "Beneficent" and "Merciful," "are both derived from *raḥmat*, signifying *tenderness requiring the exercise of beneficence . . . and thus comprising the ideas of love* and *mercy*" (3n.3), fundamental principles of Islam, manifest in Allāh, who is "the Beneficent, the Merciful," as every chapter of the *Qur'ān* affirms. Clearly, these qualities are entirely purged from Mohsin's rigidly authoritarian and self-interested idea and practice of Islam

Zahra's marriage furthers the theme of traditionalism as a hypocritical mask for self-interest and a surface manifestation of underlying economic conditions. For this marriage, like most of the other marriages in the novel, is a function, not of love, friendship, or any other human relation, but of class standing and class aspiration. In consequence, at the ceremony itself, the focal point for most guests is the dowry: "The women counted the number of clothes, the number and value of the sets of jewelry. . . . They estimated the cost of the silver bridal bed." For those present, the event is largely reducible to a monetary equivalent: "This was the information they had to pass on to others who could not be present, and by which the family would be judged" (113). The wedding ceremony is a concrete illustration of Marx's concept of the fetishism of commodities, the reduction of relations between people to relations between things, or, more exactly, relations between the monetary values of things. Here, the bride is clearly one such a commodity. As Laila puts it, expressing the sense of alienation that is a necessary part of commodity fetishism: "I felt curiously detached towards that glittering, scented bundle, no longer Zahra but the symbol of others' desires" (114)—not, of course, sexual desires, as one might expect at a wedding, but material, economic desires.

The economic point is further reenforced when one considers marriage, or more generally the regulation of sexual relations, among the lower classes. We have already seen the degree to which the entire society turns a blind eye to the casual sexual harassment of female servants, and the brutality of its response when a female servant acts on her own impulses. This is part of patriarchal structure and of the pervasive double sexual standard—not only between men and women, but between wealthy women and poor women. As Nandi puts it, "We poor people get a bad name because we cannot stay locked up. But what of all those uncles and cousins who wander in and out of zenanas? They're men, aren't they? Thieves steal the best guarded treasure." Nandi complains that a *moulvis'* daughter became pregnant, but the family was "able to bribe the midwife and get rid of her baby and then buy a husband for her." She explains, "Respectability can be preserved like pickle in gold and silver. If this girl . . . had been poor," none of that would have been possible. Indeed, Nandi weeps that "I was turned out by my father and mother for less reason" (97) when she was caught alone with a man. The point is born out by Laila herself. She çommits a graver sin in her romantic meetings with Ameer. Indeed, they are caught embracing. But no disgrace follows, as followed for Nandi.

A later scene emphasizes the cruelty of Nandi's punishment and the discrepancy between the lives of the rich and the poor. Sita "has written she will be going to England to study." The other wealthy young women feel "self-pity and envy" and discuss whether they would like to do the same. Nandi says, "I just want to go home to my parents" (106). The contrast is particularly poignant for, as we discover later, Sita's lifestyle is, it seems clear, much less chaste than Nandi's (see, for example, 292, on "Sita's conquests"). Moreover, as we shall discuss below, she hypocritically "adheres to tradition" in refusing to marry the Muslim man she loves—not out of some misplaced sense of piety, but because such a marriage would bring with it social and economic difficulties.

Nandi is not the only case where we see the mask of religious tradition ripped off to show the ugly class and gender politics underneath. Saliman is a servant girl whose "mother had been sold as a child during a famine, and given to [Laila's] grandmother" (71). The cruelty with which the masters treat the female servants filters down to the male servants as well. They imitate their "betters" in devaluing the women of their class. Ghulam Ali, one of the chief servants (121), impregnates Saliman, but denies her, much as Mohsin denies Nandi. Nandi summarizes the situation aptly: "Better to be my father's mule . . . than to be poor and a woman"—both properties, class and gender, are important. "Laila Bitia," she continues, "you don't know what life can be for us. We are the prey of every man's desires" (168).

In some ways, a more positive view of tradition enters with Laila's aunt Abida, an instance of the "strong traditional woman" character type to be found in much postcolonization fiction, especially by women. Abida's traditionalism shows the degree to which Muslim tradition, at least among Taluqdari families, includes genuine possibilities for women to develop their intellectual and other talents and to achieve considerable authority and autonomy. Moreover, Abida's wide learning and aesthetic sensitivity serve to highlight the great value of Persian/Urdu high culture, in part by separating that culture from the decadence of Mohsin and others. Nonetheless, even with Abida, the value of tradition remains highly equivocal. First of all, in keeping with the standard portrayal of this type, Abida is independent just so long as she remains unmarried. Secondly, part of Abida's strength even when unmarried rests on her complicity with the oppressive aspects of tradition. In the end, even her unhypocritical traditionalism is based on class loyalties, and thus on economy. Abida is sincere in her traditionalism not because tradition has any independent value for her, but because, unlike Mohsin, she is loyal to her class, and not merely consumed by short-term self-interest. In Hosain's materialist portrayal, even the most sincere traditionalism is ultimately based on economic class.

More exactly, Abida's traditionalism is more "orthodox," in our sense, than that of Mohsin or others. First of all, it is more sincere and, in keeping with this, more devout: "Aunt Abida . . . spent a longer time sitting on the prayer-mat in deep meditation after finishing the formal prayers. It seemed as if time meant nothing to her but its divisions into the five hours of prayer sounded by the *muezzin* from the mosque" (108). More importantly for our purposes, Abida's traditionalism is more open-minded—as is indicated by her reasoned statements about allowing Zahra to be present while her marriage is under discussion. Abida's reflective consideration of different aspects of tradition is the opposite of her elder sister Majida's unreflective conformism. When Abida and Mohsin argue, Majida objects that "to think is an added pain" (20).

Indeed, unreflective conformism is perhaps the most common attitude toward "tradition" in the novel. It is found not only in Majida and, at certain points, hypocritically, in Mohsin (see 21)—Mohsin will invoke anything that will serve his interests—but also in Zainab, and the servant Hakiman. For example, when Laila objects to a tradition as "old-fashioned nonsense," Zainab responds, "I don't think about such things. I try to do as I am told" (105). At one point, Hosain has a parrot "in his silvered cage" imitate Hakiman's voice chanting "Allah il-Allah"(26), presumably referring to the first part of the Shahādah or Kalimah, "I bear witness that there is no God but Allāh," "Ashadu an lā ilāha illā-Llāh" (pronounced "Ashadu al-lā ilāha illā-Llāh" [see Glasse]). The general significance of the parrot is obvious. The point is emphasized by the truncated and inaccurate Arabic, perhaps the fault of the parrot, but perhaps indicating that Hakiman's profession of faith is based not on understanding, but on unreflective repetition.

Abida's almost uniquely reflective attitude toward tradition is part of her great intellectual acuity. She is, according to Mohsin, "a scholar of Persian poetry and Arabic theology" (20). Later, when Laila comes upon her alone, she is "reading from her favorite volume of Ghalib's poetry." She expresses regret that Laila does not attend to this tradition: "Do you ever read the books I give you? . . . I am sorry. . . . I thought you would learn one cannot live fully out of what is borrowed. You must love your own language and heritage" (139). Moreover, her intellectual talents are not solely humanistic. She keeps accounts for the estate and decides difficult cases regarding tenants, showing great business acumen.

In addition to all this, Abida observes Islamic principles more thoroughly than the hypocritical or unreflective traditionalists who surround her. Like Laila, she too objects to the mistreatment of sweepers (see 38). Her objection, however, is not due to a universalistic, Marxist emphasis on human dignity, as with Laila (45). Rather, it is due to her Islamic rejection of the Hindu caste system. Recall how Zahra tacitly adopted that system, despite her Islamic traditionalism.

As a portrait of a strong orthodox woman, all this is important. And yet Abida is, first and foremost, a member of her class. Her decisions about tenants, if acutely intelligent, are also heartless. For example, the members of one family have been loyal tenants for three generations. Due to illness, crop failure, and other factors, the current tenant is unable to pay the rent. An old woman, a relative, pleads his case. She concludes: "You are my mother, my goddess. Have mercy!" (61). Though the reference to the "goddess" is Hindu, the attitude of mercy is, as we have seen, of central importance in Islam. The point is even more obvious if we imagine the dialogue taking place in Urdu, where the word for "mercy" would probably be *raham*, cognate with the Arabic *raḥmān* and *raḥīm*. Abida—acting more like a Goddess of destruction than like a believer in Allāh, al-Raḥmān, al-Raḥīm, and acting most like a member of her economic class—evicts the man and his family. From a Marxist perspective, it is a blatant act of class robbery. What right does Abida have to land that her family has never worked? Should the land not belong to the family that tills it and has done so for generations? The extortion of land rent under these conditions is mere legalized theft. Abida, always careful with her class ideology, masks this robbery as "a matter of principle" (62), as "justice" (61).

The same class-based rigidity leads her to chastise Laila regarding Mohsin and Nandi. As Mohsin savagely beat the helpless girl whom he had previously tried to defile, Laila ran to aid her friend, and shouted at Mohsin that she hated him. In Abida's view, it is Laila who has committed a crime here, not Mohsin: "Tomorrow when he comes you will apologise to him." Laila has opposed social hierarchy in defense of friendship and universal human dignity—the dignity of the poor, the dignity of women. But for Abida, that hierarchy is of the highest importance: "To respect your elders is your duty" (38), she says, substituting an age hierarchy for the sex and class hierarchies that are at the center of this conflict. After all, Mohsin hardly acted as an "elder" in his attempt to seduce Nandi. Unable to defend this crude submission to unjust authority, she adopts Mohsin's tactic and counsels unthinking conformism: "My child, there are certain rules of conduct that must be observed in this world without question" (38). Unsurprisingly, she tries to pass this off as traditional culture, rather than brutal class hierarchy: "You must never forget the traditions of your family no matter to what outside influences you may be exposed" (38). Presumably, such "outside influences" include those which "taught [Laila] to think of human dignity" as a universal principle superseding class (45).

In keeping with the character type—which, again, standardly presents strong orthodox women as unmarried—Abida's own independence is shattered by her marriage and its stifling traditionalism. Her unhappiness and alienation are palpable during Laila's visit, and she weeps "uncontrollably" when it is time for Laila to leave. As already noted, she almost dies from a miscarriage "because the only woman doctor . . . was away and her mother-in-law refused to allow a man to attend to her" (204). Speaking of her aunt's in-laws, Laila rightly refers to this traditionalism as "murderous hypocrisy and bigotry" (204–5).

However, even these experiences do not soften Abida's class-based traditionalism, or make her recognize its cruelties. After weeping over Laila's departure, she merely repeats the same precepts concerning hierarchy and obedience that justified her earlier criticism of Laila's independence: "Do not disappoint me. I would have you strong and"—one might expect the final word to be "independent," but no. Abida finishes her wish for Laila with almost the precise opposite—"dutiful": "I would have you strong and dutiful." Hierarchy must be retained at all cost: "Your elders are your well-wishers and guides. You must honour and obey them" ("well-wishers and guides"—again one recalls Mohsin and Nandi). She goes on to insist that one's "'self' is of little importance" and to counsel acceptance of oppression, "You cannot demand happiness and you must learn to accept unhappiness" (252). She fails to mention that, due to class and sex hierarchies, some selves are of more importance than others and some people must accept far more unhappiness than others.

Later, when Laila chooses her own husband and marries in partial defiance of her elders, Abida treats her as if she "had committed some unpardonable crime" (311). Again, it is a matter of hierarchy versus human equality, authority versus individual freedom, class aspiration versus human aspiration. "She refused to see me or reply to my letters once I had told her I could not obey her, nor my family, and deny Ameer" (312). Laila's crimes were disobedience and dishonor—crimes

against a feudal aristocracy: "You have been defiant and disobedi-
ent. . . . You have let your family's name be bandied about. . . . You have
soiled its honour on their vulgar tongues" (312). The word "vulgar" is
particularly revealing. Honor is an aristocratic concern. Laila has
reduced the family to the level of the "vulgar tongues," the ordinary
people, the commoners, who are too inferior even to speak the name of
a Taluqdar family.

Perhaps the clearest instance of Hosain's view of traditionalism and
its relation to economy is to be found not in Mohsin or Abida, but in
Zahra. We are first introduced to Zahra as the antithesis of the nonconformist Laila. Hakiman unfavorably contrasts the two. Laila explains:
"Zahra said her prayers five times a day, read the Quran for an hour
every morning, sewed and knitted and wrote the accounts" (14). When
Zahra's marriage is being discussed, her mother explains with pride that
"She has read the Quran, she knows her religious duties; she can sew
and cook, and at the Muslim School she learned a little English, which
is what young men want now" (24). She seems a perfect case of someone with a deeply—if unreflectively—traditional character. But, after her
marriage, Zahra changes entirely. She is constantly at parties and at the
race track, wearing high heels (141), imported perfume (144), make-up
(146), and the like. At one point, she is greatly concerned that some nas-
tiness about *swarāj* (national independence) might necessitate the can-
cellation of "her appointment with the only European hairdresser in
town" (156). In short, she is a complete mimic.

The change may seem baffling at first, but it is merely a matter of
"accepting the conventions of whichever society she was in" (302)—and
doing so insofar as it fit in with her class aspirations. Her husband is a
Civil Service officer (140), and so a certain type of behavior is required
of her: "She was now playing the part of the perfect modern wife as she
had once played the part of a dutiful purdah girl. Her present sophistica-
tion was as suited to her role as her past modesty had been. Just as she
had once said her prayers five times a day, she now attended social functions morning, afternoon and evening" (140). In keeping with this, however much she sets aside Islamic traditions, she remains insistently "proud
of [her] breeding," as when she exclaims to Laila, "Did you know that
Taluqdars have a right of audience with the King?" (147). Unsurprisingly,
given her class interests as a Taluqdar and as a wife of a civil servant, she
takes a dim view of nationalism (see 157), at least before the new state of
Pakistan begins to show possibilities for her husband's advancement.

CULTURE AND IDENTITY (3): MIMETICISM

Zahra provides an apt transition from tradition to mimeticism, as she herself moved from one to the other following a shift in circumstances and, thus, economic interest. Indeed, Hosain indicates that this sort of change has been part of upper-class life in the contact regions since the first years of the British Raj. Early in the novel, Laila describes three photographs hanging in her grandfather's room. In one, we see her grandfather "his brothers and cousins, black-bearded, dressed in embroidered *achkans* and caps, with jewelled swords held in their hands, sitting stiffly in high carved chairs, with uniformed retainers holding steel-tipped spears standing behind them." In the second, her grandfather is "alone, beardless . . . dressed in a suit, with shining pointed boots and spats." In the third, he is "with a group of strained pompous Englishmen standing behind Englishwomen" (32). The photographs illustrate the two aspects of Taluqdar life and culture during the British period. In one, dominating their Indian "inferiors," they dress and groom themselves in Eastern fashion. In the other, collaborating with the British, her grandfather dresses and grooms himself in the British fashion. The implication appears to be that traditional and colonial culture are much like clothes, to be put on or taken off as the situation demands, as class interest dictates.

But this is not to say that there are no differences. Certainly some characters are more likely to wear Western clothes and others are more likely to wear Eastern clothes. The most blatant case of mimeticism is Mrs. Wadia: "Her perfumes, and shoes and lace and linen and silver came from the most expensive shops in Paris and London. She went to Europe every year, was prouder of Western culture than those who were born into it, and more critical of Eastern culture than those outside it" (129). She is from a bourgeois family elevated to aristocratic status by the British: "the daughter of a Bombay scrap merchant who had been knighted after the 1914–18 war." Her family was "very popular with the English, and referred to all English officials by their Christian names."

Lest this seem a genuine assimilation to English ways, we discover later that her daughter, Perin, reverses the pattern, in changed circumstances. Perin is a sort of inverse Zahra, curiously mimicking European mimicry of India. Shortly before Indian independence, when long-term economic interests are clearly shifting, Perin's interests and manners change too: "When Perin Wadia had returned from her expensive school in Switzerland her conscious cosmopolitanism had blossomed into the even more conscious nationalism which was fashionable towards the end of the war." The phrasing here is important: her "cosmopolitanism," which is in this case a form of mimeticism, had not been *replaced* by nationalism ("traditionalism," in our terms), but had *developed into* traditionalism. Moreover, it was not a sincere development out of an internalized sense of culture, but a fashion, and a Western fashion at that: "European and American aesthetes and intellectuals and the 'smart set' of Bombay and Delhi had discovered the art and culture of ancient India simultaneously." The irony is palpable. Traditionalism here is a form of mimeticism; it is an imitation of European interest in the indigenous. The next sentence makes this perfectly clear: "It appeared at times that neo-Indians wore their nationalism like a mask, and their Indianness like fancy dress." "Black skins, black masks," to rephrase Fanon. The thing becomes curioser and curioser as Perin transposes "the Ajanta look into the twentieth century in the manner of her dress and coiffeur" and goes "to an *ashram* in the south for a period of meditation." Unsurprisingly, "She spoke of ancient culture in European idioms" (276). Perin is more akin to the bearded poet than to Abida, or Mr. Freemantle.

Nadira and her mother, Begum Waheed, form another interesting mother/daughter pair in this context. The two are perhaps most easily classed as syncretist, but, as in the cases of Zahra and her mother and the Wadias, they in fact adopt traditionalism, mimeticism, and syncretism, according to need. For example, Nadira was deeply devoted to "the greatness of the Islamic world"—insofar as this supported her family's class interests. Nadira's father was a physician who charged exorbitant fees. "After he had become successful they moved from their small house in a socially inferior part of the city, to a large house on the Mall. Begum Waheed came out of purdah, began to call herself 'Begum,' and sent Nadira to a Convent" (125–26). Later, Begum Waheed—out of purdah and with a daughter sent to study among Catholic nuns—enters politics as a candidate for the Muslim League. Her economically self-interested hodge-podge of attitudes toward tradition is evident in the reactions to her candidacy: "Progressives accused her . . . of being a capitalist and a communal reactionary, and religious fanatics attacked her for being out of purdah and addicted to immoral Western ways" (226).

More straightforward examples of mimeticism may be found in Hamid and Saira, the uncle and aunt who raise Laila after her grandfather dies. Hamid is first introduced via the standard description of a mimic: "He is more a Sahib than the English" (22). The point is stressed repeatedly throughout the novel. Laila explains that "he admired Western forms of behaviour." Moreover, "He dressed immaculately in Western clothes, and preferred to speak English" (86), even showing annoyance when asked to speak Urdu for the benefit of relatives whose English is weak (see 109). He set out to "copy . . . alien ways" (86), "adopting a Western way of living, bringing his wife out of purdah, neglecting the religious education of his sons," sending his children to England when they were still "young boys." When Laila sees their redecorated rooms, she makes the mimeticism clear: "The rejuvenated rooms reminded me of English homes I had visited with Mrs. Martin, yet they were as different as copies of a painting from the original" (120–21).

Lest anyone think that this Westernization at least had the benefit of liberating Saira, Laila explains that she was entirely "dominated" by her husband. Saira is, of course, present at all discussions with Hamid and others, but she has no real authority in any decisions—unlike a strong traditional woman, such as Abida. Moreover, Hamid often speaks to her in a demeaning way. For example, at one point, Hamid announces "pontifically" that "I have always believed in the education of girls" (109). Saira explains, "Young men want their wives to be educated enough to meet their friends and to entertain" (110). Hamid cuts her off and chastises her, saying, "I wish you would stop interrupting with your irrelevant remarks, Saira" (110). But, in fact, Saira is completely right. The education of girls is not a matter of "the principle of the thing," as Hamid asserts (110). Rather it is a response to the changing economy. Much like her own removal from purdah, it is necessitated by the increasing dominance of bourgeois social conventions, which are themselves consequential because of the connection between class-based social integration, on the one hand, and economic success, on the other.

Unsurprisingly, when it is important for their economic interests, Hamid and Saira downplay their mimetic Englishness and insist that they are syncretistic or even deeply traditional. Thus, Saira explains, bizarrely, that her children's education in England is the "only" way to "produce a perfect blending of the best of the East and the West" (87). It is easy to see how this involves the best of the West, but how could it possibly give the best of the East? And later, a Begum from Surmai is inspecting prospective spouses for her relative, the Raja of Surmai. Laila is evidently a candidate. Given the Begum's preference for tradition,

Saira explains that she believes "in education for women" only "to pre-
pare them for service." Thus, while "Laila is being educated to fit into
the new world . . . our old traditions and culture are always kept in
mind" (131). Indeed, she even goes so far as to say that, though Laila
does not observe purdah, "We observe the spirit of the Quranic injunc-
tion by limiting freedom within the bounds of modesty" (132)—a
patently hypocritical comment from a woman who has herself
renounced purdah for full Westernization.

As we have already noted, the mimetic Westernization of Hamid and
Saira is in part a concession to bourgeois convention. However, it has
other sources as well. Though it may at first seem paradoxical to say so,
it is inseparable from their commitment to the feudal order that privileges
them, for this order is visibly marked by distinction of their class from the
Indian masses and, more significantly, it has been guaranteed by British
rule. Hamid rages that "Our fathers and our forefathers handed us down
rights and privileges which it is our duty to preserve" (199)—an in some
ways astonishing use of the word "duty," for this duty is solely a matter
a economic self-interest, or, at best, class interest of the dominant elite.
Later, he repeats the point, but now suggesting the reasons why Taluqdari interests are bound up with the British: "We *Taluqdars* have ancient
rights and privileges, given by a special charter, which we have to safe-
guard" (231). The reader is reminded of Zahra's earlier insistence that
"*Taluqdars* have a right of audience with the King" (147).

In keeping with this, Hamid is vehemently opposed to nationalism.
Saleem explains the reason. It is simple: "the landlords' fear of abolition." This fear "is the basis for the formation of a new party which is
interested in keeping the *status quo* intact . . . and is fundamentally
opposed to progressive, national movements" (233). But does this advocacy of the status quo not contradict their mimeticism? In fact, not at all.
For the status quo is, again, bound up with the British. Saira puts the
point bluntly, "There is no question, it would be better to have the
British stay on than the Hindus ruling" (234). On the other hand, even
here, the phrasing is not quite right. The antagonism between Hindus
and Muslims is, at least in part, an ethnic displacement of another opposition—that between the feudal aristocrats and the national bourgeoisie.
Indeed, this particular conversation began with Saleem saying, "In the
final analysis, what you are facing is the struggle for power by the bourgeoisie" (231), which is to say, the *national*, and nationalist, bourgeoisie.
In keeping with this, when Laila subsequently refers to the Independence

"movement," Hamid again makes his attitude clear: "Movement! . . . What movement? . . . This is merely a demonstration of irresponsible hooliganism" (160). Hamid's and Saira's cultural identification with the English is founded upon a strategic alliance, a set of common economic interests extending back to the beginnings of British rule, now augmented by a shared political opposition to nationalism, whether that of a revolutionary peasantry or that of the national bourgeoisie.

Of course, Hamid and his class eventually lose out, as the aristocracy inevitably does, when confronted with the rise of the industrial bourgeoisie. "At the end of a long, legal struggle landowners had to accept the fact that their feudal existence had been abolished constitutionally as swiftly as by the revolution they had always feared" (277). The change is illustrated by the physical displacement of the aristocracy, as when Laila, on the way to her physically and allegorically decaying ancestral home, sees "three-storeyed cement blocks of cheap flats, built by Agarwal [Sita's father, who had made his fortune in part through the nationalist movement] where the Raja of Bhimnagar's palace and garden had once been" (270). Moreover, the mimeticism of Hamid and his class is ultimately reviled too. "Politically he had fought a losing battle against new forces that were slowly and inexorably destroying the rights and privileges in which he had believed. Socially he had seen that way of life going to pieces which he had cultivated so carefully; the new ruling class . . . derided it as a slavish copy of the British" (282)—even if that new ruling class did so in another sort of slavish copy of the British, in this case a mimetic pseudo-traditionalism, as the case of Perin Wadia illustrates.

CULTURE AND IDENTITY (4):
ALIENATING HYBRIDITY AND SYNCRETISM

Whatever view they ultimately take of identity, whatever relation they ultimately adopt toward tradition, Laila and her peers all begin from a sense of alienation and hybridity. Laila comments more than once that she "lived in two worlds" (124, 128). Nadira, using an aptly monetary idiom, observes that Indians of her generation—or, more accurately, her generation *and class*—"are paying for being the product of two cultures" (211). Ranjit corrects her, "Abortions, you mean" (211), the implication being that they are not so much bicultural as lacking in any fully developed culture whatsoever.

Again, for Hosain, any conflict over culture identity—including alienating hybridity—is not the result of some profound psychological crisis. Rather, it is a matter of socioeconomics; it is the result of a conflict between one's cultural capacities and the expectations defined by one's social milieu, itself defined by economic class. Some cases of this conflict between capacities and social context concern relatively trivial and local matters. For example, when Laila first goes to live with her Westernized aunt and uncle, she cannot reconcile their mensal customs with her own: "I fumbled with knives and forks, awed by the array of shining implements playing a part in a ritual" (121). Other cases are more severe. The most important and most tragic conflicts result when one has come to recognize in oneself a certain human aspiration that is stifled by society. All class-based societies stifle some human aspirations. That is necessary in order for one class to dominate another. Precisely which aspirations are stifled depends on the type of society in question. Bourgeois society involves a broad range of individual freedoms absent from feudal society, including the freedom to choose one's own spouse. It is predictable that the influence of a bourgeois society will lead members of a feudal society to recognize the possibility of choosing their own spouses, and thus to suffer when their own, feudal, society denies them that possibility. This is the dilemma of several characters in the novel, and forms the central conflict in the main plot concerning Laila and Ameer.

As we have already indicated, Hosain's implicit advocacy of individual freedom of choice in marriage is not precisely syncretistic. Rather, it is a form of universalism in which societies are seen as different, but human aspirations are the same. For Hosain, love is a human constant. Love marriages are standard in bourgeois societies and rare in feudal societies, and thus fewer people in feudal societies may be aware of the possibility of a love marriage. But there is no difference in the human beings themselves, thus no difference in their inclination to fall in love, and no difference in their propensity to choose a mate on the basis of affection. The only difference is in the degree to which that propensity is fostered, permitted, or even recognized by broader social action, expectation, and judgment.

I take this emphasis on universality to be one main purpose of Hosain's use of the story of Laila and Majnun, the paradigmatic Arabic and Persian story of romantic love frustrated by social denial. As Chelkowski points out, Laila and Majnun is "perhaps the most popular romance in the Islamic world. Versions appear in prose, song, and poetry in almost every language within the vast area stretching from the Atlantic Ocean to the Chinese border" (66) and, we might add, in every century for more than a millennium. It is a sort of Romeo and Juliet story, though it is far more culturally pervasive and has been important for many more centuries. Its transhistorical and cross-cultural popularity throughout the East indicates that romantic love and the desire for love marriage are neither recent nor Western developments, but broadly human feelings—permitted by some societies, forbidden by others, but present in all.

More exactly, Laila and Majnun are students together and fall in love, but Laila's father will not allow them to marry. Laila is forced to marry someone else, but she preserves her virginity. For years, the two lovers long for one another and write love poetry that becomes legendary throughout the world. Majnun lives alone in the desert, mad, befriended only by wild animals, composing exquisite love lyrics, and at one point joining in a desert war in the hope of gaining his beloved. Laila lives miserably in her husband's compound. Eventually, Majnun dies in the desert and Laila dies in her home.

Hosain gave her heroine the name of Laila, and had her fall in love with a man named Ameer—the clan name of Majnun being Ameer. The connection with the legend is as obvious as if an English author had named a heroine "Juliet" and her beloved "Montague." Indeed, to help us make the connection, Hosain alludes to the legend early in the novel, when a vegetable seller refers metaphorically to "the fingers of Laila, the ribs of Majnu" (58).

The parallels between the legend, most famously retold in Nizami's epic, and the novel are not perfect, but they are significant and revealing. Laila is a student and Ameer is a teacher, a slight variation from the original where both are students. More importantly, Laila's family objects to the marriage. In keeping with her Marxist and feminist principles, Hosain does not present these objections as an invincible barrier to marriage. She insists on the ability of people to act, and carefully avoids writing a work that is defeatist. At the same time, however, she carefully avoids writing a work that implies that an individual, acting alone, can successfully defeat larger social forces. Their marriage leads to monetary difficulties which could easily have been avoided, had Laila's family accepted Ameer. As a consequence of these difficulties, Ameer joins the army (316). He dies far from Laila, in the Middle East (317), recalling Majnun's death in the Arabian desert. In keeping with her overall project, Hosain explains this death not in terms of frustrated love, but in terms of political economy. While Majnun wanders in the desert, and even joins another tribe and engages in a war, because of his unrequited love, Ameer works in the desert, and even serves a foreign power during war, because of his financial need—if, admittedly, financial need rendered acute by romantic love.

Finally, Hosain's Laila does not die. Rather, having returned to her home in a state of despair comparable to that of Laila, she finds renewed—political—hope and a new, deeper, if less romanticized love. In fact, this deeper love is with Asad. In the traditional story, Laila's kind husband, who accepts that she loves another man and never forces himself on her, comes from the tribe called "Asad" (Nizami, 88). In this way, Hosain recognizes the universality of romantic love, as well as romantic politics. Yet, at the same time and in keeping with her broadly Marxist principles, she criticizes romantic love, replacing it *not* with arranged marriage, but with a nonromanticized form of personal choice based on friendship and mutual tolerance and care—as well as shared political and social commitment—rather than passion.

The other cases of romantic love in Hosain's novel are even less successful than Laila's—again, not for reasons of cultural identity, but because the economic constraints are still more severe. The first is discussed by Mrs. Wadia. "A Muslim girl, from a strict purdah family, ran away with a Hindu boy. . . . When the foolish boy's money was spent, he yielded to pressure and abandoned the girl. Her parents refused to take her back . . . and [she] killed herself" (132–33). This is in part a feminist story of the ill treatment of a woman by a man. But any simple feminist point is immediately rendered more complex, through implicit relation to class interest, by the uniform response of the women. Begum Waheed says, "She disobeyed the tenets of her religion"; Saira says, "She betrayed the cause for which we are working"; the Begum from Surmai says, "Wickedness cannot escape punishment" (133). These women do not care about some supposed feminist issue. They immediately recognize the danger of any such irregularity for the social order in which they have aristocratic privileges. Later, when Saleem mentions love to his mother, she responds, shocked, "Love? No one in decent [i.e., aristocratic] families talks of love" (180).

The point becomes clearer when we learn that the young woman in question was from a poor family and was studying at school on a scholarship. Laila responds to all of them, "She must have been brave and clever to educate herself in a poor, backward home and get a scholar-ship" (133). Indeed, this comment leads us to look back at the reason she was abandoned by the Hindu boy—he ran out of money. Of course, there is still a feminist issue here. The boy was accepted back, while the girl was not. And there is a communal issue—for the horror of the women is intensified by the difference in religious affiliation. But the underlying problems remain problems of economic class. Mrs. Wadia perceptively responds to Laila's outburst concerning the girl's back-ground, noting the type of analysis implicit in her remark, and the true danger implicit in the elopement: "What strange ideas the girl has! Dear Saira, do be careful. She may become a Socialist" (133). Saira replies, with distress, "Laila, you must be joking, defending wickedness" (133). Laila goes on, alluding to the story of Laila and Majnun and the other stories that show love to be universally human: "I am not defending wickedness. She wasn't a thief or a murderess. After all, there have been heroines like her in novels and plays, and poems have been written about such love" (133–34). Stressing the parallel between various strug-gles for independence—in love, in economy, in politics—Hosain draws a metaphor from revolutionary war to explain the consequences of this remark: "The word 'love' was like a bomb thrown at them" (134).

Sita and Kemal present a more elaborated instance of the same sort—though in this case the lovers do not run off together or marry. Sita refuses elopement, fearing the consequences. She and Kemal have been together in England and have fallen in love. But Sita recognizes the conflict between their individual feelings and the expectations of society around them. When Laila urges her to marry Kemal anyway, Sita protests, "I'm not a saint, Laila. I'm not a martyr" (216). The latter image, like that of love as a bomb, again links romantic love with polit-ical revolution, as well as individual resistance against the imposition of religious dogma; when Nita had died after being beaten in an Indepen-dence demonstration, Laila explains that "Her death was to me a mar-tyrdom" (166).

Sita makes clear that the problem is one of a conflict between indi-vidual aspiration and the broader social system of expectations and practices, a system she characterizes, in an appropriate image, as inhu-manly mechanical: "I, Sita, loved him, Kemal, and still do. Two individ-ual human beings. But it would have been the daughter of my father and mother marrying the son of his parents, with different backgrounds and different religions, two small cogs in a huge social machine" (215).

Ultimately, she marries someone else. This marriage is a purely and straightforwardly economic matter. Sita becomes "a leader in the new social world." Her husband "was ambitious . . .and glad of the progress he made because of [Sita]. He had been made a director of Agarwal's [Sita's father's] concerns." Sita's duplicity and mimeticism are captured in the image of her "beautiful house in New Delhi": "very modern and western in appearance and conveniences, very Indian and ancient in its decoration. It reflected Sita's character" (295). After her marriage, Sita reiterates the conflict between individual aspiration and social expectation, but this time from the other side: "Love is anti-social, while matrimony preserves the world and its respectability. Follow my example. I married with my mind unblurred by sentiment, and everybody is happy" (296). Of course, Hosain chooses Sita's words carefully. She says that matrimony "preserves the world and its respectability"—"respectability" is the clue that what it preserves is certain sorts of social and economic hierarchy. Moreover, it is clear that not everybody is happy. When Sita laughs, "The diamond she had taken to wearing in her nose glittered like a splinter of glass" (296). The symbol of her wealth recalls something shattered and painful.

Just as she draws the name "Laila" from the most famous love story of Persian and Arabic literature, Hosain draws the name Sita from the most famous love story of Sanskrit literature, the story of Rāma and Sītā. This too is a story of romantic love, and thus serves as further testimony to the universality of that feeling. On the other hand, the story of Rāma and Sītā is also a story of Rāma's cruel abandonment of Sītā due to social pressure—implicitly, his interests as a monarch. When Sītā is pregnant, there are rumors that she has been unfaithful. He knows they are untrue, but "in the interests of the kingdom" he nonetheless has his brother deceive her into a journey, during which he abandons her, pregnant, in the wilderness. Like the story of Laila and Majnun, it is a tragedy of lovers separated by social custom. Hosain changes the original story in two crucial ways, however. First of all, in keeping with her Marxist views, she makes clear that it is not mere social custom, but direct economic interest that separates the lovers. Secondly, perhaps in an effort to keep the woman from being a passive victim, she has Sita decide on the separation herself. In fact, in the original, Rāma eventually does decide to accept Sītā back, but Sītā refuses him. In this way, Hosain's version is consistent with the Sanskrit original, which does in the end give Sītā strength and autonomy.

Unlike Sita and Kemal, Laila and Ameer do elope. In part, this is due to Laila's greater bravery. But it is due primarily to the fact that things are indeed easier for them economically. They have difficulties, of course, and these difficulties eventually lead to Ameer's death. Indeed, Saira is displeased with Ameer from the beginning, because his family is, in her words, "very ordinary people; no breeding" (199). Later, Laila observes that "Ameer did not measure up to her conventional ideas of wealth, security and breeding" (264). But Laila and Ameer are both Muslim, and thus do not risk complete ostracism—with its attendant economic disabilities—and, unlike the couple discussed by Mrs. Wadia, Ameer has secure, professional employment. Both points are crucial.

POLITICS, ECONOMY, AND DESPAIR

At the culmination of her romance with Ameer, Laila declares that she fully recognizes the hardships that will result from their love marriage, but that she is completely willing to undergo those hardships. She then explains the importance of making such an independent choice. It is not merely a matter of achieving what one wants. It is a matter too of exercising one's free will. In keeping especially with the early Marx, she stresses the importance of developing all one's human capacities, not allowing some to atrophy. The disproportionate development of some capacities and neglect of others is what turns us into machines, in Sita's metaphor, deprives us of full human life. As Laila explains, "I have never been allowed to make decisions; they are always made for me. In the end not only one's actions, but one's mind is crippled. Sometimes I want to cry out, 'You are crushing me, destroying my individuality'" (265). Indeed, the same may be said of a nation. This is how colonialism—and feudalism, and capitalism—stifles not only individuals, but entire peoples.

But an individual act of defiance is not enough. It does not change the world. The world continues to exist, in its mechanical network of cogs, stifling the bulk of humanity with economic need. This sense of iron determination by economic necessity with no latitude for free human choice and action, a sense of entrapment and victimage, made concrete in Ameer's death—this drives Laila for a time into despair. It is only through Asad, through his broader politics of ahiṃsā, that she can overcome this despair, recognizing the greater task, the broader work of social transformation: "Asad . . . was still in prison, but his letters conveyed his faith in living without being didactic. They led me out of self-pity, through the negation of despair, into a recognition of struggle and positive acceptance" (317). It is Asad's universalist, Gandhian socialism that leads Laila out of despondency, even out of mourning for personal tragedy. I take it that, for Hosain, the point is generalizable.

Hosain is not naive about the motives of political activists. Activists are like everyone else—motivated by the same class interests. The Agarwals are committed in the independence struggle. But as Mrs. Martin points out, "For every yard of cloth burnt and unsold [Mr. Agarwal] gets a profit, because the cloth from his mill finds a market" (51). Indeed, as Hosain later informs us, Agarwal's fortunes had risen greatly in the course of the independence movement. Moreover, "He contributed generously to the funds of the Congress party, but kept on the right side of the Government" (167). Waliuddin is perhaps the most blatant case of the opportunism that pervades politics in this novel: "His political beliefs veered in any direction that promised power. He was as friendly with Congress leaders as Muslim League ones" (177). Indeed, he adopts the colonizer's technique of *divide et impera*, splitting the populace along religious lines. Saira calls him "that man who instigated Shia Sunni riots. . . . Everyone knows he secretly encouraged the rioting, and then came out as the hero who stopped it" (177). But, again, though he is an extreme case, the tendency is pervasive. Hosain even recognizes this tendency among radicals, "those earnest young poets and writers and political theorists who made the cause of every underdog their own, who hailed every Revolution as their holy war . . . who were as dogmatic as the most fanatic *moulvis* and priests, and as ruthless as Inquisitors in their determination to force their ideas on others" (315).

This opportunism and rigidity—reminiscent of corrupt traditionalists, such as Mohsin—could easily lead to cynicism and further despair. One could easily conclude: Yes, a few activists are sincere. But they are little more than pawns in the hands of the opportunists. Saleem comments "derisively" that "The Asads and Nitas of this world"—the sincere activists—"serve a useful purpose even for the Waliuddins and Agarwals" (196); in other words, the Waliuddins and Agarwals use the Asads and Nitas as unwitting tools for their own self-advancement. Zainab's bitter and consumptive brother presents a similar view of things. "'Asad is going to drive the English away,' he mocked. 'Drive them away with Truth and Non-violence. . . . What difference will it make? . . . Look around this village. The people rotted under the rulers of our own race, as they do under the English and as they will do if we rule ourselves again" (102).

In a sense, of course, Hosain agrees. Insofar as the change is merely a change from feudalism to capitalism, the poor will suffer the same oppression from different masters. But, despite this, Hosain indicates that Asad offers the possibility for something beyond a painful shift from one set of exploiters to another. He offers at a social level precisely what he has given to Laila at a personal level—escape from "self-pity, through the negation of despair, into a recognition of struggle and positive acceptance" (317). Work in solidarity with others toward the betterment of those who suffer most, and toward the human fulfillment of all in a transformed society. Laila complains that "When I think of the worries and despair, the material problems of my family and friends I cannot look objectively beyond them." Asad responds, "You will . . . if you think of those who always knew that despair" (278).

At the very end of the novel, Laila, sitting before a mirror in her decaying ancestral home, realizes that, in her self-absorption and sorrow, "I was my own prisoner and could release myself." She hears Asad approach and says to him, speaking literally and figuratively: "I have been waiting for you, Asad. I am ready to leave now" (319)—ready to leave the rotting house of her feudal ancestors, of course, but also ready to leave "self-pity" and "despair" for "struggle and positive acceptance" (317).

Self-pity and despair permeate the conflicted cultural identities of postcolonization society. The conflicts are the result of economic structures that operate to oppress the great majority of people. To adopt a certain mode of dress or to decorate one's home in the Ajanta style, to take up orthodoxy or syncretism or seek assimilation, is no solution. The only solution to the cultural problem is a response to the economic problem, and that is Asad's response to Laila's own feelings of despair: Join in solidarity with others to struggle for political and economic change, and thereby for the positive acceptance and free exercise of all those human capacities stifled in class society. Respect for and preservation of indigenous cultures, in their most humane and humanly valuable forms, can be achieved only on the basis of economic justice. Without that, culturalism can be little more than a mask for exploitation and self-interest.

SOCIALISM AND THE
POLITICS OF OTHERNESS

The problems of culturalism and colonial identity are obviously complex, and deeply felt. They do not lend themselves to easy solutions. Indeed, they involve such a variety of conscious and unconscious feelings, beliefs, impulses, social practices and interrelations, that it is difficult to imagine any measures, however complex, that would genuinely resolve the social hatred and personal pain that have resulted from colonialism. In this context, two things seem necessary if we are to make any progress in thinking about these difficult issues.

First of all, it is crucial that we have a clear, analytic understanding of what is involved in dilemmas of colonialism and cultural identity. This includes the cultural geography of colonialism, the varieties of culture that are part of colonial relations, the nature of cultural identity—its precise psychological structure and operation, the ways in which it may be formed and specified, and so on. In the preceding chapters, I have tried to establish a basic framework for such an analytic understanding. Toward this end, I have distinguished regions of colonial contact from culturally autonomous regions, the two types of contact culture from the two types of "basic" culture, and so on. I have sought to discriminate the different sorts of colony—"indigenous majority," "alienated majority," and so forth—and the variables, such as degree of severance, that bear on cultural constancy and cultural transformation. On this basis, I have undertaken to distinguish the range of relations one might have toward the various cultures involved in the colonial situation, from orthodoxy to alienating hybridity. I have tried to outline their properties and connections—for example, the link between mimeticism and reactionary traditionalism—and to detail their close relations with gender identity. After a preliminary statement in the first chapter, I have sought to expand this account in subsequent chapters, both in general terms—for example, by elaborating the concept of "nativism"—and in relation to specific cultural issues, such as Hindu notions of dharma or Igbo conceptions of cosmology and gender. In connection with this, I have drawn on Hindu ideas about law and custom to clarify the nature and variety of indigenous tradition, as well as the difference between modernization and Westernization.

In addition to this broadly social analysis, I have outlined a psychological account of the way in which "reflective identity," as I have called it, arises and operates, primarily through social attribution. It should be clear to readers that this account is radically anti-essentialist. For the properties we take to define ourselves are not based on anything intrinsic in ourselves. Indeed, as Tagore's *Gora* illustrates, these attributed properties have all their identity-defining force even when they are entirely empirically false. "Practical identity," in contrast, is an identity of habit and expectation learned in daily activity, and bound up with socially hierarchizing divisions, such as those of class, race, and sex. In a sense, this practical identity is the true repository of culture—indigenous, metropolitan, or whatever—and the most significant locus of cultural conflict under colonialism, especially in those cases where a discrepancy develops between its psychological and social components, between individual expectation and social cooperation.

My hope is that this broad range of theoretical principles and distinctions will serve to facilitate productive discussion and analysis of colonialism not only in literary study, but in more directly consequential areas of politics and culture as well.

This brings me to the second matter that provides a necessary condition for advancement in understanding cultural identity after colonization: an entirely open forum for discussion. As John Stuart Mill wrote, "Not the violent conflict between parts of the truth, but the quiet suppression of half of it, is the formidable evil: there is always hope when people are forced to listen to both sides; it is when they attend only to one that errors harden into prejudices"—a point well illustrated by Mill's own unfortunate views about the colonies—"and truth itself ceases to have the effect of truth, by being exaggerated into falsehood" (301). It is extremely important—not only to literary theory and criti-

cism, but to practical politics as well—that the recent trend toward dog-
matism in postcolonial studies be reversed. As noted in chapter 1, it
seems to be increasingly difficult even to publish in this field without
adhering to the ideas associated with Homi Bhabha, Gayatri Spivak, and
a few other poststructural writers. Again, this is not the fault of these
thinkers. Anyone's work can be raised to the level of dogma by overly
enthusiastic followers. But it is nonetheless a serious and consequential
problem, both intellectually and politically.

There is another, more local consequence of this Millian principle as
well. By its very nature, the issue of cultural identity will affect different
people differently. However socially determined it may be, identity is
nonetheless something that is experienced and asserted individually.
Even at his most stridently Hindu, Gora still affirms and feels Hindu
identity as a singular person, alone. This is poignantly made clear by the
momentary despair he feels on learning that he is not a Hindu. At that
moment, Gora recognizes not only that he might well be alone in the
future, but that he has really been alone all along—"The foundations
upon which, from childhood, all his life had been raised had suddenly
crumbled into dust. . . . What he had called the past seemed to have no
substance" (402). There is no direct connection among the hearts or
minds of people who share a commitment to one identity. Indeed, in
many ways, that affirmation of shared identity is an attempt to deny the
utter aloneness of each person's thoughts and emotions, an attempt to
overcome the painful recognition that we will never genuinely know or
be known by anyone else, that identity can never be shared, except in
name. Because of this aloneness, each person experiences his or her conflicts over identity uniquely. Certainly there are patterns. The patterns
are precisely what appear in the theory, and what we have focused on in
the preceding chapters. But there are also individual differences. And
these differences become particularly consequential when we are discussing practical responses to problems of colonialism and culture. For
what serves as a solution in one case, may not serve as a solution in
other cases. Put simply, the problems faced by Makak, Okonkwo, Nnu
Ego, and so on, are not the same. And even if the problems were the
same, the people facing them are not. There is no "one size fits all" solution to the problems of colonialism and culture.

As a result of recognizing just this diversity, I have tried to interpret
each of the preceding authors positively. I have not set out, first of all, to
criticize their views. Rather, I have tried to draw out what seems valuable,

insightful, productive in their work, what seems to contribute to a larger discussion of cultural identity after colonization—and, perhaps most importantly, what might advance a reader's sympathetic comprehension of the people involved. For these are human problems, and as such they demand not only abstract understanding, but empathic understanding as well. This does not mean that one should read uncritically. I have ended almost every chapter with some questions, some unresolved problems, some criticisms. Nor does it mean that all responses to these problems should be treated equally. Take reactionary traditionalism. I have little agreement with this position, and I suspect that this feeling is shared by most of my readers. There is no reason for us to consider reactionary traditionalism a genuinely viable response to colonialism. Nonetheless, it is important to understand what drives people into this position, and what its virtues are. The pain and love and ethical precision of Gora's reactionary traditionalism show us that this is not a position we can simply dismiss with facile phrases about "fanaticism," borrowed from the evening news. The intellectual issues, and the reality, are vastly more complex, and thoroughly human.

In this respect too, then, the active presence of many anticolonial views is important. Such a Millian multiplicity contributes to a dialectic in which some views, perhaps mistaken in themselves, nonetheless serve to highlight aspects of colonialism and neocolonialism that would otherwise be ignored and serve to counterbalance comparable colonialist views. We might shift for a moment from India, Africa, and the Caribbean to the contemporary United States. I have little intellectual agreement with such manifestations of identity politics as Afrocentrism. However, it seems likely that, in the context of a pervasive Eurocentrism, Afrocentrists help to alter the larger debate about American culture. If there were no Afrocentrism, the entire discussion would probably be even more skewed toward Eurocentrism.

On the other hand, though I believe that there is no single, complete solution to the conflicts of cultural identity, and though I believe it is important that a wide range of views be heard, and heard sympathetically, I also believe that some responses are particularly valuable, particularly consequential, and, what is more, generalizable. Though I can come to understand what sense there is in reactionary traditionalism, I cannot support its generalization, its acceptance as a broad social solution to cultural denigration and loss. Indeed, I cannot support the generalization of any particular cultural identity—syncretism, or orthodoxy, or whatever. That is the point of recognizing the individual diversity of responses to this problem. Again, there is no "one size fits all" approach to cultural identity. However, I do believe that there are two responses that are generalizable. Neither involves a commitment to one form of identity over another, one tradition over another. Moreover, both should function simultaneously to reduce cultural degradation and extinction, on the one hand, and to promote internal cultural reform, on the other. The first response is, roughly, individual—simultaneously emotive, intellectual, and ethical: universalism. The second response is economic and political: democratic socialism. Clearly, I cannot engage in anything resembling a full explication and defense of universalism and democratic socialism in the present context. However, I should like to conclude with a few observations on each.

"Universalism," as I am using the term here, has four primary components. The first is descriptive. This is the view that, at some level of abstraction, all human cultures share structures of properties and principles. This should be an uncontroversial presumption, for without it we can make no sense of the idea that these are all *human* cultures. If there are no shared structures, then we are left in the position of those colonialists—rightly denounced by Bhabha—for whom Africans shared with Europeans nothing more than a deceptively similar outward appearance (see "Of Mimicry," 131 and citations). Of course, as Appiah has noted in his defense of universalism, one must be careful in determining just what these shared structures are (58). But we have reason to believe that they are quite extensive. Work in linguistics over the past half-century has revealed a wide range of universal patterns even in the most superficially diverse languages. Recent research in literary study suggests that there is a similar universality in literature (see my "Literary Universals" and citations). There is no reason to believe that the point cannot be extended to all areas of culture.

Research on such descriptive universals is important in two ways. First of all, it is important in revealing cross-cultural continuities, the common modes of thought and action that underlie seemingly diverse practices. Second, it is important in helping us to understand cultural specificity. For, until we recognize our shared principles, we cannot fully understand what is not shared. Consider a very simple example. All written literary traditions appear to make use of allusion. The specific content of those allusions necessarily differs. But, if we are unaware of this universal, we will misunderstand, and probably undervalue, literary works from other traditions, because we will not recognize or seek to recognize the literary and other associations that often serve to give depth and resonance to a work. In Kālidāsa's *Śakuntalā*, the title character and her unborn child are partially repudiated by her husband, then taken from him and removed to heaven by her (nonhuman) mother. This scene repeats a famous episode from the final book of Vālmīki's *Rāmāyaṇa*. There, Rāma agrees to accept Sītā and their children back into the palace only if she passes through a fire unharmed. Sītā refuses, and calls on her (nonhuman) mother, who takes her away from Rāma and deep into the earth. The thematic point of Kālidāsa's scene, and much of its pathos, are necessarily lost on anyone who does not recognize this allusive connection. And no one trained solely in the European tradition will bother even to look for such connections if he or she is unaware of the shared principle of allusion. Similar points could be made about much more complex literary properties, and have been made repeatedly about language—for it is clear that we will greatly misanalyze any language, from English to Kinyarwanda, if we do not recognize the universal principles that are so crucial to all languages. No doubt, similar points could be made about ethics or religion or political structure as well.

The second component of universalism is, so to speak, experiential. It is the sense of universally shared humanity that serves as the necessary foundation for empathy. We have empathic identification with someone only when we can recognize in him or her the thoughts and feelings that animate our own actions and passions in the world, only when we feel that we can share a point of view on events, only when we overcome insular identities—of race or gender or nation or class—and imagine ourselves into common impulses, relations, and sensibilities. Lalita Pandit has called this "Empathic Universalism," and identified it as a central component of Tagore's work (207).

In the introduction, I referred to the view of Medieval Arabic theorists such as al-Fārābī, Ibn Sīnā, and Ibn Rushd, that an ethically successful literary work fosters *raḥmah*. Usually translated as "compassion" or "mercy," it derives from a root "signifying *tenderness requiring the exercise of beneficence*" (Maulana Mohammad Ali, 3n.3). This is a deeply empathic feeling that leads us to act humanely. And it is central to the ethical purpose and aesthetic force of virtually every work considered in the preceding pages. Though she was no doubt unfamiliar with the Arabic theorists and even with the concept of *raḥmah, raḥmah* is nonetheless what Jean Rhys sought to cultivate through her revision of Antoinette. It is what Achebe labored to elicit through his portrayal of Okonkwo, what Emecheta developed so painfully in the character of Nnu Ego. Moreover, in the preceding chapters, I have sought to emphasize and render more salient precisely this empathic aspect of these works. Once again, this aspect is inseparable from universalism. For without a presumption of universality, at least in the broad contours of the human heart and human mind, no contemporary European American, nor even a contemporary African American, nor even a contemporary urbanized Igbo, could open him/herself to feel for Okonkwo or Nnu Ego that empathic tenderness which entails beneficence.

The mention of ethics brings us to the third component of universalism as I am using the term—the ethical or ethico-political component. Here I have in mind, not spontaneous beneficent action based on empathy, but the sorts of ethical precepts that are enshrined in the United Nations' "Universal Declaration of Human Rights" or in the fundamental ideals of *sādhāraṇadharma* (universal dharma). These precepts do not so much lead us to understand whole cultures as to evaluate specific cultural practices. Unfortunately, universal precepts often conflict with culturally well-established practices. Does this mean that we should invariably outlaw such practices—or even that we should invariably take up the cause of opposing these practices? The answer is not entirely clear. On the one hand, it is only on the basis of universal ethical principles that we can forcefully condemn either indigenous or metropolitan practices—from Indian *sati* to American slavery, to British colonialism itself. On the other hand, such condemnations are often hypocritical, aimed only at those practices in which we ourselves are not implicated. Moreover, condemnation can prove counterproductive. For instance, as discussed above, Nandy has argued cogently that British cultural intrusions in India had precisely the reverse of their widely asserted effect, and turned *sati* from a rare practice into a virtual epidemic.

In this context, I find Tagore's ethical universalism particularly instructive. Consider some of the more ethically admirable characters from his fiction: Jagmohan, of *Quartet*, is a Brahmin who sets aside his inherited beliefs, taking up instead European utilitarianism. When a plague breaks out in Calcutta, he opens a hospital that caters to untouchables, and so dies ministering to the suffering and the outcaste. That is one end of a spectrum, and now the other: Gora is an Irish foundling who devotes himself to Hindu *ācāra*, ordinary popular custom. When tenants

on the indigo plantations are terrorized by the European planters and the
District Magistrate, Gora suffers imprisonment in their defense, while the
anglicized characters pass their leisure time flattering that same magistrate at one of his garden parties. Between these extremes, there is Nikhil,
of *The Home and the World*, a Hindu landlord who commits himself to
the *sādhāraṇadharma*, the universal dharma, of *ahiṃsā* or nonviolence
and to the support of poor Muslim tenants—a commitment that pits him
against his closest friend and against his wife. Above all these is Anandamoyi, who repudiates the exclusivist aspects of her familial tradition
and suffers ostracism from her community, after she adopts an untouchable European child whose parents died during the rebellion of 1857.

Praising the "spirit of sacrifice and willingness to suffer," Tagore
wrote that "Nothing is of higher value . . . than disinterested faith in
ideals." That is, in part, what these characters share. But that is commonplace, and hardly distinctive of Tagore. What is distinctive is the
way he extends selflessness beyond personal egoism to ethnic and racial
categories; the way he forces detachment to cross what might be called
the lines of cultural estrangement; the way he replaces the politics of
identity with what might be called a "politics of Otherness"—a refusal
to identify the good with one's own community, a denial even that there
is such a thing as "one's own community," walled off from the encompassing, shared community of humankind. Indeed, this politics of Otherness goes further still. It pushes us to condemn the faults of "our own"
far more harshly than the faults of others. It reverses the ordinary biases
of identitarian preference. It is the precise opposite of the narcissistic
moral hypocrisy that characterizes colonialism, and, indeed, almost all
human behavior.

Finally, the fourth "component" of universalism is the assumption
of common cultural ownership, the view that cultures are not tied to
particular lineages, but belong equally to all people. Though phrased in
nationalist terms, this is fundamentally the universalism expressed by
Gora, when he proclaims, "In me there is no longer any opposition
between Hindu, Mussulman, and Christian. To-day every caste in India
is my caste, the food of all is my food!" (406). Or, earlier, when he tells
Sucharita, "God has created men differing from each other in ideas and
in actions with a variety of beliefs and of customs, but fundamentally
one in their humanity. There is something in all of them which is
mine . . . which, if only we can see it in its truth, will pierce through all
littleness and incompleteness" (296). This universalism involves a radi-

cal deracialization of culture, a complete removal of culture from a hereditary group, and the extension of that culture's ideas and practices to all of humankind. As Walter Benn Michaels has discussed with particular force, culture is almost invariably defined in such a way as to tie it to ancestry and, thereby, to race (see Michaels, 137–42). The advocates of preserving Hindu or Irish or Jewish culture almost invariably have in mind preserving that culture *for Hindus, Irish people, and Jews* respectively. A universalist wishes to preserve Hindu or Irish or Jewish culture *for everyone.*

The issue of shared human culture is, however, complicated—and closely related to the much discussed topic of cosmopolitanism. Clearly, anything approaching a full treatment of this would require another book. However, there are a few things that should be said here about this aspect of universalism. First of all, in order to discuss the topic more clearly, we need to analyze practical identity further, into the part that is "transportable" and the part that is "rooted." "Transportable" practical identity would include anything one could do on one's own, away from the society of origin. "Rooted" practical identity, in contrast, presupposes one's presence in the relevant cultural community. In fact, we already suggested this distinction in the first chapter; it is a sub-variable of the degree of severance. However, in that context, we were considering cultures as wholes. Here, I am referring to practices within cultures. For example, food and music are, for the most part, transportable. In contrast, larger social activities—from communal farming techniques to such simple matters as greeting practices, activities that rely on uniform expectations and actions of the community as a whole or a sizable proportion of the community—are hardly transportable at all. Even a large group of Igbos, removed to another, culturally mixed region, will find it difficult to maintain such practices.

Common cultural ownership applies most readily to transportable culture (e.g., music). In this case, universalism suggests that we should preserve as much transportable culture as we possibly can. But we should do so in a deracialized or "cosmopolitan" form, as the common heritage of humankind. In that way, it can contribute to an individual's sense of cultural identity, but not a racialized identity. Consider music. Human culture is impoverished whenever a tradition of music is lost. But, according to this form of universalism, human culture is also impoverished when a tradition is preserved by being bound to a narrow human ancestry, by being racialized. Over the last two years, I have been working to organize an international conference on Tagore. Sometimes people—both Indian and non-Indian—would suggest that the main purpose of such a conference is introducing "the second generation" (i.e., the children of Indian immigrants) to "their" culture. According to the universalistic principles I am espousing here, and according to the principles suggested in Tagore's work, the children of Indian immigrants have no greater claim to Tagore than do the children of Irish or African or English or Armenian immigrants. As Edward Said wrote in *Culture and Imperialism* (xxv):

> We are still the inheritors of that style by which one is defined by the nation, which in turn derives its authority from a supposedly unbroken tradition. In the United States this concern over cultural identity has of course yielded up the contest over what books and authorities constitute "our" tradition. In the main, trying to say that this or that book is (or is not) part of "our" tradition is one of the most debilitating exercises imaginable. . . . For the record then, I have no patience with the position that "we" should only or mainly be concerned with what is "ours," any more than I can condone reactions to such a view that require Arabs to read Arab books, use Arab methods, and the like. As C. L. R. James used to say, Beethoven belongs as much to West Indians as he does to Germans, since his music is now part of the human heritage.

This universalism is obviously of a piece with the politics of Otherness discussed above. In fact, it is, so to speak, the initial stage of a politics of Otherness. First of all, it involves a thoroughgoing repudiation of a politics of identity, for it involves a rejection of that racializing of culture that is a necessary condition for the politics of identity. But at the same time, it equally involves a thoroughgoing repudiation of the "assimilative majoritarianism" that is regularly seen as the only alternative to identity politics. Often, when writers criticize identity politics, they seem implicitly to assume that majoritarian culture—the most common culture in any given society or the most dominant culture globally—is somehow "neutral." To take a very simple example, many people seem to assume that a sari is "ethnically particular," whereas a European-style dress is "ethnically neutral." Once one adopts this view, then an argument against identity politics tends to become an argument against "ethnically particular" ideas, practices, and the like. It tends to become an argument that everyone should conform to the "ethnically neutral" practices of the majority. Advocates of identity politics rightly respond that this distinction is false and hypocritical—dresses are no less ethnically particular than saris. Their conclusion, then, is that every practice is ethnically particular, and that each ethnic group should embrace its own ethnic particularity. The universalist view advocated here, agrees with the identitarian criticism of assimilative majoritarianism, but reverses its conclusion. In the universalist view, no practices are "ethnically particular." Every one of them is "ethnically neutral." Moreover, insofar as some of these practices are in a minority position and in danger of extinction, we all have an obligation to work to preserve them—assuming the practices in question conform to the universal ethical principles mentioned above. We have this obligation because the endangered practices are not the business of one ethnic or racial group, but are, rather, part of our common, human heritage.

But, again, this applies most readily to "transportable" culture. The issue of "rooted" culture is more complex and difficult. By the universalist principles just discussed, even rooted culture cannot be said, in principle, to belong to one group more than another. But, by definition, it is not easily shareable. It cannot be made cosmopolitan, integrated into a larger, human culture. One can wear a sari in Boston, or give a *vina* recital, but it does not seem that one can recreate the governing social structure defined by Igbo title societies. Related to this, any attempt to integrate such threatened practices into a full-fledged ethicopolitics of Otherness would be absurd. For one would actually have to live the life of the people in question. A politics of Otherness that governed, say, the English in relation to Igbo rooted culture would require that English people actually go and live in Igbo villages.

Here we need to remark on three things. First of all, it is important to recall the nature of tradition, as discussed in the first chapter. The sort of rooted culture of which we are speaking is in fact continually changing. Indeed, almost all rooted culture has been lost. The rooted culture of Africans or Indians is no less historical than the rooted culture of Europeans (as, for example, Coundouriotis has emphasized in a different context). It is no less changeable. In this way, the desire to preserve rooted culture is a mistaken desire; the ethical imperative to preserve rooted culture is a mistaken imperative. It is, ultimately, a form of reactionary traditionalism—even when it is universalized. The problem here is not that rooted culture should be preserved, but that it should not be killed, that it should be allowed to develop, to change, to have its own history. As Gora says, "I want the changes in India to be along the path of India's development, for if you suddenly begin to follow the path of England's history then everything from first to last will be a useless failure" (330).

This is related to a second point, which will initially appear contradictory with this concern to end cultural extinction, but which is ultimately consistent with it. It is mistaken to think that our highest ethical obligations regarding colonized countries are cultural. Even complete cultural extinction is not the worst consequence of colonization. It is not, in my opinion, even close. Rather, the most urgent dilemmas we face are the various forms of direct, physical suffering that result from economic inequality—the grinding poverty that is so common in much of the Third World, the disease and hunger that could easily be prevented in a more egalitarian economic system.

And this brings us to the third point, which reconciles these two concerns. Both the physical pain of colonialism and the extinction of rooted culture are the result of economic and political inequality. The case of physical pain—hunger, disease—is perhaps too obvious to require elaboration. The case of culture should be almost as obvious. The dominance of Euro-American culture throughout the Third World is one effect of the economic dominance of Europe and America. In some cases, the connection is direct, as when Euro-American media conglomerates virtually control the international market in popular or entertainment culture—music, film, and the like. In other cases the connections are indirect—as when Africans or Indians emigrate to Europe or North America seeking a level of material well-being not easily available at home and consequently are unable to continue the practices of the rooted cultures in which they were born. Cultural extinction—and, far more importantly, the extinction of individual human hope, health, life—do not result from some cultural choices or actions, and they cannot be combated effectively by other cultural choices and actions. Rather, dying cultures and peoples are the casualties of political economy—the relations of ownership, production, and distribution that define both global and local economic realities: who owns the land, how it is worked, who receives the produce.

And this brings us, at last, to the second crucial response to the broad human devastation left in the wake of colonialism: democratic socialism. This too is a form of universalism. But it is a political and economic form, associated in the preceding pages, not with Tagore, but with Emecheta and Hosain. As I am using the phrase, democratic socialism involves, first of all, a form of analysis—largely Marxist in provenance—that seeks to understand the underlying political-economic determinants of cultural degradation and human misery. Second, it is an ideal of human community and well-being. The first importance of this ideal is not cultural, but material, physical. It is an antidote to hunger, poverty, disease. But even for the purest culturalist, political economy should ultimately have pride of place in any scheme of social action. First of all, for a negative reason—the culture passes away with people. When an Igbo or Hindu or Spiritual Baptist dies of preventable hunger or curable disease, one repository of traditional culture is irrevocably lost. Second, for a positive reason—in conditions of genuine democracy and economic equality, there is no reason to suppose that there would be any serious threat to most cultures, for the usual forces that stifle cultures, directly or indirectly, would no longer exist. An egalitarian political economy will not, of course, preserve rooted culture. Nothing can or should do that. But it will allow rooted cultures to develop along the lines of their own historical change.

The works we have examined by Emecheta and Hosain illustrate the close relation between culture and political economy. They illustrate also the overwhelmingly greater importance of political economy—its determinative force, its brutal consequences. And they suggest that a concern with culture removed from a concern with political economy, an advocacy of cultural resistance without a corresponding advocacy of socialist and democratic activism, is too often the means by which exploitative domination—including domination through gender or ethnicity—is secured or concealed by powerful indigenous groups in former colonies.

Here a number of questions arise that Emecheta and Hosain cannot really address, due to their focus on cultural issues: What is the relation between economic equality and political independence? How are we to understand socialist economy? Does it involve worker/peasant ownership or state ownership? And what politics are truly democratic? Does democracy require a strong central government, or is it inconsistent with a strong central government? How are we to achieve democratic socialism—through trade unions, through the establishment of local cooperatives, or what? How can we guarantee that both the democracy and the socialism extend equally to all people, whatever their ethnic origin, gender, and so on? These issues are taken up in a rather different set of postcolonization literary works, a set of works focusing on political economy, rather than cultural identity: Ngũgĩ wa Thiong'o's *Petals of Blood*, which considers trade unionism, political revolution, and the oppressive use of neocolonial nativism; Peter Abrahams' *Mine Boy*, which addresses the conflicts between black nationalism and communist trade unionism; Kamala Markandaya's *Nectar in a Sieve*, which indirectly advocates principles of Gandhian peasant socialism, in tacit opposition to Nehruvian industrial socialism; Bessie Head's *A Question of Power*, which examines the semi-anarchistic cooperative movement of then-contemporary Botswana, and so on. Indeed, these works show that responses to political economy after colonization are as multiple and complex and differentiated as the responses to cultural identity explored in the preceding pages. Thus, they are as much in need of systematic analysis and theorization.

I have been maintaining that cultural universalism, with its politics of Otherness, and democratic socialism are necessary, if not sufficient, anodynes to the pervasive cruelty or *hiṃsa* perpetrated by colonialism. But this is clearly not the end of the story. To mention democratic socialism is not to give a final answer to the question—what is to be done after colonization? Rather, to advocate democratic socialism is to bring up a series of further, equally difficult questions, questions that have also been the topic of complex debate, not only in philosophy and politics, but in literature as well. Clearly, these debates are of deep relevance to the cultural issues we have been considering, and, more importantly, to the human hope and pain that underlie those cultural issues and give them ethical consequence. Unfortunately, however, that complexity and consequence necessarily make the debates surrounding democracy and socialism into the topic of another book.

ANALYTIC GLOSSARY OF
SELECTED THEORETICAL CONCEPTS

I. TYPES OF COLONY

A. Indigenous Majority. Colonies where the colonized people form a majority and continue to live in the same geographical region as their forebears. This combination of majority status and geographical constancy most often allows for greater cultural continuity than in other types of colony. Examples would include India, Pakistan, Kenya, Ghana, Nigeria, and Ireland.

B. Alienated Majority. Colonies in which the colonized people form a majority, but they have been displaced from their ancestral region, to which they no longer have access. Moreover, the colonized majority in this case is most often drawn from a number of different ancestral regions, with distinct indigenous traditions. This mixing of indigenous cultures and the lack of access to the communities of origin clearly alter, and limit, the relation to any indigenous tradition in such colonies. The most obvious cases of this type occur in the Caribbean.

C. Indigenous Minority (sometimes called "Settler" colonies). Colonies in which the indigenous and alienated peoples have minority status, usually forming only a small percentage of the population. Examples would include the United States, Australia, Canada, and New Zealand.

II. CULTURAL GEOGRAPHY

A. Geographical Areas

i. The metropolis. The colonizing country—England, in this case.

ii. The indigenous region. The area of the colony in which there is relatively little cultural interaction between the colonizer and the colonized—for example, interior Igboland or most of village India, during the colonial period.

iii. The region of contact. The area of the colony in which colonizers and colonized or, more properly, metropolitan and indigenous culture come into regular and systematic contact—for example, metropolitan areas such as Lagos or European plantations. The difference between indigenous regions and regions of contact is a matter of degree, if sometimes a very high degree.

B. Cultures

i. Basic cultures. The culture of the metropolis, hence English culture, and the culture or cultures of the indigenous region, for example, Igbo culture and Yoruba culture. These cultures are "basic" in the sense that they precede and form the major contributory elements for contact cultures.

ii. Contact cultures. The cultures that arise in the region of contact due to the influence of one culture on the other. There are two forms of this: metropolitan contact culture and indigenous contact culture. Metropolitan contact culture is the culture of settlers and Creoles, English culture reshaped by indigenous ideas and practices. Indigenous contact culture is the inverse of this, the culture of indigenous people as reshaped by English ideas and practices.

General note on basic and contact cultures: To speak of "metropolitan culture" or "indigenous contact culture," or to use "culture" in the singular at all, is in many ways a simplification. Cultures are best understood as sets of partially overlapping ideas, practices, and so forth. They are not strictly unitary.

C. Variables Affecting the Relations
Between Basic and Contact Cultures

i. Intensity of contact. The degree to which one's interaction with the alien culture is systematic or unstructured, occurs regularly or occasionally, affects culturally important areas of one's life or only peripheral matters, and so on.

ii. Degree of severance. The degree to which one's basic culture is accessible from or practicable in the region of contact.

iii. Degree of internalization. The degree to which any culture has become a spontaneous part of one's way of thinking about and acting in the world. An Igbo person who is born and raised in the autonomous region will have internalized Igbo custom in a way that is probably impossible for someone raised in the region of contact.

III. STANDARD RELATIONS TO CULTURES

A. Orthodoxy. Open-minded, flexible adherence to indigenous culture, with particular emphasis on large ethical or social principles, rather than on specific customary practices. Orthodox tradition is open to "modernization" in the sense of rational reform guided by both scientific and ethical principles—for example, the introduction of medical advances.

B. Unreflective Conformism. Closed-minded, inflexible adherence to indigenous culture, with little attention to large ethical or social principles and with particular emphasis on specific customary practices standard in one's immediate community.

C. Reactionary Traditionalism. A reification of basic culture in reaction against the threat posed by metropolitan culture. In postcolonization literature, it is sometimes viewed as corrupt and hypocritical. Reactionary traditionalism usually assumes one of two forms:

i. Purgative Reactionary Traditionalism and Originalism. In this version, the reactionary traditionalist seeks to preserve indigenous culture in a form purged of whatever elements make it weak in the face of metropolitan culture. Sometimes, this purgation is defended as a form of "originalism," a return to the original and thus most authentic version of the culture.

ii. Stereotypical Reactionary Traditionalism and Reactionary Nativism. In this version, the reactionary traditionalist has little direct familiarity with indigenous culture, and therefore relies on colonial stereotypes regarding that culture. When the colonial stereotype is that the indigenous people were living in a state of nature without culture, this attitude is more appropriately referred to as "reactionary nativism."

D. Assimilation. Open-minded, flexible adherence to metropolitan culture.

E. Mimeticism or Reactionary Assimilationism. A closed-minded, inflexible imitation of metropolitan culture, with particular emphasis on specific customary practices. In postcolonization literature, it is often associated with hypocrisy and corruption. Mimeticism usually assumes one of two forms:

i. Purgative Mimeticism. In this version, the mimic seeks to purge every suggestion of indigenous culture from his or her thought and action.

ii. Stereotypical Mimeticism. In this version, the mimic has little direct familiarity with metropolitan culture, and therefore relies on indigenous and, to a lesser extent, metropolitan stereotypes.

F. Syncretism. The synthesis of metropolitan and indigenous culture. This synthesis may be intentional, and aimed at the production of a new culture superior to both its precursors, or it may result spontaneously from the natural development of contact cultures.

G. Alienating Hybridity. A partial internalization of and adherence to both indigenous and metropolitan cultures, which ultimately leaves one disjoined from both cultures—emotionally, intellectually, practically.

General Note on Standard Relations to Cultures: Though here defined from the indigenous point of view, the preceding categories apply equally to settlers, with only minimal changes in the definitions. For example, from the settler's perspective, assimilation would be open-minded, flexible adherence to indigenous culture. Stereotypical mimeticism would be a closed-minded, inflexible imitation of indigenous culture as defined in metropolitan stereotypes. And so on.

IV. STANDARD GENDER CATEGORIES, CONSIDERED AS A
SPECIAL CASE OF STANDARD RELATIONS TO CULTURES

A. Orthodox Masculinity/Femininity. Gender characteristics traditionally esteemed in indigenous culture. These include competence in traditional, sex-defined practices, and conformity to indigenous, sex-defined ethical principles.

B. Unreflective Conformist Masculinity/Femininity. The unquestioning acceptance of traditional gender practices, including those that are harmful to the character in question or in violation of deeper social principles. This is most obviously a concern in feminist writings that treat the perpetuation of patriarchy by women.

C. *Reactionary Masculinity/Femininity*. Putatively traditional gender roles and ideals, rigidly asserted in opposition to the threat of metropolitan culture. Reactionary masculinity/femininity usually assumes one of two forms:

i. *Purgative Reactionary Masculinity/Femininity*. In this version, the reactionary traditionalist wishes to establish a revised set of gender practices that are purged of the degenerate traits imputed to indigenous people in colonial ideology. Such a purgation is particularly important because the reactionary traditionalist views these traits as dangerous weaknesses in an indigenous culture threatened by metropolitan culture. This purgation is often characterized as a return to an original masculinity or femininity, characteristic of an initial or foundational and thus authentic stage of indigenous tradition.

ii. *Stereotypical Reactionary Masculinity/Femininity*. In this version, the reactionary traditionalist has little direct familiarity with indigenous traditions and relies instead on metropolitan stereotypes regarding indigenous men and women.

D. *Assimilative Masculinity and Femininity* should logically occur at this point, presumably as some genuine adherence to metropolitan gender roles and ideals. However, I know of no characters that fit this category.

E. *Mimetic Degeneracy or Effeminacy*. The loss of orthodox, gender-based virtues, such as masculine courage, a loss bound up with mimeticism. Such a loss is, in a sense, always purgative. It usually incorporates a stereotype of metropolitan culture as permeated by degeneracy and by putatively feminine vices—lasciviousness, deceit, pusillanimity, and the like.

F. *Syncretistic Androgyny*. The combination of traditionally masculine and feminine traits—most often masculine and feminine virtues—associated with a synthesis of elements from indigenous and metropolitan cultures.

G. *Alienating Gender Hybridity*. The loss or painful confusion of gender identity connected with alienating cultural hybridity.

V. Types of Identity, and Despair

A. Practical Identity. The set of habits or competencies that guide one's ordinary interactions with other people, along with the communal responses one relies on in those interactions. These interactions range from "personal" practices of greeting or table manners to more obviously collective practices of work or religious ceremony. They involve implicit knowledge of when, where, and how to participate in such interactions. One's habits or competencies define the "cognitive" component of practical identity. They are completed by a set of predictable communal responses to one's actions—standard replies to greetings, coordinated or corresponding actions necessary to the progress and resolution of religious ceremonies, and so on. These communal responses define the "social" component of practical identity. An "intrinsic" view of practical identity sees the cognitive component as fixed early on. An "extrinsic" view sees it as more flexible and open to significant transformation or augmentation, as in response to changing socio-economic conditions.

B. Reflective Identity. A hierarchized set of properties and relations which one takes to define oneself. This set prominently includes sex, race, ethnicity, family position, and so forth. This set of properties and relations is first of all a matter of social attribution, not introspection. The hierarchy appears to be a function of practical identity. One's practical place in the activities of society is in part of function of attributed categories such as sex. For example, little girls play some games with some toys, while little boys play other games with other toys. The practical identity that results from the repetition of such activities is what appears to determine which properties we take to be most definitive of ourselves in reflective identity. For example, sex is almost always high in one's reflective identity, probably because it is crucial to one's practical identity. Crises regarding reflective identity appear to derive largely from conflicts between the cognitive and social components of practical identity, especially when these are accompanied or motivated by systematic denigration of one's reflective identity. (These conflicts need not derive from incompatibility, but may result from a simple racist refusal of cooperation.)

C. Despair. Insofar as practical and reflective identity provide one with possibilities and goals for the future, an idea of what one might wish or hope to do or be, despair is the complete loss of that sense of identity-based possibility and hope, the loss of those goals and wishes. There are two common forms of despair in this sense. One relates to practical identity and derives from a sense that culture is changing so rapidly that one's habits and competencies have gone completely out of joint with social practices, and that there is no way of realigning the two. The other relates to reflective identity and derives from a sense that one is part of a group that will never be able to achieve anything in culture or science or politics or anywhere else, individually or collectively. One common form of this second type of despair is what Derek Walcott calls "racial despair" ("What the Twilight Says," 21), which results from the extreme racial denigration that is so common under colonialism.

VI. COMPONENTS OF UNIVERSALISM

A. Descriptive Universalism. The view that cultures share a broad range of specifiable properties and structures—in language, literature, music, and so on.

B. Experiential or Empathic Universalism (versus Projection). The presumption that all persons share a qualitatively similar experiential subjectivity, with broadly common feelings, hopes, and so forth. This presumption provides the basis for empathic identification, and implies the importance of seeking imaginatively to adopt points of view that may at first seem incommensurable with one's own. Empathic adoption of someone else's point of view is far from infallible. Here as elsewhere specific universalist conclusions must be tentative, open to revision. It seems particularly common to confuse projection of one's own viewpoint with empathic adoption of another viewpoint. Nonetheless, the two are diametrically opposed. If Doe tends to find Igbo customs grotesque, empathic universalism will probably lead him/her to infer that Igbos tend to find European customs grotesque. Projection, however, will lead Doe to conclude that, when faced with European culture, Igbos will find their own customs grotesque.

C. Ethical Universalism and the Politics of Otherness. Ethical universalism is the view that there are general ethical principles that apply cross-culturally and can be invoked cross-culturally to defend or condemn specific cultural practices. Historically, ethical universals have been invoked against colonized cultures far more often than metropolitan cultures—

except in the case of some traditionalists, who reverse this tendency. In other words, ethical universals have been invoked in a nonuniversal way. The "Politics of Otherness" seeks to counter this tendency by an imperative that one should focus one's critical scrutiny first and foremost on one's own culture and that, in cases of real conflict—ethical or otherwise—one should give tentative preference to the alien culture, other things being equal.

   D. *Cultural Universalism.* The view that cultures are not, in principle, tied to any particular ethnic or racial group, but are the common property of all people. This aspect of universalism implies that we all have equal obligations to and interest in the preservation of diverse cultures, though diverse cultures divested of putative racial or ethnic ownership.

Works Cited

Achebe, Chinua. *Things Fall Apart: The Story of a Strong Man*. New York: Astor-Honor, 1959.

Ahmad, Aijaz. *In Theory: Classes, Nations, Literatures*. New York: Verso, 1992.

Al-Fārābī. "Canons of the Art of Poetry." In Cantarino.

Ali, Maulana Muhammad. *The Holy Qur'ān: Arabic Text, English Translation and Commentary*. 2nd, revised ed. Columbus, Ohio: The Ahmidiyyah Anjuman Isha'at Islam, Lahore, 1995 (1951).

Allan, Tuzyline Jita. *Womanist and Feminist Aesthetics: A Comparative Review*. Athens, Ohio: Ohio University Press, 1995.

Amadiume, Ifi. *Male Daughters, Female Husbands: Gender and Sex in an African Society*. London: Zed Books, 1987.

Amin, Samir. *Eurocentrism*. Trans. Russell Moore. New York: Monthly Review, 1989.

Anand, Mulk Raj. *Untouchable*. London: Penguin, 1940 (1935).

Anderson, Benedict. *Imagined Communities: Reflections on the Origin and Spread of Nationalism*. Revised ed. New York: Verso, 1991.

Angier, Carole. *Jean Rhys: Life and Work*. Boston: Little, Brown, and Co., 1990.

Appiah, Kwame Anthony. *In My Father's House: Africa in the Philosophy of Culture*. New York: Oxford University Press, 1992.

Aristotle. *Peri Poietikes*. In S. H. Butcher, *Aristotle's Theory of Poetry and Fine Art, with a Critical Text and Translation of the Poetics*. 4th ed. New York: Dover, 1951.

Asiegbu, Johnson U. J. *Nigeria and Its British Invaders, 1851–1920: A Thematic Documentary History*. New York: Nok Publishers, 1984.

Avalon, Arthur, ed. and trans. *The Great Liberation (Mahanirvana Tantra)*. Madras: Ganesh, 1963.

Baker, Patrick. *Centring the Periphery: Chaos, Order, and the Ethnohistory of Dominica*. Montreal: McGill-Queen's University Press, 1994.

Barrett, Leonard. *The Rastafarians: Sounds of Cultural Dissonance.* Boston: Beacon Press, 1977.

———. *The Sun and the Drum: African Roots in Jamaican Folk Tradition.* Kingston, Jamaica: Sangsler's Book Stores, 1976.

Beck, Jane. *To the Windward of the Land: The Occult World of Alexander Charles.* Bloomington: Indiana University Press, 1979.

Bhabha, Homi K. "Of Mimicry and Man: The Ambivalence of Colonial Discourse." *October* 28 (1984): 125–33.

———. "Signs Taken for Wonders: Questions of Ambivalence and Authority under a Tree Outside Delhi, May 1817." *Critical Inquiry* 12, no. 1 (Autumn 1985): 144–65.

Bhattacharya, Bhabani. *A Goddess Named Gold.* Delhi: Hind Pocket Books, 1967 (1960).

Black, Jan Knippers, and Howard I. Blutstein. *Area Handbook for Trinidad and Tobago.* Washington, D. C.: U.S. Government Printing Office, 1976.

Boehmer, Elleke. *Colonial and Postcolonial Literature: Migrant Metaphors.* New York: Oxford University Press, 1995.

Borthwick, Meredith. *The Changing Role of Women in Bengal 1849–1905.* Princeton: Princeton University Press, 1984.

Breiner, Laurence A. "Walcott's Early Drama." In *The Art of Derek Walcott.* Ed. Stewart Brown. Glamorgan, Wales: Siren Books, 1991.

Bronte, Charlotte. *Jane Eyre: An Authoritative Text.* Ed. Richard Dunn. New York: W. W. Norton, 1993.

Brown, Lloyd. "Dreamers and Slaves—The Ethos of Revolution in Walcott and Leroi Jones." In Hamner, 193–201.

Cameron, Deborah. *Feminism and Linguistic Theory.* London: Macmillan, 1985.

Campbell, Horace. *Rasta and Resistance: From Marcus Garvey to Walter Rodney.* Trenton, N.J.: Africa World Press, 1987.

Cantarino, Vicente. *Arabic Poetics in the Golden Age: Selection of Texts Accompanied by a Preliminary Study.* Leiden: E. J. Brill, 1975.

Carroll, David. *Chinua Achebe.* New York: Twayne, 1970.

Césaire, Aimé. *Une saison au Congo.* Paris: Éditions du Seuil, 1973 (1966).

———. *La Tragédie du Roi Christophe.* Paris: Présence Africaine, 1963.

Chakravorty, B. C. *Rabindranath Tagore, His Mind and Art: Tagore's Contribution to English Literature.* New Delhi: Young India Publications, 1970.

Chelkowski, Peter J. "Commentary: Layla and Majnoon." *Mirror of the Invisible World: Tales from the Khamseh of Nizami.* New York: Metropolitan Museum of Art, 1975.

Chomsky, Noam, and Edward Herman. *The Political Economy of Human Rights. Volume I: The Washington Connection and Third World Fascism. Volume II: After the Cataclysm: Postwar Indochina and the Reconstruction of Imperial Ideology*. Boston: South End Press, 1979.

Condé, Maryse. *Moi, Tituba sorcière. . . .* N.c.: Mercure de France, 1986.

Coomaraswamy, Ananda K., and Sister Nivedita. *Myths of the Hindus and Buddhists*. New York: Dover, 1967 (1913).

Coppola, Carlo. "The All-India Progressive Writers' Association: The Early Phases." In Coppola, *Marxist*.

———, ed. *Marxist Influences and South Asian Literature*. Vol. 1. East Lansing, Mich.: Asian Studies Center of Michigan State University, 1974.

Corelli, Marie. *The Sorrows of Satan, or The Strange Experience of One Geoffrey Tempest, Millionaire: A Romance*. New York: Grosset and Dunlap, 1895.

Cosgrove, Art. "The Gaelic Resurgence and the Geraldine Supremacy (c. 1400–1534)." In Moody and Martin, 158–73.

Coundouriotis, Eleni. *Claiming History: Colonialism, Ethnography, and the Novel*. New York: Columbia University Press, 1999.

Daly, Stephanie. *The Legal Status of Women in Trinidad and Tobago* Port of Spain: The National Commission on the Status of Women, 1975.

Dangarembga, Tsitsi. *Nervous Conditions: A Novel*. Seattle: Seal Press, 1988.

Danielou, Alain. *The Myths and Gods of India*. Rochester, Vt.: Inner Traditions International, 1991.

Davy, John. *The West Indies Before and Since Emancipation*. London: Frank Cass, 1971 (1854).

Deren, Maya. *The Voodoo Gods*. St. Albans, U.K.: Granada Publishing, 1975.

Desai, Anita. "Introduction." In Hosain.

Dharma Shastra or the Hindu Law Codes. Vol. I. Trans. Manmatha Nath Dutt. 2nd ed. Varanasi: Chaukhamba Amarbharati Prakashan, 1977.

Dicey, A. V. *Lectures on the Relation Between Law and Public Opinion in England During the Nineteenth Century*. London: Macmillan, 1905.

Dike, Azuka. *The Resilience of Igbo Culture: A Case Study of Awka Town*. Enugu, Nigeria: Fourth Dimension Publishing, 1985.

Doggett, Maeve E. *Marriage, Wife-Beating, and the Law in Victorian England*. Columbia, S.C.: University of South Carolina Press, 1993.

Doniger, Wendy, with Brian K. Smith. "Introduction." In *Laws of Manu*.

Drewal, Margaret Thampson. *Yoruba Ritual: Performers, Play, Agency*. Bloomington: Indiana University Press, 1992.

Dryden, John. "Alexander's Feast or, The Power of Music; An Ode in Honor of St. Cecilia's Day." In *Selected Works of John Dryden.* Ed. William Frost. New York: Holt, Rinehart and Winston, 1961, 75–80.

Dutta, Krishna, and Andrew Robinson. *Rabindranath Tagore: The Myriad-Minded Man.* New York: St. Martin's Press, 1996.

Eliade, Mircea. *Yoga: Immortality and Freedom.* Trans. Willard R. Trask. Princeton: Princeton University Press, 1969.

Emecheta, Buchi. *The Joys of Motherhood.* New York: George Braziller, 1979.

Emery, Mary Lou. *Jean Rhys at "World's End": Novels of Colonial and Sexual Exile.* Austin: University of Texas Press, 1990.

Engels, Frederick. Articles in Karl Marx and Engels, *Ireland and the Irish Question.* Moscow: Progress, 1971.

Epstein, Cynthia Fuchs. *Deceptive Distinctions: Sex, Gender, and the Social Order.* New Haven: Yale University Press and New York: Russell Sage Foundation, 1988.

Faludi, Susan. *Backlash: The Undeclared War Against American Women.* New York: Doubleday, 1991.

Fanon, Frantz. *Black Skin, White Masks.* Trans. Charles Lam Markmann. New York: Grove Press, 1967.

——— . "Racism and Culture." In *Toward the African Revolution.* Trans. Haakon Chevalier. New York: Grove Press, 1967, 29–44.

——— . *The Wretched of the Earth.* Trans. Constance Farrington. New York: Grove Press, 1963.

Fausto-Sterling, Anne. *Myths of Gender: Biological Theories about Women and Men.* New York: Basic Books, 1985.

Fayad, Mona. "Unquiet Ghosts: The Struggle for Representation in Jean Rhys's *Wide Sargasso Sea.*" *Modern Fiction Studies* 34.3 (1988): 437–52.

Fishburn, Katherine. *Reading Buchi Emecheta: Cross-Cultural Conversations.* Westport, Conn.: Greenwood, 1995.

Forster, E. M. *A Passage to India.* New York: Harcourt Brace Jovanovich, 1924.

Fox, Robert E. "Big Night Music: Derek Walcott's 'Dream on Monkey Mountain' and the 'Splendours of Imagination.'" In Hamner, 202–11.

Gardiner, Judith Kegan. *Rhys, Stead, Lessing, and the Politics of Empathy.* Bloomington, Indiana: Indiana University Press, 1989.

Gibb, H. A. R., and J. H. Kramers. *Shorter Encyclopedia of Islam.* Ithaca: Cornell University Press, 1953.

Gikandi, Simon. *Reading Chinua Achebe: Language and Ideology in Fiction.* London: James Currey, 1991.

Glasse, Cyril. *The Concise Encyclopedia of Islam*. San Francisco: Harper and Row, 1989.

Gregg, Veronica Marie. *Jean Rhys's Historical Imagination: Reading and Writing the Creole*. Chapel Hill: University of North Carolina Press, 1995.

Hale, Thomas A. *Scribe, Griot, and Novelist: Narrative Interpreters of the Songhay Empire*. Gainesville: University of Florida Press, 1990.

Halevy, Elie. *England in 1815 (A History of the English People in the Nineteenth Century—I)*. Trans., E. Watkin and D. Barker. 2nd ed. New York: Barnes and Noble, 1949.

Hamner, Robert, ed. *Critical Perspectives on Derek Walcott*. Washington: Three Continents Press, 1993.

Harrison, Nancy R. *Jean Rhys and the Novel as Women's Text*. Chapel Hill: University of North Carolina Press, 1988.

Hayes-McCoy, G. A. "The Tudor Conquest (1534–1603)." In Moody and Martin, 174–88.

Head, Bessie. *A Question of Power*. London: Heinemann, 1974.

Heidegger, Martin. *Being and Time*. Trans. John Macquarrie and Edward Robinson. New York: Harper and Row, 1962.

Herskovits, Melville J., and Frances S. Herskovits. *Dahomean Narrative: A Cross-Cultural Analysis*. Evanston: Northwestern University Press, 1958.

Hill, Errol. *The Trinidad Carnival: Mandate for a National Theatre*. Austin: University of Texas Press, 1972.

Hogan, Patrick. *Camps on the Hearthstone*. Dublin: C. J. Fallon, n.d.

Hogan, Patrick Colm. "The Gender of Tradition: Ideologies of Character in Post-Colonization Anglophone Literature." In *Order and Partialities: Theory, Pedagogy, and the 'Postcolonial.'* Ed. Kostas Myrsiades and Jerry McGuire. Albany: State University of New York Press, 1995, 87–110.

———. "'How Sisters Should Behave to Sisters': Women's Culture and Igbo Society in Flora Nwapa's *Efuru*." *English in Africa* 26.1 (1999): 45–60.

———. *The Politics of Interpretaton: Ideology, Professionalism, and the Study of Literature*. New York: Oxford University Press, 1990.

Holland, John, Keith Holyoak, Richard Nisbett, and Paul Thagard. *Induction: Processes of Inference, Learning, and Discovery*. Cambridge: MIT Press, 1986.

Hosain, Attia. *Sunlight on a Broken Column*. New York: Penguin-Virago, 1988 (1961).

Houk, James T. *Spirits, Blood, and Drums: The Orisha Religion in Trinidad*. Philadelphia: Temple University Press, 1995.

Hurston, Zora Neale. *Tell My Horse*. Berkeley: Turtle Island, 1981.

Husserl, Edmund. *Cartesian Meditations: An Introduction to Phenomenology.* Trans. Dorion Cairns. The Hague: Martinus Nijhoff, 1973.

Ibn Rushd (Averroes). *Averroes' Middle Commentary on Aristotle's Poetics.* Trans. and ed. Charles Butterworth. Princeton: Princeton University Press, 1986.

Ibn Sīnā (Avicenna). *Avicenna's Commentary on the Poetics of Aristotle.* Trans. and ed. Ismail Dahiyat. Leiden: E. J. Brill, 1974.

Idowu, E. Bolaji. *Olodumare: God in Yoruba Belief.* New York: Frederick Praeger, 1963.

Isichei, Elizabeth. *A History of the Igbo People.* New York: St. Martin's Press, 1976.

Ismond, Patricia. "Breaking Myths and Maiden heads." In Hamner, 251–64.

Jacoby, Russell. "Marginal Returns: The Trouble with Post-Colonial Theory." *Lingua Franca* (September/October 1995): 30–37.

Jerusalem Bible. Ed. Alexander Jones *et al.* Garden City, N.Y.: Doubleday, 1966.

Johnson-Laird, Philip N. *The Computer and the Mind: An Introduction to Cognitive Science.* Cambridge: Harvard University Press, 1988.

Kālidāsa. *The Abhijñānaśākuntalam of Kālidāsa.* Ed. and trans. M. R. Kale. 10th ed. Delhi: Motilal Banarsidass, 1969.

Khan, Israel B. *Scales of Justice.* St. Augustine, Trinidad: Legal Books, 1993.

Killam, G. D. *The Writings of Chinua Achebe.* Revised ed. London: Heinemann, 1977.

Kincaid, Jamaica. *Annie John.* New York: Plume, 1985.

Kipling, Rudyard. *Kim.* New York: New American Library, 1984 (1901).

Kloepfer, Deborah Kelly. *The Unspeakable Mother: Forbidden Discourse in Jean Rhys and H.D.* Ithaca: Cornell University Press, 1989.

Kopf, David. *The Brahmo Samaj and the Shaping of the Modern Indian Mind.* Princeton: Princeton University Press, 1979.

Kripalani, Krishna. *Rabindranath Tagore: A Biography.* New York: Grove Press, 1962.

Kurian, George T. *Historical and Cultural Dictionary of India.* Metuchen, N.J.: Scarecrow Press, 1976.

Lacan, Jacques. *Écrits.* Paris: Éditions de Seuil, 1966.

Laplanche, Jean. *Life and Death in Psychoanalysis.* Trans. Jeffrey Mehlman. Baltimore: Johns Hopkins University Press, 1976.

———, and J.-B. Pontalis. *The Language of Psycho-Analysis.* Trans. Donald Nicholson-Smith. New York: W. W. Norton, 1973.

Laws of Manu. Trans. Wendy Doniger with Brian K. Smith. New York: Penguin Books, 1991.

Lawson, Lori. "Mirror and Madness: A Lacanian Analysis of the Feminine Subject in *Wide Sargasso Sea.*" *Jean Rhys Review* 4.2 (1991): 19–27.

Lewis, Gordon K. *The Growth of the Modern West Indies.* New York: Monthly Review Press, 1968.

Lovelace, Earl. *The Wine of Astonishment.* London: Heinemann, 1982.

Lyons, F. S. L. *Culture and Anarchy in Ireland: 1890–1939.* Oxford: Oxford University Press, 1979.

Machwe, Prabhakar. "A Personal View of the Progressive Writers' Movement." In Coppola, *Marxist*, 45–53.

Mahābhārata of Krishna-Dwaipayana Vyāsa. Trans. Kisari Mohan Ganguli. 4 vols. New Delhi: Munshiram Manoharlal, 1970.

Markandaya, Kamala. *Nectar in a Sieve.* New York: New American Library, 1984 (1954).

Marx, Karl. "The Fetishism of Commodities and the Secret thereof." In *Capital (Volume I): A Critical Analysis of Capitalist Production.* Ed Frederick Engels. Trans. Samuel Moore and Edward Aveling. New York: International Publishers, 1967.

McClintock, Anne. "The Angel of Progress." *Social Text.* 31/32 (1992): 84–98.

McCord, Norman. *British History: 1815–1906.* Oxford: Oxford University Press, 1991.

McGregor, R. S., ed. *The Oxford Hindi-English Dictionary.* Oxford: Oxford University Press, 1993.

Michaels, Walter Benn. *Our America: Nativism, Modernism, and Pluralism.* Durham: Duke University Press, 1995.

Mill, John Stuart. "On Liberty." In *Essential Works of John Stuart Mill.* Ed., Max Lerner. New York: Bantam Books, 1961.

Milne, Anthony. "Derek Walcott" (Interview). In Hamner, 58–64.

Monier-Williams, Sir Monier. *A Sanskrit-English Dictionary.* New ed. Delhi: Motilal Banarsidass, 1986 (1899).

Moody, T. W., and F. X. Martin, eds. *The Course of Irish History.* Cork, Ireland: Mercier Press, 1967.

Mukherji, Probhat Kumar. (Prabhat Mukhopadhyaya.) *Life of Tagore.* Trans. Sisirkumar Ghosh. New Delhi: Indian Book Co., 1975.

Muoneke, Romanus Okey. *Art, Rebellion, and Redemption: A Reading of the Novels of Chinua Achebe.* New York: Peter Lang, 1994.

Naipaul, V. S. *The Mimic Men.* New York: Penguin, 1969 (1967).

Nandy, Ashis. *At the Edge of Psychology: Essays in Politics and Culture*. Delhi: Oxford University Press, 1980.

——. *The Illegitimacy of Nationalism: Rabindranath Tagore and the Politics of Self*. Delhi: Oxford University Press, 1994.

——. *The Intimate Enemy: Loss and Recovery of Self Under Colonialism*. Delhi: Oxford University Press, 1983.

——. *Traditions, Tyranny, and Utopias: Essays in the Politics of Awareness*. Delhi: Oxford University Press, 1987.

Nelson, Emmanuel S. "Black America and the Anglophone Afro-Caribbean Literary Consciousness." *Journal of American Culture* 12.4 (1989): 53–58.

Ngũgĩ wa Thiong'o. *Moving the Centre: The Struggle for Cultural Freedoms*. London: James Curry, 1993.

——. *Petals of Blood*. New York: Penguin, 1977.

——. *The River Between*. London: Heinemann, 1965.

Nizami Ganjavi. *Leila und Madschnun*. Trans. Rudolf Gelpke. Zurich: Manesse Verlag, 1963.

Njoku, Benedict Chiaka. *The Four Novels of Chinua Achebe: A Critical Study*. New York: Peter Lang, 1984.

Nussbaum, Martha. *The Fragility of Goodness: Luck and Ethics in Greek Tragedy and Philosophy*. Cambridge: Cambridge University Press, 1986.

Nwapa, Flora. *Efuru*. Oxford: Heinemann, 1966.

O'Flaherty, Wendy Doniger. "The Clash Between Relative and Absolute Duty: The Dharma of Demons." In *The Concept of Duty in South Asia*. Ed. O'Flaherty and J. Duncan M. Derrett. N.c.: South Asia Books, 1978, 96–106.

——, ed. and trans. *Textual Sources for the Study of Hinduism*. Chicago: University of Chicago Press, 1988.

Ogbaa, Kalu. *Gods, Oracles and Divination: Folkways in Chinua Achebe's Novels*. Trenton, N.J.: Africa World Press, 1992.

Ojo, G. J. Afolabi. *Yoruba Culture: A Geographical Analysis*. Ife: University of Ife and London: University of London Press, 1966.

Olajubu, Oludare. "Iwi Egungun Chants—An Introduction." In *Forms of Folklore in Africa: Narrative, Poetic, Gnomic, Dramatic*. Ed. Bernth Lindfors. Austin: University of Texas Press, 1977.

Olaniyan, Tejumola. "Corporeal/Discursive Bodies and the Subject: *Dream on Monkey Mountain* and the Poetics of Identity." In *Imagination, Emblems and Expressions: Essays on Latin American, Caribbean, and Continental Culture and Identity*. Ed. Helen Ryan-Ranson. Bowling Green: Bowling Green State University Popular Press, 1993, 155–71.

Oliver, Roland, and J. D. Fage. *A Short History of Africa*. 6th ed. London: Penguin, 1988.

Onunwa, Udobata. *African Spirituality: An Anthology of Igbo Religious Myths*. Darmstadt: Thesen Verlag, 1992.

———. *Studies in Igbo Traditional Religion*. Uruowulu-Obosi, Nigeria: Pacific Publishers, 1990.

Onwuejeogwu, M. Angulu. *An Igbo Civilization: Nri Kingdom and Hegemony*. London: Ethiope Publishing, 1981.

Pagels, Elaine. *The Origin of Satan*. New York: Random House, 1995.

Pandit, Lalita. "Caste, Race, and Nation: History and Dialectic in Rabindranath Tagore's *Gora*." In *Literary India: Comparative Studies in Aesthetics, Colonialism, and Culture*. Ed. Patrick Colm Hogan and Lalita Pandit. Albany: State University of New York Press, 1995.

Parekh, Bhikhu. *Colonialism, Tradition, and Reform: An Analysis of Gandhi's Political Discourse*. New Delhi: Sage, 1989.

Plato. *The Republic*. Trans. Benjamin Jowett. *The Dialogues of Plato: Volume 4*. Ed. R. M. Hare and D. A. Russell. London: Sphere Books, 1970.

Pratt, Mary Louise. *Imperial Eyes: Travel Writing and Transculturation*. New York: Routledge, 1992.

Price, Richard. "Introduction: Maroons and Their Communities." In *Maroon Societies: Rebel Slave Communities in the Americas*. Ed. Price. Baltimore: Johns Hopkins University Press, 1979.

Raizada, Harish. "Humanism in the Novels of Rabindranath Tagore." In Sharma, 62–79.

Rao, Raja. *Kanthapura*. New York: New Directions, 1963 (1938).

Ray, Sibnarayan. *Rabindranath Tagore: Three Essays*. Calcutta: Renaissance Publishers, 1987.

Rhys, Jean. *Wide Sargasso Sea*. In *The Complete Novels*. Ed. Diana Athill. New York: W. W. Norton, 1985 (1966).

Rodney, Walter. *The Groundings With My Brothers*. London: Bogle-L'Overture, 1969.

Ronart, Stephan, and Nandy Ronart. *Concise Encyclopedia of Arabic Civilization: The Arab East*. New York: Frederick A. Praeger, 1960.

Rushdie, Salman. *Midnight's Children*. New York: Penguin, 1980.

Russell, Ralph. *The Pursuit of Urdu Literature: A Select History*. London: Zed Books, 1992.

Said, Edward. "Bookless in Gaza." *The Nation* 263.8 (23 September 1996): 6–7.

———. *Culture and Imperialism*. New York: Alfred A. Knopf, 1993.

——. *Orientalism*. New York: Random House, 1978.

Samad, Daizal R. "Cultural Imperatives in Derek Walcott's *Dream on Monkey Mountain*." *Commonwealth* 13.2 (1991): 8–21.

Sarkar, Sumit. *The Swadeshi Movement in Bengal: 1903–1908*. New Delhi: People's Publishing House, 1973.

Sartre, Jean-Paul. *Being and Nothingness: A Phenomenological Essay on Ontology*. Trans. Hazel Barnes. New York: Washington Square Press, 1966.

Shanta. *Handbook of Hindu Names*. Calcutta: B. Agarwal, 1969.

Sharma, T. R., ed. *Perspectives on Rabindranath Tagore*. Ghaziabad, India: Vimal Prakashan, 1986.

Shaw, Thurston. *Nigeria: Its Archaeology and Early History*. London: Thames and Hudson, 1978.

Shetty, Sandhya. "Masculinity, National Identity, and the Feminine Voice in *The Wine of Astonishment*." *Journal of Commonwealth Literature* 28.1 (1994): 65–79.

Shils, Edward. *Tradition*. Chicago: University of Chicago Press, 1981.

Shohat, Ella. "Notes on the 'Post-Colonial.'" *Social Text*. 31/32 (1992): 99–113.

Simpson, George Eaton. *Religious Cults of the Caribbean: Trinidad, Jamaica, and Haiti*. 3rd ed. Rio Piedras, Puerto Rico: University of Puerto Rico, 1980.

Swan, Robert O. *Munshi Premchand of Lamhi Village*. Durham: Duke University Press, 1969.

Tagore, Rabindranath. *Gora*. London: Macmillan, 1910 (1907).

——. *The Home and the World*. Trans. Surendranath Tagore, revised by the author. London: Macmillan, 1919.

——. *Nationalism*. New York: Macmillan, 1917.

——. *Quartet*. Trans. Kaiser Haq. Oxford: Heinemann: 1993 (1916).

Taylor, Patrick. *The Narrative of Liberation: Perspectives on Afro-Caribbean Literature, Popular Culture, and Politics*. Ithaca: Cornell University Press, 1989.

Thomas, H. Nigel. "'Progress' and Community in the Novels of Earl Lovelace." *World Literature Written in English* 31.1 (1991): 1–7.

Thorpe, Marjorie. "Introduction." In Lovelace.

Thurston, Herbert, S. J., and Donald Attwater, ed. *Butler's Lives of the Saints*. 4 vols. Complete ed. Westminster, Md.: Christian Classics, 1990.

Tiffin, Helen. "Mirror and Mask: Colonial Motifs in the Novels of Jean Rhys." *World Literature Written in English* 17.1 (April 1978): 328–41.

Trouillot, Michel-Rolph. *Peasants and Capital: Dominica in the World Economy*. Baltimore: Johns Hopkins University Press, 1988.

Tutuola, Amos. *The Palm-Wine Drinkard and His Dead Palm-Wine Tapster in the Dead's Town.* New York: Grove, 1984 (1953).

Uhrbach, Jan R. "A Note on Language and Naming in *Dream on Monkey Mountain.*" *Callaloo* 9.4 (1986): 578–82.

Vālmīki. *Srimad Vālmīki Ramayanam.* Trans. N. Raghunathan. 3 vols. Madras: Vighneswara Publishing, 1981.

Van Allen, Judith. "'Aba Riots' or Igbo 'Women's War'? Ideology, Stratification, and the Invisibility of Women." In *Women in Africa: Studies in Social and Economic Change.* Ed. Nancy J. Hafkin and Edna G. Bay. Stanford: Stanford University Press, 1976.

——— . "'Sitting on a Man': Colonialism and the Lost Political Institutions of Igbo Women." *Canadian Journal of African Studies* 6.2 (1972): 165–81.

Walcott, Derek. *Dream on Monkey Mountain.* In *Dream on Monkey Mountain and Other Plays.* New York: Noonday Press, 1970 (1967).

——— . *Henri Christophe: A Chronicle in Seven Scenes.* Barbados: Advocate Co., 1950.

——— . "Necessity of Negritude." In Hamner, 20–23.

——— . *O Babylon!* In *The Joker of Seville and O Babylon!: Two Plays.* New York: Farrar, Straus and Giroux, 1978.

——— . "What the Twilight Says: An Overture." In *Dream on Monkey Mountain and Other Plays* New York: Noonday Press, 1970.

Weinstock, Donald, and Cathy Ramadan. "Symbolic Structure in *Things Fall Apart.*" *Critique* 11.1 (1968): 33–41.

Williams, Joseph J., S.J. *Voodoos and Obeahs: Phases of West India Witchcraft.* New York: Dial Press, 1933.

Wolpert, Stanley. *A New History of India.* 4th ed. New York: Oxford University Press, 1993.

Woolf, Virginia. *Mrs. Dalloway.* New York: Harvest, 1953 (1925).

Wren, Robert M. *Achebe's World: The Historical and Cultural Context of the Novels of Chinua Achebe.* Washington, D.C.: Three Continents Press, 1980.

INDEX

Abame, 104, 108, 127, 129, 138,
233, 239
abduction (legal status in Trinidad),
162
Abhijñānaśākuntalam (Kālidāsa). *See*
Śakuntalā
Abida, 188, 265, 266, 271, 275, 276,
282, 284–288, 290, 291
Abinash, 217, 221, 253
Abrahams, Peter, 316
absolutism, xv–xviii, 224, 253
ācarā (custom), 218–221, 233, 234,
245, 247–249, 309
Achebe, Chinua, xii, xiii, xix, 17, 22,
103–135, 137, 138, 140, 173,
216, 279, 309
Achebe, Isaiah, 107
Achille, Louis-T., 57
Acts of the Apostles, 156
Adaku, 183, 202–204, 209–211
Adim, 206
Africa, xii, xvi, 3, 5–7, 14, 15, 17,
19, 49–52, 55, 59, 62–66, 68,
72–74, 76, 78, 79, 97, 98, 100,
115, 124, 137–145, 147–150,
152–161, 167–172, 306, 309,
312
Afro-Caribbean religion, xii, 46, 51,
59, 64, 67, 139–141, 143–145,
147, 152, 153, 160, 167, 168,
170–172, 174, 180, 181, 187,

199. *See also* Afro-Christianity,
Kele, Rastafarianism, Sango,
Voudou
Afro-Christianity, xiii, 64, 140
Agarwal, Sita 264, 267, 274, 280,
283, 284, 297–299
Agarwal, Harish Prasad, 293, 298,
300
Agbadi. *See* Nwokocha Agbadi
agbala, 112, 117–119
Agnes, Saint, 87, 88, 90, 91, 101,
102
Ahmad, Aijaz, xvi, 16
Akueni, 124
Akunna, 130
al-Fārābī, xviii, 308
al-Raḥmān (Allah the Beneficent),
282, 286
al-Raḥīm (Allah the Merciful), 282,
286
alcohol. *See* liquor
"Alexander's Feast" (Dryden), 227
Ali, Ahmed, 266
Ali, Ghulam, 284
Ali, Maulana Muhammad, xviii, 282,
308
alienated majority colony, 2–3, 317
alienating denial of identity, 17
alienating gender hybridity, 23, 321
alienating hybridity, 17, 23, 278, 279,
293, 294, 320